53

THE

ROMAN REPUBLIC

IN THREE VOLUMES
VOLUME ONE

THE

ROMAN REPUBLIC

BY

W. E. HEITLAND, M.A.

FELLOW OF ST JOHN'S COLLEGE

VOLUME ONE

GREENWOOD PRESS, PUBLISHERS
NEW YORK

First published in 1909 by the Cambridge University Press

Reprinted by permission of the Cambridge University Press

First Greenwood Reprinting 1969

Library of Congress Catalogue Card Number 69-13930

SBN 8371-2077-2

PRINTED IN UNITED STATES OF AMERICA

PREFACE

I S there room for another political study of the Roman Republic?
To find defects in well-known works on the subject is easy:
to provide a fairer version of the story is, from the nature of the
evidence, supremely difficult.   No wonder that writers nowadays
concern themselves chiefly with the Empire or the Decline of the
Republic.   Yet the political interest of Roman history becomes
faint, once the Roman world has passed under the control of a
single master and his subordinates, and the tale of the Decline,
taken by itself, is but a lame story.   The great period of Roman
imperial growth, say from the conquest of Italy to the battle of
Pydna, is not only a striking phenomenon in itself.   In it the
decay of the republican system is already visible, and without it
the sequel loses most of its meaning.   Therefore I have tried to
trace the whole course of the Republic, from the dim legendary
days of the Kingdom and the early Free Commonwealth down to
the foundation of the Empire; from the single *imperium*, through
the republican magistracies and the supremacy of the Senate, down
to that concentrated extract of official powers known as the Prin-
cipate.   A large part of this range may fairly be called a historical
period, but the alternations of light and darkness make it very
difficult to keep any reasonable proportion in the narrative.   Of
Rome's two most desperate struggles, the second Punic war was so
full of recorded incidents, that no omission of doubtful matter, no
economy of description, avails to reduce the story within moderate
limits, if it is to be told at all.   With battle tactics as such I have
little to do; indeed the state of the evidence is usually such as to
forbid it.   Strategy in the large is another matter.   It often raises
questions not purely military, and reveals the state-psychology of
rival powers.   But here too the one-sided nature of most of our

evidence enjoins the utmost caution. When we come to the great
Italian war of 90—89 B.C. we are in a very different position. The
authorities are both meagre and bad. Some of the most important
points in connexion with the struggle are only known through incidental admissions, and the real features of the campaigns are lost in a
gloom seldom relieved by gleams of light. We cannot even define
with certainty when the war ended and the subsequent civil war
began. So the story can only be told in outline, and that with difficulty, though the danger to Rome from Mutilus and Silo was not less
than that from Hannibal, and the strain on the fabric of the state
perhaps greater.

The modern literature of pamphlets, articles in periodicals, and so
forth, bearing on the republican period, is immense, and I have only
been able to read a part of it. At certain points it becomes of the
first importance. A good instance is the affair of Catiline, which I
have completely rewritten in agreement with the researches (see
§ 1042) of John and others. Of course I have freely used the great
treatises of Mommsen Marquardt Lange and Holm. But I must
own a special debt to the writings of Beloch and Nissen, and to the
coloured maps of Dr C Müller re-edited by Dr G B Grundy. These,
with occasional help from the Italian survey and our Admiralty
charts, are most useful. For Rome's contact with Greece and the
Hellenistic East, much is to be gained from the writings of Dr
Mahaffy, whose refreshing independence often supplies a corrective
to the views of Mommsen and Holm. How highly I value the work
of Mr Strachan-Davidson will appear in my notes. Lastly there are
the learned editors of classical books, of whom (omitting titles) I may
name Weissenborn, Maurenbrecher, Reid, Tyrrell and Purser, J E B
Mayor, J B Mayor, Sandys, Wilkins, Holden. These scholars in their
notes and Introductions supply first and last a great quantity of helpful
material. To many others I have on occasion referred. But the accounts
given of events and the opinions expressed are my own, formed rightly
or wrongly from patient consideration of the evidence. In the matter
of giving references I have acted in a way that may seem capricious.
But I do not see much use in filling pages with references until a
period is reached in which the evidence is scattered and conflicting

and at least based on contemporary record. In the period from the Gracchi to Caesar I have tried to give every reference of importance. The help from inscriptions is of course small for the times of the Republic.

In referring to modern books I have deliberately chosen those most accessible to an ordinary reader, provided that the information there given sufficed for the purpose of the moment. This is especially the case in the matter of editions of classical authors. When drawing an inference from any passage or passages, it is of course my own opinion that I am recording. But it is often desirable to refer to the remarks of scholars as well as to the text: that these remarks are sometimes given in small school-editions is no argument against their soundness. It has been an object not to overload my notes with unnecessary references. If I have been too chary of such support, I am sorry; but I submit that it is a fault on the right side. Sometimes I have thought it well to refer to the existing indices to this or that author, as giving a collection of passages best viewed as a whole and too numerous to quote.

The maps inserted in the text are not meant to be a complete set illustrating the geography of the countries and places referred to. To attempt any such equipment was out of the question, and the Müller-Grundy series with its scheme of colours is surely far better than any set of general maps that could be prepared for insertion in the pages of this book. But there are cases in which the inclusion of details belonging to widely different periods makes a map deceptive to the eye when used for illustrating the events of some particular period. It is mainly with a view to meet such passing needs that I have prepared the little sketch-maps, the leading feature of which is the omission of irrelevant detail. This is the reason why they mostly come in the first half of the book. In the later chapters they are hardly needed. To take an instance; sufficient maps of Gaul in Caesar's time abound. To improve on them would need a rendering of the physical features of the country, hardly possible without the use of colours on a large scale.

In preparing the Index I have aimed at completeness, and have not scrupled to refer to the same detail under several different heads.

Some of the larger items, such as *Leges, Rome, Army, Colonies, Greek, Caesar, Cicero,* have been subdivided in particular headings, but to carry this out in all cases would have necessitated a separate volume for the Index. As the references are by sections, the numbers quickly indicate in what part of the book the passage referred to occurs. Roman names are given under the several gentile names. The gentile name comes in its strictly alphabetical order, but the names of individuals follow in chronological order. In one case (*Cornelii*) they are grouped under the prevailing surnames (*Scipio, Sulla, Lentulus,* etc.), each group chronologically arranged. The length of the Index is mainly due to an attempt to give a full catalogue of topics dealt with in the text. I fear these topics have not always been wisely classified under heads, for the undertaking is not easy, and it has necessitated a host of multiple references. The modern names of places are generally added to the ancient ones as these occur in the Index.

I must note a few points where I have for convenience sake employed special forms of expression. When I speak of a formal meeting for business, I use the general term *Assembly* (with initial capital), only distinguishing the several kinds of Assemblies when I think it necessary. *Centuries* and *Tribes,* when the Roman groups are meant, are spelt with a capital letter; and the same rule is followed in the word *Allies* when the Italian *socii* are referred to. The word '*period*' means a space (not a point) of time. I use the term *Aristocracy* as concrete, to represent the aggregate of the upper class actively concerned in the work of government. But *Oligarchy* is less fully established in English as a concrete term, and it is badly wanted (as set forth in § 938) to connote the peculiar qualities of a certain form of government, not Roman. I hope it is no mere pedantry to reserve it for this technical purpose. To Mr W H S Jones I owe an apology for using the term *Malaria* loosely in speaking of the unwholesomeness of certain places at certain times, and not confining it strictly to specific infection. That *gravitas caeli,* whatever its precise meaning, was a serious evil, we have the evidence of Cicero Caesar and Varro. And I think the word *Malaria* has long been used in English in this general sense.

In general I should remark that a political study is my main object. Literary military and economic history are only touched as bearing on public life, and social details as the straws that shew the set of the tide. One is apt to be greatly impressed by some isolated fact incidentally recorded, and tempted to draw wide inferences from it. But the survival of such details is largely a matter of chance, and one is liable to forget that other details, probably not all pointing to the same conclusion, have perished. I have therefore tried to walk warily. It is tiresome to be so often compelled to decline inferences and to use the language of doubt, but with the defective record of the republican period I can see no other way. I should add that my wish is to regard the politics of the Republic functionally rather than structurally. It is important to gain as correct a view as possible of the institutions of a state so extraordinary as republican Rome. But for the purposes set forth in the introductory chapter (§ 2) it is even more important to see how the institutions worked in practice. I have tried hard to keep clear of prepossessions derived however unconsciously from books that have held the field for many years, and to give a fair account of the influences at work that shaped the destinies of Rome. How far I have succeeded or failed in this attempt I cannot judge.

I should also say that I lay claim to no great startling novelties in the way of interpretation. After the labour of generations of scholars in collecting and sifting the mass of materials that compose our record, I do not see much opening for an honest reconstruction of the whole story. I do not believe that the old-fashioned views of the history of the Roman Republic are mere delusions, and that it can and should be rewritten in a sensational spirit. I do not believe that the movements of the revolutionary period are to be better understood by first attributing great importance to the action of leading men and then assuming that the characters of these leading men were one after another subject to a mysterious change. As I read the evidence, there is no justification for any such arbitrary psychology. And I believe that unbiassed students will agree with me in holding that, so far as we have any means of judging, the attempt to explain changes of policy by changes of character is peculiarly rash in dealing with such a people as the Romans. In my opinion it is only misrepresentation of the circumstances of the moment that tempts a writer to resort to such hypotheses.

To the Syndics of the Cambridge University Press I owe and hereby render my best thanks for undertaking the publication of this book. But it is not necessary to enlarge on this topic, familiar to all who have had the good fortune to receive their support. Nor need I attempt to do justice to the staff of the Press : the quality of the work employed in the production of these volumes speaks for itself.

W E HEITLAND

CAMBRIDGE

8 *September* 1909.

NOTE TO THE SECOND IMPRESSION

The contemplated reissue of this book makes it necessary for me to add some corrections and notes in a great hurry. They are of course very incomplete. Many of them are suggested by the remarks kindly sent me by Mr J. Wells, Warden of Wadham College, Oxford, shortly after the book was published. I regret that in several sections, where a more or less thorough recasting would have been desirable, I have had to content myself with indicating doubts or changes of view in these formless notes. But this is not a new edition, and it was not possible to do anything that would involve serious disturbance of the plates. I have only rewritten a very few sentences in places where a change of view was manifestly necessary. The additional notes contain much that was intentionally omitted in 1909 in order to keep down the size of the book, and is now printed in a compressed form. The sale of the first impression has been far beyond my expectations, and this reissue finds me unprepared for more revision than I have attempted here.

September 1922.

TABLE OF CONTENTS

VOLUME ONE

Book I.

Introductory.

Book II.

The Republic to the union of the Orders.

Book III.

The union of Italy under Rome.

Table of Contents

Book IV.

Rome and Carthage.

LIST OF MAPS

ADDITIONAL NOTES AND CORRECTIONS, 1922

Volume One

Preface p ix and § 3. Character, Personality, etc. See A T Mahan, *Influence of sea power upon the French Revolution and Empire* (1892) vol II p 364, on the sudden change after 1792 attributed to Pitt by some writers, absurdly. Also J B Bury, *Idea of Progress* p 303, on the case of Napoleon.

§ 5. The importance of unbaked brick as a material of early building needs to be emphasized. See Xenophon *Anab* III 4 § 7, VII 8 § 14, Ovid *Met* IV 58, and the notable passage Diodorus XIX 45 § 7. In Dion Hal fragm XII 8 λίθων may stand, meaning tufa blocks, but one may suspect that πλίνθων is the true reading. See too the remark of Columella XI 3 § 2 on the material suited for a garden wall. See below on § 1384.

§ 20. Local relation of divinity. Cf Cic *de legibus* II §§ 26—7.

§ 25. Rome, advantage of position. Recognized by Livy v 54 § 4. See below § 843 note 1. Cf Cic *de republ* II §§ 9—11.

§ 36. Gentile lands. See M Weber *Röm Agrargeschichte* pp 50—1, Mommsen in *Hermes* XIX 394. See below §§ 67—8.

§ 54. Note use of *adsiduitas* = residence on the farm, in Pliny NH XVIII 35.

§ 99. A good illustration of Massaliot enterprise is to be found in Demosth *Zenoth* § 8, p 884.

§ 102. Family records corrupt history. Recognized by Livy VII 9 § 5.

§ 110. The Consular Military Tribunes. See Livy IV 7 § 2, v 31 § 9.

§ 123. The Plebs and the land. See Mommsen, *Staatsrecht* III 84—8.

§ 139. That the great migration of Sabellian peoples into southern Italy attracted notice abroad, may be seen from the curious reference to Lucanians in Isocrates *de pace* § 50, p 169.

§ 142. For the doings of Dionysius in southern Italy see Dionys Hal fragm XX 7.

§ 147—76. 'The slow-moving revolution which ended in the plebeian victories of 339 does not in any real way resemble the socialistic out-bursts of an urban industrial proletariat.' Prof Tenney Frank, *Economic* history of Rome p 101. With this I agree.

§ 147. *pro consule*. The expression occurs in Livy III 4 § 10 under 464 BC. I take it to be informal in that place.

Tribunes. Livy x 47 § 1 seems under 293 BC to treat them as having been elected *auspicato*, but with a flaw in the auspices.

§ 187. This walling-off cities in separate quarters may be illustrated by the cases of Dyme in Achaia, Diodorus XIX 66 § 4. See below §§ 454, 593. Also by the 'Irish town' quarters in Ireland, Prendergast's *Cromwellian Settlement* ed II p 285.

§ 193 note. Cleonymus. Diodorus xx 104—5, Livy x 2.

§ 194. The Lucanians. Dionys Hal XVII 1.

§ 196. K Nitzsch, *die Gracchen* p 199, holds that, owing to the loss by the Samnites of much of their public land, small farming lived on in Samnium; and that this is why we find later a rustic population there more prosperous than the Roman *plebs rustica*. But I suspect that Roman occupation embraced chiefly the lowland districts, and that the highlands escaped the ruin of small farming here as they did in the Abruzzi.

§ 202. Messana and Rhegium. Dionys Hal fragm xx 4, 5, 16, Diodorus xxi 18, xxii 1.

§ 204. Pyrrhus in Italy. Diodorus xxii 6, Dion Cassius fragm 40 § 27.

§ 206. Pyrrhus in Sicily. Diodorus xxii 8, 10, Dionys Hal fragm xx 8.

§ 207. Pyrrhus in Italy. Dionys Hal fragm xx 9, 11, 12.

§ 221, note 2. On the *ius duodecim coloniarum* see D^r E G Hardy in Journ Rom Stud 1916 p 69, and Seeck, *Untergang der Röm Welt* ii 130—1. The chief representative of the opposite view, which finds the 12 colonies in the recusants of 209 BC [below § 354] is Nitzsch in *die Gracchen* p 65 foll and *passim*.

§ 229. Agricultural holdings. Tradition said that in the regal period 2 *iugera* was held a sufficient allotment for a citizen, and Manius Curius in the 3rd century BC was said to have pronounced 7 *iugera* enough for a good citizen. Pliny NH xviii 7, 18. See § 818 below.

§ 231. Of the rebuilding after 390 BC Livy v 55 § 3 says *tegula publice praebita est*. These tiles may have been of baked clay, as usual later. But Pliny NH xvi 36 declares on authority of Nepos that wooden shingles (*scandulae*) were the regular roofing in Rome down to the time of the Pyrrhic war. If so, we have a further explanation of the fire-danger.

The arch. Seneca *ep* 90 § 32 attributes the invention to Democritus.

§ 236. For the interest of Greek observers in Carthaginian institutions (before Aristotle) cf Isocrates, *Nicocles* § 24 p 31.

§ 238. See Diodorus xx 55 § 4.

§ 240. Punic fleet. See below § 379.

§ 245. Plutarch, *Aratus* 12, says that Aratus, driven by foul weather into the Adriatic, got a passage on a Roman ship bound for Syria. This would be about 250 BC, and the story if true suggests the existence of 'Roman' [? Italian Greek] trading vessels in the time of the first Punic war. For the earlier warfleet of Rome see Weissenborn on Livy ix 30 § 4, 38 § 2.

Galleys propelled by oars. See Index under *naval*. In 'Sea Wolves of the Mediterranean' by Comm^r E H Currey RN pp 234—7 are some interesting remarks on galleys and their weak points. The pictures are instructive. So are the models preserved in the arsenal at Venice. See on § 1126 below.

§ 254. Triumph reserved for consul. Cf Livy iv 20 § 6.

§ 259, note 1. From Digest L 5 § 3 it appears that this Claudian law was in some form reenacted by the *lex Iulia repetundarum*. That senators were not debarred from all kinds of financial enterprise, was pointed out by Mommsen (Hist ii 410 Eng trans), referring to Asconius p 94 and Dion Cassius LV 10 § 5. Prof Reid especially called my attention to this.

§ 269. Flaminius and the settlement of Gaulish lands. In this move Nitzsch (*die Gracchen* pp 25—7) sees a design to avoid disturbing the occupants of Italian *ager publicus* by a fresh distribution of allotments.

§ 318. Philip. Very instructive are his letters to the city of Larisa (about 214 BC), given in Solmsen's *Inscriptiones Graecae* pp 17—19 (Teubner 1910). A late echo of this situation is found in the fine lines of Claudian *bell Goth* 386—99.

§ 321. Contractors shirk military service. Compare the case in [Dem] *Neaera* § 27 p 1353.

§ 335. As *publicani*, these contractors were doubtless Roman citizens. But the names *Pyrgensis* and *Veientanus* suggest Etruscan origin. And the mention of one Ποστόμιον τὸν Τυρρηνόν, a pirate-captain put to death by Timoleon in 339 BC [Diodorus XVI 82 § 3] favours this inference.

§ 343. Custody of prisoners in Latin towns. An early instance in Livy IX 42 § 9. See Index under *Latin towns*.

§ 362. Livius. In Apollinaris Sidonius *carm* II 532—5, VII 555—6, we have traces of a version giving the credit of Metaurus to Livius, omitting Nero. Is this a really variant tradition, or merely due to the fact of the triumph of Livius being recorded in the *fasti*? See § 370 below.

§ 379, note 2. Meltzer II 136 treats this purchase of slaves as an exceptional measure in a great emergency, and says that rowers and sailors in the Punic fleet were ordinarily drawn from the δῆμος. But in his notes he gives no proof of this, and I doubt it. The passages Polyb XIV 10 § 4, Liv XXI 50 § 3, XXIII 26 § 4, do not really help us.

§ 402. We have record of the assignation of lands to Scipio's veterans in Samnium and Apulia. Livy XXXI 4 §§ 1—3, 49 §§ 5, 6.

BOOK I

INTRODUCTORY

CHAPTER I

GENERAL REMARKS

1. MUCH is made nowadays of the proposition that History is a Science, and I have been at some pains to make out what this means. Science is a word that now conveys very different ideas from those present to Gray when he used it to connote the Classical culture of Eton. There hangs about it the flavour of certainty, of knowledge that gives the power of foretelling exactly what will happen to various things at certain times or under certain conditions. Thus the astronomer predicts an eclipse. The chemist knows that if a certain substance be treated in a certain way certain results will follow: if the results do not follow the treatment, he infers that the substance is other than it was supposed to be, and continued experiment at last enables him to identify it as something else. Year by year new facts are ascertained and new principles evolved, and the Sciences that deal with living things are busy with experiments, in the hope that they too may attain equally certain results. And among these last is the group of Sciences that study the human individual as a living being, and like the rest are straining after certainties. How far can History, in the usual limited sense, the study of Man in communities, be compared with these Natural Sciences? I do not think anyone will maintain that History is a Science so exact that it is in a fair way to engage in successful prophecy. Neither is it experimental, for it can neither reproduce nor reverse the processes and situations of the past. Its matter, the doings of man in common life, is always changing. Difference of circumstances creates a real difference between phenomena that appear at first sight identical. It is this fact that renders the use of analogies for illustrative purposes painfully misleading, and it exposes the futile error that 'History repeats itself.' An analogy guarded by saving clauses enough to make it harmless is more likely to obscure than to illustrate. It is well that a writer should have before him the means of comparing similar incidents occurring under various conditions of place circumstance and time. But in telling his story he will do well to discard these ornaments, if he wishes to avoid producing either a false impression or fatal weariness.

2. Another definition asserts that History is past Politics and Politics present History. Now it is not clear how Politics can in any fruitful sense be called a Science; according to the current definitions it would rather be classed as an Art. There is also an old opinion widely held that the study of History is useful to the statesman. In its earlier and cruder form this distinctly implied that situations recur with such essential similarity that a policy suited to present circumstances may at once without misgiving be evolved from a knowledge of the past. When Sir Robert Walpole argued against triennial parliaments, he did not scruple to urge the inconsistency and weakness of all democracies. He can only have meant ancient democracies, that is, popular governments in societies based on slavery. He was in truth using a false analogy, as others had done and have done since. What then is the legitimate use of History to the statesman? I would answer that it is or should be an educative influence tending to produce or develop the cautious suppleness that animates all true statesmanship. Its function is not to supply parallels and patterns, but to orientate the mind and ripen the judgment which will have to deal with the shifting circumstances, not of other ages, but its own. For this purpose it is all-important that History should record truth where possible and confess ignorance where necessary; in describing an exceptionally obscure past, conclusions based on delicate combinations of doubtful or fragmentary evidence must, even though the work of a Mommsen, be offered as provisional. Such is the case with the early history of Rome, at least to the middle of the fourth century B.C., and the corruption of our record is then by no means at an end. The ceaseless efforts of a long succession of scholars to extract the truth from a mass of obscure and scattered materials may fairly be called scientific. Their methods are as exact as the conditions admit, but in the almost total absence of trustworthy statistics it can hardly be said that the goal of certainty is likely to be reached. What degree of certainty is attainable in the history of ages for which contemporary records and sound statistics are available, I do not pretend to say. But I hold that the term Science, as applied to History in the special limited sense, is no more than a name for careful study followed by honest exposition. It must never be allowed to connote mathematical certainty or suggest the solid prestige attached to exact and experimental Sciences. I would

illustrate my view in the form of an approximate proportion: History is to a Science as Politics to an Art.

3. Among the criticisms of History worthy of attention is one according to which the ordinary form of narrative, in which aims and actions are discussed and described, and the parts borne by individuals are so far as needful assigned to them, is little if at all better than superfluous. A general result must be extracted, to serve as an authority for reference when it is desired to test further conclusions of a general kind. This done, the narratives good or bad are of no further use, and should be discarded as lumber impeding the progress of the human race. There is something attractive in this view, for economy of time is good in itself, but it may fairly be doubted whether it represents an attainable ideal. So far as it refers to what is called Ancient History, I think it does not. That mere maundering is to be deprecated, all would admit. But let us take some great significant event, such as the fall of the Roman Republic. It is true that it was the outcome of a series of causes operative for a long time, causes which can be tabulated for the most part with a high degree of accuracy. To say exactly when they began to operate is much more difficult, but the movement of the Gracchi gives a convenient starting-point, more clearly marked out than is usually to be found for inquiries into such matters. A space of 100 years is filled with the conflict of tendencies and counter-tendencies, which express themselves in the aims and actions of leading characters. The length and nature of the conflict were profoundly influenced by the personal qualities of the combatants. It was not with us, but with their contemporaries, that they had to deal. The work of each generation has its feet on the past and its hands in the future. To set it in motion persons as well as principles are necessary, a fact which the non-contemporary critic is sometimes tempted to ignore. It is impossible to appreciate the Roman revolution without studying the careers and peculiarities of Marius and Sulla, Pompey and Caesar, not to mention the secondary figures such as Cicero Cato and many more. And it so happens that in reference to the movements of this period we are very fully informed, and the influence of various personalities stands out with singular clearness. Naturally enough, this stormy period has long had a great fascination for historians. Nor is it wonderful that opinions differ; the human interest of it is so immense, and the partisan evidence so copious. And here the great German no longer maintains his supremacy. A Frenchman is in a far better position to sympathize with the men of that age and appraise justly the circumstances in which they were placed. The picture drawn by Mommsen is firm in outline and painted in brilliant

colours, but a study of the evidence convinces me that the sketches of
Boissier are nearer the truth.

4. Among the many difficulties awaiting those who attempt to
write any part of the story of the ancient civilized world none is
more provoking, from a modern point of view, than the scantiness
of our information as to the condition of the free poor. What little
we have is largely due, in the first or second degree, to rhetorical
utterances, and for the most part couched in general terms. In the
story of the Roman Republic this defect of evidence meets us everywhere. In the earlier period we cannot tell with any certainty how
far the traditions of distress are genuine, how far they are back-echoes
of the agitations that marked the period of revolution. In the latter
period we are in the presence of a pauper mob the actual composition of
which we have no statistics to describe. I have tried not to blink the
difficulty, but meet it satisfactorily I cannot. As to the growth of
the power of capital and the increase of slave-industry in Italy we
are less in the dark ; but I have thought it well to give an abstract of
Varro's *res rustica*, and some account of the treatise of the elder
Cato, as having a peculiar value from this point of view. The importance of the economic relations of classes is enormous. If we turn
to Greek political terminology, and omit monarchies, to which Greeks
had a profound antipathy, we have the Few or the Many ruling Free
States. Democracy is founded on a slavery-system, hardly less so
than that characteristically Greek constitution, Oligarchy. This was
a natural result of direct or 'primary' governments, which were at
the same time only possible on a small scale. The logical Greek
mind would surely have shrunk from the conclusion that one man
could represent others save as a mere delegate to convey instructions,
and a Representative Government, the vulgar safety-valve of modern
unrest, was not yet invented. In the Roman system we find little
trace of first principles, and much make-shift and make-believe in
practice. The apparent and the real are in perpetual contrast. The
poorest citizen under the developed Republic has nominally the same
vote as the richest. The most influential senator is nominally no
more above the reach of the law than the meanest loafer of the
street. But the experience of daily life was enough to convince any
man that this was not the working truth. And we have no authori-
tative version of popular sentiment to tell us how the average poor
citizen regarded the aristocratic-plutocratic government under which
he existed. When Cicero professes to record public opinion, we do not
know for whom he speaks, and we do know that he despised the rabble
even when he affected to speak in their interest. Therefore we have
always to bear in mind that our record comes wholly from men of the

wealthier classes. Aristocrats Moderates and Progressives are alike in not being Men of the People ; they speak as partisans, and of the views of the rank and file we have no knowledge whatever.

5. I must explain why I have chosen to pass so lightly over the regal period and the early Republic. It is because I can see no means of attaining any reasonable certainty in details. The pendulum of opinion has swung to and fro pretty freely in the last 100 years, and under the influence of recent researches, especially in archaeology, is likely to go on swinging for a good while yet. There will be those whose sanguine temper leads them to believe that their present interpretation of real or supposed facts is a final solution of real or supposed mysteries. There will also be those who, like Professor Driver, warn us[1] to be on our guard against confusing the facts of archaeology with ingenious and precarious hypotheses founded upon them. And none can guess how long it may be before it will be safe to abandon an attitude of doubt on many important points. That the origin of Rome is shrouded in myth, in short unknown, is at present admitted. That numerous myths were fused and modified in course of time is certainly possible, not to say probable. But that a definite reconstruction of the process, undertaken now, is likely to be final, is surely most unlikely, and a heavy burden of proof lies upon the reconstructor. In reading the learned and ingenious *Ancient Legends* of Professor Ettore Pais, this conviction forced itself upon me with singular clearness. If the results of his method could be coherently represented in a tabular view, I feel sure that their complications would give pause even to those most inclined to accept them. To me they seem much more effective on the negative side than on the positive. Moreover, while he vigorously destroys the credit of Roman annalists, and shews that there were no genuine *Fasti* existing for the early Republic, he is at times constrained to appeal to dates which ultimately rest on such evidence, and has the air of believing more than he admits. Whether he is right in gravely impeaching the honesty of some Italian archaeologists, I cannot tell. In endeavouring to find a principle to guide me in accepting or declining his wide conclusions, I can see but one way, to accept for the time such as appear fully consistent with the advance of Rome to dominion in Italy, and with the political and social condition of the Roman people in the period regarded as historical, and to decline for the time such as do not. For the present I believe that Rome was a great city at an earlier date than his conclusions would suggest. His own severe remarks on the perils attending the hasty assignment of monuments to a particular

[1] *Morning Post* 3 April 1908.

age lead me to doubt whether the last word has yet been said as to the date of such works as the *cloaca maxima* and the 'Servian' wall. Nor can I help wondering why, in his general picture[1] of the buildings of early Rome, I can find no mention of the unbaked bricks (*lateres*) as building-material. He passes direct from wooden huts, roofed with straw or shingles, to buildings of baked bricks (*testae*) and stone. Now, if the *latericia structura* did not play an important part in the building history of early Rome, I am mistaken indeed. There is as good evidence for it in ancient writers[2] as there is for the use of wood. If this evidence is to be rejected, it at least deserves a serious refutation, which would be more to the point than to cite (as he does) the false analogy of Chicago and other cities of America.

6.   Therefore I hold it more discreet at the present stage of inquiry to deal very lightly with the period of Kings and the early Republic. Traditional dates must be given for what they may be worth. But it will be time to throw overboard the great main facts of early Roman story when they are finally proved to be figments. And this stage will hardly be reached until a rival view of the early history, thoroughly consistent with the later, has satisfactorily proved its own superiority. Meanwhile it is not necessary to praise the harsh tone of Professor Pais' criticisms, or to believe Italian archaeologists to be unprincipled rogues. The uncertainty as to the mode in which the Republic was established, as to the growth of popular liberties, especially the right of Appeal, and many other particulars, will perhaps never be wholly removed. But that these things happened at some time and in some way we do not doubt, and they profoundly influenced the course of Roman history. So too with the struggle of the Orders and the Licinian laws: it is agreed that some internal settlement was reached, and that the conquest of Italy quickly followed. Doubtful points must of course be indicated, and the details of our tradition not unduly pressed, sadly corrupted as it undoubtedly is. Another most important question is that of agrarian agitations. That the annalists transferred the phenomena of their own time to one much earlier, so that their stories are not trustworthy as they stand, is highly probable. But that there was a land-question in the early republican age, I do not doubt; nor that the struggle arising therefrom was embittered by cruel laws of debt. It would be idle to deny that anticipations and repetitions disfigure the traditional annals, or that synchronisms with events of Greek history sometimes arouse legitimate suspicion. I have called attention to the most striking of these, but do not venture to assume that no actual event of the kind occurred. Greek stories have coloured and distorted

---

[1] *Legends* pp. 238—41.   [2] Varro Sat. fragm. 524, Vitruv. II 1 § 7, 8 §§ 16—19.

Roman tradition, not merely of the regal period. A good instance is the annihilation of the Fabii at the Cremera, a parallel version[1] of the Spartans at Thermopylae, which deserves no credit. I admit that to seek for a kernel of fact in such a tale is sheer waste of time. But the explanation offered to account for the growth of the story is less satisfactory. The influence of Greek writers and the great Fabian annalist is clear, and beyond this I am not yet prepared to go. I could multiply these instances, but enough has been said in reference to the position taken up by a great scholar, whose services I appreciate highly. The tendency to connect everything in the early history of Rome with an elaborate transference and misunderstanding of ancient cults is a reaction against previous indifference, and will surely be a good deal modified in course of time.

7. A recent work[2] on the revolutionary period reconstructs the story of that age with much ingenuity and learning. I regret that I cannot agree with its main conclusions. To mention only one or two points, Ferrero's Caesar seems to me an utterly impossible figure, and the picture spoilt by the influence of too violent a reaction against the Caesar-worship of Mommsen. Nor do I think that a patching together of the scattered fragments of hostile versions gives satisfactory material for a complete rewriting of the story of the campaigns in Gaul. It is a recent fashion to know exactly from what source the later writers derived their information on any particular point. This comfortable assurance may not always retain its present freshness. Meanwhile I think it rash to build much on statements that are of value only as coming from contemporary witnesses. For that they do so come is often an assumption, however probable, and in any case we have not the works of these contemporaries before us for criticism, as we have the narrative of Caesar. If we had, and they were examined as his are, in the spirit of a cross-examining counsel, I suspect they would not leave the court without a stain on their character. That Caesar made the best of his story from his own point of view, is beyond all doubt. We need not believe all he tells us. I do not, but the new version seems to me less worthy of credit, and inconsistent with Caesar's career and the general course of events. Again, I think the talented author gives an undue prominence to Lucullus as a factor in the history of the time. As for the general structure of the book, it is my impression that the conclusions of writers on small special points are too readily received without enough consideration of their inner consistency with other parts of

---

[1] Pais, *Legends* chapter IX. Another is the ten years' siege of Veii, surely influenced by the story of the Trojan war.

[2] Guglielmo Ferrero, *The Greatness and Decline of Rome.* See note on § 946.

the narrative. And what is meant by such expressions[1] as 'the industrial democracy of Caesar's age' I have not the faintest notion. Certainly the later passages[2] in which industries are discussed do not help me much. They bear out what I have said about the predominance of slave-labour in the age of Caesar and Varro, and say nothing of democracy. Indeed to use this term here is absurd, for whatever democratic elements there were in Rome at the end of the Republic were surely not in any sound sense 'industrial.' Perhaps I have said enough to shew why I mistrust the results arrived at in this book, learned and instructive in many ways though it is. It seems misleading to give the impression that the last half-century of the Republic was a period of marked economic growth. I have shewn below that the technical improvement of agriculture cannot be taken as a proof of general prosperity, and the cases of local industries carried on in various towns do not seem to be of sufficient importance to justify such a wide conclusion. There were no doubt numerous manufactures in different places. The trades of the weaver the fuller the potter the workers in wood and metals, with other minor trades, were of course all in operation to a greater or less extent in the towns of Italy. The evidence for this is enough. But that Italian civilization had any marked industrial character, and that the age of revolution was a time of industrial[3] development, I do not believe. The export trade of Italy was evidently small, and the imports very large. Most of the articles produced in Italy were for the Italian market. The ultimate basis of finance was the money raised by the taxation and exploitation of the provinces. No doubt the peace and security established by Augustus did promote the growth of industries and revive a prosperity of considerable duration. But it is certain that, when capital found employment in manufactures, it did so largely in the form of investing in skilled slave-labour. Without statistics we can form no definite notion of the proportion of freemen to slaves in any industry. We can only speak in general terms, and we must be very careful not to imply the existence of a large class of free Italian hand-workers capable of exercising an effective influence on public affairs. To do this is surely to distort the truth. A collection of the references to the various Italian industries, such as that made by Blümner[4], clearly betrays the fact of their small importance; and part at least of this evidence cannot be used for the Republican period.

---

[1] Preface to vol. I.   [2] Vol. I c. 18, vol. II c. 8.
[3] I do not think that Ferrero I c. 6 proves this. But the passage is well worth reading.
[4] *Die gewerbliche Thätigkeit der Völker des klassischen Alterthums*, von Dr H. Blümner, in the Preisschriften von der fürstlich Jablonowskischen Gesellschaft, pp. 98—124. Leipzig 1869.

CHAPTER II

PHYSICAL GEOGRAPHY

8. THE physical geography[1] of the Italian peninsula is in the main simple and easily brought under a general view. Throughout almost its entire length the great chain of the Apennine is the dominant feature of the country: the rivers are mostly mountain torrents, the water of which rushes to the sea in headlong waste and leaves its bed dry and stony for a great part of the year. Each stream cuts out its ravine, great or small, and brings down stones sand and mud to deposit near its mouth; thus the edges of the sea are made shallower bit by bit, while the edges of the land move slowly forward, growing with the yearly tribute of the hills. This change in the shore-line is of course more remarkable in some places than in others: good instances are to be found at the mouths of the Tiber and the Arno, but as a normal phenomenon it is perhaps equally striking along the Adriatic coast. From such a conformation of the country some important consequences follow. First, there are no great river-harbours, such as London or Hamburg. And, wherever in the neighbourhood of a stream's mouth there was formed a port sufficient for the needs of ancient shipping, the tendency to silt up was a constant trouble to its owners. The Tiber is a case in point. It was to some extent a harbour-river, for vessels were brought up as far as Rome: but the uncertainties of the mouth and the labour of the upstream passage made a port on the coast-line necessary: and the remains of the imperial harbour works exist to shew how the shore has advanced and the port been pushed further out seaward by the irresistible growth of the land. In a coast-line of about 2000 miles natural landlocked harbours scarcely exist, and the help of tidal estuaries is not offered by an almost tideless sea. Nature has in short done little to promote an active seaborne commerce on the coasts of Italy, and the only great maritime city developed there in ancient times was the Greek colony of Tarentum. When Italy became Roman, the needs of commerce led to the growth of other ports in more convenient situations: but these, with the exception

[1] The work of glacial and volcanic action in different parts of Italy is fully treated in Nissen's *Italische Landeskunde* vol. I (Berlin 1883).

of the passenger-station of Brundisium, were created or improved
by art.

9. If the formation of the peninsula does not directly promote
external commerce, neither does it favour internal union. A very
large part of it is mountainous, and dalesmen living as shepherds or
tillers of the soil have always been slow to form organized states.
Each canton might have its central stronghold, important in the
event of war: but this was in no true sense a city, and no city life
was likely to arise there. We shall see that the first condition of the
union of Italy, with all its momentous consequences, was the formation of a great city, in which men's ideas could somewhat widen, and
they could learn to work together continuously for common ends.
The shape of the peninsula, which is about 650 miles long with a width
of 150 at most and 25 at least, had also an influence on its history.
The central position of Rome gave her a marked advantage over
cities to the North or South. It was not for Clusium or Capua to
achieve Italian union: tradition rightly finds the crisis of Rome's
early struggles in the conquest of Veii, a rival city only some ten
miles away. A peculiar character is given to northern Italy by the
direction of the Apennine range, here running nearly East and West
to meet the western Alps. The strip of low coast on what we call
the gulf of Genoa is small, and in parts the mountain spurs abut
directly on the sea. The broken hill country known as Liguria has
always been an obstacle difficult to pass, and its union with Italy was
only effected slowly, at the cost of long inglorious warfare. To the
North of the Apennine, reaching to the great Alpine barrier, lay a
fertile plain inviting and rewarding tillage, watered by the Po and its
many tributary streams. As Rome in her conquering and organizing
progress became more and more conscious of the Alps, it was seen
that this rich land, with its mountain frontier above and a waterway
to the Adriatic below, was an essential part of an united Italy. But
the acquisition of this district was a matter of much time and bloodshed, and only became permanent through the spread of civilization
from the South.

10. Of the islands, great and small, that lie near the Italian
mainland, Sicily alone is of primary importance in Roman history.
This is clearly seen in the struggle with Carthage. For Rome, once
dominant in Italy, the control of the island (in fact a detached piece
of Italy) was a necessity, if she meant to secure the peninsula against
invasion by sea: just as the want of control over the Alpine passes
left it open to invasion by land. Indeed Italy has attracted many
invaders from the North, and it is probable that most of the peoples
dwelling there in ancient times were descended from immigrants

who came that way. In spite of occasional winters of exceptional severity, the climate is on the whole genial, and the heat of summer is great. The olive and vine flourish in all parts of the country save the higher mountain ranges. Cereal crops and all manner of vegetables grow abundantly. The fertility of some districts, such as the volcanic land of Campania, is marvellous. In some parts, as Apulia and the south-eastern country generally, water is scarce: but as a rule irrigation presented no serious difficulty. Upland and low-land pastures afforded food to the flocks and herds at all seasons of the year, and the consequent shifting of the pastoral population no doubt contributed to keep the hill districts in a politically disunited and backward state. The extent of woodland was probably much greater in ancient times than it is now. A thick forest belt long checked the advance of the Romans in Etruria, and the great southern pine woods of Sila were famous for producing pitch: oak woods in several parts were valuable not only for bark and timber but also as a feeding-ground for herds of swine.

11. If the physical features and resources of Italy, and the position of Rome in the peninsula, had no small influence on the course of its internal history, it is equally true that the position of Italy in relation to other countries was a fact of importance. The ancient civilization that has so profoundly influenced the modern world grew up in the countries round the Mediterranean, and the long mass of Italy is carried right down into the middle of the Mediterranean world. Too much stress must not be laid on this advantage of central position: but it undoubtedly helped to bring about that which has been attributed to Roman fortune, the opportunity of dealing with enemies one by one at times convenient for Rome.

CHAPTER III

ETHNOGRAPHY

12. WE must try to form some notion of the peoples inhabiting Italy at the time when tradition professes to lift the veil and shew us the city by the Tiber bearing the name of Roma. What little is known rests mainly on (1) stray references in early writers, among whom is Herodotus, citations of early authorities (sometimes by name) in writers of much later date, and (2) researches of archaeologists and comparative philologists. I propose to give no more than the briefest outline of views widely accepted, and to avoid basing large theories on conclusions which, in spite of the learning and ingenuity of scholars, are still unavoidably vague and incomplete.

13. It seems probable that the general movement of population in prehistoric times was from North to South, immigration having taken place by land. This implies that we should look for the earlier inhabitants in the southern part of the peninsula. In agreement with this is the fact that Greek observers detected an affinity between the Itali of the mainland and the Siceli of Sicily, and preserved the tradition that the latter were immigrants from the peninsula to the island. From the Itali in the South came the name Italia, destined to be applied in course of time to the whole country south of the Alps. These, and the Oenotri not clearly distinguished from them, were probably the remains of an earlier migration, pushed into their present position by the pressure of later comers from the North. It was in this southern part of Italy that the Greek adventurers of the 8th century B.C. began the foundation of permanent settlements, colonial states, which conquered and reduced to dependence most of the old inhabitants. In wealth and splendour these outshone the cities of old Hellas, so that the South of Italy was called the Great Greece. But they, like their sister cities in Sicily, were isolated city-states. They belonged to different branches of the Hellenic stock, were bound together by no federal tie, and were always liable to quarrel among themselves under the impulse of territorial or commercial rivalry. In the South-East, afterwards known as Apulia and Calabria, were the people whom the Greeks generally called Iapygians. Their other names, such as Messapians, must not detain us here. The origin of these tribes is obscure. That they were at an early date penetrated by Greek influences is agreed: whether they were descended from a migration of the ruder Hellenic peoples beyond the Adriatic is very doubtful. The important fact about them is that they were able to maintain their independence against the Greek colonists in the South. We hear of an Iapygian chief helping the Athenians in their war with Syracuse. But later, when the Samnites were encroaching on southern Italy, they like the Greek cities felt the pressure, and sought relief from their peril by becoming allies of Rome.

14. Tradition placed the earliest of the Greek colonies at Cumae on the Campanian coast. Whatever its true date may have been, it is certain that this settlement was the forerunner of other Greek centres of influence in the bay of Naples. Here they came in contact with tribes to whom they generally applied the name of Opici (Latin *Osci*). These seem to have been offshoots of the great stock whom we find in historical times occupying the bulk of central Italy. The main body of Oscan folk were apparently still in the Apennine uplands, pressing southward by degrees. Tradition credibly represents their conquest of Campania and Lucania as a later movement. These tribes are held on the evidence of language to have been of the so-called Aryan family. They belonged to a group (Sabellian) the chief southern representatives of which in historical times were known as Samnites (Gk Σαυνῖται, Osc. *Safineis*, essentially the same as *Sabini*). In central Italy were the Sabines and a number of smaller but vigorous tribes or peoples, among whom we may mention the Marsi and Paeligni; to the south of these on the western side of the Apennine were other bodies also of Aryan race, Aequi Hernici Volsci, and in particular the Latini, who held the skirts of the hill-country and the more open land reaching to the Tiber. The northern representatives of this group of peoples may be styled Umbrian. They occupied the districts known later as Umbria and Picenum, and probably formed a part of the subject-population in what we know as Etruria. The whole group, northern central and southern, formed a great mass of kindred blood, speaking a variety of kindred dialects, and having many resemblances of customs and institutions. But they had no common political union to bind them together, and their various experiences of intercourse with other peoples naturally tended to differentiate them from each other. Nor was the difference of physical surroundings without its effect. It is no great stretch of imagination to see in the territory of the Latins a district more favourable to the growth of cities than the mountainous backbone of the peninsula could be. And the closer aggregation of men in city life surely tended to develop common interests, to promote cohesion, and favour the growth of institutions by which common action is made possible. If only the evils of Greek city-isolation could be avoided—but we must not forestall the actual sequel. It was no mere accident that in the end gave the primacy of Italy to the people among whom the notions of order duty organization and obedience were most effectively developed. It was not the power to conquer, but the skill in retaining conquests, in which the superiority of Rome was expressed. The other peoples of kindred race were quite as able to conquer as were the Latins. But the Latins under Roman leadership, as we shall see, formed an organized and progressive unit. The others did not, speaking generally, get beyond the stage of swarming bee-like whenever the increase of population called for relief. Then an outlet was found by sending out[1] a large body to win new homes. But this practice only created new communities, indifferent, and in time even hostile, to those from whom they had sprung.

15. Most mysterious of all the peoples of Italy were the Etruscans. Their racial connexion is still a puzzle to the philologists. Yet we have frequent references to them in ancient writers, and the quantity of objects discovered in their tombs is enormous. Etruscan inscriptions are numerous, but in general of small importance. Whence how and when they entered Italy is not even approximately known. It has been thought that they came from the North and were connected with the Alpine Raeti, but opinion now rather inclines to the view that they came from the East by sea. Tradition said that they came from Lydia. In historical times we find them settled in great walled cities south of the Apennine between the Arno and the Tiber. Their normal political condition was that each city was ruled by an aristocracy of warrior nobles, sometimes under a king or chief, and the number of cities was supposed to be 12. But in practice this ideal number was subject to much variation. They had been warlike conquerors, and ruled over a serf-population, Ligurian Umbrian or at all events Italian. Conquest indeed carried them far. We find them occupying two other districts, in the North the region of the Po, in the South the best parts of Campania. Tradition gave them 12 cities in each of these districts. We have at least no good reason to doubt that they did at one time enjoy great power, and were regarded by their neighbours with considerable awe. No doubt their united force could have destroyed the infant power of Rome. It is thought that Rome did for a time actually pass under Etruscan rulers. They are said to have reduced to subjection the

---

[1] This was the so-called 'sacred spring' (*ver sacrum*).

Latins Volscians and others on their way to the South. Thus at the time of their greatest expansion they were settled in three main groups of cities, and were perhaps over-lords of many lesser peoples as well. Their national character may perhaps be roughly inferred from the customs and inventions traditionally said to have been borrowed from them by others. The Romans owed to them the curule chair, the purple-edged gown, and other outward insignia of office; the arrangement of the house, with its central hall (*atrium*)

Conjectural map of early Italian peoples. Outlying seats of Etruscan power are marked E.

where the great man received his dependants; and the mysterious lore of lightning and thunderbolts, of forecasting the future by inspection of the entrails of slain animals, departments in which Etruscan specialists were habitually employed. The combats of swordsmen (*gladiatores*) are also said to have been a practice learnt from Etruria, and stage-acting to have been first introduced in Rome by Etruscan artists. To them was attributed the invention of the war-trumpet, adopted by both Greeks and Romans. The intercourse with Greeks, with whom they came into contact in all three seats of their power, seems to have had a momentous effect on their destinies. They received Greek civilization readily, and for a time this gave them an advantage over their neighbours. Greek works of art, especially the pottery of Corinth and Athens, found a market among the Etruscan nobles from an early date, and Greek mythology also found its way in. But we shall see that they did not become really Hellenized, and that they were jealous of the spread of Greek colonization in the West. Their later history, when this conquering people succumbed to the temptations of Greek luxury, will engage our attention below. In connexion with their settlement in Etruria proper we must note that they took to the sea and developed a considerable naval power, which seems to have been chiefly employed in conquest and piracy. They held Corsica and other islands, and for a time had a footing in Sardinia. It was their naval enterprises that brought them into collision with the Greeks. We shall see that this strange people, apparently destined to swallow up the slowly-emerging Rome and to become the lords of Italy, did nothing of the kind. Perhaps it may be a law of our political being that aristocracies of race must either become merged in their subject population or fall through internal decay. At all events cohesion and steady cooperation are prime necessities for such bodies as these, if they are to continue to flourish. The Etruscan cities, whether ruled by noble cliques or by single chiefs, had, as we shall see, no effective political union, and this defect was the chief cause of their fall.

16. North and West of the Etruscans were the people called the Ligurians, of whom very little is known. There are hardly any remains of their[1] language, and the only possible hope of learning more as to their affinities seems to lie in the progress of archaeology. Many facts concerning them are recorded, and from these much has been reasonably inferred. They were evidently a primitive race, occupying in the eighth century B.C. a much larger area than they did in later times. They reached at least as far as the Rhone near Arles on the West. It appears probable that they held all the Alpine country of Savoy and parts adjoining, and most of the upper plain of the Po. Southwards they reached the Arno. In historical times we find them confined to the hilly region of the north-western Apennine and Maritime Alps. Clearly they had been driven back[2] by the pressure of powerful invaders from different quarters, and cooped up in the rugged mountain country where the utmost efforts

---

[1] Now supposed to have belonged to the Aryan family.

[2] Prof. Ridgeway, in his paper *Who were the Romans*, holds that the Ligurians represent the primitive stratum of Indo-European population and once occupied the greater part of Italy.

could hardly wring a living from the scanty soil. The Celts, allied
with the Greeks of Massalia, were encroaching neighbours. The
former took possession of the plain of the Po to the North, the latter
seized most of the coast to the South, and the Ligurians were left to
become what the Romans in later times found them, a race of nimble
unruly highlanders, ever ready for raids into the lowland, and
addicted to piracy in the part where they still touched the sea.

17. At an uncertain date, but long before Rome took any direct
interest in the region of the Po, the state of things in the North was
greatly changed by two movements of great importance in their
after effects, which it may be well to mention here. From the East
a people said to have been of Illyrian origin, called the Veneti, entered
the country, probably by sea, and settled themselves in the lower
plain of the Po. From the West the Celtic tribes, having once
found the way, swarmed over the Alpine passes in successive
migrations. The Ligurians were thrust back into their hills, and the
Celts or Galli became masters of what is now Lombardy and parts
of Piedmont, and eventually of the land between the Po and the
Apennine range, now the province Emilia. This conquest was the
foundation of the Cisalpine Gaul, a momentous event in the history
of Italy. But the settlement of the Veneti was hardly of less importance, though we hear much less of the doings of this people.
The Gauls never conquered them, but the fear of a Gaulish conquest
was enough to make them take sides with Rome[1] when Rome
appeared as the defender of Italy against the Gauls. Moreover they
stood between the Gauls and the Adriatic, and so prevented the
Celtic invaders from becoming a maritime power. They were themselves a seafaring people, and had much commercial intercourse with
Greece, where their famous breed of horses was held in special
esteem. In general we must bear in mind that, while Rome was
engaged in her early struggles and laying the solid foundations of her
power as leader of kindred peoples, the region between the Apennine
and Alps was passing into new hands. The remains of former
populations, Ligurian Etruscan Umbrian, were subjects, and the
greater part of the country was ruled by tribes of a warlike and
aggressive race, ever liable to receive further accessions of strength
from their kinsmen beyond the Alps.

18. Thus the Italy in which Rome grew up was a motley
grouping of various nationalities. Into the numerous legends connected with the movements and settlements, some of native origin
others of Greek invention, we must not enter here. Nor can we

[1] See Index (*Veneti*) and Nissen vol. I p. 492.

dwell upon such side-questions as the possible kinship of the Iapygians and Veneti, of the Ligurians and the West-Sicilian Elymi, or the probability that the old inhabitants of Corsica and northern Sardinia were Ligurian, while the southern Sards may possibly have come from Africa. Archaeologists may yet achieve something towards the solution of these problems, but it is hardly likely that any discoveries in this direction will seriously affect our views on the story of Rome. The main fact, that the bulk of the peninsula was occupied by peoples more or less nearly related to the Romans, seems to be fairly well established, and it must not be lost sight of that this ethnological situation was of political importance in the long run. It made possible the Roman conquest and eventual assimilation of Italy.

CHAPTER IV

RELIGION

19. ROMAN religion as we come upon it in historical times is a strange medley. A number of great gods have their temples and worships. They are protectors of the state, and the state provides for doing them honour. Foreign influences, Etruscan Greek and so forth, are manifest, and ever growing stronger. But beside these mixed and metamorphic cults are the remains of an early native system. Its divinities are of a different character. They represent old notions fast dying out: in some cases their meaning and function are forgotten, while a name and a festival remain. Recent investigations have done much[1] towards piecing together the remnants of this earlier religion from the survivals recorded by Roman antiquaries and the remnants of the Roman calendars, and excavations in the Forum have brought to light sacred spots connected with its ritual observances. I proceed to note in general terms a few of the points interesting as illustrating the character of the old Roman people. The subject is one that has already its own literature, and our concern with it here is only indirect.

20. In the primitive Roman religion there were no images. Gods were conceived of as powers (*numina*), that is effective forces or tendencies, not as embodied in human shape or affected by human sympathies. The transition from the term *numen* to the term *deus* marks a distinct step towards the personification of superhuman power.

These powers were supposed to reside in material objects, such as a stone or a tree, and the worship of the objects themselves was probably the first stage. This is the primitive adoration of anything mysterious, known as Nature-worship, common in all parts of the world at some time or other. From this comes the belief in in-

---

[1] A good account of progress up to 1899 is given in Mr W. W. Fowler's *Roman Festivals*, pp. 332 foll. Mr C. Bailey's *Religion of Ancient Rome* (1907) summarizes results ably. Both draw from Dr Frazer's *Golden Bough*. See also E. Pais, *Ancient Legends of Roman History*, 1906.

dwelling spirits, infinite in number, which it is a man's business to propitiate.

Hence each power has its own proper place, and it may almost be said that each place has its own proper power. As religion develops, this notion of local relation cleaves to it, and when the *numen* becomes *deus* he is still conceived of as belonging to a certain place and so being the god of certain people.

The first place in which worship becomes permanently localized under a roof is the house. Domestic worship is the first to be systematized, and the last to retain the features of its origin. The gods[1] of the doorway (*Ianus*), of the hearth (*Vesta*), of the store-room (*penates*), are very early developments.

But religion is everywhere. For instance, all boundaries have a religious character. This is an ever-present fact in rural life, where boundary-stones stand as representatives of the god *Terminus*. And the dependence of the farmer on the weather, the desire to avert agricultural pests, and so forth, lead to sacrifices and festivals at fixed seasons of the farmer's year, to promote his well-being. Of rural worships those of earth (*Tellus*), corn-crops (*Ceres*), sowing (*Saturnus*), flocks and herds (*Pales*), harvest (*Ops, Consus*), may serve as specimens, and *Robigus* the spirit of mildew is an instance of malign powers to be propitiated.

A god might, and very commonly did, have a number of special attributes and functions, and be worshipped in many different places under different titles. Thus *Iuppiter*, god of the sky and celestial phenomena, appears with a great number of special names (*Fulgur, Lucetius, Elicius, Feretrius, Summanus*, are specimens) and was worshipped all over Italy. Common attributes led to identification of deities with each other, a tangle which modern inquirers find very hard to unravel. Developments too are sometimes very obscure. Thus *Mars*, a very old Italian deity, is thought to have been originally a rural god of growth, but in historical times he is a war-god.

Traces of early personification appear in the pairs of opposite sex, such as *Ianus* and *Iana* or *Diana*, *Iuppiter* and *Iuno*, *Liber* and *Libera*. The occurrence of the male and female principles is common in the early history of religions.

Survivals of early symbolism remain in *Iuppiter lapis* the sacred stone, in the spears of *Mars*, in the two-faced images of *Ianus* the door-god (*ianua*) and elsewhere. For as the state grew and set up worships of its own, it merely developed old cults with some modifications, or took over what had belonged to new members or conquered allies.

---

[1] I am not forgetting the *lares*, but omitting them because of the great uncertainty as to their nature.

Thus *Ianus* and *Vesta* become gods of Rome. *Quirinus*, said to be the Sabine analogue of *Mars*, finds a place beside him in the worship of the joint community. *Iuppiter Latiaris* is still the common god of the Latins, but his great festival (*feriae Latinae*) is presided over by Rome after the fall of Alba. *Diana*, worshipped at Aricia, is provided with a common Roman-Latin temple on the Aventine. Most important of all is the appearance of *Iuppiter* as the chief god of the state, sharing his temple on the Capitoline[1] with *Iuno* and *Minerva*, with whom he is said to have been previously associated in an earlier temple on the *Capitolium vetus*, a part of the Quirinal.

In short this crude polytheism, slowly evolving a misty theology, creating temples, and beginning to use images, was early affected by external influences. We hear of temple-builders from Etruria, and the Capitoline temple was built on an Etruscan model. But beside the general state-worships those of families, clans and *pagi* (sometimes translated 'parishes'), in fact of ancient groups not political divisions, went on.

21. All inquirers have remarked that in Roman religion there seems to have been little or no dogma; everything turned on correctness of action. The smallest flaw in performance of a ceremony vitiated it altogether: it must be begun afresh from the beginning, for the best intentions were not of the least importance. The man puts pressure on the god by doing exactly the right thing. The god, it is assumed, will take every advantage of his worshipper to evade the desired service. This quibbling precision is seen in ancient law, where form is everything, and the character of Roman religion is essentially legal. This character it kept so long as it remained Roman at all. When Greek anthropomorphism came in with Greek mythology, Greek rationalism was not far behind. And here I would make two remarks anticipating the sequel. First, when rationalism came, its sceptical influence was almost wholly confined to the educated upper classes; but by that time these classes had gained a practical monopoly of power. Secondly, scepticism tells mainly against dogma, and troubles itself little about forms; it was therefore the strictly formal Roman element in the state-religion that was best able to resist the sceptical assault. The system admired by the rationalist Polybius in the second century B.C. was still upheld by the rationalist Cicero in the last days of the Republic, and revived by Augustus.

22. We are tempted to speak of Roman religion by the name of

---

[1] According to Pais, this temple only dates from the 4th century B.C., after the Gallic fire.

superstition. But in Latin[1] *superstitio* seems to convey the notion of something futile and excessive. The spirit of sane worship is to ascertain exactly what observances are required to produce the result aimed at, and to perform these, no less and no more. This punctilious rendering of dues is *pietas*. The man who feels sure that he has successfully attained this standard may go his way and not trouble himself any more about the god until he is again in need of his services. He has no 'groundless fear of the gods.' But how is he to ascertain what is required? Here was the real difficulty, and the Roman solution was found in the creation of boards or gilds (*collegia*) composed of persons reputed to possess the necessary skill. The pontifical college was traditionally almost coeval with the foundation of the state, and the true function of the pontiffs was not so much to officiate as priests but rather to advise as a court of reference in matters that came within[2] the scope of religious law. For there was no priestly caste. As the head of the house performed the household rites, so the head of the state officiated on behalf of the community in its dealings with the gods. As time went on, and the pantheon of the state developed, particular priests had been appointed to keep up the regular observances due to certain divinities. These were *flamines*[3] (connected with *flagrare, flamma*) who performed the sacrifices of their several cults. They were under various limitations as to qualification, residence, etc. They were few in number and politically insignificant. The Vestal virgins, who were in charge of the state-hearth (*Vesta* remained a fire, not an image, to the last), were much the most important members of the special class to which *flamines* and *flaminicae* belonged.

23. With the legal notion of contract underlying the religion, with a body of official exponents of the *ius sacrum* ever concerned to retain the prestige of infallibility, it is not wonderful that we hear of most ingenious interpretations. That the prescriptions of the pontiffs had been punctually carried out, and the result aimed at not attained, was not to be admitted for a moment. Some flaw (*vitium*) in the procedure had to be discovered at all costs, and a fresh start made. Here was a situation inevitably leading to hypocrisy and imposture. So too in the case of the means employed to learn the will of the divine powers before taking any step. Signs from heaven

---

[1] See the notable passage in Cicero *de natura deorum* I §§ 115—118.

[2] Hence they had charge of the calendar. The first records of public events were their note-books, the so-called *annales maximi*, etc.

[3] The three principal *flamines* (*Dialis, Martialis*, and *Quirinalis*) were members of the pontifical college. So too was the *rex sacrorum*, of whom below § 71. See Marquardt, *Staatsverwaltung* III 242—3, 326. The other pontiffs, even the *pont. max.*, were quite free to hold ordinary magistracies, and usually did. So thoroughly secular was the office.

consisted chiefly in the flight or behaviour of birds, but also in celestial phenomena such as thunder, lightning, or (on certain occasions, such as Assemblies) a shower of rain : but anything strange[1] and unaccounted for might forebode evil. We have two terms used with reference to these signs, *auguria* and *auspicia*, not always clearly distinguished. But the verb *auspicari* strictly means 'to take the auspices,' *augurari* 'to interpret the signs,' and this probably points to the true distinction between them, *augurium* being the larger term. Auguries might be either unsought (*oblativa*) or vouchsafed to one looking for them (*impetrativa*). The seeker is *auspex* (*avi-spex*, the watcher of birds). In the state-religion he is a magistrate acting on behalf of the community for this occasion, and the right of taking auspices (*auspicium habere*) passed on from the kings to the chief magistrates of the Republic. For all important business was undertaken 'after auspication' (*auspicato*). But to infer the meaning of signs was the function of the *augur*, and tradition ascribed the institution of the augural college, as well as that of the pontiffs, to king Numa, the legendary founder of the state-religion of Rome. And the shifts to which augurs were put to explain away their failures were of course endless. But, though derided[2] by a later age, it was at the end of the Republic still thought a distinction to be an augur. Other forms of divination were later importations. The *haruspices*, whose chief function was to find signs in the entrails of victims, were Etruscan. Sibylline books and oracles were borrowed from the Greeks. On these matters we cannot dwell here. Enough has been said to shew that religion entered into every department of Roman life, from the propitiation of unseen powers surrounding the new-born child to the auspices taken before an act of war. But no general expressions can give an adequate notion of the extraordinary multitude of divine powers recognized in one form or other by families and clans or by the state. To make sure of drawing the attention of the right power, that is the one in whose department lay the granting of a particular request, it was customary, after naming certain gods or goddesses, to add a clause 'or whoever thou art,' 'whatever be thy name,' or words to that effect, in uttering a prayer. Indeed there was much to puzzle the worshipper, more particularly in rural life, where the old indistinct notions of divinity were not superseded by Greek mythology.

24. It is well to remember that the Latin word *templum* did not originally convey the idea of a building. It was an open space

---

[1] With this is connected the department of *prodigia*, which were referred to the pontiffs, who decided the expiatory acts to be performed in any given case.

[2] An instructive passage is Cicero *de nat. deor.* II §§ 7—12 with J. B. Mayor's notes.

formally marked out, especially if not exclusively for sacred purposes. Thus an augur marked out a space in which the magistrate was to remain when looking for a sign from heaven : the senate-house was a *templum*, and so was the place (later called *rostra*) from which a meeting of citizens was addressed. The notion of a building is proper to the word *aedes*, but a sacred *aedes* was of course also a *templum*. Clearly the building of a house for a god to dwell in is an indication that the god is being regarded as a person. But the Romans early began to personify abstract qualities, such as *Salus, Fides, Virtus Pudicitia, Concordia.* This was easy for a people to whom the worship of unseen *numina* had originally implied no personification at all. It has lately been suggested that the religion of Rome (the native part of it) did in effect do something for the moral guidance[1] of Roman life. It must surely be conceded that this influence was very indirect. We may grant that the devotion to precise formality was both an effect and a cause of the Roman character as revealed to us in the course of their history. A certain grim steadiness combined with minute punctiliousness (*gravitas* and *pietas*) may well have been fostered in the people by the endless observances of their public and private bargains with the gods. The word *religio* most commonly means 'scruple,' 'honour,' 'conscientiousness,' and is probably derived from a root (*lig*) containing the notion of a bond. Thus it has a legal flavour of a compact from the first. When we say that the Roman had law in his blood, it is a figure of speech, but I do not think we are entitled to say much more. Here let me end this discursive chapter, which is only intended to lead up to the scruples and difficulties of which we hear in the time of the Republic, and to which we shall often have occasion to refer below.

---

[1] See Livy xxvii 8, *Classical Review* May 1893.

CHAPTER V

THE CITY OF ROME

25. It remains to say a few words on the site of Rome as a dwelling-place, and to compare it with the neighbouring Latin towns as a place of settlement favourable to growth. The group of low hills on the eastern bank of the Tiber can hardly have been in themselves a very attractive residence. Tradition asserts, probably with truth, that the low ground between them was swamp and pools in the earliest period, and we know that the river, flowing in greater volume[1] then than in modern times, habitually flooded a great part of the site of what was afterwards the city. But the hills, which stood out more boldly then than they do now, were spacious and defensible. They were close to a wide expanse of land suitable for tillage, and the Tiber afforded a ready communication with the sea, only distant about fifteen miles. There were thus advantages of position, enabling settlers to devote themselves mainly to agriculture and at the same time to keep in touch with the outer world. The Latin towns inland, such as Tibur Praeneste and Tusculum, superior as places of residence, were cut off from the sea, and provision for their own defence against restless neighbours no doubt engaged much of their energies. Those scattered about the lower country were probably never strong communities, and we can form no clear notion of their importance, for the sites of most of them are not known, some not even guessed. Those on the coast were without the special advantages of the inland towns, and the disadvantage of being far from the centre of the district was not in their case compensated by the convenience of maritime position. For the seaboard of Latium was unsuited even to the small shipping of antiquity. What commerce there was was drawn to the mouth of the Tiber, and the control of this was asserted by Rome at an early date. To the north or the Tiber the whole coast was in Etruscan hands, until Rome secured a strip on this side. To the south the first point at all favourable to shipping was the headland of Antium, where there was some seafaring population.

---

[1] Nissen, *Landeskunde*, esp. pp. 304, 317.

But we learn that they were chiefly addicted to piracy; and Antium can hardly be recognized as a Latin town until the time when, after long contests with the Volscians, Rome finally occupied it with a colony. Moreover, if we may believe Strabo, it was along the coast that the malaria[1] afterwards common to the whole Campagna first made its appearance. Clearly the site of Rome, with all its draw-

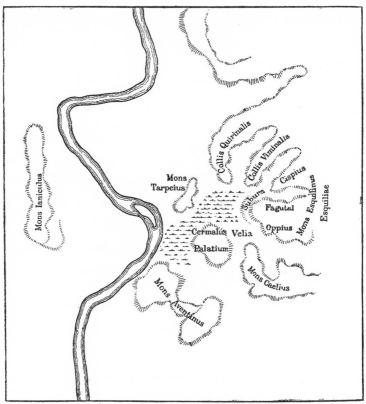

The site of Rome, roughly indicating hills and swamp.

backs, was more suited to a growing community than were those of the neighbours with whom she was connected by the ties of race and religion. But we must not let these general considerations blind us to the fact that natural advantages are turned to account by human patience and foresight. We know nothing of the heroes of primitive Rome. But when tradition, artificial and untrustworthy though it be, ascribes great and manifold energy to early Roman kings, it is probably not far from the truth.

[1] Strabo v 3 § 5 (p. 231), speaking of his own time, but the effect probably took place earlier.

26. In regard to the foundation of Rome we know little more than the assumed fact that all things have a beginning. The date assumed as a practical basis of reckoning, 753 B.C., is merely the result of Varro's calculations some seven centuries later, and need not detain us. That the growth of the city was gradual, all agree. Modern inquiries so far confirm fragmentary tradition as to make the chief stages of this growth fairly certain. No verbal description can take the place of a map, so I will speak in reference to the map

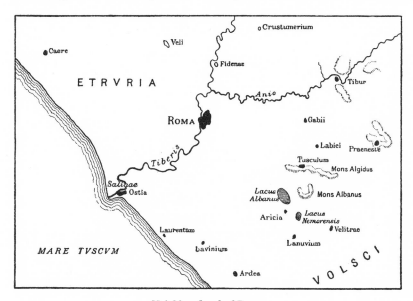

Neighbourhood of Rome.

inserted for this purpose. The first spot occupied was the *mons Palatinus* or *Palatium*, the top of which was a compact site easily rendered strong for defence by scarping and walling. Its most accessible side was to the north-east, and here stood the gate and the chief artificial fortifications. This stronghold, the so-called *Roma quadrata*, would command the land near it, in particular the piece of ground (*Velia*) running out at a lower level towards the slopes of the Esquiline. The next stage was the occupation of the Esquiline itself, which seems to have been followed by the building of a rampart of some kind including the whole of the new quarter. In the total thus formed seven parts were recognized, (1) the Palatine proper with (2, 3) its parts or annexes the Velia and Cermalus, (4, 5, 6) the three parts of the Esquiline, Oppius Cispius and Fagutal, (7) a group of houses on the north-west side of the Esquiline, called *Subura*. The existence of a town enclosed by this curious boundary is attested by the ancient festival of the *Septimontium*, which concerned only these parts of the subsequently larger city. That these parts were known as *montes*, and their inhabitants as *montani*, is strange but apparently true. The next stage was one of a different character. On the Quirinal hill to the north another settlement had been founded, of Sabine origin. Tradition suggests that the rival communities came to blows, but in the end united to form a single state. Many survivals, chiefly in the existence of separate religious observances, remained to shew that there had been such a combination of two independent communities, the headquarters of which were the Palatine and Quirinal respectively. But the latter height, and the Viminal associated with it, were known as *colles* (not *montes*), and their inhabitants as *collini*. It is probable that two other *montes*, the Capitoline and Caelian, were also included in the new circuit. The former, marked out by nature for the citadel (*arx*) of the joint community, was perhaps[1] not yet provided with a complete ring-wall of its own, but spots on and about it were devoted to religious ceremonies. The Caelian was probably not much built upon as yet, but an agricultural people would be glad of a protected open space, if only to shelter cattle in time of war. The important points to notice are, that the Aventine was not included in the city, and that the fortifications did not extend to the river. Thus far we seem to be in the early regal period of the legendary history. According to this tradition several Latin towns had already been conquered, and numbers of their inhabitants transferred to Rome. Anyhow it is clear that a great growth of population was in progress, and we are speaking of a state strong and well-established according to the standard of primitive times.

27. The last stage brings the city almost to the size and shape[2] of the Rome of the Republic. It is traditionally connected with the later kings, supposed (though this is disputed) to have been an Etruscan dynasty. The so-called Servian wall represents a bold advance. Not only was the Aventine enclosed by an extension of the wall to the south, but the line of fortification was carried down to the river. There was also a considerable extension to the north and east. Here there was no natural line of defence, for the land sloped gently up to the high ground of the eastern hills. So a large

---

[1] Another view is that the Capitoline was a separate fortress from the first.

[2] Great doubt has lately been thrown on this as belonging to the regal period. Pais holds that this stage was not reached till the 4th century B.C. See *Legends*, pp. 39, 141, 315—6. But I am not convinced as yet, for this seems to allow too little time for the subsequent development of Roman power.

part of the new enceinte on this side was strengthened by a long artificial mound (*agger*) to give the height needed for commanding the ground outside, and faced with blocks of stone.   The whole city was divided into four districts (*regiones*, 'markings-out,' connected with *regere*).   These were called 'parts' (*tribus*), *Suburana*, *Esquilina*, *Collina*, *Palatina*.   According to Varro[1], the first of these included the Caelian, which is remarkable.   The division was probably either based on an earlier one, or dictated by considerations not now to be traced.   Of one thing we may be reasonably sure, that the space enclosed by the new wall was not all covered with houses.   A good deal of the area was still open ground.   This would afford a refuge to those who dwelt on farms outside, whenever danger arose, for the function of ancient cities generally was to be common strongholds quite as much as places of residence.   Whether the whole of the new wall was actually completed in the regal period is doubtful.   Perhaps the same may be said of the drainage works[2] by which the lower levels of the city were greatly improved.   It seems that the natural line of the watercourses was followed, and eventually a system of sewers provided by arching over the channels.   Thus swampy ground was drained, rain-water no longer allowed to lodge there, and a proper outfall provided for the speedy discharge of the floods back into the river.   The *cloacae* started from the Suburan slope.   The space known as the *forum Romanum* became more regularly available for use as the common market and meeting-place of the city.   How very low its original level was may be gathered from the late excavations.   Other spaces, such as the cattle-market (*forum boarium*) near the river, would also be greatly improved by the drainage.   That the beginning of these two great works was due to the later kings seems to me probable, for it is most unlikely that the men of the early Republic were in a position to undertake such enterprises at a time when, if we may trust highly credible tradition, they were constantly at war.

28.   The above sketch is merely an attempt to state in a few words what I believe to be the probable course of the early growth of the city.   We have in truth no real knowledge.   After all that has been written on the subject, there is no general agreement even as to probabilities.   Whether our tradition is of any value whatever, is itself a matter of doubt.   Archaeologists have shewn reason for believing that the site of Rome was at least partly occupied at an earlier date than tradition indicates.   It remains to mention a few other works attributed to the kings.   The old pile-bridge over the Tiber is one.   It is set down to Ancus Marcius, and with it the

---

[1] Varro *LL* v § 46.

[2] The existing *cloaca maxima* is now said to be a late republican work.   Pais in *Legends*, p. 138.

fortification of the Janiculum, the height beyond the river. He is
also credited with the foundation of Ostia, that is with securing the
river mouth and the salt-pans worked there. That these were under-
takings of the regal period is probable, but the effective occupation of

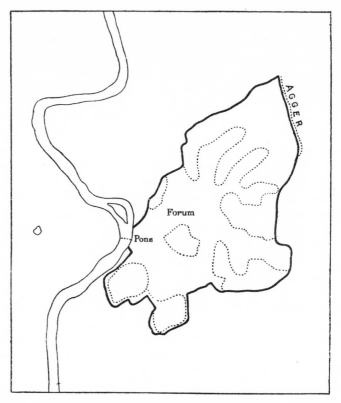

Supposed line of the 'Servian' Wall.

the Janiculum seems to be a later step. That the valley between the
Palatine and Aventine was used as a race-course is not unlikely.
That a space was cleared for the great temple on the Capitoline, and
the temple actually begun, is possible. So too with the temple of
Diana on the Aventine. But the tradition assigning shares in these
works to the last three kings is not deserving of special notice. It
has even been doubted[1] whether Rome was in any sense formed by
the union of separate communities; but the strongest argument for
this view, that two towns could hardly have existed so close together,
seems to me an arbitrary assumption, wholly insufficient to justify
us in setting aside the marked indications of two different sets of

[1] See Niese, *Grundriss der Römischen Geschichte*, § 5.

religious observances. But it must be admitted that attempts to follow out the union in detail inevitably lead to fanciful reconstructions, and are best omitted altogether.

29. Nothing will illustrate more clearly the difficulty of forming a notion of the state of the city in the time of transition from the old monarchy to the Republic than a consideration of the length of the enceinte known as the Servian wall. It is reckoned at between five and six miles. To provide men to man such a fortification would only be possible for a numerous community ; nor would mere defence save the city from famine in the long run. That an active field-army was necessary is certain. That there was such a force is proved by the fact that Rome survived and became the mistress of Latium. We have no data from which to form even an approximate estimate of the Roman population. But it is evident that it was considerable. At this point we naturally wonder how a large population contrived to get a living there. Granting that the influx of people from the country both filled up the city and provided defenders in time of war, there was still the question of food. And, the more we allow for farmers normally resident outside, the less we must allow for farmers normally resident within the walls. Nor indeed would an agriculture frequently interrupted by war be a sufficient resource to maintain a large population. The total area of Roman territory at the time (509) assigned to the foundation of the Republic was certainly very small, roughly bounded by the Alban hills and the sea. The inland extension beyond the Anio was precarious and not large. The only supposition that seems to account for the size and strength of the city on the Tiber is that the trading community was far more important than tradition suggests, or even than modern inquirers are generally disposed to admit. In short it is to the river that we must look for a reasonable explanation of much that is otherwise unintelligible. When we hear of trade-connexions such as fairs, of a treaty with Carthage in the first year of the Republic, of the foundation of Ostia, and when we hear of relations with Greeks (in particular those of Cumae), we are dealing with matters too obscure or uncertain to supply inferences in detail, but a general truth probably lurks in them. In the seventh and sixth centuries B.C. there was plenty of commerce going on in the Western Mediterranean, and it is probable that a fair share of it was attracted to the Tiber. Moreover, on this supposition we can better understand the development of town life, and with it the respect for law, which seems to have marked the Romans from very early times. Again, we must remember that there were three clearly-marked forms of political union prevalent, (1) great empires, such as those created by conquest in the East, (2) tribal systems in great variety, common among the more backward Greeks and the peoples to whom the Greeks gave the name of Barbarians, (3) city-states, common among the more advanced Greeks, and planted by them as colonies all about the Mediterranean seaboard, wherever they could expel or avoid Phoenician competitors. The first of these does not concern Italy. The second was a system good for expansion but bad for cohesion, the third was just the reverse. We shall see that the progress of Rome to supremacy in Italy was mainly due to a combination of cohesive organization with expansive power. As against tribal disunion the city-state prevailed. As compared with the isolation of city-states, the Roman methods of gradual incorporation gave what the cities had hitherto lacked, the largeness of scale necessary for competing with growing tribal communities. We shall see that the Sabellian tribes were able to overcome the Greek cities of southern Italy, only to be overcome themselves by the more compact confederacy of Rome and to be themselves added to the Allies of the conquering city. Rome brought into the world an entirely new political system, in which the consistent pressure of moral force was far more vitally important than the direct use of the sword. It has even been maintained that Rome became mistress of Italy through being less warlike than those whom she subdued, and the paradox contains a truth. But the Roman system was assuredly not the fruit of prophetic vision. The Roman methods of attaching other peoples to the civic community on the Tiber were developed gradually to meet immediate needs. How came Rome to follow a line of development so different from the ordinary methods of imperial expansion? Is it not highly probable that Rome was from the first essentially different from other cities? If so, do not the amalgamation of separate communities and a lively intercourse with the outer world afford the most probable explanation of the difference? The story that the founder Romulus strengthened the infant settlement by opening a refuge for outlaws is in form a palpable myth. But we may observe that the tendency to incorporate conquered peoples was in the historical age ever growing weaker as the dominion of Rome grew wider. Does not this, fairly viewed, indicate that in the earlier period the tendency had been even stronger? No doubt the early incorporations would be mainly Latin folk, and the core of the population Latin. But this only made it easier for the whole eventually to coalesce, and for a minority of aliens to be wholly absorbed in the mass. The community thus formed would surely be very different from that of an ordinary Latin city. And the mixed character of the population would go far to account for the internal struggles that form so great a part of the story of the early Republic.

CHAPTER VI

SOCIAL AND POLITICAL GROUPS

30. THE early Romans were a blend of stocks belonging to the so-called Indo-European or Aryan races of mankind. And, whatever other elements may have contributed to form the 'Roman People' of early days, they do not appear to have been such as to modify greatly the Latin character of Rome. The Sabines were closely related to the Latins, while of the alien Etruscans no considerable immigration seems to have taken place. It is therefore not to be wondered at that we find the primitive institutions of Rome based[1] on the Family. When we say that the Family is the basis of Roman society, we mean that it is the Family, not the Individual, of which the State takes account.

31. The primitive Roman Family consisted of

A. Father.
B. Son or Sons (by blood or adoption).
C. Wife.
D. Daughter or Daughters.
E. Slaves.
F. The estate (*res familiaris*).

And it is to be remembered that emancipated children formed no part of the family of their birth : they belonged to some other family. This Family is under the absolute rule of the Father. All the persons, and the estate also, are in his 'hand' (*manus*). But if he is supreme head of the Family, and so enjoys all the rights, on the other hand it is he who is liable for the fulfilment of all the duties. He has the estate, but out of it he must maintain the members of the Family : above all, he must see that the proper offerings and acts of worship are duly performed, and so ensure the favour of the gods. For every

---

[1] If the Family as described with its line of male-succession be really (see §§ 46, 49) a Sabine institution, this does not make it less Roman, but merely non-Latin. Then the changes of later times represent a reversion to Latin models. The institutions with which we start will be those of the aristocracy of conquest, and the course of Roman history will be the gradual self-assertion of the conquered majority. It is hardly necessary to confess my obligations to Maine's *Ancient Law*.

Family has its own gods, and its religious observances (*sacra*) must be performed by its own representative. There must therefore always be someone in the position of Father.

32. As no woman could be the head of a Family, it is clear that sons, or one son at least, were necessary for the continuance of the Family. In case no son was born to him in the course of nature, the Father could and did make good the deficiency by adopting some one as his son. The adopted son was in exactly the same position as a son by birth would have been: he was subject to the absolute power of the adopting Father, and henceforth owed worship to the gods of his new family, not to those of that in which he was born. He was thus qualified to succeed his new Father at death and become Father of the Family himself. A woman was always in the 'hand' of some man: in other words some man was always her Father. Her marriage meant that she was 'discharged from the hand' (*manu missa*) of one 'Father' into that of another. The former Father might be her real sire, her real or adoptive brother, or whoever the head of her former family might be: the new Father was her husband, whose daughter she was in the eye of the ancient law.

33. A notable but unobtrusive figure in the ancient Family was the Slave. He was included in the Family, but his condition of bondage was presumably permanent, and he could only become free by deliberate emancipation, a process which was probably rare. His condition seems however to have been a much more tolerable one than that of those who formed the brutalized labour-gangs of later times. The estate, all the goods of the Family and the acquisitions of all its members, belonged strictly speaking to the Father. If he allowed any member, even a slave, to acquire goods for his own benefit, this was solely by grace of the Father. But this universal proprietary right belonged to the Father in his capacity of *Paterfamilias*, not to him personally as an individual: if he absorbed all the rights, he was also liable for the corresponding duties. The absolute nature of the Father's power is shewn by its including the power of life and death. He was not only the High Priest of the Family, acting on its behalf in matters of religion: he was also its Supreme Judge, administering an unwritten customary law. It was however a traditional usage to consult the assembled adult free males on any important matters of family concern. This is probably the germ of an institution which in later days gives a marked character to Roman official life,—the advisory board or council (*consilium*), on whose recommendation (*de consilii sententia*) the responsible officer commonly performs his official acts. But in the last resort the official in his sphere, like the Father in the Family, is the holder of the

actual power: only in the Family the Father never goes out of office, and there is no way of calling him to account.

34. Such in the briefest outline was the nature of that marvellous institution, the early Roman Family. It was the groundwork of Roman life, for it is out of Families, not of Individuals, that the larger units—Clan, Tribe, State—were formed. Its influence is seen in the order and obedience to which the greatness of the Roman People was primarily due. That it had its weak side, that the untimely or pedantic assertion of paternal rights might end in a cruel and deadening rigidity, fatal to rational progress, is clear. But we are not bound to suppose that the voice of natural affection was always silent: even toward the offending slave the suggestions of mercy might occasionally prevail: nor is it unreasonable to allow something for the influence of common sense in times so distant from our own.

35. As the head of every Family must be a male, and sons could found new Families while daughters could not, it was natural that kinship should only be taken into account in the male line. The children of a man's son or brother stood in a direct relation to himself: they are 'born to him' in a special sense (*adgnati, agnati*): if he is a Valerius, they are Valerii too, so long as they do not by adoption (or, in case of the females, by marriage) become members of another Family. The children of his daughter or sister are 'sharers of birth' (*cognati*) with him, but legally they belong to the Families of the several husbands. What then happens when a man has a number of sons who found Families of their own, and when the sons of these sons do the same, and so on for several generations? The answer is most probably as follows. In course of time the actual evidence of agnate relationship is lost sight of in the cases where the relationship is distant. There are a number of Valerii who belong to different Families, and whose relationship to each other is marked by nothing beyond the common heritage of the Valerian name. They do however recognize a common bond in the common descent presumed by the name, and they have common worships. In fact a new social body has come into being, the House or Clan (*gens*). This body is found existing among other Aryan races: but nowhere was it so important in the history of a progressive state as among the Romans. The true name (*nomen*) of a Roman citizen is that of his Clan. Thus 'Publius Cornelius Scipio' tells us that the man is of the *gens Cornelia*, of the Family or group of Families (*stirps*) marked off by bearing the surname (*cognomen*) Scipio: Publius is his first name (*praenomen*).

36. It appears that in early times the *gens* not only had common

religious observances (*sacra*) but held property in common, like the Family from which it sprang. In the historical period this custom had died out, leaving traces. At need a Clan Council could be got together and could pass ordinances binding on its clansmen : but this was very seldom done in historical times. And as the Family had its free dependents, such as emancipated slaves or persons who had of their own will sought the protection of the *Paterfamilias*, so too the Clan had its dependents. The general name for dependents of this kind was 'listeners' (*clientes*), men ready to do the bidding of their protectors (*patroni*) who stood to them in a sort of paternal relation. Such dependents were not full members of the Family or Clan to which they were attached : but they had a kind of inferior membership, sufficient to ensure them the support of their patrons in all the affairs of life and to impose on them the sacred duty of returning these favours on any and every opportunity. In short, they came under the immemorial rule, that loyalty (*pietas*) forbids any member of a Family or Clan to do anything to the hurt of his fellows.

37. When tradition gives us our first view of the Roman State we see it organized as follows. There is the whole body of the people (*populus Romanus*), the community, as we might call it. Of this body there are sections, called *curiae*, which sections are represented as existing from the foundation of Rome. The community is only conceived as divided into these sections or wards, for the two bodies come into being together. Mommsen points out that the traces preserved in other cities indicate that the system of *curiae* was common to the communities of Latin race. In Greece the corresponding institution was the Phratry, and φρατρία is the word used by Greek writers on Rome to represent *curia*. We next learn that the Curia was made up of *gentes*. The size of Clans being necessarily various, we infer that the number of Clans in the several Curies must have varied also : and there is no real evidence to the contrary. The Curies appear as political divisions on an equal footing : and in each Curia no account is taken of the primitive grouping of its members in Clans and Families.

38. But we are also told that the community consisted of[1] three Tribes (*tribus*), Ramnenses, Titienses and Luceres. These Tribes do not appear as original divisions of the community. Indeed the first two were taken to be survivals of hostile neighbouring communities, which had each its king, fought for mastery, and then coalesced. According to Mommsen the primary notion of *tribus* is local, and the word has been transferred in use from the district to the people

---

[1] This is very doubtful, and all attempts to reconstruct the primitive organization of the community must be largely a work of imagination dealing with unsatisfactory evidence.

in it. If it ever meant the whole territory of a community, it may perhaps have stood for the community itself and so agree with the tradition which represents Rome as formed out of the union of three such bodies. Each Tribe is made up of Curies: of these there are thirty, or ten to a Tribe: and even after these three primitive Tribes disappear the Curies remain, thirty in number. Regarded as a part of the community, neither the *tribus* nor the *curia* have any organization. Neither can act independently, for want of machinery.

39. If the system of subdividing the community into sections or groups was normal throughout the Graeco-Italian world as a basis for the assignment of civic duties and rights,—and I do not dispute it— it may seem that I am laying excessive stress upon it here, as though the system were specially characteristic of Rome, which I do not allege it to be. My reason for dwelling so long upon these various groups is that I feel bound to look forward to a time when the community becomes a voting body, the recognized and (more or less) active Sovran, giving final decisions on affairs of state. We shall see that under the Roman constitution, down to the end of the Republic, all Assemblies voted not as mass-meetings by Heads, but by Groups[1] of some sort or other. In Greece the normal voting of state Assemblies was by Heads, and the importance of this as rendering possible the development of Democracy, for instance at Athens, is much greater than might at first sight appear. But of this in its own place: at present I am only concerned to account in some measure for the vitality of the group-system in Roman politics. I do not look for the cause in the absence of some great revolution such as that of Cleisthenes at Athens. It seems rather to be connected with a subtle influence working at Rome with special force and affecting Roman life and ways of thinking. The Roman of the historical period bore the name of his Clan, which the Greek had dropped. His membership of the Clan was to him a more important fact, more a part of his life, more a source of sympathies, than it was to the Greek. I suggest that the habit of being one of a group in his daily life made it seem more natural to him that he should be one of a group in political action also. I conceive that this tendency, supported by the ingrained conservatism of the Roman people, maintained the group-system to the last.

[1] That the importance of the group-system was clear to a Roman observer may be seen from Cicero *pro Flacco* §§ 15, 16.

CHAPTER VII

THE REGAL PERIOD

40. THAT there was once a time when Rome was governed by Kings is universally admitted. We believe this chiefly for the following reasons. First, tradition is clear and unanimous on the point. Secondly, in the system of the Republic there appear institutions and principles the existence of which can only be satisfactorily explained on the supposition that the republican government had been preceded by the government of Kings. Thirdly, there is no *a priori* doubt to be removed, for a monarchy of some sort or other is the normal constitution of primitive states. There has however come down to us what purports to be a history of the Roman Kings, indeed of Kings before the foundation of the city of Rome. This account connects the first beginnings of the Roman people with the tale of Troy, through the wanderings of Aeneas and his settlement in Italy. So far as we know, this story is a mere legend compiled or concocted, centuries after the events it professes to record, by Greek writers who courted the favour of Romans, when Rome was already a great and rising power. We have the story as it was dressed up for literary purposes by writers of the Augustan age—that is, about the Christian era,—who narrate purely legendary matter with as much gravity and confidence as if it were established fact. Historical criticism has destroyed the credit of these narratives, and we need not consider them in detail. There were in Rome a number of public works traditionally assigned to the regal period,—walls, drains, temples and other buildings. These works are consistent with the outlines of the traditional history in some important points. The separate primitive wall of the Palatine agrees with the story that this position was occupied first of all by the founders of the city. The great size of the Servian Wall and the Cloaca point to large resources and a good supply of labour, which can best be conceived as acting under the pressure of absolute power. We may reasonably believe that early Rome was not only ruled by Kings, but was under their rule progressive and eventually great. But it may be true that these vast works[1] are of a later date. If so, we must certainly attribute to the

---

[1] Of course the present remains of a work really ancient may be themselves of later date.

republican government a far greater activity in this department than has been generally assumed, or than I have ventured to assume. But the fact of a regal period will remain. I proceed to give a sketch of the institutions of that time, based on the researches of Mommsen and others. It is necessary to lay stress on the fact that it is a fancy-picture, the materials of which are chiefly furnished by backward inferences from survivals.

41. At the head of the Roman state stood a single magistrate, the King (*rex*), whose function it was to rule and guide (*regere*). He comes before us as leader of the people in war, as its representative in matters of religion, as its judge with jurisdiction in such legal matters as concern the people at large rather than particular Families. He is supreme, endowed with the power of commanding and enforcing commands which the Romans called *imperium*. We English have no word to express the concentrated and absolute power originally connoted by this memorable term. Nor indeed had the Greeks. The Romans were exceptional, perhaps unique, in the clearness with which they grasped the notion of ample official power and made it a chief element in their public life. The power of the Father in the Family was surely the model. The *imperium* included the power of life and death. And yet we do not find it implied in tradition that such enormous powers produced tyrannical government, until the last King's misdeeds were ended by a revolution. And then too we must remember that a King ruled for life, and consequently there existed no non-revolutionary means of bringing him to account.

42. We are not however to suppose that the Roman King was subject to no sort of restraint. All through Roman history we feel the working of a moral force under the pressure of which men, and officials in particular, were held back from the extreme assertion of their strict rights and powers. This no doubt was beginning to act in the days of the Kings. True, the King himself determined what was forbidden or enjoined by the rules of the divine law (*fas*) or the civil right (*ius*) resting on immemorial custom. But the absolute power of one over many must itself rest on a moral force of some kind, and any sane ruler would know that there must be some limits to his caprice. To conduct the business of the state by merely issuing his commands might be (as we say) 'within the Constitution': but custom enjoined that he should consult the Senate, his advisory board, on all important matters. That he did not do this is one of the grave charges made by tradition against the last of the Kings of Rome. Persistent violation of Custom (*mos*) was too great an outrage for Roman feeling to endure. Again, in case a citizen was condemned to death, the King might allow him to appeal to the popular Assembly against the sentence:

but it does not seem that he was obliged to allow it. In such cases we may believe that public feeling (which cannot be concealed) would go for much.

43. Nor must we forget that we are not dealing with Kingship in its hereditary form. The Roman King succeeded to the regal powers not as a member of some royal Family or Clan, but in virtue of election. This process was, if the tradition may be trusted, carried out in two stages, (1) the choice of a person, (2) his investiture with the *imperium*. On the first of these the Senate would probably have no little influence, but both were formal acts of the whole community assembled by Curies. The flight of birds was solemnly watched for a sign of the will of Heaven, for it was of the utmost importance that the chosen of the people should be the accepted of the gods. In an elective monarchy some provision must be made for the interval between two reigns. There must be some one temporarily charged with the power of initiation: some one at the very least competent to hold a lawful Assembly, to put a name to the meeting, and to declare the result. There is no 'Demise of the Crown' such as follows automatically upon the decease of a hereditary monarch. At Rome the gap was stopped by the appointment of a 'Between-ruler' (*interrex*), or rather of several in succession, from the Senate, any one of whom save the first could nominate a King. It is most unlikely that he should have done this merely of his own whim: no doubt intrigue and conclaves, perhaps open discussion in the Senate, went on before any Interrex came forward with a name.

44. There is not much to be said about the Senate of the regal period: the great days of this body belong to a later age. We can hardly doubt that they were originally clan-elders under a King who ruled in right of birth. But, just as we only know of elected Kings, so we find the Senate represented as made up of the nominees of the King. Custom would no doubt set limits to his caprices. But it was surely an important part of the King's prerogative that whoever sat in the Senate did so in virtue of the royal choice. The function of the Senate was simply to advise. It could not meet unless summoned by the King: it could only give its opinion on what he laid before it. To initiate and to execute were the part of the King: the Senate had in ordinary circumstances no direct responsibility or power. But in certain crises (that is, in the regal period, on a vacancy of the throne) it fell to the Senate[1] to make the necessary arrangements for the *interregnum*, for the continuity and transmission of the *imperium*. They were competent to consult the gods (*auspicia*) on behalf of the community in default of the regular representative, the King. Thus

[1] See below, § 78.

there was no break in the active sovranty, no loss of touch with the divine guardians of Rome ; for in any sudden emergency the dormant power of the Fathers awoke.

45. At the back of King and Senate we find the People (*populus*). These are the Community, the aggregate of those who are in any sense citizens (*cives*), who have any right to call themselves *Romani*. According to credible tradition they are so far recognized as the sovran power that the election of the King takes place in their Assembly. It seems however that their action is merely one of acceptance or possibly of rejection : it is not hinted, nor is it probable, that a citizen could make any other proposal alternative to the motion of the Interrex.   So too when the King allowed a condemned man to appeal to the people (*provocare ad populum*): the award of the people (*iudicium populi*) could either free him (*absolvere*) or leave the sentence to stand, but not commute it.   In the famous legendary case[1] of Horatius expiatory sacrifices are imposed, but on the offender's father, not on himself: and apparently by the authority of the King.   Legislation was no doubt very rare in these early times.   If it did occur, it would on the part of the people consist solely in the Aye or No of the Assembly to the proposal (*rogatio*, asking) laid before it.   All through there was not a trace of any popular initiative.   In the Assembly the people grouped themselves according to their Curies (*curiatim*).   The vote of each Curia counted as one.   This vote was determined by the votes of its members present and voting: and, as there were never more than thirty *curiae*, the process of ascertaining the will of the Assembly was probably not a long one.   Moreover, the tendency of Roman voting-groups in later times was to follow the lead of the one that voted first, and the order was to some extent settled by drawing lots.   Whether this was the case with the Curiate Assembly of regal times we do not know: but the practice reeks of antiquity.

46. The Roman People, when we get our first glimpse of it in history, appears as consisting of two grades or orders—the Patricians, who bear most of the burdens and have all or nearly all the rights, and the Plebeians, who bear some burdens and have (at least directly) few or no rights.   To act in any religious or legal capacity a man must be a Patrician.   The Plebeians are in every way inferior, and the history of the early Republic is mainly taken up with their struggles to attain equality with the privileged order.   The origin of these Orders is not known with certainty, and the scholars who have inquired into the matter are not yet at the end of their debate. But it is probable that the Patricians (*patricius* connected with *pater*)

[1] Livy I 26.

are the stock[1] of the old warrior-clans that made up the sovran
people when Rome first existed as a community. The name must
surely be later, when the increase of dependents of various kinds
made it convenient to distinguish those who (in the strict sense) were
'sons of fathers' from those who were not. The Plebeians are men
of the *plebs* or *plebes*, a word which Mommsen connects with *plenus*
and *pleo*, a verb found only in compounds (as *compleo, impleo*) : there
is then about it a notion of filling up, of serving to make up a whole.
It is not unlike our expression 'the Masses.' The growth of such a
class may be probably accounted for in the following way. It has
been already remarked that the old Families and Clans had their
dependents. These Clients were under their Patrons' protection, and
the bond of clientship was a very close one ; but it conferred no right
to any voice in the affairs of the Family or Clan : the client could not
be said to 'have a clan' in the true sense (*gentem habere*). Some of
them would be manumitted slaves, others would be persons of alien
birth who had sought of their own accord the protection of the
mighty. It seems also that Rome drew numbers from the cities
near, as they severally fell under her influence, partly from trans-
planting of those conquered in war, as tradition tells in the case of
Alba, partly from voluntary immigration. For Rome's position on
a navigable river, controlling a bridge[2] to which traffic would be
drawn, on what was probably a main line of communication
between Latium and Etruria, would tend to attract strangers from
the first. Now these aliens all needed protection, not those alone
who came to escape from punishment or wrong. Many of these, if
not most, became dependents of the state rather than of any particular clan ; thus their protector was the King, in whom were
gathered the active powers of the state. As time went by the
numbers of these different classes of dependents increased: a general
name was found for them, Plebs : a name implying that such people
had no independent legal status in the community, but were important only by numbers as the 'Multitude.'

47. In the inequality of conditions thus described there is nothing
inconsistent with the primitive notions and practice of the Graeco-
Roman world. In the early days of the Greek city-states we find
a privileged body of citizens and an unprivileged multitude. In Italy
too we find traces of Nobles and Commons in many cities, and of
a certain sympathy between the Nobles of different communities.
Tradition said that when the Albans were transplanted to Rome the

---

[1] For the question of race, see § 49.

[2] Assuming the *pons sublicius* to be a work of the Kings. A river-passage was always
an important point, as we shall see in the case of Fidenae.

noble families of Alba were enrolled among the Roman Patricians. The afterwards famous Julian clan was one of those that claimed an Alban origin. To be a Patrician it was necessary to be a full member (not a dependent) of some recognized clan. Mere residence, however long and continuous, could never give the full citizenship at Rome or any other city.

48. We should observe that the King might come to regard the Plebeians from a point of view very different from that of the Patricians. The inferiority of their condition would be a point of minor importance in the eyes of a ruler to whom Patrician and Plebeian were subject alike. He might find that their obedience was more habitual and cheerful than that rendered him by the proud members of the ancient clans. If great public works were executed under the kings, they were no doubt in the main products of Plebeian labour. In short it was quite natural that the kings should, as far as they dared, favour the Plebs: nor was it strange that the Patricians should resent this policy. And if the relations between King and Patricians should ever become seriously strained—if the ruler, in whom the forces of unity were embodied, and the nobles, jealous of their privileges and well used to cooperation under leaders, should quarrel—then clearly the fabric of the state was shaken, and the hour of revolution was at hand.

49. There remains the further question, political only in a secondary sense, whether any ethnological difference can be traced between Patricians and Plebeians. I have long been convinced that there was some difference not easily accounted for on the supposition that the Roman people were a homogeneous whole, varying from the first only in degrees of political privilege. In later chapters I have more than once pointed out what seem to me traces of a marked Patrician character in the cases of certain eminent Romans. A recent pamphlet[1] has furnished an ingenious provisional answer to the question. The Patricians are identified with the Sabines, and are thus an aristocracy of conquerors. The Plebeians are the ancient inhabitants of Latium, the people known as Ligurians in historical times, who were once the possessors of the greater part of Italy. Latin then is originally Ligurian, and that the conquerors adopt the language of the conquered is a familiar phenomenon. Thus the political difference is based on an ethnological one. The evidence adduced to support this view varies greatly in character and value. But the weaker parts do not invalidate the stronger. Time will bring further materials; for the present I accept these conclusions as a

---

[1] W. Ridgeway, *Who were the Romans?* 1907. See below, §§ 66, 97, for the Sabine origin of the *gens Claudia*.

probable hypothesis, with certain reservations. That there was a strong Sabine element in the Roman Patriciate, perhaps a dominant majority, seems reasonably certain, but a negative conclusion, that none but Sabines were Patricians, is hardly proved, perhaps hardly susceptible of proof. Among the points raised in evidence none is better established than the duality of burial-customs, and good reason is shewn for believing that cremation, the later custom, came in with the Sabine conquerors. But the great *gens Cornelia* clung to the practice[1] of inhumation till the death of Sulla, and to prove them not to have been Patrician will need strong evidence. I believe therefore that neither the Patricians nor the Plebeians were ethnologically homogeneous. That Sabine institutions and Sabine blood were predominant in the former, and old-Latin in the latter, seems highly probable, and this is quite consistent with the traditions of the rape of the Sabine women, and the Sabine origin of Numa, the legendary founder of the religious system. The most striking argument in favour of this view is that drawn from the customs of marriage and inheritance. For if, as Prof. Ridgeway with much reason contends, the most solemn form of marriage (*confarreatio*) and the male line of succession (*agnatio*) were not only essentially Patrician but essentially Sabine, we gain a far more reasonable explanation of the fact that the right of lawful intermarriage with the privileged Order was so long refused to the Plebeians. Here also I must remark that the converse fact of female succession among the Plebeians is at present much less satisfactorily made out. I am omitting what seem to me the less important arguments adduced by the writer, in particular the theories of migration and remigration and the zoological doctrines the soundness of which I am not in a position to test. I trust I have said enough to shew that this clever and learned inquiry has a bearing on the political life of Rome. On many matters, such as the Struggle of the Orders and the early admission[2] of the Sabines to the full Roman franchise, the views of students will be somewhat modified if they see in the Patriciate a conquering aristocracy of Sabine (or mainly Sabine) extraction, gradually becoming merged with a larger Latin substratum in a great Roman whole.

50. The most important event[3] in the internal history of Rome

---

[1] Cicero *de legibus* II §§ 56, 57 ; Pliny *N. H.* VII 187.　　　　[2] See § 226.

[3] I am aware that Servius has been pronounced a mythical character, and this reform held to belong to the Republican period. This seems to me very improbable. As a step in the genesis of the Republic it falls into a more natural place. That the details are probably anticipated from a later time is likely enough. Therefore, whether Servius be mythical or not, I leave the reform where tradition placed it, without any faith in the detail. See Pais, *Legends*, esp. pp. 140—2, but note that Livy IV 8 § 2 speaks not of the beginning of the *census* but of the *censura*, the office of *censor* as distinct from consul.

traditionally referred to the regal period is the 'Servian' Reform. By this measure the community was organized as an army under a regular scheme, in which duties were assigned to all according to their presumed capabilities: but, though the object of this reform was military, it soon led to far-reaching consequences of a political kind. I cannot here do more than give a sketch of its principal features; that is, of those points in it where the influence of the change on the later history of Rome was great and clear.

51. It would seem that the primitive organization of the community—essentially a clan-system—had been found defective for military purposes. It is probable that the Patricians found themselves under this system charged with military duties on behalf of the state out of all proportion to their numbers. And in ancient times it was not every man that could afford to provide himself with a complete suit of arms and armour and keep these in good order for war. In the Greek states we find those who could serve in full armour (οἱ ὁπλιτεύοντες) regarded as a definite class of well-to-do people. Now it was obviously desirable to ensure that those who were able to serve the state in this way should be marked out and enrolled, ready for service at need. The same would hold good of other classes in various degrees. Nor could it escape notice that young men and those of middle age would be employed to the best advantage in different kinds of military operations. What was needed was a muster-roll of all persons liable to service, on the basis of which an army could be formed without disorder or delay whenever there was a prospect of war. In preparing this roll age and wealth must be the leading considerations. Moreover the army must be as large as possible: hence Plebeians and Patricians must serve alike. Again, financial arrangements must be made for the pay and maintenance of armies in the field. It was therefore desirable that the names and properties of those who, though unable to bear arms, could serve the state as tax-payers, should be duly registered, so that the available resources of the state might at any moment be known.

52. And so the Roman community was classified as a military whole in five divisions or classes (*clases*, callings) according to property, each class having a normal equipment, which every member of the class must provide for himself. The first class had helmet, shield, greaves and corslet of bronze, and carried spear and sword. In the lower classes this equipment was gradually lessened, so that the fourth had only a spear and a light javelin, the fifth nothing but slings and stones. Such is the traditional account given by Livy, from whom we also learn[1] that the old Roman battle-order was a

---

[1] Livy VIII 8 § 3 with Weissenborn's note.

'phalanx,' that is, a formation several files deep. In this the best armed men would form the front ranks and the worst armed the rear, while it is probable that the men of the fourth and fifth classes served as light troops outside the phalanx. The cavalry seem to have been selected from the men of the first class.

53. But the division into Classes did not go far in providing a military organization. More important were the subdivisions of the classes called 'Centuries.' The word *centuria* means a hundred (of anything), but in practice we find it applied to bodies of both more and less than 100. In military language it means little more than 'company.' It is in the centuries that the distinction of age appears. For in each Class half the Centuries were made up of elders (*seniores*), or men from 46 to 60, half of younger men (*iuniores*) from 17 to 45. Thus 80 centuries in the first class = 40 senior + 40 junior; 20 second class = 10 + 10; 20 third = 10 + 10; 20 fourth = 10 + 10; 30 fifth = 15 + 15. We have here 170 centuries of combatant infantry. To these we must add two centuries of artificers (*fabri*), the primitive Artillery and Engineers, in the first class: three of musicians and other supernumeraries, in the fifth class: and one large inclusive century of the nondescript poor whose means were below the standard of even the fifth class assessment, and who were not liable to service in war. The cavalry consisted of 18 centuries. Of these, 12 were only now established: they were raised among the leading men (*ex primoribus civitatis*), that is, the wealthy: the remaining six were already in existence. We have thus accounted for 194 centuries in all, the total given by Livy. Other accounts vary slightly in detail, and make the total 193. We have only to note that the distinction of seniors and juniors seems to have been confined to the 170 centuries of foot, the horsemen, artificers and musicians being all juniors. The state found money for the purchase of the cavalry horses, and the expenses of their keep were met by a special tax on the property of non-combatants, such as unmarried women and minors. It can hardly be doubted that the strength of the several centuries varied greatly. There would be far more men between 17 and 45 living at any time than men between 46 and 60. But a field army (the juniors) needs far more reinforcement during a campaign than a garrison army (the seniors). It was therefore from a military point of view conducive to efficiency that the 85 centuries of juniors should contain more men than the 85 of seniors, as they surely did. From the numbers borne on the roll at a given time the King could choose out men enough to form one army-unit or 'picking' (*legio*), or in case of need could raise as many legions as he wanted, within the limits of the state resources.

54. The process of making this reckoning assessment or rating (*census*) was a solemn one and was brought to a close with sacrifices of purification. In the assessment it is probable[1] that only landed estate was originally taken into account, and that the inclusion of other forms of wealth came in later. The men settled on the soil (*adsidui*) were the persons called upon to defend it. On them was laid the war-rate, raised for the expenses of a war, and refunded out of booty and the enemy's compensation-money in the event of victory. For assessment purposes the territory was divided[2] into four parts (*tribus*), in each of which collectors (*tribuni*) gathered in the rate (*tributum*). These four Tribes were purely administrative units, not connected with the old clans and their religions like the three tribes of the primitive Rome. When a census was held, it placed on record the position and liability of every man able to bear arms. His class and century defined him from the financial and military points of view. When the people were assembled in their centuries on the field of the war-god (*campus Martius*) outside the walls, they were the community in arms, and were called the Army (*exercitus*). They could only be summoned and presided over by the King in virtue of his *imperium*. Throughout the period of the Republic it remained the rule[3] that only a magistrate with *imperium* could summon an Assembly of the Centuries.

55. A great number of interesting questions in connexion with this great reform have to be passed over here for want of room to discuss them. But we cannot help remarking, as we look back upon it with the experience of past ages to help us, that further change was inevitable, and not likely to be long delayed. When once all the wealth and strength of the state were organized for the purpose of ensuring its safety and defending its honour; when the people were summoned to meet as an army on such a footing that the duty of all, Patrician and Plebeian alike, was measured simply by their bodily and financial sufficiency : it could hardly be but that they would claim a voice, and that a decisive voice, in great affairs of state. We may guess that one of the first matters in which they would exercise an influence would be the approval of a declaration of war. Some think that the meetings of the Centuries were voting Assemblies from the first, as tradition represents. It is safer to say no more than that we find Assemblies voting by Centuries (*comitia centuriata*) in the earliest days of the Republic. It is also to be noted, with an eye to the period next following, that this new grouping of the people with

---

[1] See below, § 68.   [2] See below, §§ 66—68.
[3] True, the Censors had no *imperium*, but their power of calling the people together by Centuries was hardly the same as the regular Assembly (*comitia*).

no regard to the old clans and families was fraught with vast consequences. Once give up taking account of the old blood-ties, and
the political importance of the clans was doomed. To impose burdens
on Plebeians was to create a claim to rights, eventually to full
equality : but, such was the tenacity of the old families, there was a
long and weary struggle yet to come. Again, there must surely
always have been taxation of some sort. It is probable that in the
earlier days this depended solely on the will of the King, and might
at times be felt arbitrary and oppressive. It would seem that the
regular system brought in by the Servian reform acted to some extent
as a check on the King's will. If so, then, as Lange points out, we
have in it the first beginnings of limitation of the *imperium*. And the
constitutional history of Rome is, as Mommsen says, mainly the
history of the weakening of this wonderful power.

56. This great reform is traditionally ascribed to Servius Tullius,
the last but one of the Roman Kings. Nor is it unlikely that we
have in it the work of a great and powerful individual. In early
Greece we often meet with the fully-empowered lawgiver. When
internal dissensions had made the situation intolerable, one trusted
man was called in to make changes in the laws and even to remodel
the institutions of the state. In our ignorance of the internal history
of the Italian cities we cannot tell whether they ever followed this
method or not. But so it may well have been : and we must remember
that Greek cities were planted along the coasts of Sicily and southern
Italy, while the spread of Greek seafaring traffic in the West was
marked by the foundation and prosperity of Massalia in the south of
Gaul. One of the most notable among Greek reformers, Solon, had
given to Athens a new constitution in which political rights and
privileges were made to depend on the assessments of property, of
which he made four classes. To compare this system with the scheme
of Servius is very interesting, but we cannot pause here to discuss the
points of resemblance. But it is necessary to observe that, while the
main object of Servius was military, that of Solon was political. We
may however point out that the military necessities of early Rome
were greater than those of Athens in the period after the union of
Attica, and that Solon was not the military head of Athens as Servius
of Rome. The traditional date of Solon's reform is 594 B.C., and the
traditional limits of Servius' reign from 578 to 535 B.C. Whether the
system of Servius was really modelled to any extent on that of Solon,
we cannot say. The coincidences are strange, and so also is the fact
that, as the reform of Solon was followed by the tyranny of Peisis-
tratus and his sons, so the reform of Servius was followed by the
tyranny of the second Tarquin.

57. According to the traditional account Rome began her career of conquest in the regal period. We hear of the subjection of a number of neighbouring towns, some of which seem to have stood in what is now called the Campagna : several of these do not again appear in history and their sites are not certainly known. The power of Rome was pushed to the seaboard, and Ostia, the port at the mouth of the Tiber, garrisoned as a citizen settlement (*colonia civium Romanorum*). Collisions with the Etruscan powers also took place to the North : to the North-East some extension was effected at the expense of the Sabines. But by far the most important gain was made to the South-East and South, not so much in the way of direct acquisition of territory as of the attainment of a dominating position in the Latin League.

58. Loose confederations of kindred communities seem to have been common in ancient Italy. We come across collective names, Latins, Sabines, Aequi, Volsci, Samnites, Etrusci, and so forth. Each of these names stands for an unit, a sort of small nation, made up of lesser units. We know of some, and may believe of them all, that they met together at certain seasons. These gatherings were religious festivals held at some holy spot, such as a sacred grove or well, where the national gods were approached with common sacrifice and ceremonies. Fairs often grew up in connexion with these meetings, and they served also as opportunities for joint consideration of a common policy, if and when common action seemed likely to be called for. More than this we are hardly free to say. National unity was recognized, but the cohesion of these larger units was clearly very loose : each of the smaller constituent units was a community (*populus*), entitled (and probably preferring) to act by and for itself whenever it might think its resources sufficient for the work in hand. Only a great emergency, some external danger threatening several communities at once and eventually the whole, would rouse such ill-organized powers to undertake and maintain an efficient national defence. If tradition of the early times, checked by our knowledge of later events, be worthy of any trust, it would seem that the above characteristics were present in all the Leagues of Italy, whether they consisted of cities, as among the Latins, or of cantons of hill-men, as the Samnites in the dales of Apennine.

59. That these Leagues had even this slight degree of cohesion was probably due in the main to two private ties that bound citizens of different communities together in their family life. First, it was a great thing that in any other community belonging to the same League as your own you could buy and sell, hold property, succeed to an inheritance, and so forth, with the certainty that the local ruler

or rulers would protect you against wrong. In places outside your own League you would be a mere alien (*hostis*) with no rights whatever. Secondly, there was the right to contract a lawful marriage with a citizen of any other community in the League. Children of such marriages would be recognized as their Father's legitimate offspring, and would have whatever rights belonged to them as such under the local law. In outside places they would have no rights at all. These two rights, called in Latin *commercium* and *conubium*, speak for themselves. With them, common interests and sympathies tended to grow stronger: without them, all was helpless isolation. Where they existed, they went far towards creating a mutual right of settlement (as we know to have been the case in some instances), so that a citizen of one community could migrate to another and even, by formal admission, become a citizen in his new home.

60. The legendary story of the foundation of Rome makes the founders come from Alba Longa. This may be a mere inference from the fact that Alba was the religious centre and meeting-place of the Latins. This city seems to have held a sort of presidency among its fellows: not, it may be, invested with any material power, but sufficiently important to stand in the way of any other city that might desire to hold a dominant position in the League. Accordingly the first step in the encroachment of Rome is credibly reported to have been the destruction of Alba. The Albans were transferred to Rome, and only the temples on the Alban mount left standing for the yearly ceremonies of the Latin Festival (*feriae Latinae*). Henceforth Rome appears not as a simple member of the League, but as a self-organized unit, dealing with the rest of the confederates as a whole or separately, as the circumstances of the moment might require. When the Latins (or part of them) grow restive, war leads to further destruction of Latin towns and aggrandisement of Rome. Then we hear of the first King Tarquin conquering the Latin towns in detail, till he 'subdued the whole Latin Name,' and made peace. Numbers of Latins were by this time settled at Rome, added to the Roman Plebs, and the city was spreading towards the Aventine hill. We are told that King Servius induced the chief men of the Latins to aid him in erecting a temple to Diana on the Aventine as a joint Roman-Latin seat of worship, and thus to confess their acquiescence in the leadership of Rome. From the highly-coloured story of the second Tarquin we may gather this much, that the Roman King, acting it is said in connexion with the chief men of the Latin communities, extended his influence in Latium so much that he exercised an effective control over their military forces. The subjection of the Latins to Roman influence had thus already gone far. And it seems

to have been in the regal period that the joint foundation of 'Latin Colonies' began. These were settlements occupying points of strategic value, fortified bases for campaigns. We may believe that Rome was the chief gainer by this policy. It was natural that the allegiance of these garrison-folk should incline toward the one great firm growing community rather than to a slack and faltering league of jealous cities.

61. We have already treated it as a certainty that Rome was once ruled by Kings, and have dwelt on several matters in which the growth of the state during the regal period is asserted. It is not less certain that the regal period came to an end, and that the very title of *rex* was a name of horror to the Roman people so long as any real Roman people remained. But the circumstances and procedure[1] of this revolution are a mystery. The story handed down to us is a drama in the composition of which imagination, principally Greek imagination, has run riot, and old anecdotes preserved in Herodotus take the place of trustworthy detail. The catastrophe is brought about by the rape and suicide of Lucretia: for the rage of the people at the crime of Sextus Tarquinius is the immediate occasion of the expulsion of the whole royal family of the Tarquins. There is some reason to think[2] that the Tarquins were Etruscans, and it may be that Rome passed under the rule of an Etruscan dynasty whose yoke she was not able to bear. The tradition represents the second Tarquin as of war-like character, extending his power over the Latins, oppressing the Roman Plebs by forced labour on great public works, putting to death the wealthy and seizing their goods, lowering the Senate by every means in his power, and generally treating with contempt every cherished custom and precedent. He keeps a body-guard, and depends on alien support for safety at home. Even the formalities of election have been neglected, and he is a mere tyrant of the Greek type. In all this there is nothing actually impossible, and the general picture of evil government is credible enough. It seems conceivable that the doings of a bad king alarmed the old patrician citizens. They seized the moment when the King, who was naturally the protector of the Plebs, had lost popularity with them by imposing task-works, and effected a revolution. This revolution left the Patricians in possession

---

[1] Pais, *Legends* pp. 30—1, thinks that the process was a gradual one, and that the titular *rex sacrorum* (see § 71) only sank into his political insignificance by slow degrees. This sounds plausible, but I think it involves greater difficulties than the traditional' story.

[2] We know the Etruscan name *Tarchna* and there was a city *Tarquinii*. The emperor Claudius in the speech delivered at Lugudunum [Lyon. The text preserved there on bronze is given in most editions of the *Annals* of Tacitus] declared that the real name of Servius Tullius was Mastarna, and that he was a comrade of another Etruscan leader, one Caeles Vibenna.

of the effective control of the state, as we shall see. It is therefore reasonable to conclude that it was a movement of an aristocratic tendency. As for the machinery, we do not know how the change was effected. That the two magistrates of the new Republic were elected in an Assembly of the Centuries is probable. That the prefect of the city presided and laid the names before the people, as Livy[1] says, is not probable: for the *Praefectus urbi* would be a mere deputy of the King.

[1] Livy I 60.

BOOK II

THE REPUBLIC TO THE UNION OF THE ORDERS

CHAPTER VIII

EARLY DIFFICULTIES OF THE FREE STATE

62. THE traditional date for the fall of Tarquin the tyrant (*superbus*) is 510 B.C. The free Commonwealth (*libera res publica*) starts with the first pair of consuls in the following year. Here we must note another curious coincidence: the revolution at Athens, by which Cleisthenes founded the government of the Sovran People (δημοκρατία), is also placed in 509. The two events[1] are not to be connected, so far as I can see: nor would I mention the coincidence, were it not that in the first two centuries of the Republic dates and details of Roman history are still very uncertain. The narratives that have reached us are the work of compilers[2] who wrote centuries after the events described: most of the ancient records are said to have perished in 390 B.C. in the burning of Rome by the Gauls. The ingenuity of scholars in piecing together scattered fragments of genuine antiquity has led to great results in increasing knowledge of law, customs, institutions and so forth: in the history of wars and conquests confusion must remain, for we have not the knowledge of dates needed to make possible a consistent narrative. We must be content to see dimly in the mist.

63. Let us review briefly the situation of the Roman community in 509. Patricians and Plebeians were now face to face. The Monarchy that had served to weld the parts of the state together in its earlier days, that had protected the Plebs as it grew up, was gone. The new Magistrates were of course Patricians. Religion, and with it Law—not yet written down—were in Patrician hands. So was the voting-power in Assemblies, and the bulk of the land.

---

[1] But the narratives may be, and very probably are. Chronology and details of the Roman revolution are utterly uncertain.

[2] The earliest writers on Rome were Greeks, and the first Roman annalists wrote in Greek. See Plutarch *Romulus* 3, 8, Dionys. Hal. 1 6.

Such power as the Senate might then enjoy was all theirs. Meanwhile[1] the laws of debt were cruel, the prospect (if any) of getting a share of the land for tillage was less and less. For the banished Tarquins and their followers found support among Etrurian cities, and Rome lost her lands beyond the Tiber. Even the city of Rome itself seems to have been taken by the Etruscans. In a few more years there was war with the Latins. Rome survived these conflicts, and stories of Roman heroism, such as that of Horatius and his comrades holding the bridge and the tale of the great battle by the lake Regillus, were handed down to conceal the fact of defeat, and to minister to the self-complacency of Romans in later times. But it seems clear that the result was a loss for the time of Roman territory and influence, and hence a reduction in the amount of land at the disposal of the state. Meanwhile the duty of military service fell upon all citizens, and the distresses of peace were aggravated by the burdens of unsuccessful war.

64. No wonder that tradition tells us of discontent and intestine quarrels. The unprivileged Plebeians must perforce seek to better their condition, and they did. Their first objects were, to win personal protection against the harsh exercise of the *imperium* of the Magistrates, to escape from the cruel law of debt by which the insolvent debtor became the slave of his creditor, and to procure allotments of the state land (*ager publicus*) for their own use. The ruling Patricians would not give them these things. Under the existing Assembly-system the Plebeians could not extort concessions by voting-power. Besides, all power of initiating changes rested with the Magistrates: there was thus little chance that the desired concessions would even be put to the vote. Therefore, if the Plebeians were to win personal social and economic relief, they must first aim at political ends, the attainment of effective voting-power and initiative. These ends could not be achieved without combined action, nor combined action without leaders. Accordingly we find that in the period 494—449 B.C. three great steps were taken by the Plebs. First (494) they obtained the right to appoint officers of their own, 'Tribunes of the Commons' (*tribuni plebis*), with sufficient power to act as their protectors and leaders. Secondly (471) they secured the right of voting by Tribes (*tributim*) in their own Plebeian meetings. Thirdly (462—450) the agitation for written Law resulted in a rudimentary code, the famous Twelve Tables of the Decemvirs. In 449 the Valerio-Horatian laws confirmed and probably extended the privileges already won. The effect of the whole movement is

---

[1] The tradition of these evils is of course highly coloured by transference of details belonging to a later age. But that they were very old evils in some form I do not doubt.

shewn in the proposal[1] of Spurius Cassius (486) to distribute some state land in lots among the poorer citizens (if this story is to be trusted), and by the actual allotment of the Aventine hill (456). The colony founded at Antium (467) may have given some relief, but the hold of Rome on that town seems to have been precarious.

65. If we look for the means employed to exact concession, tradition gives us an account the main outlines of which deserve belief. The Plebs (at least the active part of it) withdraws from Rome to some position outside and refuses to return and form part of the Roman state unless its demands are conceded (494, 449). Each 'secession' is brought to an end by a compact, to the advantage of the Plebs. That made in 494 is said to have been a regular treaty (*foedus*) made between the Orders as between two separate communities. This amounted to a solemn recognition of the Plebs as an independent community, a sort of state within the state. The effect of this treaty was to establish the Tribunate, and the Tribunes were an active cause of later triumphs. The other means of putting pressure on the Patricians was a variety of the above. It was the refusal of army-service. Men would not 'give in their names' (*nomina dare*) till they had secured some pledge of the granting of some relief or reform. Such were the levers by which the fabric of Patrician ascendency was first shaken, and in the use of which the Roman Commons grew more and more conscious of their power.

The Tribes.

66. In speaking of the progress of the Plebs reference has been made to their obtaining in 471 the right to hold their meetings by Tribes, a form of grouping afterwards used for regular Assemblies of the whole people. It is necessary to say something of the nature and number of these groups. That the Servian reform had included a division of the city into four Tribes, tradition agrees. But some versions[2] added that a division of the territory took place at the same time, and that a number of rural Tribes were formed, bringing up the whole to a total variously stated at 30 or 31. Of this division Livy[3], though in the main following the same authorities, says nothing, and I have followed him. That there were Tribe-divisions

---

[1] He is said to have proposed to allot half the land taken from the Hernici to them and half to the Latins. This would be quite according to the treaty of 493 (below §§ 95, 96). This was unpopular in Rome, and we are told that he was accused of aiming at regal power and put to death as a traitor. But the story is too doubtful in detail, and too much coloured by later ideas, to be accepted as it stands. See Livy II 41, Dionys. VIII 70—79, Cicero *Laelius* § 28, *de republ.* II § 60.

[2] See Dionys. Hal. IV 15.   [3] Livy I 43 § 13.

outside the city at the end of the regal period is not improbable. Livy[1], no doubt drawing from one of the annalists, represents a total of 21 (the text is uncertain) as reached in the year 495. On this supposition 17 are to be accounted for between the Servian reform and 495. These are found in 16 Tribes known to have been the oldest of the *tribus rusticae*, and bearing names (such as *Aemilia, Fabia*, etc.) derived from ancient Roman *gentes*. To the 17th we will return presently. When were these 16 formed? The tradition assigning them to Servius seems to be merely the guess-work of the writers quoted by Dionysius. It seems more probable that they belong to the first years of the Republic. If so, we can hardly do better[2] than fix on the year 498, when a census was held. This is late enough to allow for the formation of the Claudian Tribe as one of the 16; for the settlement of Attius Clausus and his followers, of whom the *tribus Claudia* was formed, is placed in 504. This brought up the total to 20. One more Tribe was added, called *Clustumina* or *Crustumina* from the town[3] of Crustumerium, in whose recently conquered territory its land lay. It would seem that the districts towards the Sabine mountains were being firmly occupied at this time, for the land of the Claudian Tribe was also beyond[4] the Anio. Lange well remarks that the formation of new Tribes was regularly connected with a census, and that we hear[5] of a census held in 493 after the great Secession of the Plebs which took place in that year. He suggests that Livy has wrongly put the formation of the 21st Tribe before the Secession instead of after it. I believe that in assigning it with Lange to the census of 493 we shall not be far from the truth. The number[6] stood at 21 for more than 100 years. Meanwhile the Tribes had become voting bodies. Future additions were always made in even number, so as to preserve the odd total convenient for this new purpose.

67. If this account of the numbers be accepted, we are driven to wonder what was the relation of the 17 rural to the four city Tribes. Did the Servian division include the country districts? If so, it must either have been superseded by a later one, or we are wrong in assigning only four Tribes to it. No certainty is attainable, and opinions differ widely. We must never forget that the 'parts' or Tribes were certainly not as yet voting-groups. Voting at all must have been excessively rare in the regal period, and the groups would

---

[1] Livy II 21 § 7. Dionysius also assumes the total of 21 Tribes in the year 491, see VII 64.

[2] The view of Lange, *Röm. Alt.* I pp. 510—1.

[3] This precedent of naming after a locality was henceforth followed.

[4] Livy II 16.   [5] Dionys. VI 96.   [6] See Livy VI 5 § 8.

be *curiae*. What then was the object of the Tribe-division? We do not know. That it was an administrative measure of the early Republic, designed to facilitate the work of the consuls by providing them with a larger staff of assistants (so many to each Tribe), is possible, but pure conjecture. The fact of the gentile names given to the first 16 rural Tribes is notable. It seems to be a survival recalling a time when the old clans as such held land as a common estate. Mommsen's theory[1] is that the rural Tribes grew out of the *pagi*. The *pagus* or 'parish' was a local unit widely recognized in Italy. If *pagi* were commonly named after the *gens* that held all or most of the land in each (the evidence for which is pitifully slight), it was naturally easy to transfer such names to the new Tribes when that grouping was adopted. Thus the Tribe including (or co-extensive with) the *pagus Lemonius* would become the *tribus Lemonia*. But it is known that the *pagi* were more numerous than the *tribus*, and there is no reason to think that the total of the former was a multiple of the total of the latter. It would seem then that the two sets of groups stood in no direct relation to each other. And the *pagus* was a natural growth from within, and had its own religious observances. The *tribus* was an artificial creation[2] of the state of which it was a part, and had no *sacra* of its own. The two stand for two different stages of development, and mark a momentous change. How the change was effected it is evident the Roman antiquaries of later days themselves did not know.

68. Another point calls for some notice. The two chief purposes for which we find the Tribes and Tribe-registers employed in the historical period are the army-levy and the raising of the war-loan (*tributum*). The four 'Servian' city Tribes seem to have been approximately equal in numbers, and it is probable that the same was at first the case with the rural Tribes. The persons registered were landholders (*adsidui* = settled on the ground), that is landholding families, each under a head. It is generally assumed, probably with truth, that no account was taken originally of property other than land and its appurtenances[3]. It is most unlikely that no citizen owned land in more than one Tribe. How then was he registered? Liability to military service forbade his being entered in more than one Tribe. We may suppose that at first his place was determined

---

[1] Mommsen, *Staatsrecht* III 169, 170, 116, 117.

[2] Hence additions, not continuous with the original district, could be made to a Tribe. It had no meetings of its own, but was a part of the Roman state.

[3] *ager privatus, servi, iumenta*. It was to these only that the ancient solemn form of transfer (*mancipatio*) was applied. Mommsen points out that the state-domain (*ager publicus*) was not included in the Tribes.

by his hereditary connexion or by residence, and this might meet the difficulty for a time, so long as cases seldom arose. But it is obvious that the question would soon become of practical importance as cases grew frequent. And it is clear that the compulsory war-loan, raised in the form of a percentage of a man's registered property, took account of it all, in whatever Tribe-district it was situated. That the difficulty was a real one, we may infer from the fact that in course of time the determination of a man's Tribe ceased to depend directly on the ownership of land in a particular district, and became more and more the hereditary membership of a particular political group.

69. In order to understand the composition of Tribes regarded as groups of citizens, we must speak of two classes, one of which was included in the Tribes, while the other was not. Those whose property did not reach the lowest amount assessed for taxation (that is, liable to *tributum*) were registered as persons simply : each one had only his *caput* to declare. Hence they were called the 'assessed by the head' (*capite censi*) or 'men of offspring' (*proletarii*), as contributing nothing but themselves and their brood to the resources of the state. But they were *tribules*, members of Tribes, for they were citizens. As they were not taxed, so they were not called upon to serve in war. The true inferiority of their position appears when we reflect that the voting Assembly of the early Republic was organized by Centuries, and unconnected with the Tribe-organization. All these poor citizens were packed into a single Century, and had a vote of no value whatever. The introduction of voting by Tribes meant to them the acquisition of an effective franchise. It was no less than a second revolution. We may wonder why it took about 200 years to get finally rid of patrician privileges and supersede the Assembly by Centuries as a legislative organ. Old prestige of the clan-nobles and conservative influences of religion may partly account for this, but it is quite possible that the very poor were less numerous in these early times than tradition would suggest. Very different was the position of those whom the chief magistrate (afterwards the *censor*) for any reason declined to enrol on a Tribe-list. This was not a question of poverty, but of disgrace. There might be good reason for it, but the power of the magistrate was only limited in two ways. First, there was the force of precedent backed by public opinion, a very effective check in Rome, at least in early republican times. Secondly, there was the fact that his acts were only valid for his term of office, in the census department until the next census. When he placed a man on the list of the 'tax-liable' (*aerarii*), he left him in the position of one whose relation to the state was that of liability to arbitrary taxation for its benefit. But the man remained

potentially a citizen, and at the next or a later census he might be restored to his former status with all its rights and duties. The same power that struck him off a Tribe (*tribu movere*) could put him back again. Beside these degraded citizens were other *aerarii*, namely freedmen, for in the early Republic the taint of former slavery could not be shaken off. But we are not to suppose that the *aerarius* of either kind was a common figure in Roman life. The number of such persons was probably very small.

CHAPTER IX

THE CONSTITUTION, 509—449 B.C.

70. WHETHER the revolution by which the Roman Kingship came to an end, and the new government was set up, was so sudden a movement as the tradition makes it appear, it is not possible to say. We must take the tradition for whatever it may be worth: it is at least not inconsistent with the sequel. The first point to notice is that, while the King was driven out, the kingly 'power of command' (*imperium*)[1] was not destroyed. Two Magistrates were appointed, in each of whom the full *imperium* was understood to reside. But the use of the *imperium* was really limited in practice. First, the equal powers of the two rulers could lead to a deadlock: each could block the action of the other. Secondly, they held office for a year only. True, there was no actual means of turning them out of office at the year's end, other than the moral pressure of their fellow-citizens' disapproval. But the fall of Tarquin had shewn that even Roman patience had its limits; and, by the time that this event had become a mere memory, the force of custom was established. The liability to impeachment[2] after retirement from office was a possible danger that very rarely found effect: indeed it was until the days of the Empire very seldom possible to punish retired officials for official acts. Thirdly, while the King was able, but not obliged, to allow a condemned man to appeal to the People (*provocare ad populum*) from the royal sentence, in the very first year of the Republic we hear of a law compelling the magistrate to allow appeals in all cases. The fourth limitation was that of the establishment of the Tribunate of the Commons in 494 B.C. Thus we see that, while the regal *imperium* was in appearance retained, its effective force was materially weakened even in the first years of the Republic. This contrast between appearance and reality should be attentively remarked; for it illustrates the method of progress observable throughout Roman

---

[1] The power of appointing a deputy (*praefectus urbi*) during absence in war or at the Latin festival remained to the consuls.

[2] The impeachments of ex-consuls of which tradition speaks are acts of vengeance for opposition to Plebeian claims. These form part of the struggle of the Orders rather than of a scheme of official responsibility.

politics. Fact and theory were constantly at variance; a system of 'make-believe' to which even the history of England can hardly afford a parallel.

71. The remaining strength of the *imperium* was upheld chiefly by its being for the present lodged in two officers only. They were at first called 'leaders' (*praetores*), perhaps 'judges' (*iudices*), but soon, we do not know exactly when, the term 'colleagues' (*consules*) became their official title, and I shall therefore refer to them as Consuls. The various survivals of the regal system are interesting. The title remained in that of the *rex sacrorum,* an unimportant priest, who was 'king' for certain ceremonial purposes, and who in later times must still always be a Patrician. A trace of the life-tenure of office may be detected in the absence of any formal means of turning a magistrate out of office. If it be true that the Consuls at first appointed their own Quaestors, this must be a survival of the King's wider power of appointing subordinates. And an useful piece of machinery survived in the *interregnum.* The election of Consuls could only be conducted by a magistrate holding the *imperium.* It very seldom happened that a Consul was positively unable to preside over the Centuries for this purpose: but when it did happen, the old plan of *interreges* was resorted to, as in the days of the Kings. But emergencies might and did occur when the danger of the state demanded that absolute power should be placed in one man's hand. Whether this contingency had been provided for at the time of the Revolution or not, we learn that in 501 a temporary King was appointed to deal with the Latin war. His title was *magister populi*[1] or *dictator.* His term was to be six months, during which time he had entire control of the state and its resources. He was not elected by the Centuries, but nominated by a Consul. For about three hundred years we find Dictators appointed in moments of danger without or within.

72. In the department of Religion we find what may even be a trace of the King's life-tenure. For his headship of state religion was in effect inherited by the Head of the college of Pontiffs, the so-called *pontifex maximus,* and this officer held office for life. He lived in the 'King's House' (*regia*), said to have been the palace of Tarquin, and was a person of the first importance. The Pontiffs had the charge of the Roman calendar, and issued monthly notices of the coming Festivals, indicating what days were unlucky (*nefasti*), and so barred for public business. Other days were lucky (*fasti*), but of these only some were available for Assemblies (*comitiales*), the rest were free for proceedings at law. Prodigies, that is, any strange occurrence in which a divine warning was supposed to be given, were

---

[1] This appears to have been the original title.

also interpreted by the Pontiffs, who ordered the proper ceremonies to comply with the heavenly will. Signs from the flight or feeding of birds were got by the magistrate, but the principles on which this very ancient divination proceeded were regulated by the college of Augurs. All Assemblies were opened by taking the Auspices, and the slightest flaw vitiated the proceedings. Enough has now been said to shew that the great religious colleges wielded an immense political power. In this period their members were all Patrician, and used their power in the Patrician interest.

73. The appointment of the first Tribunes of the Commons in 494 was the effect of the great Secession. It shewed that the Roman Plebs was awake to its needs. Henceforth the Plebs is a recognized body in the state, and has recognized leaders, who are secured against the violence of the regular (Patrician) magistrates by a mighty oath taken by the whole plebeian army before their return to Rome. When they swore to protect their Tribunes, the practical effect of the oath lay in the conviction that it would be kept: and the privileged order wisely abstained from provoking a rising that would have been the ruin of Rome. The first duty of the Tribune was to give 'help' (*auxilium*) to any plebeian against the magistrate's *imperium*. His 'coming between' (*intercessio*) annulled any official act. He could thus bring to a standstill all the machinery of state. No doubt this wide power grew up by gradual encroachments, but it grew very fast. That such an institution, an embodied negative, did not speedily ruin the state, was due solely to the good sense moderation and patriotism of the men of the early Republic. The Tribune could call together the Plebs and address the meeting on any subject, and none might interrupt him. He had ample power to enforce his will in the 'constraint' (*coercitio*) which he could use by fines and arrest, even against the consul himself. Here was indeed a powerful protector for Plebeians. Yet with all this the tribune was not a Magistrate of the Roman People, and there were in fact limitations to his power. In the first place he had no *imperium*. Power or 'competence' (*potestas*) of a general kind he had in plenty: but that special power which would have enabled him to command an army was absent. Consequently he could not act beyond the city precinct—the first milestone in any direction outside the walls. For at this point the *imperium* became regal again: from being the 'Home-command' (*imperium domi*) it became the 'Field-command' (*imperium militiae* = command on service), and the negative power of the Tribune was silent in the presence of martial law. Besides, he had colleagues. At first there were only two Tribunes, but the number was soon raised to five, and in 457 to ten. And on the regular Roman

principle, that the full powers of an office resided equally in all holders, any one Tribune could block the action of the other nine. We shall see later on that it was this rule of 'equal power' (*par potestas*) by which the political force of the Tribunate was paralysed for some 200 years. Lastly, there was the time-limit of yearly tenure.

74. The Magistrates proper were distinguished by their dress and symbols of authority. On ordinary occasions the Consul wore a gown with a border of scarlet (*toga praetexta*). At festivals, or when in command of an army, he donned the full royal red. Twelve marshals or 'summoners' (*lictores*) waited on him, bearing the bundles of rods (*fasces*) that marked the presence of the *imperium*. The axe no longer formed the core of the bundle as in the regal days, at least in the city: in the field it reappeared, and with it the power of life and death. In the city it was the custom for the Consuls to officiate in turns, and to 'have the Fasces' for a month at a time. In the field other arrangements were made, which will be considered on a later page. All men were bound to shew respect to the magistrate: he sat while others stood before him. In view of this a sort of folding seat (*sella curulis*) was carried in his train: and the 'curule chair' gave its name to the 'curule' offices of the next age. All these outward marks of dignity were wanting to the Tribunes. They were merely officers of the Plebs. Accessible to all their fellow Plebeians by day or night, unimpressive but efficient, hearing complaints and redressing grievances, they needed no show of dignity to remind themselves and others of their great and growing power. Two points[1] deserve notice, in which Consul and Tribune are alike. First, there was the right of issuing public notices (*ius edicendi*). This was a normal attribute of official power. An 'edict' might be simply a command, or a warning of what the official would do in this or that contingency. Secondly,—and this is most important—all officers of state were unpaid. It is hardly too much to add that all were elected, for the Dictator is hardly a true exception. And I may well call attention once more to the great amplitude of official power characteristic of the Roman system.

Note on Chronology of the Republic.

75. Now that we are come to a time in which the names of normally annual magistrates are used to give the date of a transaction, it is necessary to explain briefly why the ordinary method of dating is adopted. To write as though we were

---

[1] Here I purposely omit consideration of the Quaestors, subordinates of the Consuls, and the Aediles, subordinates of the Tribunes, in order not to obscure the general view with details of secondary importance.

dealing with a series of exactly-reckoned years of (say) 365¼ days each on the average, and with a succession of magistrates whose official years were of equal length and conterminous with the civil years, is in effect to forestall the Julian calendar of 46 B.C. and the series of changes by which the date of entering on office became fixed. But some such makeshift is absolutely necessary. Mommsen[1] has no difficulty in proving that in the early Republic magistrates went in and out of office without regard to the civil year, and that in practice their tenure was not strictly annual. Between 509 and 295 the variations were extreme. In the period 276—223 it seems that the regular date for consuls to enter on office was the first of May. A later change placed it on the 15th March, and in 153 it was finally fixed on the first of January. This caused that date to be gradually accepted as the civil New Year, instead of the first of March, but it was not so recognized officially till the Julian calendar. Religious scruples were of course in the way. Moreover the pontiffs responsible for the civil calendar kept it so that it was habitually out of order. Annalists had to form some kind of chronology for their own use. At the cost of sundry inexactitudes, a list of magistrates was made out from the beginning of the Republic, which was placed in the year we call 509 B.C. By adding to this an assumed period (244 years in Varro's estimate) for the reigns of the Kings a date was found for the so-called foundation of Rome. Thus were established two eras (1) *post reges exactos*, a frequent point of reckoning in Latin writers, (2) *post Romam conditam* or *ab urbe condita*, which came into use later. The official list of the chief magistrates set up in the Forum soon after the fall of the Republic, the fragments of which are known as the *Fasti Capitolini*, also contained inexactitudes. In the endeavour to make a complete list harmonize with the total of years, errors crept in, as Mommsen has shewn. Therefore it must be admitted that in the history of the Republic there are points where the exact chronology cannot be recovered with certainty. But for my present purpose these minute and subtle errors are quite unimportant. I have accordingly taken the nominal years as real ones, and done the best I could with them in the usual way. But a full consciousness of the looseness of this method leads me at this stage to insert a warning.

76. The Senate of the Republic is the old advisory board of the King, lasting on though the kingdom is at an end. As the King chose his councillors, so now did the Consuls. I cannot believe that any Plebeians were chosen by these Patrician magistrates in the early years of the Republic. It is quite probable that, as tradition tells, the numbers of the Senate, depleted under the tyranny of Tarquin, were raised to their proper strength (300) by the inclusion of new members. That these (numbering 164 according to one account) were Plebeians, is I believe a mistaken inference of writers writing long after the event. It is said that the new senators were at first described as 'added to the roll' (*conscripti*), and that in time, the distinction between *patres* and *conscripti* being lost sight of, the famous title '*patres conscripti*' came into use as a single form of address including the whole House. However this may be, it is at least certain that in the early Republic the Senate was a stronghold of the Patricians, an

---

[1] Mommsen, *Röm. Chronologie* chapters II, III, *Staatsrecht* I 576—582.

organ of dogged conservatism. Whether it was or was not an understood principle, that senators held their places for life unless and until their names were left out of the roll by the revising Magistrate, is quite uncertain. That this became the custom we know: indeed the life-tenure was probably in practice normal from the first. And it can hardly be doubted that an ex-consul, if not already a senator, would have a first claim to be chosen at the next revision of the list. Already there was beginning that which characterizes the Senate of later times, its permanence and inclusion of all magisterial experience. Though it was not directly possessed of legislative judicial or executive power, it was beginning to gain influence over the Magistrates and at their expense. A consul with only a year of office would generally be glad to secure for his acts the moral support of the great Council. Why then, we may ask, did the influence of the Senate at first grow so slowly? The cause is to be found in the decline of the Patrician order as a political force. Once the struggle of the Orders was over, and the Senate a mixed body, the patricio-plebeian Senate became the real government of Rome. Till then, Rome was in effect governed by Patrician Consuls and Plebeian Tribunes, each backed by powerful support: and the balance of power inclined this way and that by turns, until wealth finally superseded birth as the basis of social distinctions and a new political equilibrium was found.

77. The Senate could only meet on the summons of a Magistrate and discuss such matters as he laid before it: members could only give their opinions if and when called upon by the presiding Magistrate to do so. In early times the amount of speaking was probably small. In a division, the Senate voted by heads, and hence was the only important meeting of Romans in which the majority was certain to prevail. It seems also to have been the case that all or nearly all the senators lived within easy reach and could readily be summoned to special meetings at need. This would lead to more frequent consultation of a body whose advice could be got at once: for in days of warfare and crises it was often necessary not only to act wisely on behalf of the state but to do it without delay. Hence it was in matters of foreign policy that the Senate first gained a predominant influence.

78. Though it lacked initiative, and had in the main only such authority as respect might attach to its opinions, the Senate had at least two definite political rights. In the event of an election having to be held by an Interrex, the Fathers (*patres*) made the arrangements needed: they retained, that is, the power of investing that functionary with temporary *imperium* and the right to take auspices, sufficient for the purpose in hand. We have already remarked that

such a contingency was very rare. It appears that only Patrician senators were qualified to take part in the proceedings, and this too after Plebeians had been admitted to the Senate. We may perhaps fairly infer that this right was not felt to be of serious importance. The second was the 'sanction of the Fathers' (*auctoritas patrum*) to which Roman writers often refer. In law *auctor* is one who takes responsibility for anything: he guarantees it, for instance the title to an estate. So in the Roman constitution the validity of such public acts as election and legislation had to be confirmed by the sanction of the Fathers (*patres auctores facti*). Here was an opening for stubborn refusals leading to a deadlock, and there are traces of this situation occurring now and then, but not for long. A deadlock seldom gave a lasting advantage to the Patrician cause, and the wary Elders well knew the practical limits to the use of their power. How this cause of friction was removed will appear later. We have only to add that both these two prerogatives seem to be survivals from a very early period, when clan-elders composed the King's council, and when much depended on the loyal cooperation of the Clans.

79. When once the Roman state was governed by yearly magistrates, it was natural that Assemblies of the people should gradually come to play a larger part in the decision of great matters of state. It is a pity that we know so very little about these Assemblies, for they must have been the scene of the famous Struggle of the Orders. The old Assembly of the Curies still existed, indeed as a formal meeting for certain legal purposes it lasted on into the times of the Empire. Whether it included Plebeian members or not, is hardly certain: if it did, they would probably vote as Clients of Patrician Clans. The thirty Curies, composed of *gentes*, were groups formed on a footing of presumed community of blood and actual community of religious observances. Since the Servian reform and under the tyranny of Tarquin this body had probably lost much of its practical importance, which it never recovered. Traces of its former competence remained, as in the right of formally ratifying the *imperium* of a magistrate (*lex curiata de imperio*). But it seems that this was a mere formality which was never refused. Certain forms of adoption and wills were also executed in the presence of special meetings of the Curies. On the whole the Curiate Assembly passed more and more into the position of a Survival.

80. Popular action in matters of state now found expression in the Assembly of Centuries. Speaking broadly, the citizen-army had become a political Sovran. The wars in which the young Republic was involved would no doubt lead to somewhat frequent meetings, and the working of the body as a voting Assembly, clumsy and

complicated though it was, would be made more easy by experience. But it had essential defects. The poor citizen, scantily equipped, might be content to stand behind his wealthier comrades in battle-array, and to let the brunt of the fighting be borne by the fully-armed : but, when it came to voting on home questions in which his own interests were concerned, he would grumble to find his vote ineffective in the time of peace. Yet ineffective it was, for a majority of the Centuries was controlled by the wealthy, and against this majority, if solid, nothing could be done. Nay more, it was the rule to call the Centuries to vote in the order of financial and military precedence, and to close the voting so soon as a majority had voted one way. So that the poorer voters—that is, counting heads, the majority—might often not be called to vote at all. And in these early days, when the territory was small, and the outlying voters would generally be able to attend, the political impotence resulting from the structure and rules of the Centuriate Assembly must have been particularly galling to the poorer citizens. These would be nearly all Plebeians. It is clear that, if the Roman Commons were to make their power felt in the state, they must provide some other organ than the system of the Centuries.

81. That the Plebs had begun to hold meetings of its own may be gathered from the election of its Tribunes and from the early history of the Tribunate. But these were informal gatherings, not recognized by the state. If a law (492) forbade under severe penalties all interruption of a tribune while engaged with a meeting of the Plebs, this must have been a sort of corollary of the compact after the Secession of 494. In itself it could not strictly be a law (*lex*) at all. How these meetings were organized we do not know. Mommsen holds that they voted by curies, which I find very hard to believe, and no brief discussion of the question is possible. In 471 we are told that a law was passed (the *lex Publilia* of Volero) giving the Plebs the right to meet and elect their officers by Tribes. The registers of the several Tribes would include only the freeholders in the several districts : to the Plebeians of this quality, the backbone of the Plebs, the power was thus given. The value of all votes would be approximately equal, for the number of voters at this time would probably be much the same in all the Tribes. Thus were established the *concilia plebis tributa*, which went on by the side of the regular Assemblies down to the end of the Republic, and in their time exercised a vast influence in Roman politics. At what date the system of voting by Tribes was first used in formal Assemblies of the whole *populus* we do not know Such Assemblies there were in later times. From a reference to a 'greatest' Assembly in the Twelve

Tables it has been argued that there must be implied the existence of a less great one, and that this can only be the Assembly of the Tribes. It is possible. In that case the date of its origin would fall between 471 and 451 B.C.

82. Formal or informal, these gatherings have one important principle underlying all alike. They vote in groups. The vote of the group is determined by the majority of its members present and voting, and it counts as one. To illustrate this, let us shew in a supposed case what strange results might follow from group-voting. Take the Tribes at the time when they were 21 in number. Let us assume that all are of equal voting strength and that an equal percentage in each Tribe are present, say 1000 voters per Tribe. In mass-voting 10,501 votes give a majority. But what is needed here is to win the votes of 11 Tribes. These may be carried each by 501 to 499. In the other 10 Tribes the whole of the votes may agree with the minorities of the 11 Tribes. Classifying them under Aye and No, we get this:

$$\text{Ayes.} \quad \text{11 Tribes at 501 votes each} = 5511,$$
$$\text{Noes.} \quad \left. \begin{array}{l} \text{10 Tribes at } 1000 = 10,000 \\ \text{11 Tribes at } 499 = 5489 \end{array} \right\} = 15,489,$$

and the Ayes have it, being 11 to 10. So extreme a case would not occur in practice, so far as the voting was concerned, but the Tribes in course of time became more unequal in number of members, and unequal percentages of attendance must have been a common state of things. In short, there was not in Roman Assemblies any system of voting in which the majority (counting heads) could make sure of defeating the minority. Nor do we hear of any attempts at reform directed to this end. The will of the mass of the people prevailed now and then in some great stirring crisis, when a wave of popular feeling swept all before it: but such moments of impulse are not without their danger, and such capricious forces are unsuited to the conduct of ordinary government.

83. Every formal Assembly of the whole community (*populus*) was called *comitia*. This word is plural, and the use of a plural term to describe a single Assembly is notable. Whether it arose from the fact that each Assembly was composed of a number of Groups, I cannot say. But such is my belief. For clearness' sake I use the word 'Assembly' to render it, and 'Meeting' for the *concilium* of the Plebs. The meeting-place of the Curies was in the space known as the *comitium* at the northern end of the Forum. The Centuries, being the army, were not allowed to meet in the city. Their place was the Field of the War-god (*campus Martius*) on the north-west side of the city. The Tribes could meet within the precincts, and their normal place seems to have been the open space on the Capitoline hill (*area Capitolii*) in front of the temple of the Capitoline Jove.

84. It remains to sketch the respective functions of the Centuries and Tribes. It will be convenient to consider this subject under three heads—Election, Jurisdiction, Legislation. The Centuries elected the magistrates of the community, who had the *imperium*: that is, in this period, the Consuls. The meeting of the Plebs by Tribes (perhaps by Curies before 471) elected the Tribunes of the Commons and the Aediles. The formal Tribe-Assembly as yet was not an electing body. In jurisdiction, cases affecting the life or legal status of a citizen (his *caput*) were reserved for the Centuries. Questions of fines and other penalties to be inflicted on magistrates who molested the Tribunes, or in any way violated the rights of the Plebs, came before the Plebs in its *concilium*, and later before the formal *comitia* of the Tribes. It is thought that this jurisdiction was the first purpose for which *comitia tributa* were employed. If the Plebs by itself did ever (as we are told) claim the right to judge a Patrician on a capital charge, the ultimate basis of this claim can hardly have been other than a threat of force. Of legislation in a strict sense there was, as usual in primitive communities, very little. The legislative Assembly was that of the Centuries. The Plebs soon began to pass 'resolutions of the Commons' (*plebiscita*). These only bound the Plebs, and needed acceptance by the Centuries to become laws (*leges*). It was later, after long struggles, that they became binding on the whole community.

85. In another respect these gatherings are exactly alike. Neither *comitia* nor *concilium* could do more than answer the question (*rogatio*) put to it by the presiding officer. There was no debate. If speaking was needed, it took place in a mass-meeting (*conventio, contio*). The *contiones* were quite informal, and probably very rare in early times. Serious business began with the voters breaking up into their groups. And nothing could be done before sunrise: with sunset all business for that day came to an end. All the citizens of whom we have been speaking had a vote of some kind, though the effective value of the various voting-rights differed very greatly. But a man might be a citizen and yet have no vote at all, as for instance those who at a Census were[1] for any reason not put upon the rolls of the Tribes. New citizens[2] not yet enrolled had also no vote. In fact the term *civis* marks a man's relation to a state, not necessarily his possession of the full rights of a citizen in that state. In relation to other states he is simply an alien.

[1] See above, § 69. [2] See below, §§ 854—856, 874, 889.

CHAPTER X

THE DECEMVIRATE AND THE VALERIO-HORATIAN LAWS

86. A GRIEVANCE common in ancient states, where a large unprivileged class existed by the side of the privileged nobles, was that the laws, though of public effect, were not matter of public knowledge. Law was custom that had come down from time immemorial, closely connected with religion. The exact knowledge of this custom, and of such interpretation as might be needed for its application to the affairs of life, rested with the Pontiffs. Furthermore, that a legal rule might take effect, minute observance of certain forms and ceremonies was necessary: nothing was easier than to vitiate legal acts, such as contracts or conveyances, by some trivial slip. Great power therefore lay in the hands of those who knew the law and its formalities: these were in early times all Patricians. We need not wonder that the Plebeians found the situation past bearing. In 462 B.C. the Tribune Gaius Terentilius Harsa began the agitation by an attack on the consular *imperium*, threatening to define and limit it by means of legislation. The Patricians stubbornly resisted him, and a regular struggle between the Orders went on year after year, till in 454 a compromise was reached. It was recognized that the drafting and publication of a written code was now a question of practical politics. Accordingly three commissioners were sent abroad to study the legal systems of the Greek states, in particular Athens and the famous laws of Solon. During their absence the parties forbore their strife: in 452 they returned, and the tribunes insisted that a beginning of the work should be made at once.

87. The Romans now resorted to a strange expedient. A body of ten Commissioners (*decem viri*) were elected for 451. There were to be no Consuls, no Tribunes, while the Ten held sway: there was to be no appeal to the people from their decisions. The Plebeians consented to let the whole Ten be chosen from the Patricians, stipulating that certain existing laws affecting Plebeian interests should not be repealed. The traditional story represents these Decemvirs as having ruled with justice and moderation, and their leader, the haughty noble Appius Claudius, as courting the favour of the Commons by the arts of a demagogue. The Ten posted up a draft of laws on ten tablets (*tabulae*), and invited public criticism. Then, having amended the draft in the sense of suggestions received, they called together the Centuries, and the vote of the Assembly confirmed the ten Tables as statutes of Rome. But it soon got out that to finish the work, to make up a complete body (*corpus*) of the Roman law (that is, of statute-law), two more Tables were needed: and this was made a pretext for continuing to suspend the constitution and electing Decemvirs for the following year. Appius now gave himself up to mere popularity-hunting in view of the election. His colleagues sought to tie his hands by appointing him presiding officer. No one but a Tribune had ever received votes for himself and declared himself elected: and this was thought low. But Appius did not care. He secured his own reelection, and the election of nine others, some of whom were Plebeians. They were his creatures, and he was now master of Rome.

88. Hereupon, says the story, the mask was dropped: Appius and his colleagues appeared as ten tyrants. It was whispered that they meant to hold no elections, and so to perpetuate their rule. The draft of the two supplementary Tables was published, but no steps taken to pass them into law. Rome was now the scene of a reckless orgy of violence and wrong. It was chiefly Plebeians that suffered: a gang of young Patricians were in attendance to back up the wicked Ten: scourgings, judicial murders, confiscations, were at last the ordinary business of this reign of terror. Men wished for their Consuls and Tribunes once more, but the Ten remained in office. Hope dawned in the shape of foreign invasion. The presence of Sabine and Aequian armies on Roman territory led to the summoning of the Senate. A stormy debate followed, and the levy of armies, and disastrous war. At this point come in the stories of the murder of Siccius, a popular leader, by order of the Ten, and the rescue of Verginia from the lust of Appius by death at the hands of her father. The Roman field armies now marched on the city. But the Ten did not finally give way until a 'secession' of the Plebeian forces had taken place. The safety of the state demanded their return. So under pressure from the Senate the Decemvirs abdicated, and the constitution was restored. Machinery for the election of Consuls existed in the *interrex*: to hold the election of Tribunes the Chief Pontiff was called to preside. The consuls of this famous year (449) were Lucius Valerius Potitus and Marcus Horatius Barbatus, who had distinguished themselves in the senate as champions of liberty and moderation. But, if Livy's version is to be trusted, the choice of Tribunes was first made, and it was not until the Plebs had met and passed resolutions, condoning the mutiny of the army and

claiming the right of appeal, that the consular election took place. It seems not unlikely that the formal confirmation of the two supplementary Tables was procured by the consuls, though the whole Twelve are generally referred to as the Decemvirs' work. We shall speak of the Tables below. Meanwhile we must deal with the constitutional legislation which marks out this year as a great epoch in the history of Rome.

89. The actual contents of the *leges Valeriae Horatiae* cannot be discovered with certainty. As the story of the Decemvirs is tainted with the party spirit of later writers, so the account of these laws is muddled by their misunderstandings. Perhaps we may fairly extract the following residuum as probably near the truth. First, some means was provided by which a resolution of the Plebs could easily be converted into a law binding on the whole *populus*, Patricians included. What the machinery was, is most uncertain. Some think that, when a *plebiscitum* had been carried, the consul was bound to lay the question before the Assembly of Centuries without delay: anyhow it was something that strengthened the Tribunes' hands. Next, the right of Appeal was restored and safeguarded by enacting that any magistrate who acted as president at the election of a magistrate from whom there was to be no appeal should be held an outlaw whose slaying was justified by divine and human law. Thirdly, the persons of the Tribunes were in some way further protected, under threats of awful penalties: and some similar protection given to the Aediles and a court of Ten judges[1] (*iudices decemviri*) of whom we know little. Care was also taken of records: the Aediles were to keep the Orders of the Senate in the temple of Ceres. When the consular laws were passed, the Tribunes came forward with measures to secure their gains. On a Tribune's motion the Plebs passed a resolution threatening scourging and death to any election-president who should 'leave the Plebs without Tribunes' or take part in electing a magistrate from whom there should be no appeal.

90. We have no time to dwell on the picturesque details of the fall of the 'Wicked Ten,' and the moderation shewn by the exasperated Commons in their hour of victory. A general enthusiasm now prevailed: the war interrupted by civil dissension was resumed, and the armies carried all before them. It is said that Patrician sulkiness led the Senate to refuse the popular Consuls the honours of a triumph, and that it was granted them by the people on the motion of a Tribune. What demands our attention is that the Roman constitution had been set aside to make room for an experiment, and had been restored in such a form and under such conditions as to

---

[1] See Keller, *Civilprocess* I § 5.

strengthen the position of the Plebs. The direct outcome of the Decemvirate was the Twelve Tables of the statute Law. We must now say a few words upon the nature of this legislation and its importance as an episode in the long struggle of the Orders.

91. A number of fragments of the 'Twelve' are preserved to us; a few of them purport to be verbal quotations, but these are probably somewhat modernized. Traces of antiquity appear: an alien is still called *hostis* (not *peregrinus*). And the right to cut up (*secare*) an insolvent debtor may be an ancient survival and refer to his human body; though some hold that his estate is meant. The style of the fragments is short and jerky. Subject and object are constantly omitted: you are not told who is to do what, or to whom the doer is to do it. And yet the meaning, quibbles apart, is generally pretty certain. But this sort of statute language seems to imply that the construction to be put on the various clauses might become a kind of Science in the hands of qualified interpreters. That this was the result, we know: that those who drafted these statutes had this in view, I dare not affirm. The form of conveyance by the 'bronze and scales' points to a time before coined money. But one of the progressive acts[1] of the Decemvirs was to use coin (not cattle) in their laws for expressing fixed sums when dealing with judicial wagers or fines. It seems that the Consuls were still spoken of by their original title of Praetors.

92. The following enumeration of some of the matters that we know to have been included in the Twelve Tables will shew how wide their scope was, and how much reason we have to lament the loss of the full text. There were the rules of procedure at law, among them the very ancient *actio sacramenti*, in which the parties each staked a deposit and the loser forfeited his deposit to the state: but, it seems, none of the set forms of words (*actiones*) in which pleadings had to be conducted. There were rules of execution for debt and the treatment of insolvent debtors: of emancipation of sons, divorce of wives, succession of posthumous children, wardship of women: of intestate succession: of wills, perhaps legalizing the Plebeian will (a kind of sham sale to the heir) which had come into use as more convenient than the old will made before the Assembly: of contracts and conveyances, here also perhaps making procedure somewhat easier: of title to estates acquired by prescription, and title to wives on the same principle, thus recognizing a newer and simpler form of marriage,

---

[1] Mommsen, *Strafrecht* p. 13, points out that they not only borrowed from Solon's statutes but borrowed a Greek word (*poena* or *poenae*). This is all the more natural if, as he holds, the Decemvirs introduced coinage into Rome. See *Münzwesen* pp. 175, 302. Thus the use of metal bars taken by weight was superseded. Marquardt, *Stvw* II 6, 7.

in which the husband only acquired the full marital authority after a
year of unbroken cohabitation : of easements, such as rights of way
and watercourses, etc.: of civil wrongs, incantation, assaults, witch-
craft, arson, burglary, theft, usury, fraud of guardian against his ward
or patron against his client, false witness: of the limits of justifiable
homicide and the right of association, forbidding night-clubs and
meetings for unlawful purposes.   So too there were rules of a public
state character (*ius publicum*), forbidding the passing of laws relating
to individuals (*privilegia*), and reserving trials affecting the civic
existence (*caput*) or life of a citizen to the Assembly of Centuries.
This reminds us that there was strictly speaking no Criminal Law :
if an act was viewed as an injury to the state, the offender was
brought to the bar of the Assembly, whose verdict took the general
form of an act of legislation, often by simply declaring him to be a
traitor or public enemy (*perduellis*).   The law also mentioned the
'investigators of murder' (*quaestores parricidii*), to whom fell most of
the work of prosecution.   Another head was the sacred law of funerals,
with rules for mourning, for checking extravagance, for interment or
cremation, for sepulchres : all burials were to take place in future
outside the city.   The two supplementary Tables seem to have
contained the famous clause forbidding lawful marriage between
Patricians and Plebeians, probably recognizing an existing custom :
also a clause providing that in case of conflicting statutes the later
in date supersedes the earlier.

93.   We may I think detect three main influences at work in this
legislation.   First, there are the remains of ancient customary law,
now put into writing and becoming statute law.   Secondly, changes
in the way of preferring newer and simpler customs to older and
more elaborate ones.   Thirdly, changes and additions suggested by
Greek models.   We might call them Survivals, Simplifications,
Borrowings.   That the first was the most important I do not doubt.
But the general effect of the famous 'Twelve' was undoubtedly to
leave the Plebeians in a better position than before.   If, however,
the Patrician leaders fancied that the Plebs would be satisfied with
this reform, and so be content to do without Tribunes in future, they
were, as we have seen above, doomed to utter disappointment.

CHAPTER XI

94. THE relations of Rome to neighbouring powers in the period 509—449 B.C. are in outline as follows: first, a struggle for existence; next, a wise policy of alliances; thirdly, an improvement in the position of Rome, only checked by the weakening effect of internal dissensions. But the details of the campaigns and battles are so confused in our authorities, and the results so misrepresented under the influences of national self-complacency and family pride, that it is hard to construct with any confidence even a general survey of events.

95. We have already referred to the Etruscan war of 508. It is now generally thought that Porsenna actually took the city of Rome. If so, why did he not occupy it or restore the Tarquins? Perhaps the Etruscan cities, never very good at cooperation, were causing him some uneasiness. Perhaps he was not sorry to have a 'buffer-state' between Etruria and the Latins. So we might go on guessing: the one certainty is that we do not know. The Latin war of 501 is also connected in legend with the Tarquins. What we are most concerned to notice is the fact of Rome being at war with the League in which she had as chief member attained a dominant position. Perhaps the confederates did not all combine against her: Livy says that Praeneste went over to Rome. In 493 we hear of a most important step. A new treaty of alliance[1] was made between Rome and the Latins: its terms are said to have been mutual support in war and equal shares of booty, and community of private rights between citizens of Rome or any Latin city. Rome hardly appears as the mistress of the League; but, as one against many, she retained the natural advantages of her unity.

96. In 495—4 we begin to hear of the Volsci and Aequi as enemies of Rome. The Aequi were a cluster of hill-communities to the N.E. of Rome and Latium, the Volsci inhabited a hill and coast district to the S.E. These peoples were constantly at war with Rome

---

[1] This was the famous treaty of Spurius Cassius. A copy of it seems to have been in existence in the time of Cicero. See Dionys. VI 95, Weissenborn on Livy II 33, Reid on *Cic. pro Balbo* § 53.

and the Latin lowlanders. The endless raids and devastations of territory on both sides make one wonder how anyone survived at all. We do hear of famines at Rome, and importations of corn : but the Latins, whose lands lay directly in the track of these inroads, must have been the greatest sufferers. This wearing and indecisive warfare went on with occasional breaks till 431, when the power of the Volsci and Aequi was broken : and even after that there were rebellions. It was their pressure that led to the first typical achievement of Roman foreign policy. Between these two peoples, in a small hill district, dwelt the Hernici, a brave little people, who are said to have given the Romans some trouble in 495. In 487 the Roman army beat them in the field : in 486 an alliance[1] was concluded with them, modelled on that lately made with the Latins. It seems pretty clear that this was on the face of it a favour to the Hernicans : they seemed to have secured powerful allies and to have strengthened their somewhat precarious position. So indeed they had : but Rome always took care not to have the worst of a bargain. And now, while the forces of the two Leagues, added to that of Rome, were, whenever they cooperated heartily, more than a match for their enemies, it was the Latins and Hernicans who bore the brunt of the border wars. Their lands were invaded first, and the Roman army would reach the seat of war in time to share the glories of victory and claim her third part of the spoils. And by the Hernican alliance Rome ensured that the Aequi and Volsci should be watched on two frontiers and parted off from each other by a wedge of territory friendly to Rome. Furthermore, from a note of a Roman antiquary[2] it is inferred that in the treaty of 493 it was agreed that the chief command in war should be held in turn by a Roman and a Latin, apparently in alternate years. We have no such note about the Hernicans, nor is a triple arrangement probable. We know that at some time uncertain this privilege of the Latins, if it ever existed, fell into disuse. It may have been the effect of the Hernican alliance that caused the command-in-chief (probably soon) to become the prerogative of Rome.

97. Thus far we have said nothing of the Sabines. Tradition tells of many wars with them, and several hard-fought battles : but they do not seem to have been such inveterate enemies of Rome as were the Volsci and Aequi. Perhaps their position between the Aequi and the Etruscans may have rendered them less hostile to Rome. A simple independent hill-folk, they seem to have had in-

---

[1] Sp. Cassius was again consul. Livy II 41, Dionys. VIII 68, 69.

[2] Festus p. 241 M. Mommsen, *Staatsrecht* III 619, rejects this inference, denying that we have any trace of an alternating command.

ternal dissensions. Legend, perhaps truly, says that in 504 a Sabine chief, Attius Clausus, worsted in party strife at home, migrated to Rome with his following of clients. He was welcomed and admitted to the Patrician[1] order, and received lands for settlement of his followers on the Sabine-Etruscan frontier. The Romans called him Appius Claudius, and from him the great Claudian clan took their origin. The details are not trustworthy, but the main fact is probably true.

98. We must return to the relations between Rome and the Etruscans. Their powerful fortified cities, ruled by aristocracies of wealthy lords, were slow to cooperate for common ends. It was possible to be at war with some of them while on friendly terms with others. From about 481 B.C. there was frequent warfare between Rome and the great south-Etruscan city of Veii. This struggle seems to have made a great impression on the Roman mind, for the traditional account abounds in legends. But in truth the Etruscans had already seen their best days. In 474 they were thoroughly beaten in a sea fight by Hiero, the tyrant of Syracuse, off Cumae on the Campanian coast. They never again were formidable at sea, and their power in Campania was quickly lost. Shortly before (480) Phoenician power in Sicily had received a great check by the defeat of the Carthaginians at the decisive battle of Himera. Etruscan and Carthaginian had been accustomed to work together. Thus did the Greeks in their great age help to secure for the Italian races the freedom to work out their destinies untroubled by alien control. It is well to notice that the chief strategic point, taken and retaken by either side as Rome or Veii got the upper hand, was Fidenae. At this point there was a bridge or crossing over the Tiber, which the town commanded. It had been an old bone of contention between Latin and Etruscan, and Rome never held it securely till Veii fell.

99. In connexion with the foreign policy of Rome in this period I cannot omit a further reference to the relations between Rome and the Greeks. Greek influences entered Rome very early, chiefly by the way of trade. But we find indications of friendship, if not of alliance, with Greek states such as Cumae. And most noteworthy of all is the tradition preserved of a very early alliance with Massalia on the coast of Gaul. It is said[2] that in the days of the first King Tarquin the Phocaeans, wandering in search of a resting-place, put into the mouth of the Tiber and made friendship with the Romans, after which they went on their way and founded Massalia. Their fights in defence of their spreading commerce, their colonial forts

---

[1] See above, § 49, for the probable Sabine affinities of the Roman Patriciate.
[2] See note on § 143.

and factories, their steady and cautious aristocratic government, the importance of their little state as a centre of culture and enterprise, all mark them as worthy forerunners of Venice and Holland. We shall meet with the Massaliots later on, always deserving respect, always loyal allies of Rome. I believe the early alliance of the two cities to be a fact, and would note that before Rome set herself to become the mistress of Italy she was not unwilling to gain useful friends beyond the seas. As the Latins and Hernicans bore the brunt of most of the border warfare, so no doubt the Massaliots kept down Etruscan piracy, and afforded to Rome such share as she might claim in the trade of the Western waters.

100. As to the armies with which Roman policy was in this period carried out, they were probably organized on the Servian system referred to above. The battle order was that of a phalanx or column of foot, with the best-armed men in the front ranks. Cavalry, and to some extent light troops also, played a more important part than in the later system. This probably indicates that the wealthier Romans were doing their duty well. They cheerfully served in the cavalry and heavy infantry, and the poor were available as skirmishers. To secure conquered lands and occupy strategic points the Roman-Latin-Hernican confederates founded 'Latin Settlements' (*coloniae Latinae*) in the districts taken from the Volsci. These were Suessa[1] Pometia, Cora[1], Velitrae[1], Norba, and perhaps Antium. Signia was reinforced with new settlers. Of these garrison-towns I have spoken elsewhere.

---

[1] Beloch, *Ital. Bund* pp. 135, 191, points out that these early joint colonies became members of the Latin League, and so do not appear as colonies later on; hence they are not among the 30 referred to in Livy XXVII 9, 10, under 209 B.C. These three are assigned to the regal period. Norba is placed in 492, and seems like the refounded Signia to have become a *Colonia Latina populi Romani*. Antium became in 338 a citizen colony.

CHAPTER XII

THE LEGENDS OF THE TRADITIONAL NARRATIVE

101. To deplore the meagreness of our knowledge of the early history of the Republic will not indeed help us to increase it, but the defects of the record must be steadily borne in mind. It is not merely that doubt hangs over the chronology owing to the loss of documents in the Gaulish fire of 390 B.C. This may account for our hearing so little: but after all what gives us most trouble is the unsatisfactory nature of what we do hear. All our authorities wrote centuries after the events. The lawyers and antiquaries of the Empire or the last age of the Republic have preserved a number of detached rules, customs, forms, phrases, and so forth, upon which they comment: and it is to be hoped that in the main these comments are sound, and that we understand them aright. But these do not make a continuous history. The continuous narratives, of which that of Livy is the most important, are sadly vitiated, not only by unwise use of materials but by the perverted aims of the writers.

102. Documents, such as lists of magistrates, treaties, records of the priestly colleges, and the like, can never have been very plentiful for this period: if any still existed, genuine survivals and later restorations were almost certainly not distinguished by the critics of the time of Augustus. The works of earlier writers, none of them contemporary with the events (or nearly so), were freely used, but on no sound principles and with no steady judgment. Perhaps Livy never shews to more advantage than when he at times gives conflicting stories and owns himself unable to decide between them. And with these insufficient authorities there is mixed up a quantity of matter taken from sources even less worthy of trust. Such were family records, including the speeches said to have been delivered at the funerals of the illustrious dead. Of these records the great Patrician Houses in course of time accumulated stores, and we may be sure that historic accuracy seldom checked the tendency to glorify a man's self or ancestors. In the period now before us we find a glaring instance of the way in which these private memorials have tainted the books that to us are sources of Roman history. The reader of Livy is struck by the continual recurrence of the name Fabius among

the consuls of the years 485—477 B.C. The general glory of the Fabii reaches a climax in the latter year, when we are told that all the males of the clan perished fighting for their country, and the only surviving Fabius was a boy left behind at Rome. Yet the *gens Fabia* produced not a few men of note in later days. Possible the traditional story of the Fabii is, probable it is not. And, when we remember that the first of the Roman annalists, Fabius Pictor (contemporary with Hannibal), served as a leading authority to the later writers, it is almost a moral certainty that we have found the source of the Fabian legend. As we hear the best of the Fabii, so on the other hand the Claudii fare badly in the traditional narrative. Mommsen has shewn that we cannot trust the accounts of them at all. This family of reformers is pictured to us as a series of harsh obstructive aristocrats, inveterate enemies of the Plebeian cause. The details of the picture are neither probable nor consistent as they appear in Livy and Dionysius. The misrepresentation is perhaps, as Mommsen says, derived from the works of the malignant annalist Licinius Macer, who wrote about 80—70 B.C., when the Claudii were really conservatives and Macer a vehement supporter of the other party. Another source of doubtful stories was found by Niebuhr in ancient lays sung on public occasions. We all know and value Macaulay's attempt to give us a restoration of this minstrelsy, but I believe that the part actually played by such lays in the generation of the Roman legends was very small.

103. Enough has been said of the materials used, tainted with partisan feeling and family pride. It remains to add that historical criticism was in a rudimentary state. Authorities were sometimes weighed, but often only counted. The practice of borrowing a bit here and a bit there from different sources, all inexact and many of them loose in chronology, led to multiplication of incidents: the same event was repeated as something new in different years, taken from different authorities with various colouring. But the most serious vice of the writers of Roman history was the perversion of their aims. The Greek Dionysius is ready to pander to the vainglory of his Roman masters, but he seeks also to glorify his own race by making out that Rome was essentially[1] Greek—a Greek colony, in fact. Livy is a man with a mission. To him the greatness of the Roman past only intensifies the alarm with which he views the present. His task is to help on the work of Roman regeneration with his pen. His means are found in the brave deeds of the Romans of old : with these

---

[1] That Greek influences, chiefly from Italiot and Siceliot Greeks, operated very early in Rome, I do not doubt. Whether to the extent and in the precise manner asserted by Pais (*Legends, passim*) is another matter.

'precedents' or 'patterns' (*exempla*) he preaches his long impressive sermon, the gist of which is, that Conduct is the main thing : he has set forth in concrete cases what men should follow or shun. It is the voice of one crying vainly to a people that has lost its vigour and is nevertheless degenerately greedy of renown.

104. Authors that write with a moral purpose are justly suspected as exponents of historic truth. And in the age of Augustus we must allow much for a very sinister influence—that of the rhetorical training in vogue. Originally popular as a preparation for the debates of the Senate, of mass-meetings, of the law-courts, its chances of practical application were now sadly reduced. One strong hand quietly controlled all, and the appeals to the passions of men who were free agents were felt to be out of date. Unable to express itself in practical oratory, rhetoric took possession of literature. This movement had a bad effect, worst of all perhaps in the department of history. It was the fashion to declaim on imaginary themes, to compose speeches in the character of historical persons, to produce by the artifices of descriptive detail a more poignant rendering of traditional scenes. Straining after effect is fatal to sober reverence for truth. We can easily trace the workings of Rhetoric in the artificial heightening of contrasts, in elaboration of descriptions, in the habit of filling in a picture with added motives and explanations. Here the materials are supplied by fancy, and imagination, in itself necessary to the historian, becomes rather the substitute than the handmaid of research. This evil betrays itself in various ways. A common slip is 'anticipation,' the introduction of references to institutions at dates when they did not yet exist. The custom of putting speeches—set orations—into the mouths of historical characters (Dionysius reports a speech of Romulus at the foundation of Rome) gave frequent openings to these mischievous tendencies of Rhetoric. It was no new custom : we find a very bad instance of it in Herodotus. But it is a childish folly. Perhaps Thucydides alone had any considerable success in thus imposing on his readers. And the experience of ages did not improve the practice of writers : in Livy (not to speak of Dionysius) the neat and eloquent harangues— pure inventions—lend an air of unreality to the whole narrative. But Fashion rules, and History had to be written thus.

105. When we have made allowance for these shortcomings, and for an average amount of human ignorance and carelessness, it is clear that in basing our history of early Rome on these accounts we must use a watchful and candid criticism. And we must remember that unhistorical stories may at times have an historical value. Fiction may give us an insight into a people's ideals : and this is strikingly the case with the Roman legends. They were the moral food of the Roman youth, and they tell us much of the temper of the old Roman people. The characters are mostly (perhaps all) real persons : the details largely fiction. I proceed to give a few specimens.

106. Collatinus, the colleague of Brutus in the consulship (509), was a Tarquin. Brutus appealed to his patriotism, and he resigned his office and went into voluntary exile rather than remain at Rome with the prospect of being a disturbing element in the new Republic. Soon after, a conspiracy for restoration of the Tarquins was discovered. The two sons of Brutus were implicated in it. The consul had to try and condemn them, and even to preside at their execution. The Roman father had feelings, but they were overridden by the Roman consul's duty to the state. The consul Valerius was building a house on the Velian hill : this was thought to indicate an ambition beyond the limits of true patriotism. Hearing this, he at once pulled it down[1] and built on the low ground instead. Next comes the Etruscan invasion (508), and the famous defence of the bridge by Horatius and his comrades, which we need not recount here. This is followed by the attempt of Mucius to assassinate Porsenna. He fails and is caught. In prospect of torture and death, he defies the king, declares himself only the forerunner of a series of assassins. To prove his constancy he burns off his right hand in the altar fire hard by. Even when Porsenna forgives and releases him, he does not abate his threat of the avengers to come. He is henceforth nicknamed Scaevola (left-handed), and the name is proudly borne for ages by the Mucian House. Next comes the virgin Cloelia. The Romans had to give hostages to Porsenna, and she was one. She puts herself at the head of the maids, eludes the guard, and brings the whole company back safe, swimming the Tiber under shot of darts. In the great secession (494) of the Plebs, we are solemnly told that Menenius, the envoy of the Patricians, brought the Commons into a milder frame of mind by telling them the fable of the belly and the members. To the years 493—488 is assigned the famous story of Marcius Coriolanus, the hero of the Latin and Volscian war. His quarrel with the tribunes, his life in exile among the Volscians, how he led their armies to victory and humbled Rome, how in the last straits the Romans owed their safety to the intercession of the hero's mother and wife, while he came to some miserable end—this is not history, but drama, as the eye of Shakespeare saw. A little later (479—8) we meet with the story of the 306 Fabii, how they under-

---

[1] To him was attributed the first law granting the general right of Appeal. He received the kindly nickname of *Publicola*, the People's Friend.

took to guard the Roman frontier against the men of Veii, and how, after a successful career as wardens of the border, they fell into a trap and were cut off to the last man.   In 458 there came a moment of great peril.   A consul with his force were surrounded by the Aequi, and could not cut their way out.   A whole army was in jeopardy, and L. Quinctius Cincinnatus was made Dictator to save it.   His public spirit was already known.   The story of Cincinnatus tilling his plot of ground is a commonplace of literature.   The deputation of senators come on their serious errand : the sturdy farmer is requested to put on his gown and hear it.   Washed and gowned (*togatus*) he is saluted Dictator, and steps from the spade or plough straight to the head of the state, apparently without the least exultation or nervousness or even surprise.   Coolly he gets together a relieving army, every man bearing twelve stakes, three or four times the usual number, beside his food and arms.   The dictator marches off and reaches the seat of war about nightfall, and during the night surrounds the surrounding Aequi with a palisade.   This part of the story is childish, but the rescue of the army and defeat of the enemy are possible enough. Lastly there is the famous episode of Verginia and the Decemvir Appius Claudius.   It is surely not necessary to repeat this immortal tale.

107.   If now we take a general view of this wonderful collection of legends, caring little whether the details be wholly or in part imaginary, but regarding the heroes and heroines as at least a gallery of moral types, we may gain a fair notion of the kind of greatness that carried Rome the city of the Tiber to the headship of the ancient world.   It is simple enough.   There is a plain devotion to duty, a disregard of personal inclinations, a pride that disdains submission, a constancy of the finest temper.   There is a clear grasp of the object of the hour and a willingness to take the necessary steps.   That there was a worse side to these fine qualities, we have much reason to know : narrowness of mind, bigoted obstinacy, hardness and cruelty, all meet us in Roman history.   But all persons and peoples have their faults, and Roman faults cannot discredit Roman ideals.   We are not dealing with a clever people, like the Greeks.   Here there is no constellation of brilliant stars, but a succession of good citizens, able to cooperate and to obey, and preeminent among peoples ancient or modern in unfaltering steadiness of nerve.   Far be it from me to disparage the *Iliad* and *Odyssey*.   Early Rome has no poems to compare with those glorious works.   But, if we compare the types of character offered by the Greek and Roman legends respectively to the admiration of youth, I think the Italian series is the better suited to build up good citizens.   Good, I should say, for an age of contests.

Anyhow the course of history lends countenance to this opinion. Rome struggling is successful mainly by the possession of the harder civic virtues ; Rome triumphant rapidly decays, and is largely ruined through that awkward stiffness which hinders her from moving with the times. Brutus and Cincinnatus had their day, and a great day it was. But when a more supple and original type of man was needed, the want could not be met, and the conquering Republic blundered to its fall from sheer incapacity for reform.

CHAPTER XIII

THE CONSTITUTION, 448—367 B.C.

(a) *The Magistracy.*

108. THE great crisis of the Decemvirate was over: the Valerio-Horatian laws had strengthened the Plebs and its leaders the Tribunes. But the Roman government at the beginning of the period 448—367 B.C. was still a very simple machine. Positive power to perform the acts of state rested almost wholly with the two consuls. Checked in the city by the negative power of the tribunes, in the field they were supreme. They were in fact an Executive with general un-defined powers; a common form of primitive government. The written laws of the Twelve Tables doubtless gave a body of known and fixed rules and did away with many judicial vagaries, but the Consuls were still at the head of the judicial system, such as it was. Administration in all departments was still directed by them. Wars often kept them at the head of armies. They had in fact too much to do, and it must surely have happened in any case that a specializing process would detach various functions from this great office, and create new offices for the discharge of those functions. In other words, the scope of the *imperium* must be reduced. This at least is what happened. But at Rome this movement was complicated by its connexion with the struggle of the Orders. The Patricians were not inclined to lessen the importance of an office to which they alone were eligible: but, when it became clear that their prerogative was seriously threatened, this reluctance was exchanged for a desire to hand over to the Plebeians as little as possible.

109. The first sign of the narrowing of the scope of the *imperium* occurred probably in 447, as a sequel of the Valerio-Horatian reform. It seems that the Quaestors, hitherto each appointed by a Consul as his assistant, were ordered to be elected by the people (*populus*), and from later indications it is thought that this means the Assembly of the Tribes. A Consul presided at the election, and the Quaestors chosen were to be the assistants, not of himself and his colleague, but of the Consuls of the next year. One can see that this step tended to make the Quaestorship into an independent office, as it did. But the office never became one of high rank. Its original connexion with the detection and arrest of murderers gradually disappeared, while its financial duties were developed. We find the Quaestors in charge of the State Treasury (*aerarium*) containing money, documents, military standards, etc., and engaged in the collection of moneys due to the state. In 421 we find the number of Quaestors raised from two to four, and Plebeians made eligible. In 409 three of the four were actually Plebeians.

110. The next step was taken in 445. The Tribune Canuleius, the author of the famous marriage-law, agitated for having the Consulate thrown open to the Plebeians. The movement, taken up by his nine colleagues, was only foiled by a counter-move of the Patricians. This consisted in an arrangement by which, in any year, the place of consuls might be filled by Military Tribunes with Consular Power, who might be either Patricians or Plebeians. This curious office, which occurs 51 times in the period from 444 to 367 B.C., seems to have been evolved thus. There were in a legion six *tribuni*, but the number of legions varied with the needs of each year. Thus the number of *tribuni militum* would be six or a multiple of six. It was now left for the people in their Centuries to elect and endow with consular powers a number of these Tribunes not exceeding six. Thus a number of military posts were converted at a stroke into offices of government, civil or military. In the earlier part of the period we find usually three Tribunes thus qualified, then commonly four, and in 405 and later regularly six. The years in which consuls were appointed belong nearly all to the earlier part. At first the choice of the Centuries, controlled by the rich, fell wholly upon Patricians, and the Plebeians seemed to have gained only the right to be not elected though eligible: but as time went on Plebeian Military Tribunes with Consular power began to be chosen and the Plebs saw their own Order sharing the highest office. In a time of many wars it was probably convenient to have more than two magistrates holding the *imperium* that qualified them for the direction of civil jurisdiction and also for the command of armies. When tradition says that the great soldier Camillus was more than once elected a Consular Tribune with five colleagues who were meant to do his bidding, and did, this is very likely true: though of course only the presence of a born leader in a time of danger would make such an arrangement work. There is indeed a story that the need of more chief magistrates was the real ground for the introduction of Consular Tribunes. This account, preferred by Mommsen, may very likely be the truth. Anyhow the restoration of the consulship in 367 was accompanied by the institution of the Praetorship, probably to meet this long-felt need.

III. The institution of the Censorship[1] is fully accounted for by the need of providing in some regular way for duties which the Consuls were often too busy to perform. We can hardly connect this change with the struggle of the Orders in any more direct way than as an attempt to increase the efficiency of the consulship. Since the great Servian reform it had been clearly necessary to hold a periodical revision of the register of citizens and their properties: otherwise the whole system of Classes and Centuries (that is, the Army and the Sovran Assembly) must fall into confusion. The duty of keeping the register up to date had passed from King to Consuls: but it was found very difficult to accomplish it amid the pressure of a crowd of other duties in the narrow limits of a year of office. The revision was probably intended from the first to recur regularly in a fixed period[2], which seems at first to have been every fifth (in our reckoning fourth) year. Later, it was every fifth year as we should reckon it. But, what with wars and other urgent business, the work had at times to be neglected, and the consuls by whom it was left to stand over to another year were perhaps nothing loth to transfer a tiresome burden to other shoulders. The proceeding itself was called *census*, meaning an assessment or rating fixed by the official according to the best of his judgment (connected with *censere*, to think, reckon, judge). To conduct a *census* implied a decision in the case of every individual citizen, a decision on which depended his position in Army or Assembly till the next revision came round. Most cases would admit a prompt decision, but many would not: and there is reason to think that the process of drawing up the roll of citizens, with all its many subdivisions, was toilsome and long. With this main function were combined other important duties, such as making up the roll of senators, a proceeding which threw much power into the censors' hands; and the control of such matters of public economy as state contracts (*publica*). These last fall into two main classes, the state dues (*vectigalia*), the collection of which was leased out to farmers who paid a lump sum down for the privilege, and public works of construction or maintenance for which contractors tendered[3] (*ultro tributa*) and for which the Censors made contracts at a fixed price. The general name for persons holding state contracts was

---

[1] The traditional date is 443 B.C., but Mommsen would place it in 435. The *census* belongs to the Servian reform.

[2] Mommsen derives the four-year cycle from the Greek Olympiads. The irregular recurrence in practice was not overcome until the Senate became supreme in the state and the vagaries of the magistrates were checked. See below, § 622.

[3] Literally 'voluntary assignments,' that is, sums which the state did not get in, but went so far as to pay out. The contract placed the state in the position of debtor. For details see Mommsen, *Staatsrecht* II 434 foll.

publicani, and the contracts held good until the next revision. If even after the appointment of Censors the five-year period was not strictly observed (and there was great irregularity), this was due in the main to interruptions caused by war: but we are not to forget that a contractor-class was steadily growing up, whose interests would be favoured by delay, and that no force tells more surely in politics than the vigilance of personal interest. The publication of the register of citizens was followed by a religious ceremony of 'cleansing' (*lustrum*) in which the acting Censor purified the assembled people (*exercitus*) with solemn sacrifice, thus fulfilling the vow made to the War-god at the last *lustrum*, and renewing the vow forward to the next. We do not know that the censorship was ever closed to Plebeians by law. We know that it was many years before (351) a Plebeian first became Censor. The remarkable thing is that the religious act of the *lustrum* was not performed by a plebeian censor till 280. Religion was the last stronghold of the failing Patriciate. The actual term of office was a year and six months, only extended to meet special needs such as the watching of some important contract. In other respects also the Censor differed from an ordinary magistrate: he had no *imperium*, and could not of himself summon Senate or Assembly. Strictly speaking, the office was never of the first rank. But it soon became a post of dignity, assigning to each citizen his due position in the state, visiting scandalous conduct with recorded disgrace. It was a characteristically Roman office, with wide undefined powers. Its holders were men of repute, nearly always ex-consuls, and it was thus regarded as the crown of a successful official career.

112. We see that, while the pressure of the Plebs was more and more felt, the Patrician Order stood its ground. Not only was it generally able to control the Assembly of Centuries, but it no doubt enjoyed the prestige that usually attaches to an experienced governing class in times of danger and distress. Its stubborn defence of the consulship against plebeian claims is marked in many ways, amongst others by the frequent use of the Dictatorship. We hear of Dictators in no less than 15 years of this period: Camillus, the hero of the age, was Dictator five times. No doubt the urgency of external danger was the cause of most of these appointments, but there were times when, in view of popular discontent, the concentration of executive power in one strong hand was the real object of the ruling class: thus Camillus was employed in the crisis of the Licinian laws, first to prevent their passing, afterwards to mediate between the extreme partisans and conclude the legislation in peace. The Tribunes of the Commons appear in this period as making use of

their established position now guaranteed by the Valerio-Horatian laws. The tradition represents them as able by 'intercession' to block decrees of the Senate. This probably shews that they had reached the stage of sitting by the senate-house door and watching in the interest of the Plebs the proceedings of the council. They were gaining recognition, they were on the way to seats in the Senate and to the position of Magistrates of the Roman people; but these results were not achieved as yet. And it seems as if the senators managed at times to do what in later days they did habitually, to neutralize the tribunician power by the veto of tribunes. Thus in 417 a land-bill was brought forward by some Tribunes, and blocked by others, and in 376 the same use of Intercession blocked for the time the passing of the Licinian laws. The true explanation of this occasional weakening of the Tribunate is doubtless to be sought in the different interests of the richer and poorer Plebeians. These interests had been gradually diverging ever since the Servian reform, and the real line of division was coming to be not that of blood between Patrician and Plebeian, but that of wealth between Rich and Poor. This division appears clearly in the struggle for the Licinian laws. And it was chiefly the wealthier Plebeians that were elected Tribunes: and it suited the Patrician leaders to gratify some of them in various ways (such as leases of state land) and so to induce them to betray the cause of the needy multitude. When at last the economic situation became intolerable, and the Plebs was really aroused to put forth its strength, the wealthier Plebeians used the needs of the poor to win the Consulship for themselves, Licinius and Sextius led unanimous colleagues and an united Plebs, and Patrician obstruction was surely and speedily overcome. Of the Consulship we have already spoken under other heads. It was the chief bone of contention between the Orders in the political strife of this period; and, when once the Patricians lost the exclusive possession of this office, the complete equalization of the Orders was simply a question of time.

(b) The Senate.

113. It is of the first importance to appraise rightly the condition of the Senate in the period 448—367 B.C. We observe a gradual change in its composition, gradual formation of its character, gradual growth of its influence, by which we are prepared for the splendour of its later history. It was no longer the advisory board consulted now and then by a life-long King: it had sixty years of experience as the adviser of yearly magistrates. Some sort of continuity was necessary in the interests of the state: and the members of this

permanent and easily-summoned body must by this have become
conscious of their own essential superiority to the holders of transitory
power.　But the Patrician Order was becoming more and more hope-
lessly a minority in the state, and the Senate, if not wholly Patrician,
was to all intents and purposes a Patrician body.　The introduction
of Plebeians was necessary if the Senate was to retain and increase
its power.　And this was done, but at what date exactly a beginning
was made it is not easy to say.　Still, as the Decemvirate had been
open to Plebeians, as the consular Tribunate and Quaestorship were
also open, we may fairly place the regular admission of Plebeian
senators somewhat early in this period.　However few they may
have been, every such admission was the concession of a principle
certain to bear ample fruit.　Membership of the State Council was
no longer dependent on membership of one of the ancient clans.

　114.　In later times, from which our information comes, we find the
Senate working under well-established rules of procedure.　A large
part of its code of practice may well have grown up in this period.
What concerns us here is that it was and remained the true centre
of Roman discussion of state affairs.　Haranguing multitudes is not
debate.　In the Senate alone opinions of all kinds could find expression, probably brief in these days.　Various proposals came before
the House, the audience were the voters, each with a single vote, who
passed judgment on the motions.　The presiding Magistrate laid the
matter in hand before the House and called upon members in a
regular order of precedence to give their opinion.　The magistrates
and ex-magistrates came first.　By these speakers the various motions
(*sententiae*) were made.　They were bound to give an opinion of some
sort, even if it were no more than a proposal to defer the matter.
Those of a less dignity simply declared their adhesion to the views
of this or that speaker.　When the president thought fit to take a
vote, he told the Ayes to go to a certain part of the chamber and the
Noes to another part.　Thus the voting was strictly by Division
(*discessio*).　The president declared that one or other side had the
majority: if in doubt, he could count the numbers.　When the proceedings issued in the passing of a regular Order (*consultum*) in
answer to the original question of the magistrate, it was duly recorded
in writing: this was generally done on the spot, and several senators
(whose names were recorded) served as witnesses to the correctness
of the draft.　If the *intercessio* of a Tribune forbade the passing of a
formal *senatus consultum*, it was not unusual to record the result as
a Resolution (*senatus auctoritas*).　The difference between a valid
Order and an invalid Resolution was this, that the latter could not
be carried out owing to the opposition of an irresistible power.　It

must not be confused with that between a Statute and a Bill. A Bill is meant to become a binding Statute: if blocked, it is nothing. But the Senate could not legislate: in point of form it only expressed its opinion (*censere*) on the matter before it. Hence a mere Resolution might in certain circumstances carry considerable weight. In fact *auctoritas* is the word that best expresses the position of the Senate. That House might be, and often was, blinded by partisanship and prejudice; but it could never be a wholly indifferent matter that this or that policy had received the express 'support,' 'sanction,' 'guarantee,' or 'approval' of what all men knew to be the most competent body in Rome.

115. This very inadequate sketch of the procedure of the Senate must suffice for our present purpose. We must now consider the nature of the business that came before it. There were matters connected with religion, such as the admission or exclusion of new gods and provision for the proper worship of the old: matters connected with jurisdiction, when magistrates sought advice in the face of some situation where precedents were lacking, or when safe-conduct (*fides publica*) had to be given to a witness, or a particular magistrate chosen to conduct an inquiry. War too was the Senate's concern: not the declaration of war, but the number of troops to be levied and the provision for placing armies in the field: any special questions that a general might shrink from deciding on his own responsibility: to decree a public Thanksgiving for victory, to grant a general the honour of a Triumph and vote money for its cost: to decide what should be done with conquered lands, and so forth. We are told that Camillus asked the Senate how he should dispose of booty. In the department of Finance (with which most other departments are always connected) the Senate early began to interfere. Ordinary matters were settled by the magistrate, extraordinary by the Senate, and it would often be doubtful to which class a particular outlay belonged. The creation of the Censorship increased the Senate's power. The office was an intermittent one, and concerned with many matters of an exceptional kind, and thus easily fell under senatorial influence. It became the regular practice to procure an order of the Senate for the assignment of money to any exceptional public purpose, and this soon grew into the effective control of the state treasury. Rewards for public services, expenses of festivals, purchase of corn in time of dearth, seem all to have been voted by the Senate: and the frequent failure of the Tribunes to carry agrarian laws shew how firm was its hold on the management of the public land.

116. An important sphere of senatorial action was a general

administrative care of the city and Home affairs, such as public order and police. This power was indefinite but generally effective. It consisted chiefly in advising and supporting magistrates in situations of doubt. We find the Senate consulted on the question whether Consuls or Consular Tribunes should be elected for the coming year: and the appointment of a Dictator often takes place in consequence of a vote of the House to that effect, sometimes, it would appear, even including the mention of a particular name. In matters involving religious scruple the Senate had at disposal the expert advice of the colleges of Pontiffs and Augurs. But it was in the sphere of external policy that the Fathers played the most conspicuous part. The receiving or sending of embassies, the discussion and conclusion of treaties, were matters within the competence of the Senate: indeed there was nobody else to do these things, for the magistrates were fleeting figures, here today and gone tomorrow, and the Roman People in Assembly had not yet learnt to interfere mischievously in delicate negotiations. The end of a war was normally brought about thus. The Roman commander made a temporary arrangement with the enemy: for terms of peace he referred their ambassadors to the Senate at Rome. Sometimes he returned himself to the city and presided at a meeting or meetings of the House in which terms were discussed. In any case he sent notice of his own views. But the decision on the Roman side was the work of the Senate. As the Senate settled terms with the enemies of the state, so it exercised a general supervision over the Allies and their relations to Rome and to each other. Disputes, questions arising out of treaties, the treatment of rebels, and other such matters, were matters for the Senate. Finally, in all sudden and dangerous emergencies it was the Senate's part to find a policy, to give firmness to fluttered Magistrates and wavering citizens, and somehow or other to save the state. Whether in this period the Fathers already claimed and used the right of arming the Magistrates with absolute powers, as they are said[1] to have done in 384 to deal with the sedition of Manlius, is more than doubtful. More probably a later practice has by 'anticipation' been foisted into a story of earlier times.

117. To consider the position of the Senate in general:—we must never forget that this period was for Rome one of great trouble and strain both within and without, and that the government of primitive states is apt to consist very largely of dealing with emergencies. Popular Assemblies were hardly suited for this duty: Roman citizens as a rule looked for a lead to Senate and Magistrates. Yearly officials naturally looked about for every means of strengthening their hands.

[1] Livy VI 19.

Their most ready help lay in securing the advice and support of the body in which were gradually accumulating all the traditional and practical knowledge of public affairs. That body was at hand, so that it could be quickly consulted : it voted, so that its real opinion could be learnt. The Magistrate acted, the Senate only advised. But when the advice was regularly sought, it was soon found impossible to neglect it. The process begins in earnest in the period 448—367. The Senate is becoming the director of state policy, and the Magistrates are losing power. But while the growth of precedent is strengthening the influence of the Senate, the actual sovranty rests with the People, whenever they have made up their minds to exercise it. Wisely then did the Senate at the close of this period give way in time and consent to the passing of the Licinian laws.

(c) *Assemblies.*

118. In connexion with the popular Assemblies there is in this period little of importance to remark, beyond the fact of the rise of the Assembly of the whole people summoned by Tribes (*comitia tributa*). The Centuries were still the sovran Assembly : they declared war and performed other legislative acts : they elected the regular Magistrates of the Roman People. We have already seen that the wealthy voters controlled a majority of the Centuries. The wealthy were no doubt still mostly of the Patrician Order : but we begin to come upon traces of a class of wealthy Plebeians whose interests did not always coincide with those of the needy multitude. It seems that they were now and then able to hold the balance between the Patricians and the Plebeian poor : hence it naturally followed that the benefit of the reforms of this period was in effect chiefly theirs.

119. We have already seen the meetings (*concilia*) of the Plebs voting by Tribes. In their origin these Tribes were local divisions, and at some time in the preceding period they reached, it is said, a total of 21. In this period (387) four new ones were formed, bringing up the total to 25. It is the use of these groups as the basis of a voting Assembly of the whole people (*comitia*) that calls for attention. That it gave great opportunity to the Plebeian poor of making their votes felt is on the face of it clear. The Tribes were in these days probably not very unequal in number of voters : voters, rich or poor, old or young, had each one vote in his own Tribe. It sounds as though the Patricians had been swamped utterly. But the Assembly by Tribes had not yet acquired an independent legislative power. Indeed it could not vote on anything beyond the question put to it by the presiding Magistrate. And the rich men who controlled the

Centuries were little likely to vote away their power into the hands of an Assembly where the will of the poor majority was certain to prevail. So the Tribe-Assembly did not become the normal exponent of the People's will for a good while yet. It soon gained the right of electing the Quaestors, and it was in this minor office that the actual choice of Plebeians first became usual. But at first the activity of the Tribe-Assembly shewed itself chiefly in jurisdiction. To bring obnoxious persons to trial on a capital charge necessitated the summoning of the clumsy Assembly of the 193 Centuries. Men who were in a position to offend seriously would almost certainly belong to the well-to-do class. Acquittal was therefore likely, even if some religious scruple did not cause the total failure of proceedings. If then a popular Tribune wanted to bring an offender to justice, it was simpler and more effective to lay on him a heavy fine and bring the case on appeal before the Tribes.

120. The passing of the Canuleian law (445 B.C.) is one of the most important events of the early part of this period. The tribunes of this year were active reformers : while Canuleius' bill legalized marriages between the Orders (*de conubio patrum et plebis*), his nine colleagues proposed to throw open the Consulship, that is to empower the people to elect Consuls from the Patricians or Plebeians at will. We have a traditional account of the embittered strife between the Orders aroused by these schemes. It is said that the Patricians at last gave way and accepted the marriage-law, that is, they allowed the necessary steps to be taken for turning the Resolution of the Commons into a regular statute. By this concession they hoped to divert the attention of the Plebs from the other proposal, which however bore fruit indirectly in the Consular Tribunate, as we have seen above. The non-existence of the right of *conubium* between the Orders[1] was probably a survival of the irregular way in which the Roman Plebs had grown up. Marriage belonged to the sphere of the old religious family law. With this system of immemorial custom the Plebeian, existing in the community on sufferance, had from the first nothing to do. Hence while the Latin (probably the Latin Patrician only), had under the rules of the League *conubium* with the members of the old Roman clans, the Roman Plebeian had not. And further, the ancient religion of the state entered into everything. The Magistrate had to consult the gods by taking the auspices (*auspicium*, watching birds) before every important public act at home or in the field : he had to offer sacrifices : and to do these things he must be in himself a duly qualified person. This qualification came by birth. Either a man belonged to a house recognized by the gods, or he did

---

[1] See above, §§ 49, 59, 92.

not. Thus the religious and social disability of the Plebeian carried with it a political disability.

121. When the Canuleian law legalized the marriages of Patricians and Plebeians, its immediate effect would be that children of such unions would follow the status of the father according to the principles of the old family law. But to admit that the son of a Plebeian mother was a Patrician must have been a shock to the prejudices attested by the superseded rule. In truth the concession gave up the Patrician case from the religious point of view, just as the device of Consular Tribunes did from the political. The contention that none but the stock of the old clans were acceptable to the divine powers had lost much of its force. And in course of time religion became more and more a mere affair of state, and its traditional connexion with the Patrician Order died away. In conclusion we must notice the very exceptional circumstance that the law of Canuleius directly repealed a statute of the Twelve Tables only passed five years before.

122. The process of reform-legislation may be illustrated by the struggle for the passing of the Licinian laws. After a conflict in the course of which the administration of the state had suffered from a sort of deadlock, Licinius and Sextius procured the ratification of their Bills already decreed by the Commons (*plebi scita*). This ratification is generally thought to have required two[1] steps. First, the Bills must be passed by the Centuries: secondly, the 'sanction of the Fathers' must be given. Thus they formally became Statutes. The former concession was no doubt mainly due to the fact of wealthy Plebeians being eager to capture the Consulship: the latter was a confession on the part of the Patrician leaders that abandonment of obstruction was better policy than an appeal to force. And so, as ever in the wholesome politics of early Rome, a great crisis was surmounted without the banishments and shedding of blood that commonly attended the party struggles of the brilliant city-states of Greece.

---

[1] I accept this view not without some misgivings.

CHAPTER XIV

THE LICINIAN LAWS.

123. THE wealthy Plebeians wanted to attain the Consulship, that is, to share the *imperium* with the Patricians. The attempt of Canuleius and his colleagues had been foiled by the introduction of the consular Tribunes. The experience of many elections had shewn the indifference of the poorer Plebeians to the claims of the richer. Seldom indeed had a Plebeian been elected a consular Tribune. Hence it had become clear to the leading Plebeians that, if they meant to hold the chief magistracy, they must secure a reserved place, secured from Patrician encroachments. It was not worth while to struggle for eligibility, if they were in practice never likely to be elected. Having once made up their minds what to aim at, they proceeded to gather their forces. No help could be looked for from the Patricians: tough and sly, the old families had staved off the pressure for a time by giving the wealthy Plebeians a share in the beneficial occupation (*possessio*) of the state land, and by allowing inter-marriage to take place. A means must be found of securing the effective support of the mass of the poor Plebeians. Now what these needed was economic relief: their outlook did not include political honours.

124. It is remarkable that the agitations for allotment of land were in this period mostly abortive. The land bills were a great feature of the years 416—410, but either the proposers withdrew them or their fellow Tribunes blocked them. No doubt this failure is a sign of the slackness brought about on the Plebeian side by divergent interests. It was not due to the cessation of land-hunger as the Senate well knew. To appease this we find allotments of land provided; in 393 the conquered district round Veii, in 383 the Pomptine land taken from the Volscians, was parcelled out thus. The same may have been the case in 418 with the land of Labici, which Livy treats as a Citizen Colony. Of the so-called Latin Colonies we find five founded in this period: Ardea (442) in the Rutulian country, Satricum (385) and Setia (382) among the Volsci, Sutrium (383) and Nepete (383) in Etruria. Romans who joined these Colonies became 'Latins,' citizens of a new Latin community, and so satisfied their

land-hunger at the expense of their Roman franchise.   This last plan
no doubt found favour with the leaders of state policy, the Senate, as
tending to keep down the growing numbers of poor Plebeian voters.
But such concessions could not permanently meet the difficulty.   The
colonies were garrison posts, and therefore exposed to inroads of the
neighbouring enemy: the uncertainty of reaping the fruit of their
labours was ever present to the farmers in the allotted lands near the
border.   It was no wonder that the champions of the poor clamoured
for the free allotment of the 'public lands,' the state-domain, of which
the rich were enjoying a practical monopoly at a nominal rent which
they sometimes managed to evade.

125.   Failure had also attended the attempts to alleviate the
sufferings of the poor under the laws of debt.   The pictures drawn by
Livy and others of the poor Roman called from his farm or other
work to fight for his country, finding all ruined on his return home:
the seizure of all his goods by a creditor, followed by the seizure of
himself: the soldier with his honourable scars becoming the half-
starved bondsman of a heartless capitalist: these stories are worked
up by a skilled rhetorician, no doubt; but they may be not far from
the truth.   In times of trouble the rate of interest is sure to be high,
and early law knows no pity for the debtor.   We hear that in the
debt-crisis of 385 a Patrician, M. Manlius, the man who had saved
the Capitol in 390, gave up all his property to redeem debtors from
bondage.   Rightly or wrongly, he was said to be aiming at regal
power, and this cry was used to get him done to death and save the
Republic.   The general strain on the resources of the poor is indicated
by other signs.   In 428 and 400 we hear of drought and frost.   In
440, 433, 411, 392, there was suffering from dearth.   To import corn
from abroad was not always easy: something was done, but discontent remained.   A wealthy Plebeian, Spurius Maelius, gained great
popularity by relief of distress in 440.   But he was charged with the
design of overthrowing the Republic, and means were found of putting
him to death.   In 433, 428, 412, 401, 392, we read of epidemic
sickness.   And in 390 came the inroad of the Gauls, in which the
city was burnt and the land laid waste; a disaster the effects of
which were no doubt felt for many years.   On the top of all these
various burdens and sufferings we hear that in order to strengthen
the city a great work[1] of wall-building (378) was necessary, and that
the levy of the rate (*tributum*) for this purpose aggravated the financial
distress.   The time for an effective reform movement seemed to have
come at last.   Two wealthy Plebeians, Gaius Licinius Stolo and Lucius

---

[1] Livy VI 32.   Whether this refers to the repair of the 'Servian' Wall, or whether that
wall was now first built, I do not venture to say.   Its date is matter of dispute.   See § 27.

Sextius Lateranus, were among the Tribunes of the Plebs. They came forward with a scheme by which they hoped to unite Rich and Poor, and so overcome Patrician obstruction by the solid forces of the Plebeian Order. It is usual to consider it under three heads, though it is not unlikely that, in order to make sure of the whole passing, the movers finally brought it to a vote in the form of a single Bill.

126. First, there was Debt. It was proposed that whatever sum a debtor had already paid in the way of interest should be deducted from the principal of the loan; the balance still left due to be paid off in three instalments within three years. This was clearly a temporary provision for relief of debtors in the present crisis, only excused by the downright necessity of finding a way out of an intolerable situation. Secondly, there was Land. It was proposed that no one should be allowed to occupy more[1] than 500 *iugera* of land, that is, state land. This was meant to prevent for ever the evil spoken of above. The state domains were not in future to be so monopolized by the rich as to leave little or no chance of allotments to the poor. The proposal was not in the ordinary sense an agrarian law (*lex agraria*): it offered no distribution of allotments at the moment. But it would, if enforced, go far towards providing material for future agrarian laws, and this explains both the enthusiasm for the measure and the opposition to it. In connexion with this we hear also of a provision limiting the number of cattle and sheep that anyone might keep on the land recognized as public pasture: and it may be that this tradition is trustworthy. Another story, that, in order to protect free labour, a clause specially required the employment of free men in a certain proportion to the slaves, is not credible. Had the Roman country-side been already given over to slave-gangs, the victorious wars between 366 and 200 B.C. could hardly have taken place. It is true that we hear of a slave-conspiracy in 419, but it is spoken of as a city affair. The mention of a 'free-labour' clause in connexion with the Licinian laws is surely another case of 'anticipation,' drawn from the circumstances of a later period. Thirdly, there was the Consulship. It was proposed that no more Consular Tribunes should be elected, and that one of the two Consuls of each year should be chosen from the Plebs. The Patricians were to be debarred from evading the struggle by shelving the Consulship itself: the apathy of the Plebeian poor was no longer to be allowed to leave the Patrician Order in virtual possession of the chief magistracy. Here at last was a plain issue that had to be faced. All must have seen that with the enactment of such a law the struggle of the Orders would be practically decided in favour of the Plebs.

[1] The *iugerum* was about ⅝ of an English acre.

127. Of all the constitutional struggles in the history of Rome this was the most famous. It lasted for ten years. The Plebeian leaders were re-elected Tribunes year by year. At first the Patricians tried to neutralize their power by inducing other Tribunes to block the proposals of their own colleagues. To meet this, Licinius and Sextius blocked the elections of the regular magistrates: it is said[1] that for five years no magistrate with *imperium* was elected. Only under pressure of danger from the public enemy did they allow the appointment of Consular Tribunes to be resumed. But they had given an impressive display of their power: as a negative force the Tribunes of the Plebs were irresistible. The weary fight went on. In 368 the stubborn Patricians turned to their last resource: a Dictator was named, the old hero Camillus. By this time Licinius and Sextius were becoming exasperated at the vicious obstruction of colleagues. They prepared to override even the sacred *intercessio*. It is said that when the Tribes were already voting, and the bill was in a fair way to pass[2] in spite of the blocking Tribunes, Camillus intervened and succeeded in breaking up the meeting. He resigned his office, but a successor was found. At this point we hear of a renewal of the differences between the rich and poor Plebeians: the latter were ready to drop the law about the Consulship, and pass the rest. But the bold leaders stood firm, and plainly told the people that they must take all or none. The end of the struggle was foreshadowed in the carrying of a separate proposal of the Tribunes concerning the *duumviri sacrorum*, whose chief function was the custody of the Sibylline Books, a collection of prophecies consulted in great emergencies. There were in future to be ten guardians instead of two, and half of them to be Plebeians. The year 367 saw Camillus Dictator for the fifth time, to repel an inroad of Gauls. This done, the old man returned to the political strife in Rome, where he seems to have played the part of a mediator. The Bills passed into law. The first Plebeian Consul was L. Sextius himself. So the Patricians were forced to give way. But with their usual tenacity they managed to extort a concession which minimized their defeat, at least for a time. The ordinary civil jurisdiction in the city had for some time been felt to be more than the Consuls, generally otherwise engaged, could regularly discharge. Now that the state was about to return to its two yearly Consuls and drop the more numerous Consular Tribunes, a good pretext was found for detaching this function from the Consulship and assigning it to a new officer specially appointed for the purpose. The new official was a regular magistrate with *imperium* (this was necessary for jurisdiction), a colleague of the

---

[1] Livy VI 35, and Henzen on the *Fasti Capitolini*.   [2] As a *plebiscitum*.

Consuls (but inferior to them), called by the same title (*praetor*). He
was to be a Patrician. At what exact point in the final negotiations this compromise was agreed to, is far from clear, nor does it
greatly matter. Two 'curule' Aediles were also appointed, to carry
out the festival with which the restoration of concord was celebrated.
These new Aediles were at first Patrician.

128. And so at last a settlement was reached. The wealthy
Plebeians had gained a solid triumph : the Consulship once secured,
their attainment of the other magistracies was a mere matter of time.
The gains of the poor were less substantial. The relief of debtors
was not permanent, and the hard old laws of debt remained in force
as written in the Twelve Tables. As for the state land, the difficulty
lay not so much in passing laws as in getting them carried out. It
seems that a heavy fine was the penalty for breach of the new rules,
and that it had to be exacted by the Aediles, who brought offenders
to justice before the Assembly of the Tribes. But Aediles generally
belonged to the wealthy class among whom the offenders would be
found. In 357 we read that Licinius Stolo himself was fined for
fraudulent evasion of his own law. No wonder that the law gradually
became a dead letter. What economic relief did follow in the next
period was due rather to the extension of Roman territory by conquest,
and the allotments and plantation of colonies, than to the beneficent
operation of the Licinian laws.

CHAPTER XV

FOREIGN POLICY AND THE ARMY

129. THE period 448—367 B.C. is a critical one in the foreign relations of Rome. It includes the hard struggle for the Etruscan borderland, the Gaulish inroad of 390, and the beginning of serious differences with her Latin and Hernican confederates, which come to a head in the next period. The Etruscan cities seem always to have lacked the power of effective cohesion, and Rome was able to deal with Veii Capena and Falerii, the chief places of South-Eastern Etruria, without provoking a general war with the Etruscan powers. As before, Fidenae, commanding the passage of the Tiber, appears as the regular bone of contention, while the main stronghold of the enemy is the great city of Veii.

130. In the dawn of Italian history we get glimpses of a great Etruscan power spread over a large part of the peninsula. Of this mysterious people we have spoken above[1]. They seem to have been a conquering race, settled in fortified cities and forming in each a local aristocracy, to whom the rest of the population in town and country were subject as serfs. Their own tongue lived in the cities but never became the language of the country: its affinities have been guessed at, but never satisfactorily traced. Some maritime activity they displayed in the way of piracy and perhaps of commerce; but I see no reason to think that they were a first-rate naval power, and their imports from Greece were probably carried in Greek bottoms. It would seem however that they had little love for the pushing inquisitive Greek. Their real sympathies were with the Phoenician, and we find them cooperating with Carthage to check the advance of Greek mariners in the Western seas. The Greeks called them Τυρρηνοί, the Romans *Etrusci* or *Tusci*, but it is said that *Rasenna* was their name in their own tongue. The Romans were much impressed by the dark and gloomy religion of their neighbours and their solemn ceremonial. That there was some fatal defect in their political system may be inferred from the fact that they produced neither a true homogeneous nation nor a great

[1] § 15.

centralized empire under a leading power. And so, when the blows
began to fall, their scattered forces gave way and their weakness
was exposed, even in Etruria proper, where they were at their
strongest.

131. Since their naval defeat in 474, their hold on Campania had
no doubt been weakened. And a new and terrible enemy had for
some time been pouring over the Alps. These were the Gauls, who
overthrew[1] the Etruscan power in the region of the Po. Their
swarming tribes were pressing on during this period, occupying
lands north of Apennine, and threatening the great cities of Etruria.
That Veii was left to her fate was probably in part due to the fact
that the northern cities were preoccupied with their own peril.
Tradition[2] affirmed that the great wealthy city of Melpum was
sacked by Gauls on the very day of the capture of Veii by Camillus
in 396 B.C. In 424 the Samnites[3] took Volturnum (later Capua),
and Etruscan power in Campania fell with the fall of the chief city.
In 391 the Gauls crossed the Apennine into eastern Etruria, and
assailed the city of Clusium. Rome, appealed to on the ground of
a common danger, sent ambassadors to warn the enemy off. Unable
to come to terms, these envoys wickedly broke the law of nations
and fought for Clusium in the ensuing battle. The Romans refused
redress, says the story, and elected the offenders Consular Tribunes
for the next year. The enraged barbarians marched on Rome and
fell in with the Romans posted on the little stream of Allia. After
a charge and a rout, the Roman army for the time ceased to exist.
To reconstruct the true story of what followed is not possible, so
utterly has it been perverted and coloured in the interests of Roman
vanity. It seems that the city of Rome was sacked and burnt. The
citadel on the Capitoline hill held out for more than six months.
Legend told that a night-surprise was very nearly successful: even
the watch-dogs, let alone the sentinels, slumbered on: only the sacred
geese were awake and alarmed Marcus Manlius in the nick of time.
How a Fabius, rather than leave unperformed the sacred rites of his
clan, passed through the enemy's lines on the appointed day and did
sacrifice as usual on the Quirinal hill: how Camillus in his exile at
Ardea refused to command the now rallying forces of Rome until
duly authorized by the Senate and people in the Capitol: how
Cominius floated down the river in the night and climbed the hill:

---

[1] Livy v 33—35, Polybius II 17.

[2] Pliny, *N. H.* III 125 (after Nepos). Melpum was probably on or near the site afterwards occupied by Mediolanum (Milan). Felsina afterwards Bononia (Bologna) was another
of the great Etruscan cities of the North.

[3] Livy IV 37.

how he returned safe bringing the news of Camillus' recall and his nomination as Dictator: how, yielding at last to hunger and despair, the besieged were fain to buy the departure of the Gauls with a heavy ransom: how, at the very moment of payment, when the words 'woe to the vanquished' were in the mouth of the insolent barbarian, Camillus appeared with his army and won back both gold and freedom with the Roman steel:—these and other tales in sundry variations afforded matter to generations of Roman writers and served to stimulate and edify the Roman youth.

132. We may with some confidence infer from the traditional stories that the Gauls, terrible as they were in battle-onset, were incompetent to conduct a siege, and that from shortness of supplies and want of knowledge how to adapt their habits to a treacherous climate their forces were melting away. Such has been not seldom the fate of northern armies in Italy. But we hear, and may well believe, that their foraging parties were cut off, and thus their position rendered precarious[1] by direct Roman efforts. Rome in short was burnt, but her power had not permanently collapsed. After the first shock of disaster was over, parties began to assemble in arms and wage a guerrilla warfare with increasing success. The newly taken Veii[2] is said to have been the chief centre of this resistance. This striking demonstration of the vitality of the Roman state will meet us again on a larger scale in the disasters of the Hannibalic war. It may remind us that the struggle of Patricians and Plebeians, of which we hear so much in this period, and which at times appears to absorb all the forces of the state, was not really the whole interest of Roman citizens. There was more unity among Romans than traditional history would suggest: the occasions when we read of differences being laid aside in order to present an united front to an enemy are perhaps the most genuine indications of the normal temper of the people.

133. The actual warfare between Rome and the Etruscans during this period may be ranged in three stages. First, there is the continuation of the old border wars, 438—425. Secondly, there is the ten years' war of Veii, 406—396, ending with the capture of that city by Camillus. Thirdly, in the years 395—383, we find a picture that is simply astounding. In 395—1 Rome pushes on to the northward,

---

[1] According to Polybius II 18 it was the news of an invasion of their own country by the Veneti that caused the Gauls to return home. This is probably the true story.

[2] We may ask why Veii was not made into a Latin Colony. Partly perhaps from the fear of its growing too powerful, expressed in the story of the proposed migration from Rome to Veii. Partly, I think, because there was weakness in Etruria, and it was found possible to plant colonies at Nepete and Sutrium, further north. So the land of Veii was added to the *ager Romanus*, and in 387 four new Tribes made out of the new territory.

takes Falerii, chastises Volsinii and other towns, allots the conquered lands of Veii to a number of her own poorer citizens, and in general appears so strong and so firmly established in Etruria that she can afford to drive Camillus into exile on a charge of embezzling booty, while Etruscan Clusium turns to her for aid against the Gauls. The year 390 sees her laid low, shattered in the Gaulish storm. But in 389 she deals successfully with a number of enemies and revolted allies. An Etruscan war is but one item in the list. She operates now in the district of Tarquinii, perhaps the leading city of Etruria: and after sundry victories asserts her predominance in southern Etruria by occupying with colonies the strategic posts of Sutrium and Nepete, which she maintained in spite of stubborn opposition.

134. That there are exaggerations and misrepresentations in parts of this tradition is only too probable. The tale of the Alban lake is a strange legend. The water rose to an unusual height in 398, while the siege of Veii was in progress, or rather at a stand. It got abroad that an ancient Etruscan seer had declared that Veii was safe so long as that lake was not drained. A stout young Roman trapped and kidnapped the old Veientine. Put to question before the Senate, the seer repeated his prophecy. A deputation was then sent to Delphi, and the response of the great oracle of Greece confirmed the prediction of Etruscan lore. The lake was drained, and Veii fell. It was taken at last, after a siege of Trojan duration, by a mine[1] driven under the city, opening into the citadel. Even Livy cannot believe the tale that a sacrifice on which the city's fate depended was in progress at the moment when the Romans emerged from the ground, and that the rite begun in the interest of Veii was ended in the interest of Rome.

135. The onward movement of Roman history is brought home to us as we observe that in this period the long struggle with the Aequi and Volsci comes to an end. Many campaigns and many tales of battle have been recorded by the annalists in the usual confusion. But the two notable points are; first, the great conflict of 431, when the Romans, supported by the Latins and Hernicans, beat their old enemies so thoroughly that they never recovered their former strength: secondly, the war of 389 and 386—1, when we hear of Latin and Hernican volunteers serving on the Volscian side. Rome was then in distress, and enemies were assailing her in many quarters: the narratives are untrustworthy: but we seem to have come to an end of the serious Aequo-Volscian wars and to have reached the far more serious discontents of the old and faithful allies of Rome.

---

[1] This seems to correspond to the wooden horse in the tale of Troy.

136. That some change took place in this period in the relations between Rome and the Latins is not to be denied: the exact nature and form of the change is a matter of great uncertainty. No direct account of it, no clear reference to it, have come down from antiquity: we have only acute inferences based on doubtful materials, which it is to be hoped are rightly understood. The prevailing view (Mommsen) is that about 385 or 384 Rome closed the Latin League: that in it there were then included 47 members, either old Latin cities or Latin colonies: that of these 47 only 30 were full members with votes in the federal diet, though the other 17 were partakers in the Latin festival: that the Latin communities founded after this date were not admitted members of the League: that the limits of the district regarded as Latium were henceforth definitely fixed: and that the new communities had no reciprocity of private rights (*commercium* and *conubium*) with the older Latin cities or with each other, but with Rome only. Some of these points are made out to a high degree of probability. Perhaps we may safely say that the change, whatever its details, tended to bring out the fact that the League was really controlled by Rome, and made a beginning of Rome's new policy towards allies. To keep them isolated from each other but severally connected with the central power is henceforth the principle of Roman imperialism. To apply such principles now was certain to provoke discontent and disloyalty. Rome was still staggering under the disasters of 390: the conquests in southern Etruria had extended her dominion, but she was now, from the Latin point of view, less necessary as a bulwark against the Etruscans, whose weakness was apparent: on the other hand, the need of Latin support to Rome would be evident to men who knew, as the Latins surely knew, that great new powers were growing up behind them to the South-East, and that southern Italy was full of fighting and unrest. Truly it was a bold step at this juncture to resolve, as the Romans seem to have done, that, while the Latin race[1] should be encouraged to spread and to occupy lands hitherto belonging to the Aequian the Volscian or the Etruscan, this expansion should aggrandize not the League but Rome. Yet this was what the planting of 'Latin colonies of the Roman People' really meant. No wonder the Latins were discontented. But they did not yet see clearly enough, or feel warmly enough, to rise in a body against their mistress; and Rome was left to consolidate her forces for the inevitable conflict in a respite of some forty years.

[1] For my part I believe that Roman Plebeians, migrating to gain allotments of land, formed a great part of all 'Latin' colonies, and tended to give them from the first a connexion with Rome rather than with the old Latin towns.

137. The details of the friction between Rome and the Latins in the years 386—370, and the various outbreaks of actual war with some of the confederate cities, are untrustworthy. In general unofficial help was given to Rome's enemies, and the smouldering embers of Volscian resistance kept alive. In particular there was constant recurrence of trouble in connexion with the colonies of Antium Circeii and Velitrae: other colonies, such as Setia, had to be reinforced: old Latin cities, as Praeneste and Tusculum, revolted. In 381 we hear that Tusculum made complete, submission and received the Roman citizenship. Whether this was the full *civitas* including enrolment in a Roman Tribe and the right of voting, or the *civitas sine suffragio* of which we hear so much later on, is a doubtful question. In either case it would surely imply that the community was in future to have no political connexions with any other power than Rome. We read of Tusculum being attacked by the enemies of Rome, and relieved by Roman armies.

138. Highly important from the point of view of Roman history were the changes taking place in southern Italy and Sicily during this period. They include the growth and advance of the Samnites; the frittering away of the resources of the Western Greeks and the decay of their power: a decay hastened not only by the pressure of the Italian tribes but by the long-delayed vengeance of Carthage. The danger awaiting the Greek cities that fringed the coast of southern Italy from encroachments of the up-country natives had been seen in 473, when an army of Tarentines and others was utterly defeated by the Iapygians. But the Greeks were strong as yet, and it was not till the great southward movement of the Samnites that the pressure on them became serious.

139. The Italian stocks classified as Umbro-Sabellian were of Indo-European descent, cousins of the Latins. In the North the Umbrians seem to have been driven back by the advance of the Etruscans, and in historical times we find them occupying only a hill district of moderate extent and perhaps surviving as a subject population in southern Etruria. Their southern kinsmen, the Sabines and others, known under various tribal names, passed along the Apennine highlands and were pressing onward, forming settlements as they went. Where resistance was slight, they overflowed into the lowlands, chiefly toward the north-eastern coast: the greater compactness of the Roman-Latin league barred their advance to the South-West. But as time went on these vigorous and fertile dalesmen found their lands too narrow for their numbers: swarms issued from the parent stocks to win new homes in the country beyond. Hence came the great people known as Samnites, whom we find about the middle of the fifth century B.C. established in the mountain district known as Samnium and extending down to the coast of the Adriatic. To the South-West of them lay the fairest region of Italy, the rich and genial lowlands of Campania, the seaboard fringed with Greek cities, but for the most part in the possession of the Etruscans, once powerful and linked to their greater kinsmen of Etruria, now isolated and effete. Into this land the invading Samnites poured. Etruscan Capua (424) and Greek Cumae (420) alike fell into their hands, and they were soon masters of all Campania save Neapolis and a few other spots where the Greeks still held their ground. But in thus becoming the lords of Campania they came under influences which modified their character. Town life and the enjoyment of wealth and splendour engendered a reckless pride in the descendants of the simple mountaineers. If their military prowess still remained, cavalry rather than infantry were their most important arm. As they multiplied, they had no mind to emigrate and win new homes in less favoured lands. Mercenary service abroad became an ordinary career, and we find bodies of Campanian soldiers of fortune serving under the banners of Carthage or Syracuse. All sympathy with the Samnites of the hills seems to have died out. It is strictly consistent with their traditional character that a deputation sent from Rome to buy corn in a time of dearth (411) is said to have met with a haughty repulse. But the occupation of Campania did not bring the spreading of the Samnites to a close. By the end of the fifth century B.C. the continuation of their onward movement had placed a large section of them in possession of a wide district reaching from the Tuscan sea to the gulf of Tarentum, which after them was called Lucania: and soon the wild region extending to the strait of Messana was also occupied by a body of seceders from the Lucanians themselves, known as the Brettians or Bruttians.

140. The contrast offered by this rapid and steady expansion of the Sabellian stock over so large an area to the slow and painful development of the Latins headed by Rome, is one that no observer can ignore. But in truth expansion is not development: and the ties that bound the southern Samnites to those who stayed behind in Samnium seem to have been no more effective than was the case with the settlers in Campania. No doubt, as they moved south, they coalesced with the remains of the earlier occupants of the land: also they came more and more into touch with the Greek cities that held all the best portions of the coast. But any differences that might thus arise between the various branches of the great Samnite family would hardly serve to explain the political failure of so vigorous a race. We must in the main ascribe this failure to the radical defects of their organization. They seem to have been grouped in loose confederations of minor units which we may call Cantons. Independence was dear to them, as to hill-folk everywhere: but effective common action was checked by jealousy or frustrated by delay. Voluntary cooperation was in practice but a poor substitute for a regulated obedience: and, in the absence of a great dominant centre of political life,—that is, of a great city or a great king—there was no recognized leader to obey. In the isolation of mountain valleys local and sectional interests overpowered the calls of brotherhood, generally expressed in appeals for help. And so one cried and the other dallied, and what was done was often done too late. In short the Samnites never developed into a true nation, nor were they welded into a consolidated empire of their own: and the finest military race of Italy succumbed to the persistence of a smaller body who had learnt to act together and to obey.

141. If want of cohesion was the great defect of the Sabellian peoples, it was directly fatal to the existence of the Western Greeks. Founded mostly from the eighth to the sixth century B.C., their cities had prospered mightily, and were most numerous and splendid in Sicily and southern Italy. Their growth alarmed the Phoenicians and Etruscans: but the Carthaginian attack on Sicily in 480 was decisively repulsed, and in 474 the Etruscans defeated at sea. Rich and powerful, eminent in intellectual life and the gifts of a brilliant civilization, glorified by victories in the athletic festivals of Hellas, they were the wonder and envy of the Greek world. But their successes in war had been achieved by concentration of power under 'tyrants,' usurping monarchs whose rule was never regarded as lawful government in the political ideas of Greece. And so their fall left the Western Greeks without effective leaders, the cities swayed by factions, the stronger states threatening the weaker, Dorians seeking to absorb Ionians. Outwardly splendid and apparently secure, the political incompetence of the Greek city-state was bearing them to their doom, while Carthage sullenly bided her time.

142. In 510 the great city of Sybaris in Southern Italy had been destroyed by its sister Greek city of Croton. In 443 Athens, at the height of her power, founded Thurii near the site of Sybaris, and thus betrayed an interest in the affairs of the West. The quarrels of the Sicilian Greeks next engaged her attention: from 427 onward she strove to interfere with effect by naval expeditions or diplomacy. The ill-judged Sicilian Expedition of 415—3 ended in fatal disaster. It might seem that the Western Greeks, with triumphant Syracuse at their head, were doubly secure against the assaults of their enemies. But once more their political futility brought them to ruin: they

could not give to each other in the hour of danger a prompt and whole-hearted support.   When Carthage poured her armies of mercenary barbarians into Sicily nothing was ready for resistance.   In the war of 409—5, city after city fell by storm or siege or flight of the citizens : some of them never to regain their former greatness, others wiped out of being to rise no more.   Only a strip of territory in the east of the island was now held by the Greeks : even Syracuse, the

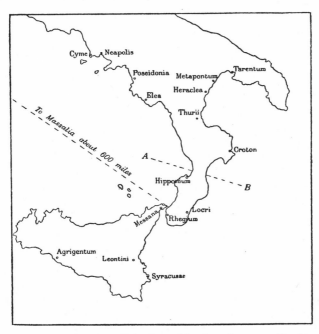

The region of Magna Graecia.   Only those cities that play a considerable part in Roman history are marked.   *AB* indicates the barrier-scheme of Dionysius.

refuge of the survivors, was in jeopardy.   At this juncture a saviour appeared in the famous Dionysius, who rose by craft from demagogue to tyrant, concentrated the stricken remnants of the Greeks, hired mercenaries, baffled the Carthaginians and brought them to terms, enlarged and strengthened Syracuse, and ruled there as absolute master for nearly forty years.   At his death in 367 Syracuse was a naval and military power of mark, with possessions far up in the Adriatic, and feared in the Greek world.   But his career had a bad effect on the fortunes of the Western Greeks : his policy[1] was wholly

[1] For the scheme said to have been contemplated by him, of cutting off the toe of Italy by a wall or trench, see Grote's *Greece* part II ch. 83.

selfish. Some of the Greek cities in Italy he took, others he weakened: when some of them renewed old alliances to withstand the pressure of the Lucanians (393), he did not scruple to join forces with their enemies.

143. So it was that in the earlier part of the fourth century Greek civilization in Italy and Sicily shewed every sign of decay. Not only did many of the lesser cities perish: the Greek character of those remaining was in many cases grievously impaired. We shall see in the next period that as yet their hopes looked eastward for a deliverer: but a few indications in the present period already point to connexions and sympathy with Rome. The deputation of 411 are said[1] to have been well received in Sicily after their repulse in Campania. Rome seeks guidance from the Delphic Oracle. A Roman gift to the Delphic God (394) is captured[2] at sea by the Greek pirates of Lipara, who waive all claim to the prize and escort the Roman vessel to Greece. From another source[3] we learn that the offering when it reached Delphi was lodged in the storehouse or 'treasury' belonging to Massalia. This is perfectly credible. It is also said that the faithful Massaliots[4] raised a fund in aid of the Romans when suffering from the invasion of the Gauls. Whatever be the truth as to these particulars, we may gather that in general Roman and Greek were on friendly terms.

Thus we see Rome in the period 448—367 B.C. advancing into southern Etruria, becoming the champion of Italy against the Gauls, drawing the restive Latins more directly under her control, generally friendly with Greeks, and becoming, so to speak, conscious of the spreading power of the Samnites.

144. We must glance briefly at the Army, the active organ of most of the foreign policy of a growing state. This period saw momentous changes in the military system. We have no exact dates, but the changes are not improbably connected with the name of Camillus, who is the soldier-hero of the age. It is said that the long siege of Veii made winter campaigns necessary, and that this led to the regular payment of the troops. It may have been experience gained in more continuous service that made possible the introduction of the new battle-order, the beginnings of which at any rate belong to this period. The old phalanx-formation (which had perhaps proved a failure against the Gauls) was given up. The regular infantry of the legion was divided into 30 companies or 'maniples' (*manipulus*, a hand-

---

[1] Livy IV 52.   [2] Livy V 28.

[3] Diodorus XIV 93.

[4] For Massalia and Rome see Justin XLIII 5, Strabo IV 1 § 5 (p. 180), and the note on Thuc. I 13 in Classen-Steup (*Anhang*, pp. 346—8).

ful), each of which consisted of two 'centuries.' The century was strictly the half-maniple, so that in fighting or working the sections could operate in turns on an orderly principle of relief. It is clear that to carry out this system efficiently a far more exact training was required than would have sufficed for the simple movements of the old phalanx. Accordingly the position of the men in battle-order was made to depend, not on their wealth (that is, on their ability to provide a full equipment), but on experience and fighting skill: the young and nimble led the attack, the veterans behind were a trusty reserve, while between these stood the men in the prime of their bodily powers. When the system reached its full development we find the legion thus ranged in order from front to rear:

    10 maniples of *hastati*   at 120 = 1200 men,
    10   „   of *principes* at 120 = 1200 men,
    10   „   of *triarii*   at 60 = 600 men.

Besides these 3000 troops of the line the legion contained 1200 light troops (*velites*), better equipped and organized than the *rorarii* of the earlier time, and 300 cavalry. The maniples of the foot were drawn up with intervals between company and company equal in width to the front of a company: but the companies of the three lines stood, not one behind the other, but like the squares of one colour on a chessboard. The spaces between the companies gave room for taking open order, so that the soldier might use his weapons freely: they allowed the light troops to advance skirmishing and to retire quickly when their work was done: if the attack of the first line (*hastati*) failed, they could fall back through the intervals of the second (*principes*), whereupon the latter would at once take open order and assail the enemy. In a stubborn fight the turn of the *triarii* would come in due course: it was their duty to restore the fortune of a stricken field. To describe the equipment of the men is not possible here: but we must notice one point of great importance. This is the introduction[1] of what soon came to be regarded as the characteristic Roman weapon, the *pilum*. This was a javelin of some 6½ feet in length, half wood half iron. Into the stout wooden shaft the iron shank was firmly fixed, and at the other end was a barbed head. It must have been a very heavy and clumsy missile: but practice taught the Roman soldier to hurl it with good aim and force as he came near the enemy: if it missed the corslet, it pierced the shield and rendered it useless: before the man could disengage the *pilum* and recover the use of his encumbered shield, the advancing Roman was

---

[1] Perhaps borrowed from the Sabellians. See Sallust, *Cat.* 51 § 38, and pictures in Baumeister's *Denkmäler*, pp. 2048, 2075.

upon him sword in hand. The improved sword was a short two-edged weapon with a sharp point, handy for close combat, business-like and deadly.

145. No doubt the manipular legion was a great improvement upon earlier formations. Inasmuch as each company had a separate existence and a proper duty, it did not necessarily fall into confusion because the company next it had been broken : and the new legion was far better able than the old phalanx to operate on uneven ground. The *pilum* and sword were more effective weapons of attack than the old spear. The spear had its merits in meeting an enemy's onset, and hence it was retained as the distinctive weapon of the third line. The cavalry were in the period of Camillus still an efficient arm, but in course of time the Romans seem to have neglected it and to have relied too exclusively on the legionary foot. For this they were to pay dearly. The legions could be rolled up into a mass by successful cavalry charges, so that the bulk of the men, jammed in a crowd, could not use their weapons. It was by such tactics that Hannibal overcame superior numbers, using to the full the efficiency of his horse. It was the rule to post the Roman legions in the centre of the line of battle, with the allied forces flanking them to right and left. The Latin and Hernican contingents were good troops, organized after the Roman model : but it is open to doubt whether they ever reached quite the same standard of efficiency. Gathered together in small detachments from a number of scattered communities, they can hardly have developed the same technical skill and cohesive power as the Roman levies. Nor was there always unanimity of feeling among the cities. But under the leadership of Rome an iron discipline prevailed : soldier and citizen were still the same, two characters in one person : he was carrying out, not the terms of a mercenary bargain, but a duty to which he had been born. Such was the moral foundation of the steadiness of Roman armies.

146. It was of a piece with the Roman habit of regarding it as more important to hold than to acquire that the construction of camps formed a great part of military duty. Every change of position implied the building of a defensible camp on a regular plan, with its earthen lines and palisade. Defeated it might be for the moment, the soldier knew that he had quarters for shelter and rest a short distance in the rear. He was not left to scuttle from the field he knew not whither : the presence of the camp steadied his nerve for the moment and renewed it for the morrow. The moral importance of this camp-system can hardly be overrated. It was not for nothing that the great conquering people of antiquity were the greatest users of the spade.

I have remarked above that we cannot fix the exact date of the introduction of the new military system. Some changes may have been made before the time of Camillus: some were no doubt gradually evolved in the course of the great wars of the following period. But it seemed best to give this brief sketch of them in treating of this period : for I cannot doubt that much was due to Camillus' initiative. I have dwelt only on those points that seemed to have a direct bearing on the history of the Roman people, and its relations to other powers. It can hardly escape observation that the tendency of military reform was to obliterate social and political distinctions, and to create an uniform ideal of a citizen's duty to the state.

BOOK III

THE UNION OF ITALY UNDER ROME

CHAPTER XVI

THE CONSTITUTION, 366—265 B.C.

(a) *The Magistracy*

147. THE passing of the Licinian laws restored the consulship
to the position of normal chief magistracy of the Roman state. The
two Consuls, equal colleagues, held for a year the full *imperium*, once
lodged for life in the single person of the King. Nominally their
power was unimpaired, but in practice, compared with that of the
consuls in the first age of the Republic, it was no longer what it had
been. The wide range of its functions had been narrowed by the
establishment of the Censorship, and it had of late suffered a loss of
prestige. For many years the Romans had done without it, and the
Consular Tribunate, inferior in dignity and held by more numerous
colleagues, had served for a substitute. There had been a sort of
dilution of the consular power, a subtle weakening. Nor was there
any prospect of an effective restoration of its strength. The consulship had just been thrown open to Plebeians, men not members of
the old clans, not connected by blood with the original citizens of
Rome of whose hereditary institutions the sacred *imperium* was one.
If Plebeians were henceforth to take the auspices, to ascertain the
will of Heaven on behalf of the state, it was clear that the state was
thereby to some extent 'secularized.' No wonder that Patrician
obstinacy strove for a time to nullify in practice the newly enacted
rule, or that the divergent interests of the rich and poor Plebeians
made possible the election of two Patrician consuls in defiance of the
law. But in 342 some legislation was threatened, and perhaps carried
through, in the form of a Resolution[1] of the Plebs declaring both

[1] Livy VII 42. This comes in quite casually, as a story preserved by some annalists, and
appears as a part of the general agitation connected with the mutiny of the army in Campania, one of the most obscure matters in the ancient historians. A rule against re-election to
magistracies, save after an interval of ten years, is part of the same tradition. This matter
will come up for consideration in a later chapter. It is significant that the Resolution about
the magistracies is mentioned immediately after one forbidding usury, the chief bugbear of
the poor.

consulships open to Plebeians. The tradition is most obscure, but it seems that the main object, the observance of the Licinian law, was henceforth secured. Meanwhile the range of consular functions had been narrowed by the establishment of a new office to which the civil jurisdiction was attached, and which was for that purpose equipped with the indispensable *imperium*. But, on the other hand, the activities called for in this great period of conquest must have tended to enhance the importance of the consuls. As generals abroad and presidents at home they had plenty to do, and these were the parts of public duty held most in honour. In 326 we meet with the first instance of a practice common in later times: a consul commanding an army in the field was not superseded at the end of his year of office, but retained[1] in command 'in a consul's stead' (*pro consule*). Here was a substitute, different from the appointment of a Dictator, for the automatic succession of the yearly consul to a military command. Again, it seems certain, though we can point to no law and give no exact date, that the Tribunes of the Plebs were now recognized as Magistrates of the Roman people, not merely of the Commons. Furthermore, the circumstances of this period led to the appointment of a great number of Dictators. From 363 to 301 we hear of more than thirty cases. But beyond all these movements, and far more effective in lessening the real importance of the regular chief magistracy, was the gradual growth of the power of the Senate. Thus, by the tendency to divide (and eventually more or less to specialize) functions, by the use of extraordinary measures, and by the encroaching control of a great directing Board, the consuls' field of action was practically limited, and their powers, though still very great, were less than they had been of yore.

148. I have spoken of the great number of Dictators in this period. Most of them were of the regular sort, appointed to see the state safely through a crisis needing a concentration of military power. We must remember that a Dictator was the colleague of the consuls but superior to them (*maior collega*). He was named (*dictus*) by a consul, not elected by the Assembly. In a period of great wars, such as 366—265 B.C., it is not strange that the appointment of Dictators should have been often resorted to. This was not an episode in the struggle of the Orders, for we find a Plebeian Dictator as early as 356, with no mention of any special legislation to legalize the step. It seems that the opening of the consulship carried with it that of the office to which a consul nominated: the

---

[1] Livy VIII 24 §§ 11, 12, 26 § 7. This gave him a continued *imperium* in his own sphere of operations, not in Rome. His triumph thus came after he had ceased to be a regular magistrate (*acto honore*), which was a new thing. See Index under *Triumphs*.

imperium, fundamentally the same for all its holders, was open to the Plebs, and there was an end of the matter. But we have to notice a change in this highest of Roman magistracies. We begin to find a Dictator described as appointed 'for business' (*rei gerundae causa*), which implies that there were some other kind or kinds of Dictators whose duties were of less capital importance; in other words, to whom there was no intention of entrusting the command of armies in the field. And of such Dictators we hear, appointed to hold elections in the absence of the consuls and for other special purposes, such as the formal act of driving a nail (*clavi figendi causa*) in a temple wall to appease the wrath of the gods. These Dictators for special purposes appear first in 363. But there seems to have been no legal means of confining a Dictator to so narrow a sphere: indeed we are told that on this first occasion[1] L. Manlius proceeded to levy an army, and was only prevailed upon to desist by the opposition of all the tribunes, no doubt backed by popular discontents. But he did not remain Dictator; he resigned office.

149. The truth is, the Dictatorship was essentially a military office, and the practice of using it as a convenience for special ends was but the beginning of a process which finally led to its disuse altogether. The consuls, not the Dictator, were the true representatives of the old regal *imperium*. The Dictator represented it only on the military side. Such an appointment was in effect the declaration of a state of siege, a digression from the ordinary course of state administration. Hence we do not find the Dictator at the head of the civil jurisdiction. Hence he was, it seems, less dependent on the support of the Senate than the consuls were, though this point is somewhat obscure. Hence there was at first no right of Appeal to the people against his decisions: both in Rome and abroad (*militiae*) he ruled with power of life and death. When the Dictator's sentence was first made subject to *provocatio* is not certain: Mommsen conjectures that it may date from 300 B.C., when we hear[2] that the Valerian law of Appeal was re-enacted for the third time. Hence also the Intercession of the Tribune was barred as against a Dictator, and this seems to have held good until some time in the next period.

150. The Dictator's term of office was limited in three ways. First, it could not exceed six months in all, a rule probably suggested by the duration of the ordinary campaigns, the soldier's working year. His command was never extended. Secondly, he went out of office when the consuls of the year, by one of whom he had been nominated, came to an end of their term. Thirdly, it was the custom, of strong moral obligation, for him to resign as soon as his work was done.

---

[1] Livy VII 3—5.   [2] Livy X 9.

Some held office for a few days only. And no doubt the practice of appointing Dictators for special duties of minor importance tended to promote these early resignations. Slight and doubtful are the traces of a reluctance to resign this terrible magistracy: but while held it was usually wielded with a strong hand. All this was thoroughly Roman. Roman too was the jealousy with which it was regarded, and the way in which that jealousy operated. The office was looked upon as a temporary revival of the regal power, as in some respects it was. It was felt to be unrepublican, and we know that it was doomed to disappear. But for the present it was useful, and remained in use. Signs of its decline may be detected in what has been said above: but the gradual growth of the Senate's influence affected it most. If we may trust tradition at all, it seems that in this period the Senate not only called upon a consul to name a Dictator, but often requested him to choose a particular person. Such an instruction had the effect of a command. On other occasions, if the person nominated was obnoxious to the influential nobles, the scruples of religion would suddenly awake, and it would be discovered that there had been some flaw in the proceedings attending his appointment: thus he was driven to resign.

151. That the new magistracy, the Praetorship, was a most useful help in the administration of the Roman state, is clear. It appropriated the ancient title of 'leader,' originally the general term for Chief Magistrate, and gradually gave it the special connotation of 'leader in civil jurisdiction.' Not that the consul was deprived of his powers in this department—that was not the Roman way,— but the new officer was entrusted with the duty, and the old one, in deference to the new arrangement, ceased to exercise his powers in that particular sphere. The consideration of the Praetor's judicial activity may best be reserved for the next period. For the present we may remark that he had the same yearly tenure of office as the consuls, and the same *imperium* ; he was their colleague, but inferior (*collega minor*): in case of difference, the Praetor must give way. But . the possession of *imperium* qualified him, not only for the charge of the civil jurisdiction, but also to act as the consul's assistant in all the functions of the office. In the absence of the consuls he was their natural substitute in Rome. He could summon the Senate and preside at the meeting; he could (at least on the request of the House) call an Assembly of the people and lay proposals before it, or at need even undertake the enrolment of an army. His practical importance is seen in the disuse[1] of an old office, that of the 'city praefect,' a temporary deputy left in charge by the chief magistrates

---

[1] Retained only for form's sake during the Latin festival on the Alban mount.

when their duty kept them in the field. But the Praetor, having *imperium*, had a wider competence than this. He too could command an army, and in time of need we find him doing so. He too, like the consul, could have his command prolonged and act 'in a praetor's stead' (*pro praetore*). In our present period we see that the Praetorship was from the first an eminently useful office. In later times we shall find Praetors and ex-Praetors doing a large part of the work of government. It seems that, as Mommsen holds, this office was never closed to Plebeians by law. At least we know of no statute either closing or opening it. And the law of immemorial custom had at the time of its foundation just been set aside by the Licinian law in the case of the consulship. True, the Patricians seized on the Praetorship and held it as long as they could. An office connected with administration of law was almost as precious as one dealing with religion. A Plebeian was first Praetor in 337. This was Q. Publilius Philo, one of the leading statesmen of Rome, who had previously been consul and dictator.

152. Of the Tribunate of the Plebs in this period it is necessary to say but little: but that little is significant. The fruits of the united action of rich and poor Plebeians had been reaped in the Licinian laws, and the rich at least soon managed to secure their share. A stream of wealthy Plebeians was steadily passing into the Senate: the political power of the Patrician Order as such was slowly dying out. The Tribunes were not men of the poorer class: they were no doubt generally in sympathy with the Plebeian senators. And we find them now regarded as Magistrates of the Roman people. We find them sitting and speaking in the Senate. Whether they had after 367 assumed the right to summon the House is doubtful: probably not at first. But they were fast becoming the useful servants of the Senate, and their vast negative power, given them as a weapon to protect the Commons and their interests, was quietly and surely being turned into a means of controlling the administrative magistrates, and their fellow Tribunes also, in the interest of the Nobles. When we hear of them taking an active part in public affairs, other than the mere carrying out of the Senate's will, it is generally as champions of the Plebeian nobility that they come forward. When[1] the augurs (Patrician) dislodge a Plebeian Dictator from office (327) on the pretext of a technical flaw in his appointment, the Tribunes protest. When[2] Patricians invoke their aid (314) against a Plebeian Dictator, they refuse it. When[3] the question of admitting Plebeians to the sacred colleges of Pontiffs and Augurs came up (300), they were at first divided, but unity was soon restored and the bill passed.

[1] Livy VIII 24.   [2] Livy IX 26.   [3] Livy X 6—9.

They are seldom hostile to the Patricians as such. Even in the
cònflict[1] aroused by Appius Claudius' refusal to lay down his censorship (310) at the end of 18 months we hear that the intention of some
Tribunes to coerce him by force was thwarted by the 'intercession'
of others. So too the opposition[2] of some Tribunes to the celebration
of a triumph by a Patrician consul (294) was rendered ineffective.
When old Fabius Rullianus[3] declined (298) to be made consul for the
following year, on the ground of a statutory impediment, the Tribunes
offered to procure a vote of the people to dispense him from the law.

153. But when the power of their office or the interest of the
Plebeian leaders is menaced, they are still bold in maintaining the
rights of the Commons. In 357 we hear[4] that a consul commanding
in the field held an Assembly of the Tribes in his camp and there
carried a law, apparently harmless in itself and of financial benefit to
the state. But the Tribunes saw that this sort of thing would never
do: men bound by the military oath were hardly free agents. So
they took strong precautions against any future attempt at legislation
away from Rome; that is, out of reach of tribunician power. In
353 we hear[5] that the Dictator wished to secure the return of two
Patrician consuls for 352. The Tribunes blocked the election till
the Dictator's term of office came to an end. Then followed a series
of *interreges*, and the struggle went on, until the Patricians gave way,
and the Licinian law was observed. The threat of 342, by which
this illegal Patrician encroachment was finally stopped, has been
referred to above. It is to be noticed that these revivals of the old
vigour of the Tribunes fall in the earlier part of this period. We
hear that the mass of the Plebeians were far more concerned about
the laws of debt than about these questions of constitutional right
and privilege: indeed it seems that laws limiting or abolishing
interest on loans were necessary to induce the poorer voters to support the other measures of the Tribunes. Later, in 287, we hear that
the intolerable pressure of debt led to civil strife, to a last 'secession'
of the Plebs, and to the famous law of the Dictator Hortensius. We
can hardly doubt that the Tribunes took an active part in this crisis,
but our authorities for that time are so meagre that no record of
their action has survived.

154. Now that the Tribunes were Magistrates of the Roman
people, they seem to have taken in hand the business of bringing to
justice offenders against the state generally, not the Plebs alone.
But the instances[6] of this procedure are so very few in this period

---

[1] Livy IX 34 § 26. [2] Livy X 37. [3] Livy X 13.
[4] Livy VII 16. [5] Livy VII 21.
[6] See the list in Mommsen *Staatsrecht* II, section on the Tribunate.

that the consideration of it had better be deferred.   About three
cases occur, in which misconduct during tenure of office was visited
with prosecution after the offender's return to private life.   In contrast to these political offences, akin to treason, are the public
cases of breaches of statute law.   These were dealt with by the
aediles.

155.   The censorship was first held by a Plebeian in 351 B.C.
It was the same man, Gaius Marcius Rutilus, that won the dictatorship for the Plebs in 356.   We may well believe the tradition that
the Patricians opposed his election, for the influence of this great
civil magistracy was far-reaching, and the control of the list of
senators must have been particularly important in this period.   The
victory of Marcius was followed up by one of the Publilian laws of
339, enacting that of the Censors one at least must be a Plebeian.
In 280 the religious ceremony of the *lustrum* was performed by the
Plebeian Gnaeus Domitius Calvinus.   The complete equalization of
the Orders is perhaps most clearly signalized by this act.   The
Censors of this period had important duties to perform.   New citizens
were being placed on the rolls: in 332, 318, 299, new Tribes were
added, two on each occasion, bringing the total up to 33.   Among
the public works were the famous road and aqueduct named after
Appius Claudius, whose censorship has left a great mark on the
traditional history.   We hear of his being Censor in 312 with
C. Plautius.   The force of Appius completely overbore his milder
colleague.   In revising the senatorial list he disregarded precedent,
introducing members who would back up his policy, even sons of
freedmen, tainting the House in a way that moved the indignation of
the Nobles.   Plautius could not face the storm of unpopularity, and
resigned office.   In drawing up the roll of citizens Appius took an
even bolder step.   He enrolled the 'masses of the market-place'
(*forensis turba*), that is the artisans and town-folk generally, in all
Tribes alike.   This promiscuous distribution threatened to weaken
or destroy the power of the freeholders in the rural Tribes.   To come
to Rome for an Assembly was an effort, not to say a sacrifice, for the
yeoman working on his farm: the townsman was already on the spot.
Thus the voice of a rural Tribe might easily be given in opposition to
the wishes of the majority of its members, if weather or farm-work
chanced to keep the country-voters at home in considerable numbers.
In short, Appius appears as aiming at power by favouring the urban
element in the state: with him begins the civilian type in the
series of republican worthies.   As the difference between Appius and
Plautius illustrates the competence of either colleague to act in the
face of anything short of definitive refusal of consent by the other, so

the naming of public works[1] after one Censor when they had been begun by both records the validity[2] of the acts of a single Censor. That these acts only held good until the next revision is seen in the actiòn of the Censors of 304, who enrolled the urban mass in the four city tribes only, undoing the work of Appius. As for the Senate, we are told that the consuls of 311 ignored[3] the revision of Appius and summoned meetings of the House on the basis of the old list.

156. But worse was to follow. When his eighteen months[4] came to an end, Appius refused to retire, thus violating not merely the custom of the constitution but the Aemilian law[5] of 434 B.C. as well. Employing the quibble, that his election was a later act of the people, superseding the law of 434, he argued that the law did not apply to his case. A Tribune attacked him for his conduct, and, as he still remained stubborn, ordered him to be placed under arrest. Six other Tribunes supported their colleague, but three interposed on his behalf. So Appius cared for none of those things. One version[6] of the story adds that in 307, while still censor (this makes him hold office for 5 years), he stood for the consulship. A Tribune blocked the elections till Appius at last did resign: whereupon he was elected consul. In this highly-coloured and probably garbled tale we see clearly that Appius and the nobles are opposed. The Tribunes hostile to him are the tools of the Senate. He is painted as the haughty wilful aristocrat, but there is no doubt that the real offence for which he has been pilloried by Roman annalists was his reliance on the support of the multitude. What the true version of the story may be we simply do not know. The nature of the materials is seen in the explanation of the name 'Blind' (*caecus*) borne by the great Censor. According to one account his blindness came on him years after his censorship, but in consequence of divine wrath at some of his censorial innovations. Another tradition is that on retiring from the censorship, wishing to avoid the Senate, where he was unpopular, he shut himself up at home, pretending to have lost his sight. To the latter part of this period belongs the censorship of Fabricius, who is said to have expelled from the Senate an ex-consul of great distinction, on the ground of luxurious extravagance, finding that he kept ten pounds of silver plate. True or not, the story illustrates the arbitrary and inquisitorial nature of the censorial power.

[1] See Livy IX 29 with Weissenborn's notes. Another account (Diod. XX 36) says that Appius exhausted the treasury by his public works, without the Senate's leave.

[2] Mommsen, *Staatsrecht* II 339, suggests that the story of Appius' continuance in office is a perversion of the fact that his term was extended by *prorogatio*. But the instances of this procedure are of much later date, and I cannot think the suggestion probable. It seems to me that his acts were not invalid, because what was done could not be undone.

[3] Livy IX 30 § 2.

[4] Livy IX 29—34.

[5] Livy IV 24, probably a confused tradition.

[6] Livy IX 42 § 3.

157. Before the changes of 367 B.C. there had been two Aediles. They were Plebeian officials, assistants of the Tribunes. In 367 two Curule Aediles were added. It seems to have been intended to confine this office to Patricians, but the restriction was set aside in a very short time. The two new officers enjoyed the external privileges of using the official chair (*sella curulis*) and the gown with purple border (*toga praetexta*): they were elected by the Assembly of Tribes, not by the meeting of the Plebs. But the functions of the two sorts of Aediles were so rapidly assimilated that for our present purpose it is not necessary to distinguish them. Naturally the office to which all citizens were eligible was regarded as more dignified than that tenable by Plebeians only, for it was more strictly a Magistracy of the Roman people. But in the decay of tribunician activity, which was brought about by the equalizing of the Orders, the Aediles gradually took their place in the administrative system as subordinate to the Consuls rather than to the Tribunes.

158. Their duties were miscellaneous. Their chief business was the charge of the city. This included the oversight of streets and public places generally: and public buildings were in their care, though contracts were reserved for the Censors' department. Water-supply, scavenging, public order, corn-supply, inspection of weights and measures, market-regulations, and other matters, were in their charge, and they were expected to keep an eye on religious observances, no doubt reporting anything of importance to the Senate. To them fell the duty of providing for the games held on public festivals, an obligation which as time went on became more serious with the increase of these shows. To enable them to carry out their various duties they had the power of seizing pledges and of fining the disobedient. A fine above the regulation amount was subject to an appeal to the people. They had also the duty of bringing to justice offences against the community, that is infractions of public law involving penalties. This kind of justice, penal rather than (in our sense) criminal, was administered by the assembled people, before whom the Aedile brought the accused, acting as prosecutor himself. Usury, adultery, and the occupation of public land beyond the legal maximum, are specimens of the offences. Heavy fines were often inflicted: these were paid over to the Aediles, who used the money for some public work, a roadway, a temple, or a statue, and the like. Most of the above functions are directly assigned to the Aediles in the traditional accounts of this period. The Aedile with his clerks (*scribae*) and other attendants was one of the familiar figures in Roman life. It soon became customary to hold this office as a step towards the praetorship and consulship. It offered many opportunities of gaining popularity, and we shall see later on that it came to be chiefly regarded from this point of view.

159. The Quaestors fill much the same place as in the preceding period. The Quaestorship was now a junior magistracy, subordinate to the consulship and praetorship. What attracts our notice most in this period of great wars is perhaps the military duty. This function, dating from the increase of the number of Quaestors in 421, must have become more important as the wars were carried on at a greater distance from Rome and the armies remained longer in the field. On service abroad the Quaestor was definitely attached to the staff of a particular general, and he not only managed the financial affairs of that general's army but served at need in a combatant capacity. He had a special tent (*quaestorium*) corresponding to that of the consul (*praetorium*). He often commanded a part of the army in a battle or was left in charge of a camp. Somewhere about the year 267 the number of Quaestors was raised[1] to eight. The four new posts were created for administrative duties in Italy, but of the details of their departments very little is known.

160. There were also other officers, elected by the people, and regarded as magistrates, but of inferior grade. Such were those of the military tribunes who were known as *tribuni militum a populo*. The people had got used to electing military tribunes instead of consuls, and it seems that the restoration of the consulship in 367 did not satisfy the appetite of the people (or rather of their leaders) for power of patronage. So in 362 they won the right to elect six military tribunes, in 311 the number was raised to 16; finally at some date unknown in the period 291—219 it was put as high as 24. The remainder of the requisite number for the legions of the year (6 to a legion) were nominated by the general. In actual service all, magistrates or not, seem to have been simply military officers. Under stress of disaster these elections could be dropped for a time and a commander left to appoint his own nominees.

161. We find also a pair of officers charged with the repairs and equipment of the fleet. These were the *duumviri* (or *duoviri*) *navales*. That there was in early times some sort of Roman fleet seems certain from their operations against the cities of the coast ; and in this period from their movements against the maritime Greeks of Campania and beyond. But it seems equally clear that the naval command was a mere department of that on land, and that the consuls entrusted it as need arose to subordinates of their own nomination. In 311 we hear[2] of a *plebiscitum* being passed ordaining that the appointment of

---

[1] See Tacitus, *ann.* XI 22, Livy, *epit.* 15, Mommsen, *Staatsrecht* II 557.

[2] Livy IX 30 § 4.

Duumvirs should be made by the people.   Whether there had been
Duumvirs previously is not at all clear.   Probably not: but anyhow
these two officers would now by virtue of popular election become
magistrates.   Their number corresponded to that of the consuls.   But
the office seems to have been only filled up in time of need, and the
neglect of naval efficiency was, speaking generally, all through the
republican period a weak point in the armaments of Rome.

162.   To take a general view of the Roman Magistracy in this
period, let us first recall the fact that this period is marked, internally
by the equalizing of the Orders, externally by the conquest of Italy.
The growth of Roman power is continuous and lasting: long before
265 B.C. we are already dealing with one of the great organizations of
the ancient world.   If we now enumerate the Magistrates by whom
the administration was carried on at home and abroad, taking a year
in which a census was held and also a dictator appointed, we have

> [Dictator   1],
> Consuls   2,
> [Censors   2],
> Praetor   1,
> Aediles   4,
> Quaestors 4,

that is, 14 administrative magistrates.   Besides these there are the
10 Tribunes, whose position in the state is fast becoming anomalous
through the union of the Orders.   Their old occupation gone, they
are henceforth, in spite of occasional revivals of activity, rather a
hindrance than a help in the work of government, except so far as
they are instruments of the Senate.

163.   The smallness of these numbers attracts our attention.   The
Roman system is one of few offices and short tenure.   As a rule, each
office is held by two or more colleagues at once, each colleague being
fully competent to perform any act within the range of the particular
office, or to bar its performance.   But the increase in the number
of offices did in practice limit the range of each: no office was so far-
reaching in its competence as the consulship of the early Republic had
been.   Nor was the clashing of the power of colleagues so troublesome
in practice as might appear likely: the moral force of public sentiment
was against such bickerings.   And there were ways of avoiding them:
the colleagues might take turns of duty, as had been customary in the
alternate months of the consuls, or they might agree to assign the performance of special duties by casting lots.   In war we find a consul
leaving to his more experienced colleague the direction of a campaign.
In short, as the magistracy grew out of the subdivision of the wide powers
inherited by the consuls from the Kings, so also we begin to detect

the first beginnings of a specializing tendency, which worked very slowly, and did not have its full effect till the time of the Empire. The first great step was the separate Praetorship. Definite duties were assigned to a single officer who had no really equal colleague. As the interference of his superior colleagues, the consuls, would be ineffective unless they were agreed to thwart him, the Praetor would for the most part be left with a free hand in their special sphere of civil justice: and we see later on that, as more praetors were appointed, special functions were assigned to the new offices. The same holds good of the quaestorships. We may say that we have here the germ of a great change, by which the departments or 'charges' (*provinciae*) are divided among offices rather than among the officers of a particular year. Formerly a Fabius and a Valerius might come to terms as to which of them should command this or that army or perform the routine duties in the city for this or that month. The day was to come when a number of praetors and quaestors were to hold praetor-ships and quaestorships each carrying with it a special group of proper duties: when these offices would be virtually departments, and the notion of the concurrent competence of colleagues would cease to be of any practical importance. This doctrine lingered on more effectively in the case of the censors: hence probably arose their quarrels of which we hear later, and the disuse of that office in the last century of the Republic is partly to be ascribed to this cause.

164. It has already been pointed out that the responsibility of ex-magistrates for their acts while in office seldom came to a practical enforcement at Rome, if we set aside those accusations that were due to the activity of tribunes in giving effect to Plebeian revenge. This is very clear from the rarity of these accusations in the present period. Patrician privileges disappeared fast; consuls and tribunes were drawn from classes that were assimilating more and more in aims and sympathies. The bitter strife of the Orders was at an end, and consul and tribune learnt to work together. The department of the state in which Patrician privilege endured longest was naturally that of the great religious colleges. But this stronghold also was forced in 300 B.C. when after a sharp contest the Ogulnian law[1] was passed, raising the number of Pontiffs from 4 to 8 and of Augurs from 4 to 9. The new places in the colleges were reserved for Plebeians, but it does not appear that the right of existing members to choose (*cooptare*) their own colleagues was taken away. If we find, as we do, that harmonious cooperation was now the ordinary state of things with the Roman Magistracy, though unpaid and ever changing, this is primarily due to the solid moral forces at work. Patriotism and a sound public opinion

---

[1] Livy x 6—9.

went far: but the possession of a permanent organ of state policy in the Senate was of incalculable value. For the Senate's power was mainly a result of its moral prestige: its encroachments were submitted to, since no efficient substitute could be found. Even in this period many acts of the Assemblies seem to have been merely formal acceptances of the Senate's will. In all emergencies the body that can act promptly is certain to gain power.

(b)   The Senate.

165.   Little need be said in detail concerning the Senate of this period. It continues, much as before, directing the finances of the state and the management of state property, the government of the city, the equipment of armies. It receives and despatches embassies on behalf of the state, discusses treaties and prepares terms of peace for the Assembly to confirm. The relations of Rome to her allies and conquered enemies, the appointment of commissions of inquiry, the assignment of districts to commanders in war, and endless other matters, were settled, either normally or in critical emergencies, by the Senate. For, even where it was constitutionally correct to submit a question to a popular vote, the Senate had often to take upon itself the responsibility of a prompt decision. Nor does such action seem to have been seriously challenged. It seems strange perhaps that a body of normally 300 men should have gone on extending its power by constant usurpation, as it was now steadily doing. But it was characteristic of the Roman Senate that its power rested on custom: and custom is ever being developed, for the justifiable innovation of one year is the precedent of the next. And so long as the general condition of the state was sound, so long as the Roman Assemblies were gatherings of patriotic and responsible citizens, not mobs led by agitators, the system worked well: the lack of legal sanction for various acts of the Senate caused no alarm. The Senate had itself no legislative power, at least under the Republic. But if its Orders were respected and put in force by Magistrates, as they generally were, and if this went on for a series of years, then what began in the form of advice to a magistrate would set and harden into a custom of the constitution.

166.   In this period, as we said above, the Senate is more and more able to control the magistrates. Consuls and dictators take instructions from it: the tribunes are mostly the instruments of its policy: refractory magistrates, such as Appius and Postumius[1], are already very rare. The Senate is well on its way to become the effective Governing Board of Rome. The transition was inevitable, as

[1] See below, § 174.

we may see from three considerations. First, there was the strength of the new Nobility as compared with the old Patriciate. So long as the Senate was identified with the cause of a decaying Order, so long the decline of that Order weakened the Senate. But now the vacancies in the Senate were being fast filled by wealthy Plebeians : the power of money was blending with the prestige of birth to form by inter-marriage and community of interest a new ruling class : a class stronger in numbers than the old Patricians, and not hampered by the odium incurred in a vain struggle to retain exclusive privilege. The Nobility of the new model based its pretensions on tenure of public office. The attainment of one of the higher magistracies gave a certain character not only to a man himself but also to his family. They were 'known' or 'distinguished' (*nobiles,* connected with *noscere, nomen,* etc.), and the abstract quality *nobilitas* soon took the concrete sense as the collective name of the noble class. On the face of it this new 'nobility' depended on popular election. But Rome was now getting past the stage of political development in which poor men were raised to the highest offices of state : the tradition of such impartiality remained, recording the open-minded innocence of ancient times. In short the new Nobility, while claiming no formal birthright, tended to close its ranks and become an Order : to belong to a family already 'noble' improved the chances of a candidate for office. And the power of the new Nobility was growing, and its growth strengthened the Senate.

167. Secondly, the Senate was a permanent body, and was thus at a great advantage in dealing with ever-changing magistrates. The right of censors to strike off the senatorial roll the names of unworthy members was but seldom exercised, perhaps in these days seldom called for : seats were generally held for life. The revolutionary revision of Appius was simply disregarded. To act in defiance of the expressed opinion of such a body, the manifest guardian of the con-tinuity of Roman policy, was more than an ordinary Roman official would do. If he did, the Senate could let loose at him a tribune or two when he went out of office, and an acquittal by the court of the Tribes was not always easy to secure. Lastly, the composition of the House was such as to exert, automatically, a powerful pressure on the individual magistrate. Though there clearly were in this period mem-bers who owed their seats simply to the choice of the censors, it must already have been the case that many vacancies were filled by past holders of office. The higher magistrates had the right to sit, speak and vote in the Senate, whether their names were on the roll or not. In the course of an official year each would or might have presided in the House when his business was under discussion. It

was morally impossible to avoid adding the names of such persons to the permanent list of senators at the first opportunity. Thus, when a magistrate faced the House, he saw before him rows of ex-magistrates, generally indisposed to countenance any evasion of the obedience that had formed the dominant habit of their own careers. To withstand the moral pressure of such a company would need exceptional moral courage: to carry through resistance to a successful ending was hardly possible.

168. Two survivals of old Patrician privilege call for brief notice. First comes the *interregnum*. In this period we find several occasions on which this institution is seen at work. It has been described above. Here we have only to note its continued existence, and to repeat that the *interreges* were Patricians. The political importance of this function was small, and so it was left on its old footing. If in any year the election of consuls for the year following could not be got over before the present holders went out of office, recourse was had to *interreges*. But they could not on such occasions influence the result seriously: if they did attempt anything of the kind, it would be merely[1] as tools of the Senate. The other institution is that known as the 'sanction of the Fathers' (*patrum auctoritas*), which has sorely troubled the writers on the Roman constitution. Laws and elections, if not sentences in popular trials also, required this sanction in order to have full validity. True, the sanction was in this period turned into an empty form by being made to precede the act to which it gave validity—a typical specimen of Roman statesmanship—; but it remained necessary. Now, who were these *patres*? Some have identified them with the Assembly of the Curies, a view against which tradition and probability alike protest. Others think that the Senate as a body are meant, and the use of *patres* in sundry passages as a name of the Senate lends colour to this view. But it is clear that the institution was now only a formal survival of what had once been an effective exercise of power. This does not suit the present position of the Senate, which was not growing weaker, but gaining more control of the government year by year. It is therefore best to regard these *patres* as the Patrician members of the Senate. We thus find a survival of the time when the Senate was wholly Patrician; and this is Mommsen's view. A distinction between Patrician and Plebeian senators survived in the case of the *interregnum*, and the contrast between formal necessity and practical insignificance is marked clearly in both institutions. But we need not hold that the 'sanction' was originally the act of the Senate as the

---

[1] The instances of both consuls being Patricians between 356 and 342, some of them elected under an *interregnum*, may be accounted for thus.

state-council. If the Senate, as I believe, grew out of a council of the clan-elders, it may well be that the 'sanction' is a trace of the primitive days when the Roman state was only in course of formation, and when no common act could be effective without the approval of the heads of clans.

(c) *The Assemblies.*

169. Throughout this important period the Assemblies, and beside them the Meeting of the Plebs, went on as before. A stray notice[1] under the year 310 B.C. even reminds us of the existence of the Assembly of Curies, still performing the solemn acts required by the custom of the constitution. But the expression of the popular will takes place in the Assemblies of the Centuries and Tribes and in the *concilium plebis.* These three gatherings existed side by side. All three were in use as organs of legislation, and before the end of this period all were equally competent in this respect: for the Hortensian law of 287 removed the last disabilities of the separate meeting of the Plebs. That this meeting should have been kept in existence, after the Tribe Assembly had become established in possession of sovran powers, is a typical case of Roman unwillingness to abolish any institution. Its survival may well be connected with that of the tribunate. The tribunes were retained, though their proper work was done: to abolish the peculiar plebeian meeting, with which the tribunes were traditionally connected, would not have been the Roman way.

170. That the three organs of legislation were put on the same level of competence does not imply that they were active in an equal degree. It seems quite clear that for this purpose the Centuries were passing out of use. Nor do we hear of any great struggle to promote or prevent the transference of legislative activity from the Centuries to the Tribes. Yet we know that the former Assembly was so constructed as to give a preponderating influence to wealth and age, while in the latter there was no such arrangement; indeed there was no inequality beyond the fact of a vote in a small tribe being somewhat more effective than a vote in a large one. And this is the period in which the political distinction between Patrician and Plebeian disappears, and the true line of cleavage, that between Rich and Poor, shews clearly. It is usual to assign the greater simplicity and easier working of the Tribe Assembly (29 Tribes in 358, raised to 31 in 318), compared with that of the 193 (or 194) Centuries, as the true and sufficient reason for the growing use of the Tribes in legislation. That it was a reason, may be freely admitted: but it is hardly enough by itself to account for the change. We must note that the regular

---

[1] Livy IX 38 §§ 15, 16.

presidents of the Tribe Assembly were the regular magistrates of the 'people'—consuls, praetors, curule aediles—for it was a gathering of the *populus*, not of the *plebs* only. As these offices became occupied by Plebeians, to whom the traditions of the older Assembly were hardly congenial, it was not unnatural that they should prefer to lay their proposals before the newer Assembly. And it is not clear that there was anything in the Roman constitution to prevent them. Once an Assembly of the *populus* by Tribes had been recognized as a lawful exponent of the will of the community, any attempt to keep it from legislating, from accepting or rejecting the proposal laid before it by a Magistrate, was hardly likely to succeed. Soon its convenience began to tell, and it rapidly became the ordinary Assembly of Rome.

171. This process was gradual, and in this period it is, owing to the loose expressions of Livy and other writers, often impossible to say with certainty in which Assembly this or that law was passed. The year 300 supplies a good instance of this difficulty. We have two important laws[1] passed in the same year; the Ogulnian, admitting Plebeians to the two great religious colleges, which is expressly assigned to the Tribes: and the third Valerian, reenacting in more stringent terms the right of appeal. In this latter case nothing is said as to the Assembly, and the fact of the proposer being a consul proves nothing. But, as its effect was to reserve capital punishment for the decision of the sovran people (that is, the Centuries), we should probably infer that the Centuriate Assembly passed it. The same may be said of the famous law of the dictator Hortensius in 287, but the indications pointing to this conclusion are very slight. Any decision of a competent Assembly was in the strict sense a *lex*. The term includes various orders (*iussa*) relating to affairs of state. Such were the resolution for declaring war (*lex de bello indicendo*) against an enemy, passed by the Centuries. Such was the 'law' for the punishment of the people of Tusculum, rejected by the Tribes in 323. Such was the dispute about the departments (*provinciae*) of the consuls in 295, when the Senate had voted the Etrurian command to Fabius. Decius protested, claiming to have the commands assigned by lot, and carried the question to a popular vote: but the Tribes confirmed the decision of the Senate. When the citizenship without the right of voting was given to Acerrae in 332, the law was probably passed by the Tribes.

172. The long struggle to secure equal powers of concurrent legislation for the 'Meeting of the Plebs' is marked by three laws as to the exact purport of which we are in the dark. They are a Valerio-Horatian law of 449, a Publilian law of 339, and the Hor-

[1] Livy x 9.

tensian law of 287, referred to above. All three are described in general terms as enacting that Resolutions of the Commons (*plebi scita*) should be binding on the whole community (*omnes Quirites* or *universum populum*). The rest of our knowledge consists of delicate inferences from doubtful indications. At first sight it seems as if a statutory rule of the constitution had been ignored in practice, and had therefore been simply reenacted, probably in a more stringent form, until all evasion was at last successfully barred. Some such procedure is directly suggested by Livy[1] in the case of the laws guaranteeing the right of Appeal. But, however much the Senate and Magistrates might be able to frustrate the observance of a regular constitutional law in occasional circumstances, it is hard to believe that such usurpation would be tamely submitted to for so long periods of time. The view now prevalent is on the whole more probable, that on each occasion some definite step was taken, the exact nature of which our loose and meagre authorities do not enable us to ascertain. This seems confirmed, in the case of the Hortensian law, by the language[2] of the later jurists, who date the equivalence of *lex* and *plebiscitum* from the passing of that law. It is possible that, in order to become valid, a *plebiscitum* at first required reenactment by the Centuries, which in its turn required the patrician sanction (*patrum auctoritas*). In 339 we are told[3] that this sanction was made merely formal: it was to be given in advance, before the Centuries voted. If the law of 339 gave the meeting of the Plebs an independent status so far as the Assembly of Centuries was concerned, it may still have left the *plebiscita* subject to the 'sanction of the Fathers,' and it may have been this irritating cause of friction that was removed in 287. But this is hypothesis.

173. We have now reached the stage when Rome had three popular bodies competent to pass laws. In election too the three bodies were all active, but each had its own clearly-defined sphere. The Centuries chose consuls, praetors and censors. The Tribe Assembly chose curule aediles, quaestors, and a number of minor officials. The Meeting of the Plebs, also grouped by Tribes, chose tribunes and plebeian aediles. The power of presiding magistrates to influence elections by refusing to 'accept the name' of an obnoxious candidate, and thus restricting the choice, had been great in the early days of the Republic. It now died out. There are only a few traces of it in this period, by the end of which the choice of

[1] Livy X 9.
[2] See quotation of Laelius Felix (2nd cent. A.D.) in Gellius XV 27 § 4, Gaius I § 3, Pliny, *N. H.* XVI 37.
[3] Livy VIII 12 § 15.

the electors was practically free.   Cicero[1] tells a story belonging to
these times, of how the famous Appius Claudius was presiding at
a consular election as *interrex*, and refused to take the name of a
plebeian candidate, in defiance of the law.   But the great Manius
Curius, who was then tribune, by some means induced the *patres*
to give their sanction in advance—apparently to the election of the
plebeian named, or of a plebeian simply.   It is implied that this
thwarted Appius' design, but the story is incomplete.   This was a very
great achievement, adds Cicero, for the Maenian law had then not
been passed.   This Maenian law seems then to have required in the
case of elections the same anticipative sanction as was required in
the case of legislation by a Publilian law of 339.   When the Maenian
law was passed, we do not know for certain, but it is a probable view
that it was in or soon after 287, as a sequel of the Hortensian law.

174.   With respect to the third department of popular activity,
jurisdiction in public trials, it is not necessary to say much.   Capital
cases went before the Centuries.   Other cases, in which a money
penalty was aimed at, went before the Assembly of the Tribes.   Of
these latter, the cases of a political nature, such as the trials of ex-
magistrates for offences directly injurious to the state, were regularly
taken up by the tribunes: the common offences against the law were
prosecuted by the aediles, as has been said above.   The political cases
were becoming rarer as the levelling of the Orders proceeded, but
we hear of a remarkable one[2] late in this period.   L. Postumius
Megellus, consul in 291, was a man of mark.   He had been consul
twice before, and was a successful general.   He now entered on
strange courses.   First, he bullied his colleague till he extorted the
right to take the command in the campaign of the year.   When he
had raised his army, he marched a number of them off to his private
estate and compelled them to work as farm-labourers on his land.
When he took the field against the Samnites, he behaved in the same
arbitrary manner.   A consul of the previous year was already in
command of an army in Samnium as proconsul.   Postumius ordered
him to withdraw: and, in defiance of messages from the Senate, persisted in his despotic action, even to the length of threatening force.
The other man at last went home, to spare his country the dangers
of discord in the field, and Postumius carried on a victorious campaign.   This done, blind to various signs of disapproval on the part
of the Senate, he openly expressed his irritation, divided the war-
booty among his troops, discharged his army before his successor
appeared, and wound up by holding a triumph without the leave of

[1] Cic. *Brutus* § 55, Orelli's *index legum*, under *Maenia*.
[2] Dionysius, fragm. XVII (XVIII) 4, 5.

Senate or people.   When he went out of office, he was at once brought to trial by two tribunes, and condemned to pay a large fine by the unanimous sentence of the Tribes.   The story is very likely not accurate in some details, and the man may have been mad, as Dionysius suggests: but it well illustrates the still absolute power of the *imperium* in the hands of a reckless man, and shews the machinery for the punishment of such doings in working order.   It seems that trials still took place before the separate Meeting of the Plebs, but they were probably rare.   We must remember that trials before these popular courts arose originally out of the right of appeal against a magistrate's sentence, and that the procedure still normally, if not always, took this form.   Mommsen holds that appeals to the *concilium plebis* were from tribunes and plebeian aediles.   But the tribunes could now prosecute before the regular Assemblies, even before the Centuries: so in this period most of the cases judged by the Plebs were no doubt from aediles.

175.   To describe the forms observed in these various popular gatherings, whether *comitia* or *concilia*, from the taking of auspices before sunrise to the adjournment or dismissal before sunset, is out of the question here.   Yet without details of the kind it is hardly possible to convey any notion of the clumsiness of the whole system, or of the hindrances that caused meetings to be dismissed without arriving at any result whatever.   Except in elections, the people had no initiative: in legislation, no amendments could be proposed: in public trials, the rule was to have three hearings of the case at three sittings with intervals between them, and a fourth for the voting.   Votes had to be given in person: notice of meetings was given in Rome only: many voters lived at a distance from the city.   We can hardly wonder that the actual work of government passed over more and more into the hands of the Senate: the marvel is that under such a system as that of Rome the popular will should have been able to make itself felt at all without a revolution.   Indeed it came to that in the end, but the time was not yet.   For the present, the good sense of a people remarkable for patience enabled the system to work.   But we get a momentary glimpse of great public discontents ending in a movement of revolutionary character in the meagre tradition of the events that led to the passing of the Hortensian law. This consists of a few words in the surviving abstract of the lost eleventh book of Livy.   They tell us that the Plebs was suffering from pressure of debt, that hence arose long[1] and serious seditions, ending in a 'secession' to the Janiculan hill, from which place they

---

[1] The institution of the police officers (*tresviri capitales*) in 289 may be in some way connected with the early stages of these discontents.

were brought home (*deducta*) by the dictator Q. Hortensius, who died
during his tenure of office.   A very broken fragment[1] of Dion Cassius
probably also refers to this struggle: it seems to preserve a tradition
of the vigorous effort to secure economic relief, the hope of the rich
that the movement might be frustrated, the gradual extortion of concessions by the Plebs, and their consequent determination to extort
more.   We see suffering, indignation, a 'secession' (the last) after the
old model, the appointment of a dictator (Plebeian) to deal with the
crisis: we may fairly infer that, beside the famous constitutional
law, measures were taken to relieve debtors.   This is all we know
of one of the greatest constitutional crises of Rome: as usual, it was
a compromise consisting of concessions to the Plebs.   At the same
time a change was made in the official Calendar, the effect of which
seems to have been to lessen the number of days available for regular
Meetings of the Plebs.   This may, as Lange[2] suggests, have been a
move on the part of the nobles to check the activity of a meeting
which they regarded as a nuisance.

176.   Yet after all, when every allowance has been made for the
defects of the system under which it had to work, the Roman People
was still in this period a great and vigorous body.   It was perhaps
not wise that such matters as a treaty of peace, or a proposal to
dispense some public man from the operation of a statute, should be
brought before a large Assembly, not educated (like the Ecclesia of
Athens) by frequent meeting, by habitual consideration of alternatives, and by the stimulus of genuine debate.   At Rome this political
education was confined to the Senate: and it was no doubt mainly
by the influence of the Senate that the popular Assemblies were
'kept straight.'   This influence would act as a rule indirectly through
the Magistrates, without whose summons no meeting could legally
assemble, and to whose question their decision must be an answer.
This affected the plebeian *concilia* as well as the regular Assemblies.
This also may explain why we never hear of collision between any
two of the concurrent legislating bodies.   There was no Supreme
Court to have acted as umpire in such a conflict, had it occurred: and
in this period the three bodies were not yet composed of practically
the same persons.   But the Senate handled matters so that there
was no collision; and prevention was better than cure.

---

[1] Dion Cass. fragm. 37.
[2] Lange, *R. A.* II 108.

CHAPTER XVII

THE CONQUEST OF ITALY

177. It is hardly possible to exaggerate the importance of the Roman conquest of Italy. From being one of a number of local Italian powers, a power the superiority of whose organization to those of her neighbours was as yet not fully understood, victorious Rome takes her place openly as one of the Great Powers of the ancient world. The hundred years that followed on the achievement of her internal unity through the Licinian laws were a momentous period in world-history. We may arrange it in four stages. (1) While Rome was dealing with the defeated Latins and doubling her strength, Philip of Macedon was putting an end to the free action of the city-states of old Greece. (2) While Rome was engaged in her great Samnite war, proving herself stronger than her strongest Italian rival, and consolidating her much-extended power, Alexander had won his enormous empire, out of which since his early death several great kingdoms were being formed. (3) By the time when Rome had shewn herself able to withstand a combined assault of her Italian enemies, and was acting as the leading power of Italy, the second generation of Alexander's 'Successors' were passing into possession of the various thrones, and the Federal revival of old Greece was at hand. (4) The completion of the subjugation of Italy by Rome brings Rome directly into touch with the Successor-Kings: Pyrrhus tries to repeat in the West the eastern exploits of Alexander, and fails miserably: and the discerning Ptolemy Philadelphus seeks the friendship of Rome. And all through this period there runs a capricious and disturbing influence, the pressure of the Gauls. The Romans have now learnt how to beat them, and they no longer gain ground in Italy, but their warlike prowess and ferocity were well known. About 280 further swarms in search of new homes invaded Macedon and Greece, and their settlement in Asia Minor created one of the troublesome problems of the East.

	Latins and Hernici	Gauls	Etruscans	Samnites	Gree
366 to 338	368 Rumour of Hernican revolt. 363–58 War, and ? treaty renewed in favour of Rome. 360 Latins uneasy. Tibur helps Gauls. 358 ? treaty renewed. Latin contingents help Rome. 349 Latins refuse contingents. 346 Volsci urge them to revolt. 343 Latins ready for war, but wait. 341 They take up war with Samnites (?) 340–39 Great war of Latins with Rome. 338 Settlement of Latium. League dissolved.	361–58 War. Gauls are beaten with help of Latins. (*Manlius Torquatus*) 350–49 War. Gauls are beaten. (*Valerius Corvus*)	356–1 War. Etruscans are beaten. Truce for 40 years with Tarquinii and Falerii. Caere receives Roman citizenship without right of voting.	354 Embassy to Rome, and treaty of alliance. 343–1 War. Samnites beaten. Treaty renewed.	349 Greek pirates infes of Latium.
337 to 303	307 Hernici detected aiding Samnites. 306 Hernican rebellion put down. Settlement.	332, and again 330–29, False alarms of Gaulish inroads. 311–08 General war with Rome, victories of Rome. Fabius pierces Ciminian forest.	327–04 Great war with Rome. 321 Affair of the Caudine Forks. 318 Truce for 2 years. War extends to most parts of Italy. Rome wins by securing her gains. 304 Temporary peace, and treaty renewed.	332 Alexande lands in Lu defeats a for nites, Lucar He makes f vances to I dies. 327–6 Affair o lis. Greeks to Rome ar trate at Nea rentine intri 320 Tarentine tervene betw and Samnite 307 (about) I friendly t treaty) with
302 to 282	295 Strong Latin contingents in Roman army.	299 Gauls threatening Etruria. 296–5 They join combination of Etruscans, Samnites, &c. Battle of Sentinum. 284–3 Gauls join Etruscan revolt. Senones victorious at Arretium, then crushed by Rome, and lose their lands. Etruscans and Boii beaten by Vadimonian lake. 282 Boii defeated again, and make peace.	301 Rome restores the Cilnii to power at Arretium. 299–4 War with Rome. The great combination of 296–5 fails. Some cities make truce with Rome. 293 Revolt of Falerii suppressed. 285–3 Revolt. Gauls called in, but the rising fails.	298–0 War renewed over Lucanian question. 296–5 Great combination fails. 293 Exhaustion of Samnites, desperate efforts. 292 Capture and execution of C. Pontius. 290 They sue for peace. Treaty renewed.	289 Death of A End of Sic sure on Itali Tarentine i S. Italy. 28 on Roman capture an Thurii.
281 to 265			280 Romans defeat Etruscans of Volsinii and Volci and make peace. 265–4 Roman intervention (in favour of aristocrats) at Volsinii.	280 Samnites join Pyrrhus and share his failure. 272 They submit to Rome, but there is a small rising in 269.	281–72 Pyr failure of Py rentum surre Rome. 281–71 Affai gium. Hi Romans. 273 Embassy andria. T Ptolemy II.

age	Volsci, Aurunci, Campani, Sidicini	Apuli, Lucani, Bruttii	Paeligni, Marsi, Aequi, &c.	Sabini, Umbri, Picentes	S.E. corner of Italy
	353 Volsci threaten Latium.				
assy to d treaty ce.	348-1 Volscian intrigues and hostile acts, headed by Antium. They try to detach Latins from Rome, 340 and aid Latin revolt.				
gratula-bassy to	345 Aurunci beaten. 343 Sidicini call in Campani against Samnites. Campani seek Roman protection. 341 Campani join Latins against Samnites (?). 338 Settlement of Antiates and Campani, submission of Aurunci.				
	336-5 Ausones (?=E. Aurunci) conquered by Rome. 314 Mixed up in Samnite war and are crushed. 330-29 Some Volsci finally submit. Revolt of Privernum put down. Settlement. A sequel of Latin settlement. 321 Roman army from Caudine Forks kindly treated at Capua. 318 Roman *praefecti* first sent to administer justice at Capua. 314-0 War carried on in Campania. Romans take Nola and Nuceria. *via Appia.*	326 Apuli and Lucani allied with Rome, but soon detached by pressure of Samnites or Tarentine intrigues. 324-0 Samnite war. Romans lose and regain Luceria. 318-7 Romans conquer Apulia. 314 Affair of Luceria (?) repeated. Colony sent. 317 Romans invade Lucania.	325 Vestini, joining Samnites, are defeated by Romans. 308 Marsi and Paeligni help Samnites. Defeated by Romans. 304 Aequi revolt. 303 Alba colony, revolt is renewed. Crushed. 304 Marsi, Paeligni, &c., join Roman alliance.	310 Fabius' envoys penetrate to E. Umbria and make friends. His raid alarms W. Umbri. 309 Easy victory over them. 308 Rebellion, defeat, surrender of Umbri. 303 Brigand band destroyed.	
assy to nd new					307 War with Sallentini (Messapii, Iapyges).
	295 Strong contingents of allies in Roman army (a picked body of Campanian horse).	298 Samnites invade Lucania, expelled by Rome (new alliance). 297 Rebellion in Apulia put down. 296 Romans suppress Lucanian seditions, backing aristocrats. 291 Great colony at Venusia. 289-2 Several interventions of Rome to protect Thurii from Lucani, &c. First collision with Bruttii.	302-0 Treaty with Vestini. Small risings of Marsi and Aequi put down.	300-299 Umbrian rising put down. Treaty with Picentes. 296-5 Umbri join the great combination against Rome, and share its failure. 290 Sabine rising put down. They surrender and become Roman citizens without right of voting.	302 Cleonymus' raid on Sallentini repulsed.
al treaty me.				270 War in N. Umbria, final conquest 266. 269-8 Revolt and conquest of Picentes. Some transplanted. 268 Right of voting given to Sabini.	
fleet at causes standing e.		280-72 Lucani join Pyrrhus, and are conquered after his failure. Bruttii conquered at the same time.			267-266 Conquest of the Sallentini. Rome gains Brundisium.

179. But important though this period surely is, it is hardly possible to construct a satisfactory account of the wars in a narrative form. The results in general outline may be accepted as true: but the details of the story are often corrupted by the carelessness of annalists, the prepossessions of writers of family[1] memoirs, or the determination of later authors to find on all occasions an edifying moral. It has therefore seemed best to arrange the chief matters of the traditional accounts in a tabular form, that the course and connexion of events may, in spite of some confusion, appear more readily to the eye. We shall thus be able to speak of the period in more general terms (which is all that our authorities will justify) without losing ourselves in a maze of generalities. The period 366—265 has been shewn in four divisions, each of which records a stage in the advance of Rome: the general import of these four stages is indicated above.

180. In treating of the last period we noted the growth of discontent among the old allies of Rome, the Latins and Hernicans. Private volunteers helped to keep alive Volscian resistance. Rome had now to bring this state of things to an end. Of her war with the Hernici we know next to nothing. Roman tradition claimed the victory, and we can only infer that the war ended in some sort of advantage for Rome. At this time the Gauls again appeared. The mass of the Latins seem to have been true to their allegiance: but, if we may believe the story that Tibur helped the invaders, this was rather from antipathy to the Gauls than sympathy with Rome. We have a tradition that a 'peace' was made with the Latins (358) before the final battle with the Gauls: but to what discontents or hostilities this may point, and on what terms cooperation was restored, we cannot say. The story of the single combat in which young T. Manlius slew a gigantic Gaulish champion, from whose golden collar (*torquis*) he won himself the name Torquatus, is an episode of this war. The next struggle[2] was with the Etruscans, who seem to have suffered as usual from imperfect combination. How uneasy the Romans felt at this time, being aware of the alienation of their allies, is seen in their alliance with the Samnites, concluded during the Etruscan war. It is represented as made on the request of the Samnites. That this step was resented by the Latins we may probably infer. In 350—49 Rome had to resist another Gaulish inroad,

---

[1] See for instance Livy VII 9 §§ 4, 5.

[2] It was a result of this war that Caere, which had previously been on terms of *hospitium* with Rome, was incorporated as a dependent community, receiving *civitas sine suffragio* as it was called later, a precedent often followed afterwards. It seems to have kept some local government for internal affairs, but the Caerites were not enrolled in a Roman Tribe. See Marquardt, *Stvw.* I 29, 30, 45; Beloch, *der Ital. Bund* 120—1.

and the usual Latin contingents were not forthcoming. Great efforts were made, and the Gauls again beaten off. In this war we meet with the tale of M. Valerius, how a raven perched on his helmet and helped him to overthrow a Gaulish champion in single combat: these duels are specially frequent in the Gaulish wars.

181. But it was now manifest that the Latins were passing out of Roman control. The remaining Volscian communities seem to have fomented the Latin discontents in hope of securing their own freedom by supporting a Latin revolt. The headquarters of the anti-Roman movement are said to have been at the piratical and rebellious port-town of Antium, a city on which the Romans had long and vainly tried to keep a permanent hold. In 343 Rome and the Samnites came to blows over the Campanian[1] question, Rome having taken under her protection the Campanians, who had been worsted by the Samnites in a war provoked by themselves. We read that the Latins were ready for revolt, but were induced by the Roman victories over the Samnites to turn their attention elsewhere. One may suspect the true version to have been that they were well content to see two hated neighbours weakening each other. A stranger tradition follows: when the Romans made peace with the Samnites in 341, it is said that the Latins took up the war on their own account, allying themselves with the Campanians. But we also find this move described as a pretext to cover the preparations of the Latin-Volscian army against Rome: and we do not hear of any serious conflict between them and the Samnites. The truth is, we do not know what happened. In 340 we read that a Latin deputation came to Rome with the demand[2] that one of the two consuls should be a Latin, in fact a demand for political equality. The rejection of this demand led at once to the great Latin war. In this most critical struggle the Roman forces can have had little help from allies: one account said that a Samnite army came to support them, but came too late. And against them were arrayed Latins, Volscians, Campanians, to whom Roman methods of campaigning were familiar, and most of whom had learnt the art of war by service in Roman armies. Nothing can be more confused than the traditional account of the campaign: we gather that two hard-fought battles secured the victory for Rome. Picturesque details survive. The greatness of the peril enjoined stern maintenance of discipline. In

---

[1] The story of the mutiny of the army in Campania, aiming at securing certain military rights to soldiers and (perhaps successfully) at a cancelling of debts, is omitted here, as I can find no satisfactory solution of its difficulties. See Livy VII 38—42 Weissenborn.

[2] Livy VIII 5. One may perhaps see in this demand a reminiscence of a time when joint armies were commanded in alternate years by Latin and Roman generals in turn. There was a tradition of such a system. See § 96.

particular, irregular combats without the consuls' leave were strictly forbidden. Young Manlius, son of the consul Manlius Torquatus, accepted the challenge of a Latin champion and slew him. The father paraded his troops, and in presence of the army put his son to death for disobeying orders. Before the first great battle of the war a dream, confirmed by the seers' inspection of victims, warned the consuls that victory would fall to the side that lost its commander: the colleagues therefore agreed that whichever of them saw his part of the army giving way should willingly devote himself to death, satisfying the requirements of heaven to win the day for Rome. It fell to P. Decius Mus[1] to carry out this agreement, which he did with a detailed solemnity hardly credible in so critical a moment: but after the exact performance of the proper rite—such was the view of Roman religion—the gods took the only course open to them, and gave Rome the victory. These two stories afforded endless matter for moralizing in later ages. Beside these we find two other details of equal interest and less liable to distortion. First, it appears that the wealthier Campanians (the 'horsemen') took no part against Rome; a fact which reminds us that the regular Roman policy was to favour the aristocratic parties in the states with which Rome had relations: one Latin town (Laurentum) also held aloof from the rising. More notable still is the story[2] of Lanuvium. The citizens of this town were against Rome, but they wasted time in discussions: so at the time of the first Roman victory, when the Latins were already beaten, the Lanuvine contingent was just starting to join the army of the confederates. Some had passed the gates, when a messenger met them with news of the disaster: upon which they marched back again, and their commander remarked 'the Romans will make us pay heavily for this little trip.' Here we have a specimen of the way in which Rome's confederated enemies—not only Latins—gave their chances away. We hear[3] that the Latins had two *praetores*: these probably corresponded in position and power to the Roman consuls, and the general military system was on the Roman model: but each city would be more or less impatient of control by the central authority, and each contingent had its own *praetor*, whom the general Praetors would not always venture to coerce. The wonder rather is that the Latins made so good a fight of it: what chance had they against a solid people ruled and led by such men as Manlius and Decius?

[1] The glory of this Plebeian hero, handed down no doubt by some Plebeian annalist, is in favourable contrast to the harsh discipline of Manlius. It is to be noted that the threat by which Patrician attempts to monopolize the consulship were stopped (see § 147) was only two years before, and the *leges Publiliae Philonis* the year after.

[2] Livy VIII 11, §§ 3, 4.   [3] Livy VIII 3 § 9.

182. The Latin League had either to obey or to conquer Rome. It had shewn that it would not do the first and could not do the second: so its hour was now come. Before we describe the dissolution of the League, let us bear in mind one direct result of the Roman conquest. Latins and Campanians alike lost a large part of their lands. The importance of this is not only that allotments were found for many of the poorer citizens of Rome, though that was a great advantage to the Roman state: the great confiscation must have left a number of dispossessed farmers in every township of Latium, eagerly looking for land in the place of what they had lost. The leaders of Roman policy were probably well aware that a desperate struggle awaited them in a not distant future: at any rate they set to work at once reorganizing[1] on a practical and permanent footing the resources over which they had won control, building up a solid fabric destined to foil the assaults of mighty enemies. The first object was to place the Latin cities in such a position that their strength might add to the strength of Rome, while the risk of its being used against Rome was removed for ever. A mere general scheme of subjection would not effect this. If they were not to be always looking for a change, the lot of the conquered must be one with which they might gradually become content. Some of the Latin cities therefore received the full Roman citizenship. In other words, they ceased to exist as separate communities and became part of the *populus Romanus*. As the elders died out, any regrets for the past would disappear: the new generation would be proud of being Romans. Others remained nominally independent, but their relations with Rome were regulated and defined by separate treaties, different in each case, but all alike placing the military force of the allied community at the absolute disposal of Rome: such were Praeneste and Tibur. Not to enter into details many of which are doubtful and obscure, the general principle followed was this: either a community was by incorporation merged in Rome, or it was bound closely to Rome and isolated from all others. The old League with its mutual rights between city and city, with its federal meetings at the spring of Ferentina, ceased to exist: meetings (*concilia*) of the Latins were forbidden. The ties that grew up through intermarriages were also broken: there was to be the right of *conubium* between each city and Rome, not between one Latin city and another. So too with the *commercium*: a citizen of a community that continued to exist was placed in this position: his right to buy and sell, to succeed to an estate and to hold property, was protected by law so far as the transaction concerned himself and citizens of his own community or himself and Romans. But the citizen of Praeneste

---

[1] Livy VIII 14, Weissenborn.

could not enter into business relations with the citizen of Tibur. In short, the Roman citizen was in a position to exercise his rights anywhere: the Roman ally paid dearly for his nominal independence by being put under galling local restrictions. Yet what other power was there likely to afford him more protection or grant him better terms?

183. Beside the Latins, there were the Volscian and Campanian rebels to be dealt with. The general course adopted in Campania was to give the people Roman citizenship without the right of voting or holding office (*civitas sine suffragio*). By this step they became merged in Rome and were liable to perform civic duties without enjoying civic privileges. They were not entered on the regular Tribe registers but in a separate list. This treatment, which from this time onward[1] was often applied to Rome's subjects, was first employed in the case of the people of the Etruscan Caere in 351. Roman magistrates could henceforth exercise authority in Capua without breaking any treaty, and the way was prepared for the introduction of Roman law. Local government, as at Caere, was not suppressed: this was probably a concession to the Campanian knights, who had stood by Rome, and in whose favour the municipal constitution was now restored. As for the Volscian towns, it is hard if not impossible to distinguish them from the Latins: they are practically all 'Latin' in a political sense. *Latium* was originally a merely geographical expression: its limits were variously understood: with the suppression of the Latin League we may begin to regard it as including the Volscians. One city called for a special treatment, the ever-restless Antium. The Romans took this matter seriously in hand. They took away the fleet—the ships of war, the organ of piracy—and forbade its renewal. A colony of Roman citizens was sent there, and the troublesome city reorganized as a part of the Roman state. The Aurunci, a small people lying between the Volscians and Campania, were conquered at this time. Roman dominion now enveloped the Volsci. Sulky and restive, as the later revolt of Privernum will shew, they had now no resource left to delay the inevitable Romanizing of the land. Rome had now so dealt with her more important neighbours, that every year severed them from each other more and more, and bound them more firmly to herself. There was no rival power to tempt a transfer of their allegiance by the display of an equal constancy and moderation: she could now wait in patience for the effect of time.

184. The years 337—303 include the great Samnite war of 327—304, which is the turning-point of the conquest of Italy. How the Samnites spent the ten years preceding it we do not know. The

---

[1] Livy VII 20, VIII 14, Weissenborn.

Romans turned them to good account. The Auruncan or Ausonian district between the Volscian land and Campania was more fully subdued, Cales between the Liris and the Volturnus was founded as a Latin colony, while a citizen colony at Anxur extended Rome's hold upon the coast. Clearly the leaders of Roman policy did not mean to let the communications with Campania be interrupted by land or sea. Connected with these movements was the final pacification of the Latin-Volscian district not included in the settlement of 338. The revolt of Privernum, its main incident, was quickly put down. The general policy followed was that of incorporation with Rome. Much land was confiscated, and allotments provided for Roman citizens. The old inhabitants became citizens without voting rights. And to clinch matters a Latin colony was founded at Fregellae, commanding the inland route to Campania and watching the Samnite border. Rome had now the Latin and Volscian country completely in her power. Time was strengthening her hold upon her allies; her fortresses secured the chief strategic points on the lines of advance: and she commanded a large part of the vast resources of Campania. True, she had not yet made a final settlement with the discontented Hernici: that was to come. And any slackening of Gaulish alarms in the North might set the Etruscans free to attack her in the rear. Meanwhile the Etruscan aristocrats kept their truce, and Rome was left to face the Samnites.

185. Southern Italy was in a state of unrest. The weakness of the Greek cities invited the encroachment of the inland peoples. In the far South some cities had been more or less completely absorbed in the Bruttian confederation. In Campania the Greeks held their ground with difficulty. The cities round the gulf of Tarentum were threatened by Lucanians and Samnites: Tarentum alone, strong in her wealth and advantageous position, was still able to have a policy of her own. But this policy seems to have been fitful and inconsistent. The wish to play a great part on the continent, to keep the Italians at bay and dominate the neighbouring Greek cities, was not supported by willingness to bear in person the hardships and sacrifices of war. The philosopher Archytas, who had guided them wisely, was now dead, and inferior demagogues led the indolent mob. In any strain they looked round for a deliverer from outside, as Greek states had been used to do : yet the champion's presence was soon felt to be a burden. King Archidamus of Sparta, the first of a series, was defeated by the Lucanians and fell in battle (338). Soon after we find Alexander, king of the Molossians, come over from Epirus to uphold the Greek cause. He was an uncle of Alexander the Great, and a man of power. He defeated both Lucanians and Samnites, and is

said to have made overtures to Rome. It would seem that he aimed
at conquering Italy with Roman help. His imperial schemes soon
brought him into conflict with Tarentum, and the old story of Greek
rending Greek was repeated in Italy. Mixed up in the party feuds of
the Italians, he was murdered (332) by a Lucanian exile. These
movements in the South no doubt give the explanation of the peace
between Rome and Samnium in the years 340—328. Rome was
steadily consolidating her power and encroaching on a district claimed
by the Samnites, the upper valley of the Liris. Against this menace
it was time to be up and doing : but for the present the impatient
hillmen were constrained to wait. As the troubles in the South
died away they once more turned their attention to the North and
West.

186. Now begins the long struggle commonly called the second
Samnite War, lasting from 327 to 304. Of this great struggle, in
which the question of Italian supremacy was virtually decided, we
have in Livy what professes to be a narrative, but is in truth a jumble
of traditions from which we can extract but a few solid facts. The
general result, the names of a few famous leaders, and stray notices
from which inferences may be drawn, are all we gain. How far the
meagre statements preserved by Diodorus are deserving of preference,
is very uncertain : we have not got the authors from whom Livy and
Diodorus drew. And the help derived from scraps of other writers is
extremely slight. Repetitions, inconsistencies and absurdities abound
in the tradition of this war as in those of earlier times.

187. The immediate occasion of war was found in Campania.
A double[1] city, with an old [Palaepolis] and a new [Neapolis] quarter,
the forerunner of modern Naples, stood on the shore of the bay. It
was Greek in origin, and, though there was a Campanian element in
the population, was still essentially Greek. Rome now owned most
of Campania, and it was alleged that the Neapolitans had made raids
into the Roman territory. In hope of resisting the impending attack
of Rome, they looked abroad for help. Tarentum talked and dallied:
the Samnites and Southern Campanians sent a garrison. The
Romans laid siege to the city : the trade of the port was interrupted :
the presence of the garrison was found oppressive. As usual, the
chief men seem to have been inclined to Rome. Secret negotiations
were opened, the Romans offered liberal terms, and the town was
betrayed to them. Under the protection of a most favourable treaty

---

[1] This obscure topographical matter is discussed by Beloch, *Campanien*, pp. 60—62.
The division of a city into Greek and Barbarian quarters is known in other cases. For
Emporiae in Spain see Livy XXXIV 9, Strabo III 4 § 8 (p. 160). I believe that some such
precaution (for the quarters were walled off) is to be traced at Syracuse also. See *Journal of
Philology* XXIII, p. 54.

the Neapolitans enjoyed a long prosperity as the loyal Allies of Rome, bound to provide a naval[1] contingent, as they were well able to do. The siege lasted long enough to be the occasion of a momentous constitutional step : for the extension of the command of the consul Quintus Publilius Philo as *pro consule* was the beginning of the Roman pro-magistracy. Rome was now at war with Samnium, and tradition tells us that both sides were well aware that Italian supremacy would be the victors' prize.

188. And now the loose unpractical constitution of the Samnite league, and the border feuds with some of their neighbours, told against the Samnites. Roman diplomacy won allies in Apulia, where the lowland peoples feared and hated the raiders from the hills : even the Lucanians were for a time brought into alliance with Rome, and neutralized the hostility of the southern Greeks ; while little help could be looked for on the Samnite side from the smaller Sabellian peoples to the North. So the war opened with Roman successes. An invasion of Samnium brings before us two of the Roman heroes of the period, the dictator L. Papirius Cursor and his master of the horse Q. Fabius Maximus Rullianus. Other Fabii and Papirii also play parts as the war goes on, and our tradition is no doubt largely derived from the partial records of these and other great houses. Fabius, left in temporary command by Papirius, engaged the enemy in defiance of orders, and gained one or more victories. From the wrath of the dictator he fled to Rome, thus escaping execution. Papirius followed him, and was only prevented from putting him to death by the entreaties of the whole people. The story is dressed up in all the colours of rhetoric to illustrate the stern discipline of this Golden Age of Rome. But while the dictator is chasing his subordinate we feel that his proper place is at the head of his army, and that the story as it stands is worthless. As the war went on fortune varied. Rome held the northern Sabellians in check, and seems to have pushed into Apulia : but we hear that the Lucanians were by Tarentine intrigues brought into revolution : the democratic party prevailed, and the country fell under Samnite influence. Rome however had the best of it[2] on the whole, and peaceful overtures of

---

[1] Beloch, *Ital. Bund* p. 207, points out that they seem also to have been bound to maintain a body of cavalry.

[2] Pliny, *N. H.* VII 136, preserves a strange story that one of the consuls of 322, L. Fulvius, was a Tusculan. In 323 the Tusculans (for their status, see above § 137) had been accused (Livy VIII 37) of having supported the late rebellion of Privernum and Velitrae. Their prayers for mercy had procured their acquittal from the Roman Tribes. Fulvius, says Pliny, had been *consul* at Tusculum. He went over to the Romans, and was made Roman consul at once. Thus he triumphed over the people whose consul he had been (and so a *hostis* of Rome), within the space of a year! In the *Fasti triumphales* he is made to triumph *de Samnitibus*

the Samnites are said to have been coldly received in 322. No doubt the most has been made of the pride that went before the fall: the next year brought the disaster of the Caudine Forks. By reports of the imminent danger of Luceria, the loss of which post would mean the loss of the Roman hold on Apulia, the consuls were induced to advance to its relief. Time was precious, so from their quarters in Campania they set out to force a way through the heart of Samnium. They walked into a trap, found themselves unable to cut their way out, and were forced to capitulate. The Samnite general Gavius Pontius made them agree on behalf of Rome to withdraw from the districts claimed by the Samnites, dismantle the new fortresses [Fregellae], and renew the old alliance on equal terms: at the same time he would not dismiss the captive army without making them pass, stripped of armour and outer clothing, under the 'yoke' [*iugum*]. This public insult to their defeated enemy was all that the Samnites gained by victory.

189. In point of form the peace was not binding: the Roman senate and people had not accepted it, and the consuls could not bind the state by exceeding their powers. And at Rome forms were all-important in public affairs, just as in law and religion: no wonder that now, in the hour of disgrace, formality overrode the claims of honour. The terms were repudiated, the consuls handed over to the Samnites, who refused to accept this sham satisfaction: they raged, while the Romans quibbled: it was now too late to challenge Rome to send back her army into the death-trap of Caudium. Such in outline is the story, the details of which are to be regarded with distrust. The rival powers, embittered by the incident, continued the struggle. Rome had lost prestige, and the Samnites took Fregellae. Two of the heroes of this period, Publilius Philo and Papirius Cursor, were consuls in 320. While the latter marched round into Apulia, the former made a direct attack on Samnium, beat the enemy, and forced his way through to his colleague, who was besieging Luceria. The Samnites drew their forces together for its relief. A battle was imminent, when an embassy from Tarentum appeared. They required both parties to cease hostilities, and announced that, if either were contumacious, the Tarentine forces would fight on the side of its opponent. In defiance of this intervention—nothing came of the threat, of course—the Romans fought and conquered. Luceria fell, and Roman influence in Apulia, backed by the powerful city of Arpi, was strengthened. Communications by the Adriatic coast route were

Quirinalibus. The whole story is suspicious, and the local title for the chief magistrate of Tusculum seems to have been *dictator*, Livy III 18, VI 26. The affairs of Tusculum are particularly obscure in our tradition. See Livy VIII 14 § 4.

secured by a victory over the Frentani, a Samnite people. We now hear of a temporary truce between the two belligerents, of the spread of Roman dominion in Apulia, including an invasion of Lucania, of the organization of Roman jurisdiction in the incorporated districts of Antium and Campania, and of the formation of two new Tribe-districts between Rome and Capua, where much land had been allotted to Roman citizens. As usual, growth and consolidation followed the victories of the Roman sword.

The southward advance of Rome.

190. War soon broke out again on the border of Campania. Each side captured some fortresses. Further north, Rome lost but soon regained Sora on the upper Liris (314): and it seems that there was severe fighting in the country between the Volscian and Samnite lands. This implies a vigorous offensive on the Samnite side, and probably at least one victory. But Rome pulled through the danger, and now taught her neighbours a sharp lesson. The little people of the Ausones were massacred on suspicion of contemplated rebellion. In Apulia we hear that Luceria, betrayed to the Samnites, was recovered at once, and this important post occupied by a strong Latin colony. Rome was determined to keep in touch with this district: that the Samnites could not prevent this move, marks them as the weaker side. There was also a conspiracy at Capua, which according to one account reached the stage of actual revolt. This was quickly put down, and the Samnite army, sent to cooperate with the rising, was beaten back and followed into Samnium. Next came the easy recapture of Fregellae, and an advance of the Romans in southern

Campania. Here their chief gain was the important city of Nola, which became, probably on favourable terms, an Ally of Rome: as elsewhere, the aristocratic party seems to have been placed in power. The occupation of important strategic points was resumed in the planting of Latin colonies at Suessa and the Pontian islands, followed shortly by one at Interamna on the Liris: and the permanent improvement of the coast road from Rome to Capua was carried out by the censor Appius Claudius. Rome had now two lines of communication with Campania, and we may assume that important points, such as the bridge of the Volturnus, were guarded with forts. That the statesmen of the Republic were deliberately aiming at the conquest of all Italy, is perhaps too much to assert. But they must have seen that it was likely to become a necessity: neighbourhood of states on an equal footing was not a system used in antiquity: it was necessary to eat or to be eaten.

191. The grip of Rome was tightening on the failing Samnites: with their fall Italian freedom would be virtually at an end. At last, already too late, the cities of Etruria rose in arms. They were a shrunken confederacy, for Rome now held southern Etruria: but the pressure of the Gauls in the north seems to have relaxed for the time. The year 312 passed in preparations: in 311 the Etruscans laid siege to the Roman frontier fortress, the Latin colony of Sutrium. A victory gained by the consul Aemilius relieved it, but, as it seems, not effectively. Fabius Rullianus his successor again saved the town, and the enemy fled into the wild upland known as the Ciminian Forest, a border tract which had hitherto served[1] as a buffer between Roman and Etruscan, avoided by traffic and reputed to be impassable to armies. This barrier Fabius resolved to pierce. A Roman who spoke Etruscan went with a single slave to spy out the land, and is said to have penetrated far, even into Umbria. On his return Fabius pushed forward at once, crossed the forest, and laid waste a large stretch of the rich land of Etruria. The Etruscans now mustered an enormous host in self-defence. Somewhere (where, traditions differed) Fabius routed them with great slaughter, some of the chief cities sued for peace, and were granted a temporary truce. A last effort of despair was foiled by Fabius' great victories at the Vadimonian lake in 310 and near Perusia in 309. The war died out in marches and capture of posts, followed by a futile rising in Umbria. The chronology is in great confusion, but in 308 quiet seems to have been restored.

192. Meanwhile the war went on in Samnium. We hear of the capture of the chief Samnite town, Bovianum, and of a Roman

[1] Livy IX 36, 37.

victory: of operations against the Marrucini, a small people somewhat further North: of Roman successes in Apulia, and the capture of forts in Samnium : of a naval expedition to southern Campania, including a raid against Nuceria, which ended in disaster to the Roman force. Not much progress was being made, and the Samnites with vast exertions managed to bring a splendidly equipped army into the field. But the dictator Papirius beat them in a great battle, and sent loads of magnificent shields to deck the festivals of Rome. Nuceria was now taken. In this hour of Roman triumphs, it seems that the northern Sabellians, Marsi and Paeligni, threw in their lot with the losing side and shared their defeats : a short campaign brought them to submission. Next year (307) came the turn of Rome's old Allies,

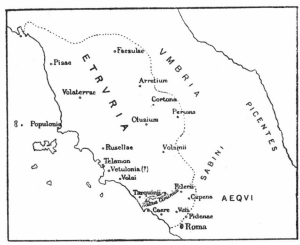

The chief Etrurian cities.

the Hernici. Hernican volunteers were found in numbers among Samnite prisoners taken in battle: explanations were demanded and refused : and a great part of the Hernican league—even when it was too late they were not unanimous—declared war against Rome. The rising was promptly and firmly put down, for it would not do to neglect the control of the hill country between Rome and Samnium. The rebels were incorporated[1] in the Roman state without voting rights: the loyal communities were allowed to remain as free Allies under their own laws, entitled to meet in federal diets and enjoying the privilege of intermarriage. The Hernici as a people drop out of

---

[1] Livy IX 43 §§ 23, 24. Among the rebel towns, which became *municipia* of the lowest class, without local governments, was the chief place Anagnia.

history: the diversion effected by this rising enabled the Samnites to seize Sora and a few other posts and in 305 to invade Campania once more. But defeats awaited them, the towns seized were lost again: in 304 they sued for peace, and gained a renewal of their old treaty. Such an ending of this weary war surely shews that the Roman accounts, with their tales of constant victories and enormous slaughter of the enemy, are at least partial and overdrawn.

193. During the last five years or so of this war there seem to have been one or two expeditions into the S.E. corner of Italy, where the native Iapygian, Messapian or Sallentine communities were being drawn into the struggle. Tarentum[1] had enough to do to keep her independence in face of the general agony of the Western Greeks: for the monster Agathocles was in the midst of his bloody and violent career at Syracuse. So Rome turned to settle matters with the northern Sabellians. Massacre and confiscation put an end to the Aequi, her enemies of yore. The Marsi, Paeligni, Marrucini, perhaps even the Frentanian Samnites, submitted and were now enrolled as Allies of Rome. Latin colonies at Sora and at Alba near Lake Fucinus helped to secure the fruits of the war. The pacification of the Umbro-Sabellian lands to the North and East was steadily carried out and small risings put down. The colony of Carsioli (298, perhaps 302) followed Alba, securing the way through central Italy: Narnia (299), the ancient Nequinum, commanded southern Umbria and the way to the North. We hear that Rome had also intervened in Etruria, to support the aristocratic party at Arretium, and that fighting had ensued. In 299 things become somewhat clearer. The growth of Rome is marked by the formation of two new Tribe-districts, the result of the allotment of confiscated Hernican land to Roman citizens. And now trouble was again brewing in the North. The Gauls were once more on the move, and the Etruscans sought by bribes to hire them for a war with Rome. The Gauls took the money and went home, and the alarm died away: a small campaign in Etruria is recorded, but the chief result was that Rome made an alliance with the Picentes, no doubt on favourable terms: the district of Picenum had a strategic value in prospect of a struggle the approach of which was surely foreseen.

194. For the unconquered Samnites were making ready to renew the fight for freedom. They had learnt that singlehanded they were unequal to the task. But their emissaries were active in Italy, in hope to form at last a grand coalition and overthrow the growing

---

[1] The barren expedition of the Spartan prince Cleonymus with a Greek mercenary force on the invitation of Tarentum had no influence on the fortunes of Italy, save that it may have kept the Lucanians occupied, and left the Greek cities rather weaker than before.

power of Rome. With the Lucanians persuasion failed, and coercion
was employed to compel alliance. The Samnite party was placed in
power: a Lucanian embassy (from the nobles, no doubt) made
complaint in Rome and were received as Allies: redress was claimed
and refused by the Samnites, and war[1] was declared. The war in
Etruria was dying out, and Fabius and Decius the consuls of 297
both led their armies into Samnium. Fabius beat the enemy in a
desperate fight, and the combined armies laid the country waste with
fire and sword. Decius had routed a force of Apulians, who had been
induced to support the Samnites: so there was little open resistance
for the time. It is said that the Samnite army at last left their own
land and marched into Etruria in hope of involving the Etruscans
and Gauls in a great general war. This is put in 296, and in that
and the following year we find Rome facing a grand coalition,
Samnite, Umbrian, Etruscan, Gaul. A second Samnite force made a
diversion in Campania, but was in due course driven off with heavy
loss. But the attempt caused alarm, for the security of the Appian
way was menaced and great damage done in the country. So two
colonies of Roman citizens were founded on the coast at Minturnae
and Sinuessa. Meanwhile the issue of the death-struggle was decided
in Etruria.

195. It is a pity that the tradition of this great crisis should have
come down to us in a tangle of confusion. The conflicting claims of
family pride corrupt the annals as usual, and the reappearance of Appius
Claudius as consul in 296 brings in the misrepresentations of the anti-
Claudian annalists. It would seem that a Roman army invaded Lucania
and restored the aristocratic party to power. We hear of a Roman
victory in Etruria over a combined Samnite-Etruscan force: but it was
clearly not decisive, and the Gauls and Umbrians now appeared in arms
to join the coalition. Great was the alarm in Rome. Old Fabius
Rullianus and his former colleague Decius were made consuls for the
next year: immense forces were raised, and the Latins and other Allies
gladly furnished contingents of unusual strength. Such loyalty attests
the judgment of contemporaries on the merits of the Roman system
in that day. Rome was not merely a successful leader: she was firm
and consistent, she did not draw back from the responsibilities of her
position, she supported her Allies and smote her enemies: and she

---

[1] The dark uncertainty of the history of all these events is illustrated by the famous
epitaph of L. Cornelius Scipio Barbatus, consul in 298. It ascribes to him victories in
Lucania and Samnium. But Livy, following his annalists, places Scipio's campaign in
Etruria, and the *Fasti triumphales* assign a double triumph (Samn.-Etr.) to his colleague
Cn. Fulvius, none to Scipio. See Livy x 11, 12, and for attempts to reconcile discrepancies
Mommsen on *CIL* I 29, 30. Probably the epitaph is wrong, facts being distorted by family
partiality. But much of Livy's narrative of these early times rests on no better authority.

was still the one trusty bulwark of Italy against the Gauls.   Above
all, her policy was intelligible, a quality that has, alike in ancient and
in modern times, brought to steady governments a great reward.

196.   Before the new consuls reached the seat of war, a disaster had
befallen the Roman arms.   A legion left on guard at Clusium was
cut to pieces by a force of Senonian Gauls.   But on the advance of
the Roman armies the enemy retired, and concentrated their whole
forces north of the Apennine at Sentinum in Umbria.   The consuls
followed them : the invasion of Etruria by the spare armies, raised for
the protection of Rome, drew off the Etruscan confederates to the
defence of their country : and the coalition was represented by the
Samnites and Gauls on the day of battle.   The stubbornness of the
fight, the self-devotion of Decius, who, like his father in the Latin
war, gave his life to stay the wild onset of the Gauls, the completeness
of the victory, all made the battle of Sentinum a famous memory.
A remnant of the Samnite army, making for home, was cut up by
the Paeligni as it passed through their territory.   War still went on,
however : conquest and punishment of the chief cities brought peace
in Etruria (294—3) : in Samnium the fiercest resistance was still
offered to invading armies.   A serious reverse befel the Romans in
Apulia.   But the resources of the Samnites were failing : town after
town was taken : all attempts to beat back the Roman advance were
foiled.   In despair they turned to solemn oaths and horrible ceremonies and dragged their last reserves into the field.   But this also
was a failure, and the conquest went on.   In 292 they won their last
victory, utterly defeating the consul Fabius Gurges, son of old
Rullianus.   But the old general averted the wrath of the Senate by
offering to serve as his son's lieutenant or chief of staff, and achieved
a great and final victory.   Pontius the Samnite leader was taken
prisoner, led in the consul's triumph, and beheaded.   Such was the
mercy of Rome.   Resistance was now stamped out, and the intention
of Rome to keep a firm hold on southern Italy manifested by the
foundation of the great Latin colony of Venusia.   It was in the
Daunian district of Apulia, close to the borders of Lucania and
Samnium.   While the number of men sent to Latin colonies was
normally from 2500 to 6000, Venusia received 20,000.   In 290 the
Samnites sued for peace, and the old treaty was once more renewed.
This sounds strange, after all these years of bloodshed and ruin.   But
Rome was no doubt eager to be relieved of the sacrifices entailed by
the war.   She had defeated a great coalition, and her supremacy was
now assured.   She did not hurry to pluck unripe fruit from the tree
of conquest.   Far more powerful than the sword as a Romanizing influence, her system would bring the fruit to ripeness in years of peace.

197. We now begin to find ourselves among a new generation of Roman heroes: the chief figures now are Manius Curius Dentatus and Gaius Fabricius Luscinus, names on which Roman literature loved in later times to dwell, as patterns of patriotism and courage, of an incorruptible frugality and honour. M'. Curius as consul in 290, after sharing the last campaign of the Samnite war, conquered the Sabine mountaineers. Why the Sabines were at war with Rome, and why the war broke out at this moment, we do not know. After a speedy conquest, they were incorporated as citizens without voting rights, and seem to have been easily Romanized. Next year Curius commanded as proconsul in the South. The Lucanians had now served their turn, and Rome could no longer allow them a free hand. So she took up the cause of Thurii, beat the Lucanians, and saved the Greek city. She was not unwilling to appear as champion of the Greeks, whose value she knew. But just now Agathocles died: Syracuse ceased to be a menace to the other Greeks of the West: and the Tarentines, able to pursue their own designs more freely and dreading those of Rome, became active promoters of anti-Roman policy, though at present not venturing on war. Hence it seems southern Italy was for several years in a state of unrest. Campaigns took place, of which the record is lost. But it is clear that the Romans held fast to Thurii and made their way in those parts. In 282 Fabricius triumphed as conqueror of the Lucanians and Bruttians. This sort of thing did not suit the Tarentines, who had far sooner have seen Thurii destroyed. In the South therefore a crisis was at hand.

198. Meanwhile Rome had to face more troubles in the North. About 285 we hear of war in Etruria, but in the dim twilight of our tradition[1] we only get glimpses of a repetition of the old story. The Senonian Gauls are called in, and begin by cutting to pieces a Roman force: then comes Roman revenge, and the Senones are annihilated. Then the Boian tribe appear, rally the failing Etruscans, and share with them a crushing defeat by the Vadimonian lake. Next year the Boii fight the Romans again with the same result, and a peace is made. The foundation of colonies also shews that Rome was busy to the North of Apennine. Most important was the citizen colony of Sena on the coast of Umbria, which marked the expulsion of the remnant of Senones from the strip known as *ager Gallicus*, and the Roman annexation of the land. We will now turn to the fourth stage of this period, which includes the war with Pyrrhus and its sequel, the completion of the conquest of Italy.

199. In 282 the inevitable collision with Tarentum came at last.

---

[1] Chiefly Polybius II 19—21; Livy, *epit.* 12.

This city stood in a position of such exceptional strength that to take it by force was impossible with the appliances of antiquity: to starve it out was hardly less difficult, owing to its magnificent harbour[1] and ready access to the sea. The trade of the port was great. The state kept up a considerable navy, and the decline of Syracuse had probably left it the first maritime power in Italo-Sicilian waters. A treaty existed binding the Romans not to send a fleet to the north of the Lacinian headland. One day ten Roman ships appeared off Tarentum. The Tarentines manned a fleet, attacked the Romans, sunk some of their ships and took the rest, sold as slaves or put to death their prisoners, raised an army, and marched upon Thurii, where they drove out the Roman garrison and sacked the town. So far there is little cause for doubt, and the ancient tradition represents the Romans as meaning no harm, the Tarentines as acting in passion at the instigation of light-headed demagogues. Whether the Romans were in truth so innocent, merely voyaging to their new Adriatic colonies (as Mommsen would imply), or whether they were acting in collusion with a pro-Roman party in the city (as Ihne suggests), is more than we can now decide. That the acts of the Tarentines have been put in the most unfavourable light, to exhibit Greek democratic levity as a foil to the serious moderation of Rome, is highly probable. No part of Roman history has been more wilfully turned into a moral lesson for readers than the Pyrrhic war.

200. The Romans moved cautiously. An embassy was sent to Tarentum to demand the redress of injuries and the restoration of the *status quo*. Not to dwell on suspicious details, it was met with refusal and insult. Perhaps the Tarentines were already treating for the protection of Pyrrhus, and this may account for their confidence and for the caution of Rome. War however was declared, and a Roman army entered the territory of Tarentum. Its mission was as much political as military: it must have had full information from Roman partisans, if it be true that only the properties of the democrats were laid waste: the offers of peace already made were repeated sword in hand. Tarentum was filled with intrigues, and the aristocratic party came into power for a moment, only to be overthrown at once on the arrival of Cineas, king Pyrrhus' chief minister. He announced that the king would shortly bring his army to their aid, and the popular party, restored to power, abandoned all thoughts of peace.

201. The country of Epirus, corresponding roughly to the modern Albania, is wild and mountainous. Its inhabitants, hardy and brave, were of the same stock as the Greeks, but difference of conditions had

---

[1] See Map, below § 337.

made them a different people. In the brilliant life and grand achievements of the Greek city-states—a chapter of Greek history now closed—they had borne no part. Like the Macedonians before the great Philip took them in hand, they lived under a tribal system: the Molossian tribe was the most powerful. Its chiefs claimed descent from the hero Achilles: in short, the institutions and traditions of the Epirotes belonged to the Heroic age of Greece. Now, when Philip and his greater son Alexander had run their course, and the vast empire of the latter was being carved into great kingdoms; when the humbled cities were dependent on the will of the warrior kings of the age; the backward tribes came to the front. They were still in full vigour, their traditions pointed to monarchy of some sort, and the Macedonian system supplied a model. Of the second generation of Alexander's successors, the most striking figure was the Molossian prince Pyrrhus. Richly gifted in body and mind, his youth was passed in hair-breadth escapes and adventures in exile. He won back the Molossian throne, established himself firmly in Epirus, and entered into the struggles for the kingdom of Macedon, which he even won for a moment and lost again. But he strengthened and enlarged Epirus, and seems to have been an admirable ruler of a devoted people. To this bold and brilliant being the Tarentines now turned for help, promising him numerous allies among the sulky Italians lately subjugated by Rome, and the resources of the Italian Greeks. No doubt they reminded him that their navy had helped him to recover Corcyra. In an evil hour, fired by the legends of Achilles and the deeds of Alexander, he set out to win glory and empire in the West.

202. The Romans raised large forces to receive him, and did their best to secure quiet in restless districts by marches of troops, taking hostages, and posting of garrisons. In particular, wishing to prevent operations on the coasts of Latium and Campania, they threw a legion of Campanians into the Greek city of Rhegium, as a guard of the Sicilian strait. These men (nominally Roman citizens) saw on the opposite shore the city of Messana, held by the Mamertini ('sons of Mamers' the War-god), a body of Campanian mercenaries formerly in the service of Agathocles. Paid off after his death, they had treacherously seized Messana, killed the men and married the women, and were now a free-state of robbers. The object-lesson inspired the Roman-Campanians to do the same sort of thing in Rhegium: and in the present crisis Rome had to defer punishment of the mutineers. Meanwhile Pyrrhus reached Tarentum after losses in an Adriatic storm, and took matters into his hand. He drilled the citizens into soldiers, and turned the city into a camp.

Discipline and restraints were odious to men habituated to licence
and pleasures: and they soon hated a deliverer in whom they had
found a master. But Pyrrhus rightly persisted, and formed a respectable army. His own Epirotes were splendid troops, but 20,000
pikemen of the phalanx with a few archers and cavalry were surely
not enough for his enterprise, and he had of course to garrison
Tarentum. But he brought to Italian warfare 20 elephants, a force
esteemed in the East. The Tarentine levies at best were no match
for the conquerors of Gaul and Samnite, and the promised allies
from Samnium and Lucania discreetly awaited the result of a
battle.

203.   In 280, while one consul quieted some local movements in
Etruria, the other faced Pyrrhus. They met near Heraclea on the
Lucanian coast, and Pyrrhus won the day. It may have been that
the stiff phalanx had the better of the supple legions: it seems
certain that the elephants did produce some panic: but the king's
generalship was no doubt the chief cause of his victory. Pyrrhus
pushed on into Campania and vainly tried to gain Capua and Neapolis. Dogged by the Roman army, he pushed on again towards
Rome. But his hopes of Etruscan support were disappointed. Besides
the army beaten at Heraclea, now reinforced, he had before him the
other consul with the troops set free by the pacification of Etruria.
He could effect nothing, so he withdrew his army, having reached
Anagnia (or perhaps even Praeneste), to winter in Campania. Many
Samnites and Lucanians had joined him after his victory: these no
doubt felt evil forebodings when they saw their champion driven to
retreat. And in the southern Greek cities, of which he was now
master, there was always a pro-Roman party, and to hold them with
trusty and sufficient garrisons was beyond his power. He had already
sent the persuasive Cineas to propose a peace, probably on the terms
of the independence of the Greek cities. Tradition says that the
Senate had faltered: old and blind, Appius Claudius came to the
House in a litter, and recalled the wavering Fathers to their duty.
Cineas returned with the message that the Romans would not treat
for peace while Pyrrhus remained in Italy, and full of admiration
for all he had witnessed in Rome. The calm dignity of the Senate,
the incorruptibility of the leading statesmen, the refusal of jewels
by Roman ladies, the sturdy patriotism of all, impressed him
deeply: even his skilled cajolery had failed. And that a public
man should refuse a bribe was to a Greek always a matter of genuine
surprise.

204.   And now, while Pyrrhus was busy with preparations at
Tarentum, he was visited by a Roman embassy of whom Fabricius

was one.   The king is said to have hoped that peace was the object of their mission, but it was merely the redemption of prisoners.   He tried all his arts to work upon the ambassadors, but in vain : no prospect of peace was held out.   Neither the most splendid offers nor the sudden appearance of a huge elephant could allure or unnerve Fabricius.   We are gravely told that the king, not to be outdone, now released his Roman prisoners without ransom, or at least let them go home on parole to return, a promise which was honourably kept.   Fabricius read the king a lecture on frugality as a shield against temptation.   The campaign of the next year was in Apulia, where Pyrrhus gained another victory at Ausculum (or Asculum).   But the Roman army was not broken up : while the king's motley force of Epirotes, Tarentines, Greek and Sabellian mercenaries, was nowise fitted to stand the strain of long indecisive operations.   News of troubles in Epirus barred the hope of further supplies of good troops from home : Pyrrhus himself is said to have been wounded.   At all events he seems to have retired to Tarentum, where he brooded over a change of plans.   For the present he had little prospect of success in Italy.   Rome, with her well-planted fortresses and her resources within easy reach, was able to wear him out.   Even on his march towards Rome he had remarked that the districts under Roman dominion were rich and prosperous, while the land of his allies lay waste.   Rome protected allies, and he could not.   Besides, there was no bond of sympathy between him and his allies : each side sought to use the other for its own profit, and the Italians complained of losses from the marauding of his troops.   He had come to Italy as leader and champion of the Greeks, doubtless with an eye to those of Sicily as well.   Meanwhile the Carthaginians were carrying all before them in that island.   To the Greeks all depended on the relief of Syracuse, now besieged.   If the city fell, Sicily was lost.   Pyrrhus had been son-in-law of the late tyrant Agathocles.   The despairing Syracusans offered him the crown and called for his aid, and he resolved to undertake the task.

205.   His designs were known or suspected, and not unnaturally were regarded by Rome and Carthage from different points of view. The former wanted to get the troublesome invader out of Italy, and to win Tarentum : the latter to keep him out of Sicily, at least till they had won Syracuse.   Rome was suffering under the losses and strain of the war, and longed to be able to consolidate her power in peace.   Carthage knew that her Eastern kinsmen had been struck down by Alexander, and that old-Greek Rhodes and new-Greek Alexandria had succeeded to the commerce of Phoenician Tyre. She hoped at last to settle scores with the Greeks, whose competition had plagued her in the West for quite 500 years. Both powers saw the great danger of leaving two such commanding positions as Syracuse and Tarentum in the hands of an able ruler of imperial instincts. Rome and Carthage therefore, acting on a common interest, leagued together[1] for mutual defence against Pyrrhus. They had long been in diplomatic relations. Two if not three[2] treaties had preceded the present one : but their purport had been to define the spheres of influence of the two states and to recite the privileges conceded to the citizens of each in the dominions of the other. The clauses of all the treaties quoted by Polybius betray mutual jealousy. This of 279 is no exception : a story, that a Punic fleet visited the coast of Latium and that the Roman government politely declined the proffered help, illustrates the fact that no sincere alliance was possible between two powers, each wholly devoted to its own interests.

206.   Early in 278 Pyrrhus crossed to Syracuse. He left garrisons in Tarentum and Locri, and promised to return. He took all power into his own hands, formed an army of the local Greeks to support his expeditionary force, and took the field amid general enthusiasm. He then drove back the Punic forces, winning battles and taking towns at such a rate that by the middle of 276 he held the whole island with exception of Messana, where the Mamertines still remained, and the western sea-fortress of Lilybaeum, where the Carthaginians stood at bay. Carthage now offered peace on condition of her keeping this stronghold, but Pyrrhus would not consent to leave her a base from which her forces might at any time advance to reconquer Sicily. Yet he could make no impression on Lilybaeum by land : in the hope of blockading the port he set himself to create a fleet. But the Greeks, already galled by his severe and arbitrary government, found his further exactions unbearable. The rescued cities abandoned the cause of their deliverer, and made overtures to their enemies. After one more fruitless victory over a Punic army, he threw up the venture in disgust and sailed for Italy, leaving the Sicilian question unsettled, and having wasted blood, money, reputation, and the opportunities of three momentous years. As he left the shore, he is said[3] to have remarked to his staff 'what a cockpit we are now leaving for Carthaginian and Roman to fight in.'

207.   He was indeed wanted in Italy, for the Romans had not been idle. In spite of a disaster, due to blundering generalship, they

---

[1] Polybius III 25.

[2] Discussed by Mommsen *R. H.* I appendix, and by Mr Strachan-Davidson in appendix to his Polybius.

[3] Plutarch, *Pyrrhus* 23.

had quieted the Samnites: movements in the South had been put down and the Greek cities taken: but to besiege Tarentum was beyond their power and skill. Pyrrhus did not even make the crossing at his ease: a Punic fleet attacked him and he lost a number of ships. He landed near Rhegium, and had to fight with the Roman mutineers and the Mamertines of Messana. He cut his way through to Tarentum, taking most of the Greek cities on his line of march. His gains in men and money from these exhausted places can only have been trivial. His desperation is shewn in his seizure of the temple treasures at Locri. The end was now near. True, he had as yet not lost a battle, but his resources were failing. Many of his Epirote veterans were dead, and he could no longer find numerous allies or inspire hope as in the past. Early in 275 he advanced into Samnium. Near Beneventum he fell in with the consul Manius Curius. A night march miscarried: elephants had lost their terrors for the Romans, who plied them with fiery darts till they turned and trod down the ranks of their own side. Here was a decisive victory at last. The king fell back on Tarentum, where he left a garrison to hold the city, and embarked with the relics of his army for Epirus. He plunged into wild adventures, and perished ignobly a few years later in a street-fight at the siege of Argos.

208. If anyone still doubted that the Romans meant to be supreme in Italy, he must have been enlightened in the course of the next few years. The Lucanians and Bruttians were at once beaten into submission. Risings in Samnium were put down. The defeat of the Umbrians of Sarsina and the conquest of Picenum gave Rome a firmer hold on the North. Some of the Picentes were transplanted[1] to southern Campania. Everywhere confiscations of territory took place, by which either the state-domains of Rome were enlarged or room was found for the planting of colonies. Above all, it was necessary to secure Tarentum. The situation there was very complicated. The pro-Roman party had been driven to occupy a fortified post in the neighbourhood, and the democrats, led by men to whom a Roman conquest meant death or ruin, were in possession of the city. But the city was commanded by the citadel held for Pyrrhus by Milo with an Epirote garrison. While the Romans vainly beset the city by land, a Carthaginian fleet made at least a show of blockading it by sea. With the death of Pyrrhus Milo's interest in Tarentum came to an end, and his main object was to withdraw his forces safely to Epirus. He knew that the people in the city wished to surrender it to the Carthaginians, but a city mob was of small

---

[1] Strabo v 4 § 13 (p. 251); Pliny, *N. H.* III 70.

account in the eyes of a military man trained in the school of Pyrrhus. He knew the value of the Tarentine citadel to either of the two expectant powers. Probably he found that he could make a better bargain with Rome: it was more important for Rome to prevent Carthage from setting up a Lilybaeum in Italy than for Carthage to gain such a foothold there. Anyhow Milo withdrew his force with all their belongings under a convention, and handed over the key of southern Italy to the Romans. The Carthaginian admiral had now no choice but to withdraw, protesting that the intentions of his government had from the first been most friendly. But Rome, not unnaturally suspicious, seems to have required and received diplomatic assurances of friendship from Carthage. The citadel of Tarentum now became a Roman fortress. The Roman partisans returned to the city, and no doubt to power. Tarentum as a Roman Ally was left to conduct its own internal government: but another great Greek city had succumbed to the irresistible growth of Great Powers. Tarentum was still a city; it was no longer a city-state.

209. The mutineers at Rhegium were not forgotten, and Rome could now attend to them. They may have looked for help from Messana or even from Carthage. But Carthage shrank from a step that meant war with Rome, and the Mamertines had their hands full. After Pyrrhus left Syracuse a young soldier named Hiero had come to the front as leader. He attacked Messana, and was on the point of taking it, when Carthage intervened to rescue the Mamertine robbers. Henceforth the town was held by a Punic garrison: it was plain that Carthage meant to command the strait. When the Romans appeared to besiege Rhegium, Hiero, though busy with Messana, sent them useful help. After desperate resistance, Rhegium was carried by storm: no quarter was given, save that 300 wretches were sent to be scourged and beheaded in the Roman Forum as a lesson to Italy. Rome now came forward as a patron of Greeks. Old citizens of Rhegium were invited from the retreats whither they had fled to escape the mutineers, to form a nucleus of population. The city was refounded as a Greek city in alliance with Rome on favourable terms, and in that character rose again to considerable prosperity. The extreme south of Italy was now secured. With the subjugation of the Sallentini of the South-East, and the capture of the port of Brundisium, the work of conquest was complete.

210. The planting of colonies and the extension of good roads went on steadily, to secure what the sword had won. On the coast of the Tyrrhenian or 'lower' sea Cosa in Etruria and Paestum in Lucania (a revival of the extinct Greek city Poseidonia) strengthened Rome's hold of the seaboard. On the northern coast Ariminum did

the same, and served as a border-fortress to watch the Gauls. It was followed up by the planting of Firmum (264) in Picenum, where ground had lately been cleared. Thus the Roman citizens settled in and near Sena received a welcome support. Finally the yoke was placed on Samnium. A strong colony was planted in the commanding position of Beneventum followed in 263 by another at Aesernia. Thus the Samnites lost territories and were watched by fortified towns in the heart of Samnium. Any active cooperation of the various cantons was made more difficult than ever. Meanwhile the Sabines, long connected with Rome and loyal in the recent time of trial, received their reward. In 268 they were raised[1] to the full citizenship, and could henceforth vote in Assemblies and hold office. A less genial lesson was afforded by the fate of the great Etruscan city of Volsinii in 265—4, which virtually belongs to this period. The ruling caste of nobles had here, as elsewhere in Etruria, sunk through luxury[2] and self-indulgence into a deplorable state of political weakness. Their subjects—or slaves, as the tradition[3] calls them—controlled the government and maltreated their lords. An appeal addressed to Rome by the latter only led to more insult and violence. At last Rome intervened : stubborn resistance was followed by bloody retribution, and the once famous leading city of Etruria[4] was destroyed. Speaking generally, Roman policy in Etruria was not one of annexation, but of alliances with the separate cities : the failing aristocracies were useful agents.

211. And now this new world-power of Rome was a fact that the judicious could no longer ignore. She had for some time been on friendly terms with the wealthy commercial city-state of Rhodes, and with her nearer neighbour Apollonia on the Adriatic. Syracuse had recently done her a good turn. Her oldest ally was Massalia. She was the protectress of the Italian Greeks in the stead of Pyrrhus repulsed from Italy. She had in fact begun the policy that eventually made her the head of the whole Greek world. Such a result was far beyond her present horizon. But Greek influences and Greek sympathies soon took hold on the Romans. And among Greek antipathies was one, deep and old, to the Phoenicians. Carthage not only threatened to extinguish the Greeks of Sicily. Among the anxieties of the Macedonian dynasty in Egypt was the fear of Punic jealousy and aggression. Carthage hated Alexandria, and the Egyptian

---

[1] Velleius I 14 §§ 5, 6.
[2] The authorities cited in Athenaeus XII 14 (pp. 517—8) probably refer to this period.
[3] Valerius Max. IX 1 § 2 *ext.*; Florus I 16; Zonaras VIII 7; Orosius IV 5 §§ 3—5.
[4] Now Orvieto. Refounded later on the site now Bolsena.

province of Cyrene lay exposed to an attack from Carthage.   So the far-sighted ruler of Alexandria, Ptolemy II Philadelphus, took the opportunity of Pyrrhus' defeat to send an embassy[1] to Rome.   A Roman embassy returned the compliment, and friendship, perhaps[2] an alliance, was established, a step fraught with great consequences in time to come.   We may look on this step as an admission by a competent judge that Rome was one of the chief factors in the international life of the Mediterranean world.

[1] Dion Cass. fragm. 41.   Dionys. Hal. fragm. xx 14.   [2] See § 428 below.

CHAPTER XVIII

CAUSES OF ROMAN SUPREMACY

212. MANY causes contributed to make Rome supreme in Italy. A Roman would no doubt have boasted that the result was mainly due to the stubborn bravery of his fathers, and this would in part be true. But the conquered also were brave, and it was the care devoted to the military system in general and in particulars that slowly and surely established the superiority of Roman armies. Discipline was at its very best. The tactics of the manipular formation were no doubt developed greatly in the wars of this period. Some have thought that the method of attack, hurling the *pilum* and then rushing in sword in hand, was devised to deal with the stiff phalanx of Pyrrhus. Be this as it may, for the elastic formation of the legion in maniples a higher kind of discipline was needed than for a rigid phalanx. Tradition paints Pyrrhus as lost in admiration of the Roman legionaries. Their dead lay on the battlefield with their wounds all in front, their faces set in a grim frown of defiance : recruits poured in to fill the vacant places of the fallen : like Hercules lopping off the Hydra's heads only to see new ones grow, the king could make no real progress. 'With troops like these,' he said, 'I would conquer the world.' The cavalry was in this period still good, though it hardly kept pace with the improvement of the infantry : the fleet hardly calls for much notice till after 265. Beside the legions of full citizens there appear in the course of this period other legions of half-citizens, as they are often called by modern writers, and other bodies formed by contingents of Allies (*socii*).

213. Even more important than the military system was the positive nature of Roman policy. At the bottom this policy was simply a resolve to keep what she had got. But from the first she grasped and followed the law of imperial being—that whoever would not go back must go forward. From the first too her diplomacy had been subtle and consistent. Taking advantage of the jealousies and selfishness of the various peoples, she concluded a series of alliances, and made way in Italy by turning one power against another : without seeing what they were doing, the peoples served the interest of Rome.

By the side of the Roman army as an engine of conquest we must set the Senate, by whom policy and diplomacy, alliances and incorporations, were directed.

214. Nor must we leave out of count the superiority of the Roman government to other governments of the day. If absolute independence was out of the question, was not the Roman system, with all its faults, better than any other? Hard and formal, masterful and crafty, Rome had a better name than others for honesty and justice combined with consistency. The ease with which she gained control of the northern Sabellians (Sabines Marsi Paeligni &c.) seems to be a case in which the character of Rome served her well. Fortune too served her greatly in the advantage of a central position. Rome could divide her enemies and deal with them in detail, for she held the 'inner lines' more and more firmly as time went on. To cut off the Etruscan from the Samnite and keep open the way to Apulia was the object of the colonies founded 303—298. We see that the gift of fortune was clearly understood and turned to good account. Closely connected with the colonies was the great road-system begun in this period. Lastly, we may point to the skilful treatment of acquisitions, whether by alliance or incorporation. We may call it a system of graduated privilege. It will form the subject of the following chapter.

CHAPTER XIX

ORGANIZATION OF ITALY

215. NOW that we have reached the time at which the supremacy of Rome in Italy was established, we must take a general view[1] of the relations of the Italians to Rome and to each other. It was the nature of these relations that enabled Rome to pass triumphantly through the long struggle with Carthage : it was the changes for the worse in their practical working that led in the decline of the Republic to the ruinous conflict of the great Italian War. We may for the present include in Italy the peninsula as far North as Ariminum : the conquest of the Gauls in the region of the Po comes later. All this Italy was in some way or other bound to Rome, and we may classify the various forms of connexion as follows :

A. The connexion by *civitas*, either (1) the full or 'active' franchise, including the right of voting in Roman Assemblies and of holding Roman magistracies, or (2) the incomplete or 'passive' franchise, including all the burdens of citizens and only the 'private' rights such as *commercium* and *conubium*. Besides the ordinary citizens of the Roman Tribe-districts, this class contains (*a*) the *municipia* with or without local self-government, (*b*) the citizen colonies.

B. The connexion by *foedus*, either with (1) old existing communities, or with (2) new communities founded or refounded by Rome. This class includes (*a*) the treaty-states, (*b*) the Latin colonies.

The one rule that applies to both these classes is the obligation to military service under the general direction of the Roman government. The differences between them arise from the difference of the processes by which the two classes were severally created. These processes, Incorporation and Alliance, were kept clearly and fundamentally distinct.

The members of class (A) were all in some sense *cives,* and in course of time the half-citizens tended to become full Roman citizens. Their districts or towns were not separate *civitates*, but parts of the

---

[1] My obligations to Marquardt, Lange and Beloch in this chapter are so obvious that I need not confess them in detail.

Roman *civitas*. Their law was gradually accommodated to Roman law. For war purposes they were organized in legions on the Roman model, commanded by *tribuni*.

The members of class (B) were politically *socii*. In theory their districts or towns were independent *civitates*. The Roman law regarded them as aliens (*peregrini*). For war purposes they were organized in *alae* (horse) and *cohortes* (foot), bodies smaller than those of class (A). The gradual disappearance of the class of 'half-citizens' left the *socii* in a relatively worse position : they tended to become mere subjects.

216. Let us now consider these various categories one by one, and first the *municipia*.

The practice of incorporating into the state persons from outside was used at Rome from very early times. Tradition asserted that in the regal period whole communities [Alba Longa and other towns] were bodily transplanted to Rome and merged in the Roman People. Then we find communities merged without change of residence, as Gabii under the Tarquins. This appears as effected by mutual consent[1] under the terms of a treaty : and the same may be true of Capena (395) after the fall of Veii, of Tusculum in 381, and of Lanuvium, Aricia and other places in 338, if we hold that the citizens became full citizens of Rome. But to non-Latin populations it was not desirable to give the full franchise. Accordingly we begin to hear of another device. A community was merged in Rome without the 'public' rights of voting and being voted for. The franchise thus conferred carried the 'private' rights, but was in the main a means of imposing burdens [tasks, *munia*] and asserting the subjection of such half-citizens to the authority of Roman magistrates. It may be that this capacity for bearing burdens was called *municipium*: we only know the word in the concrete sense of a community of such 'burden-bearers.' The earliest *municipium* was the Etruscan city of Caere in 351. It seems that the Caerites retained a local government for internal affairs. But they were brought under Roman law, and Caere was now a subordinate commune within the Roman state. The same treatment was applied to other incorporations, whose status was accordingly defined as the 'right of Caerites' [*ius Caeritum*]. Instances are Fundi, Formiae, Arpinum, and Capua with its group of associated townships. But for various reasons it was found more convenient as time went on to do away with the local governments when incorporations took place. Thus, in dealing with the rebellious part of the Hernici in 306, Anagnia the chief town became a Roman *municipium*, but was

---

[1] In later times these towns are called *municipia*, and the title *municipium foederatum* seems to have existed. But that the name was used of them from the first is not proved.

deprived of self-government. This treatment was applied in a number of cases, and machinery that might serve the purposes of disaffection was thus removed. In the case of a country district like that of the Sabines [290] such a system would be especially effective. But the status of both classes of the *municipia* was only temporary. Whether it was or was not from the first meant to be a transitional stage, the spread of Roman law and the increase of personal relations[1] between *municipes* and full citizens tended to the levelling of distinctions, and the former were in course of time admitted to the full franchise of Rome. Thus the Sabines received it in 268, and by about 150 B.C. the half-citizens as a class had disappeared. The *municipia* of the later Republic are communes of full Roman citizens.

217. We now come to the citizen colonies (*coloniae civium Romanorum*).

It was from very early times the custom of war to take from the conquered part of their territory, commonly one-third. This land could either be sold, or kept as domain-land [*ager publicus*] of the conquering state, or assigned by that state to its own citizens. The assignation was in the form either of allotments to individuals or of the foundation of a colony. The latter plan was preferred when the conquest included a town the position of which suggested the advantage of holding it in the interest of Rome. A Roman garrison (usually 300 men) were sent, not for temporary occupation, but as permanent residents, who settled there with wives and families and were provided with means of subsistence by allotments of confiscated land. These men were the *coloni*. They formed a kind of local aristocracy, a ready-made Patriciate, so far as the town itself was concerned, and the original inhabitants a kind of Plebs. We see here a copy of the traditional Roman model. All power seems to have rested with the Roman *coloni*, who chose their local magistrates and senate from their own ranks. But the most important characteristic of a citizen colony was that the *coloni* retained their full Roman franchise as being simply a part of the *populus Romanus*. Each man was a Roman citizen: the aggregate were only regarded as a body because their special duty to the Roman state could only be performed by them jointly. This was the only difference between them and other members of Roman Tribes. Their garrison duty was treated as an equivalent of service in the field, which was therefore not required of them. By their side was the mass of the old inhabitants. In the early days of the Republic we have traditions of conflicts between these and the privileged *coloni*,

---

[1] Through *conubium*. This the half-citizens had with Rome and with other *municipia*. Even the rebel Hernican towns seem to have had it with Rome after 306, but (by express restriction) not with each other, if Livy IX 43 is to be believed.

whom they sometimes managed to expel. In the period 366—265 this seems not to have been the case. Possibly some cause of the former friction had been removed. The prevailing view is that the old inhabitants were half-citizens with only the 'private' rights. It is indeed most probable that such was their position, for without the existence of *conubium* and *commercium* between the two classes of inhabitants we can hardly account for the fusion which undoubtedly took place. But this may not have been so from the first: indeed the invention of the new status of *municipes* in the case of incorporations would rather suggest that it came in as a remedy for the evils of a former system of complete isolation of the two classes. In any case we know that with the conquest of Italy the Roman *coloni* gradually lost the character of a garrison, the inhabitants were blent together into one body, and all were full Roman citizens alike, long before the great Italian war. As to the situation of the citizen colonies, we must remark that their first design seems to have been to secure the coast. When we find them (about 184) beginning to be planted inland, this is for other reasons, and their character is completely changed.

By the growth of *municipia* and citizen colonies the half-citizens of Rome were spread further and further over Italy: and the spreading of the full citizens is marked by the allotments of freehold land and the creation of new Tribes. But all who were in any sense citizens were under Roman Law, and to administer this by a single Praetor sitting in Rome became impossible. Accordingly we find that it became the practice for the Praetor to appoint[1] deputies (*praefecti*), who visited the chief places and held courts there. In those centres where no local government was left, they probably had to perform some administrative duties also. The size of the districts seems to have varied, and with the size the number of deputies. The most important was the Campanian Prefecture. The details of the *praefecturae* are little known, and beyond our present scope.

218. We must now turn to the communities linked to Rome by compacts of various kinds, and first to those called Treaty-States (*civitates foederatae*).

It is hard for us, living in an age when it is a simple matter for a citizen of one state to be naturalized in another, to understand and bear in mind the jealous exclusiveness of ancient times. Yet the modern principles are of very recent date. In antiquity religions were local, the international influences of industry and commerce were very weak, civilizations were largely of a military character, and expansion of states took almost without exception the form of

[1] See Livy IX 20 Weissenborn, Mommsen *Staatsrecht* II 593—5.

conquest. The pioneers of progress, the Greeks, rolled back the Persian invasion, but were unable to form by union a great organization strong enough to guarantee their own freedom and peaceful development. No wonder it was held for an axiom in foreign policy that the good of *A* was the evil of *B*, and mutual suspicion was the rule between neighbours. Yet intercourse between peoples was necessary: the sacredness of envoys was generally recognized: the declaration of war and conclusion of peace were generally accompanied by oaths and religious ceremonial, and punctilious formalities laid the first foundations of public international law. But to establish friendly relations in time of peace between two states some sort of direct compact was necessary; for if they were not friends the presumption was that they were enemies. No state of antiquity was better served by a policy of alliances than Rome. Sometimes she merely entered into general friendly relations with another power, sometimes into terms of reciprocity (*hospitium*) for the benefit of individual citizens of each state visiting or trading in the other. But a treaty (*foedus*) in the full sense defined the rights and duties of the two partners (*socii*) to each other as sovran states, in particular the terms on which each was to help the other in war and the limitations (if any) on the right of either partner to enter into alliance with any third power. When the conditions were the same for both sides, the treaty was said to be 'fair' or 'level' (*aequum*); when one side was in some respect bound while the other was left free, it was 'unfair' or 'hard' (*iniquum*). Cases of the latter sort might vary infinitely in the degree of restraint imposed, from a trifling limitation to a point at which the sovranty of the inferior partner became nominal.

219. At the time when Rome became the mistress of Italy far the greater number of the Italian communities, whether cities or cantons or groups of these, were bound to her by treaties. They were thus recognized as states (*civitates*), and their sovranty was shewn in conducting their own administration, in jurisdiction under their own law, in coining under their own name. They were bound to supply naval or military contingents: the latter were not put into the legions, but were organized in other bodies, commanded by their own officers, and kept quite distinct from the citizen troops. Whether any Treaty-state was nominally free to contract alliances with outside powers or not, was of no practical importance: no doubt the great mass of the treaties barred such a step, and Rome was not likely to allow interference with her prerogative in foreign affairs. The highest degree of sovranty known is that including the right of mutual reception of exiles. The citizen of state *A* could settle in state *B* and become a citizen there, a course men often took to escape penalties

in the state of their birth. This was no small degree of freedom, and was more highly valued than the full Roman franchise. It was enjoyed by a few cities such as Praeneste Tibur and Neapolis, which had obtained their treaties at times when their adhesion was specially valuable to Rome. But the great bulk of the Allies were in a much less favourable position. Their treaties varied, but in general the subordination of their interests to those of Rome[1] was clearly marked. How far the citizens of the Treaty-states enjoyed the 'private' rights of *commercium* and *conubium* with citizens of Rome or other Treaty-states is one of the most doubtful points in Roman history. Perhaps in this respect also there was[2] variety. It is hardly credible that the old Roman policy, of isolating those whose union seemed dangerous to Rome, was abandoned after the settlements of the Latin and Hernican towns [338, 306].

220. A special class of Allies, with peculiar privileges of their own, were found in the so-called Latin colonies. We have already spoken of the practice, common in Italy from very early times, of founding new towns as fortresses to guard border districts and secure newly acquired territory. Rome had founded such strongholds in partnership with the Latins and Hernici. After the Latin and Hernican Leagues were broken up and the several towns had become either Roman *municipia* or Treaty-states, Rome must have felt the want of a body of trusty allies specially attached to her, as the members of the old Leagues had been. It is not to be wondered at that she went on vigorously founding Latin colonies, creating, as Beloch says, a new Latium. For these colonies stood to Rome in the same sort of relation as the old Latin cities had done formerly: only they were not members of a joint League : their connexion was with Rome, not with each other. Their military character was clearly marked from the first in the ceremonies of foundation. Three commissioners appointed by decree of the Assembly, acting under a charter (*lex*) approved for the purpose, conducted the colonists in military array to a place carefully chosen on land acquired by Rome, and there, after solemnly marking out the line of the walls, established them as a *civitas*, sovran in its internal administration, but bound to perpetual alliance with Rome. Latin colonies were founded sometimes on the seaboard, but more often inland. They were closely connected with the road-system : roads and fortresses helped to support each other. As they were

---

[1] In some of them Rome had even the right to keep a garrison, as at Tarentum.

[2] Beloch, *der Ital. Bund* p. 222, seems to have come to this conclusion, but thinks that in most cases the Allies had the *conubium* both with each other and with Rome. I doubt this, and the reference to ὁ τῆς ἐπιγαμίας νόμος in Diodorus XXXVII 15 is in dramatic context, not a very serious authority.

generally planted[1] in districts where they had hostile neighbours, former owners of the soil, round about them, it was necessary that the number of colonists should be large. The 2500 sent in the cases of Cales and Luceria seems to have been too small: Interamna Sora and Carsioli had each 4000, Alba 6000: the distance and importance of Venusia required 20,000. Like those old Latin towns that were not incorporated with Rome, these new 'Latins' shared the 'private' rights with Roman citizens, and old and new made up the favoured class of Allies known as the 'Latin name.' We may shew the situation in a table:

$$socii \begin{cases} \text{old Latins} \\ \text{new Latins} \\ foederati \text{ simply.} \end{cases} \begin{array}{l} nomen\ Latinum, \text{ who are} \\ foederati \text{ and something more.} \end{array}$$

All are *peregrini*, and their territory *ager peregrinus*.

221. The colonists were drawn from various sources. After the break-up of the old Leagues and confiscation of much Latin and Hernican land, some of the dispossessed people were no doubt available for the purpose: but this supply must soon have failed. Allies from the Treaty-states were also admitted, and probably in increasing numbers. A considerable percentage however seem to have been Roman citizens. By going to a Latin colony they became 'Latins.' But the Roman franchise was in this period not yet (as it was later on) greatly sought for its incidental advantages, and the passionate desire for a vote as a vote can hardly be traced in Roman history. And the allotments of land to Latin colonists were large: so the poorer Roman gladly exchanged his old franchise for that of a colony-town with Latin Right, in order to secure a substantial farm. It appears that the citizen of a Latin colony was allowed to migrate to Rome and become a Roman citizen, provided that he left behind him in the colony a son to represent the family. But this right was further restricted[2] later on, perhaps from 268 onward. The restrictions would be expressed in the charters of the later foundations: and, if this change really took place, we have in it a warning of the more oppressive treatment that was to come.

---

[1] I do not mean that they were planted in uninhabited spots. But when an existing town was made a Latin Colony it received a new population and started afresh.

[2] That is, beginning with the case of Ariminum. See Cicero *pro Caecina* § 102. I believe the view of Mommsen *R. H.* book II cap. 7 to be sound, though it has been questioned. See Index, *Colonies*.

222. COLONIES OF THE PERIOD 366—265 B.C.

Period	Citizen colonies	Latin colonies	Where situated	Remarks
Period 366—38	338 Antium ...	... ...	Volscian coast	Refounded as a citizen colony in connexion with the Latin settlement.
Period 337—03	329 Anxur ...	334 Cales ... 328 Fregellae... 314 Luceria ... 313 Suessa ... 313 Pontiae ... 313 Saticula ... 312 Interamna ... 303 Sora ... 303 Alba Fucens	Volscian coast ... ... N. Campania Volscian coast Volscian land Apulia Auruncan land Volscian island-group Campano-Samnite border Volscian land Volscian land Aequian land	
Period 302—282	296 Minturnae ... 296 Sinuessa ... 283 Sena Gallica ... 283 Castrum Novum	299 Narnia ... 298 Carseoli ... ... 291 Venusia ... 289 Hatria	S. Umbria Aequiculan land Coast of Aurunco-Campanian border Apulia Picenum ager Gallicus, coast of Umbria Coast of Picenum	
Period 281—65		273 Cosa[1] ... 273 Paestum ... 268 Ariminum 268 Beneventum 264 Firmum ... 263 Aesernia ...	? Coast of Etruria Coast of Lucania ager Gallicus, coast of Umbria Samnium Picenum Samnium	This is a continuation of the policy followed at Beneventum, and really belongs to this period.

1 It has been held that the colony Cosa must have been in Lucania or Campania. But a careful consideration of the evidence led me

223. On the face of it the position of the Allies was not a bad one. In their internal affairs they enjoyed much freedom, and the prevention of wars[1] between the various cities and peoples no doubt promoted the general prosperity of Italy. In practice all disputes were referred to the arbitration of Rome. The duty of furnishing contingents to the Roman armies was not so onerous as the maintenance of forces to defend their separate freedom. The maximum contingent of each state seems to have been fixed by its treaty or charter : it was recorded in a covenanted assessment (*formula*). Copies of the *formulae* were enrolled at Rome, and requisitions for troops were addressed by the Roman magistrates to those of the several states. Only in case of dire necessity was the whole contingent called out. The *census*, which included the preparation of the service-roll, was in the case of the Allies conducted by the officials of the several states. For each state had its own laws, though it might by its own act adopt Roman law. It had its own constitution, and there was no general constitution of the whole confederacy, nothing analogous to the Latin League of early times. But the influence of the Roman model was no doubt widely felt in the allied states. And, in case of internal dissension, the wealthy minority, who had most to lose by disturbance and were liable to depend on external support, knew that they could count on the sympathy of Rome. And so Rome could generally count on their services.

224. But if the yoke of Rome was not heavy, judged by the standard of conquerors in the third century B.C., if the presence of a dominating and organizing power gave to Italy a new security against the assaults of external enemies, it was a yoke none the less, and as such no doubt galling. In these early days of Roman supremacy, when the yoke was lightest, there was still the fresh memory of former independence. Conscious of the danger from ambitions fostered by such memories, the statesmen of Rome pursued a policy calculated to break up any cohesion existing in peoples connected by affinity of race. They made their separate treaties either with single cities or with the smallest possible groups of tribes or townships. Thus the single city was the unit in Etruria, Umbria, Western (Campanian) Samnium, in the Iapygian districts of the South-East, and the Greek cities of the coast. The Sabellians of central Italy, Marsi, Paeligni, Marrucini, Frentani, Vestini, were received each as a single people. So too were the Pentri, to whom the name Samnites was now specially applied: so the Hirpini beyond them to the South-East, the little confederation[2] of cities in Southern

---

[1] The phrase of Vergil *Aen.* VI 852 *pacisque imponere morem* is classic.

[2] Nuceria and its dependent confederate towns. See Map below § 310

Campania, and the Lucanian and (probably) Bruttian town-confederations. Besides, the units where dangerous were cut off from each other and kept under observation by Latin colonies, each with a solid block of territory, as Beneventum between the Pentri and Hirpini. And across Central Italy ran a belt of territory now held by Roman citizens with Latin colonies to North and South of it, a block designed to keep Etruria and Samnium apart. And thus there was no doubt as to the real subject position of the Allies. Fair words were used, but the decision of all questions of peace and war rested with Rome. Treaties of commerce and alliance with foreign powers were made by Rome. It seems too that after 268 the right of Allied states to coin[1] in their own name was restricted, probably not in all cases at once. But the difference in the position of Rome's various subjects was sure to tell in her favour as time went by. The half-citizens might look forward to the attainment of the full franchise: of the Allies, the most depressed might hope to rise, the privileged would fear to fall. Cooperative rebellions were discouraged, and the subjects gradually became used to circumstances and fitted into their places in the great system. And under the training of manifold experience the Roman Senate developed the supple tenacity that made it the most efficient public body in the politics of the ancient world. Judged by the possibilities and standards of the age, the ruler of Italy was worthy of her crown.

---

[1] See below § 227 as to the coinage of silver at Rome. Beloch *Ital. Bund* p. 213 suggests that what was done was to limit the currency of local coinages to their several districts. Then the Allies, bound to pay their own contingents wherever serving, would find it convenient to use money of general currency instead of their own local coin.

CHAPTER XX

225. WE shall in due course come to a time when the old Roman People, the conqueror of Italy and winner of the lordship of the Mediterranean lands, is either dead or scattered or degenerate. What remains of it will be found wholly unable to act as an effective political force: its great name will be fitfully and inconsistently usurped by a worthless mongrel rabble, and a greedy and wasteful nobility. Such a Roman People could never have rivalled the great achievements of the past. It is therefore necessary to review however lightly the condition[1] of Rome and the Romans in their golden age, when Roman virtues were at their height, and when Rome became the Head of Italy but had not yet claimed the primacy of the world.

226. Most of the old Patrician clans seem to have been still in existence, and Plebeian clans had grown up in imitation of the old model, at least among the wealthier Plebeians. But the political importance of the clans was a thing of the past. They were kept alive by social and religious traditions, and by common rights under the civil law. Peculiar customs survived in particular clans: thus the *gens Cornelia* clung to the ancient practice of burying not burning their dead right down to the time of Sulla: in one clan the ladies[2] never wore garments of linen, in another they eschewed ornaments of gold. That great institution the Roman family was still in full vigour. The normal state of things was that the father of the house attended to the farming of the family land and performed the duties laid upon him by the state, while the mother managed the house and taught her handmaidens to spin the wool. Slaves there were, male and female, and the wars no doubt had increased the supply. But the institution of slavery had not reached the brutal industrial stage, in which the slave is worked like a modern machine, a productive chattel, bringing in an economic profit. Speaking generally, he was the servant[3] of the family, not a mere item of an owner's

---

[1] The help got from the *Staatsverwaltung* and *Privatleben* of Marquardt, and from Middleton's *Ancient Rome*, in this chapter is of course great.

[2] Pliny *N. H.* XIX. 8, XXXIII 21.

[3] See Pliny *N. H.* XXXIII 26, 27.

capital. Skilled slaves worked as tradesmen for the profit of their owners, but this system was not yet organized on a large scale. The place of the clients attached to great houses in earlier times was now occupied by freedmen : for emancipation seems to have been frequent, indeed we hear[1] of a law passed in 357 imposing a tax on manumissions. The government of the household was still on the ancient model : the power of the father, the dignity of the mother, were its chief features. A new form of marriage, of Plebeian[2] origin, which did not necessarily place the wife in the full power of her husband, was now in use. But the power (*manus*) could be acquired after marriage in a definite legal way, and it is not to be assumed that there was in this period any effective diminution of marital control. The old elaborate form, which required the presence of certain great priests and ten witnesses representing the community, still survived among Patrician families, kept up by sentiment and by the rule that only the offspring of such marriages were eligible for certain religious functions. Obedience of children was a matter of course. Education, narrow, practical, and unprogressive, was a family matter. It consisted mainly in a kind of apprenticeship, the sons following the father, the daughters the mother : the rudiments of reading, writing &c. might be imparted by a slave : the real formation of character rested with the parents, enjoining reverence for ancestral custom (*mos maiorum*), the great corner-stone of Roman morality. Thus were built up the self-sacrifice and patriotism that marked the Romans of the golden age. But this glory was bought with a price, for it was associated with a rigidity, an unadaptability incapable of necessary change, the evil effects of which were in due time destined to appear.

227. The houses of this age were simple, even in Rome itself. Thatched roofs had probably disappeared, at least in towns, but we hear[3] of wooden shingles in use down to the time of the Pyrrhic war. A ground floor and nothing[4] above it was the regular scheme, and the accommodation of the ordinary house consisted of one large room or hall (*atrium*) out of which small bedchambers and offices opened. In this hall were the images of the household gods, the hearth with the family fire, and, in the case of distinguished families, the waxen masks of famous ancestors, kept in cupboards near the door. It was not the custom among the Romans to wall off a part of the house for the women only, as was common in many Greek states : the

---

[1] Livy VII 16 § 7.   [2] See §§ 46, 49, 66, 92 above.
[3] Pliny *N. H.* XVI 36.
[4] Tradition supplies few traces of houses with upper storeys. The *tertia contignatio* in Livy XXI 62 § 3 is on the low ground of the *forum boarium* (B.C. 218). No doubt it was in the lower parts of the city that high building first began.

Roman matron moved freely in her domestic sphere and was not
a toy.   In all houses of any importance there was a money[1]-chest,
and some provision was made for the keeping of records of family
interest : where members of the family had held offices of state, public
official documents, left in their hands, were commonly preserved
among their family records.   Nor must we forget the account-books,
for to keep accounts carefully was one of the first duties of a Roman
father.   To know his exact financial position, to keep and increase
the family estate, was his pride : to be shiftless, to leave the estate less
than he found it, was a recognized disgrace.   Meals were few and
simple : little fleshmeat was used, and food was taken sitting.   Of the
fruits of the earth wheat was the staple grain.   The earlier spelt [*far*]
was passing out of use.   Oats served for feeding domestic animals.
Barley was in use, but of ill repute as a food : to be put on a barley
diet was in later times a military punishment.   Grinding corn and
baking bread seem never to have wholly superseded the old plan of
beating grain in a mortar and making a porridge of the meal, particularly in rural districts.   Garden vegetables were consumed freely :
beans lentils peas onions garlic leeks cabbage gourds pumpkins
lettuces fennel mustard and a host of others supplied the Roman
table.   Of fruits there were the fig and the grape : and the olive was
now well established in Italy : there were also various nuts.   But the
great advance of gardening and the introduction of numerous foreign
vegetables and fruits belong to a later period.   Nor were Italian
wines yet famous.   Flesh, as that of the wild boar, came sometimes
from the chase : and we find the swine and the goose domesticated :
but pork was largely cured and smoked so as not to call for immediate
eating but to be ready for festival days as required.   Bacon [*laridum,
lardum*] was a time-honoured dish.   Fish seems as yet to have been
hardly used as food.   The goat and sheep were chiefly valued for
their milk and wool, the ox and the ass for their labour.   To kill the
ox for food was long regarded as wicked.   Milk was an important
article of diet.   Honey supplied most of the needs now met by sugar.
Salt was prepared by evaporating sea water in pans on the coast :
the salt-pans by the mouth of the Tiber were one of the earliest
acquisitions of Rome.   In short, there was abundance of necessaries
but little in the way of luxury, and women were forbidden the use
of wine.

---

[1] A silver coinage began at Rome in 269, no doubt necessitated by the conquest of Italy,
particularly of the Greek cities.   The *denarius* (= 10 *asses*) was practically the equivalent of
the Attic drachma, a coin widely current in the Mediterranean, and doubtless well known
in Rome.   Silver had long been used by weight.   See below, §§ 249, 403, for the later
changes in the currency.

228. The sound simplicity of life was shewn also in the clothing of which the almost universal material was wool.   Country folk doubtless made much use of skins.   Linen was used to some extent, but apparently more in Samnium than in the Roman districts : we hear of it also as a writing material [*libri lintei*].   Spinning and weaving were already well-developed arts : dyeing probably less so, but the crimson borders of the garments of the young and of official robes shew that it was not neglected.   Shoes were of leather, and varied with the sex age or position of the wearer.   The regular underclothing of both sexes was a kind of woollen jersey [*tunica*] the shape and name of which seem to have varied with time.   The over-garment was the flowing gown [*toga*], worn originally by both sexes, but perhaps now giving place to the long frock [*stola*] in the case of women.   Weather and convenience suggested additions to this equipment.   For manual labour the *toga* was laid aside : and the working folk did not wear it at all.   For war it was girt up in a special way, and was eventually discarded for a more convenient[1] uniform.   But it was the proper costume of the Roman citizen in public, and so it remained.   The Roman Allies throughout Italy, liable to service in the Roman armies, were officially styled *togati*, the wearers of the gown.   The use of valuable ornaments seems to have been very rare. The man's ring was of iron ; of gold only when he was acting in a public[2] capacity, as that of ambassador, on behalf of the state.   But we hear of complimentary crowns of gold granted in honour of con- spicuous bravery in the field.   Gold ornaments were worn by ladies, and the use of the metal was clearly growing.   That we hear of golden spoils taken from Samnites and Sabines need cause no wonder: a metal of high value, not yet used in coinage, was not only a likely ornament but a means of hoarding natural to rude peoples, and we meet it again in the golden collars of the Gauls.   Hair was worn long, and beards : but the razor was a very old invention.   Its common use belongs to a later age.   Shears or scissors are said to have been introduced in 300 B.C. from Sicily.   Ostentation in funeral ceremonies was checked by law as early as the Twelve Tables.   But a funeral in an illustrious family was a great affair.   The most characteristic feature was the presence of the famous ancestors of the deceased.   Men wearing their portrait-masks, and dressed to represent them, went in the procession to the platform in the Forum, where they sat and listened to the family representative descanting on the merits and glories of him who had just gone to join their company in the

---

[1] The *sagum*. Varro *L.L.* v § 167 says the name is Gaulish.   Livy VII 34 § 15 mentions *sagulum gregale*, x 30 § 10 *saga*.

[2] Pliny *N. H.* XXXIII 11.

spirit world of ancestors.   We are of course dealing only with the
case of the great houses: little ceremony would be used in funerals of
the common sort: but Rome was no home of levelling ideas, and in
social matters the great houses were Rome.   In country districts too
all things would be in a simpler style: but the citizen, wherever
resident, was a citizen of Rome: Rome was the centre and the
type.

229.   But agriculture was the great Roman industry, and it seems
to have been in a generally healthy state during this period.   We
hear much less of dearth distress and debt than in earlier times.
Attempts were made by laws to restrict the rate of interest on loans:
in 357 to 10 %, in 347 to 5 %, in 342 to abolish interest altogether.   In
326 or 313 some restrictions[1] were placed on the power of the creditor
to imprison the debtor: the exact details are uncertain.   Much of
this legislation must have been futile, but it seems to indicate that
capital was more abundant, the rate of interest tending to fall, and
the poorer citizens fully awake to the chance of bettering their condition.   Something, probably not much, may have been effected to
the farmers' benefit by the working of the Licinian laws.   But the
increase of the Roman territory through conquest was the main
thing.   Assignations of land to individuals went on freely from time
to time: large blocks were set apart for Latin colonies, in which
Romans settled: plenty was left to increase the state domain-lands,
chiefly monopolized by the rich.   Thus the clamorous Plebeians were
in great part removed from Rome and its neighbourhood, while the
nobles enjoyed the perquisites of power.   The system was not likely
to last for ever, but for the present it did not work badly, and the
agricultural interests on the whole were doing well.   The holdings
were generally small: the typical Roman of the period was a yeoman
tilling his own land with the help of his sons and it might be a slave
or two: hand-work of this kind was honourable.   To this age belong
such stories as that of the great Manius Curius, found cooking his
meal of herbs by the envoys from Samnium, and refusing the gift of
gold that they had brought.   The public approval of frugality is
recorded in the renown of Fabricius.   Not content with a simple life
and incorruptibility amid the temptations of Pyrrhus, he is said as
censor to have struck off the roll of the Senate an ex-consul, whose
offence was the keeping ten pounds of silver plate.   However much
the legends of this period may have been overcoloured by the later
Romans, eagerly seeking an effective contrast to the degeneracy of
their own day, they shewed a true instinct in admiring these farmer-
heroes.   It was the true strength of Rome that victory sent her

[1] Livy VIII 28 Weissenborn.

soldiers to the plough and mattock, while the public danger could at
short notice recall them to the javelin and the sword.   The Republic
sometimes had soldiers: it always had men.

230.   A number of trades were carried on in Rome and elsewhere,
but mostly on a small scale.   The cobbler tanner carpenter potter
smith were everywhere, the goldsmith as needed.   Weaving and
baking were departments of home life: the piper and the butcher
were needed for the service of the gods.   The shops seem to have
been generally wooden booths open to the street, easily put up and
taken down.   The sedentary trades were not held in honour like the
tillage of the soil.   It was recognized that such a life unfitted men
for the toils and hardships of war: and to bear a part in national
defence was a man's first duty to the state.   Only in great emergencies
(as in 329) were the operative and artisan classes[1] called out for
military service, and it seems that they were equipped by the state.
The trade products were meant for the home market, and were
probably of an ordinary kind.   Goods of a higher class were no
doubt already imported from abroad.   Phoenician Etruscan and Greek
merchants brought cargoes to Ostia and it is not to be doubted that
there was a brisk traffic on the Tiber.   It is most unfortunate that
we have hardly any record of this traffic, which was of great importance in promoting the development of the city of Rome.   That there
was some Roman shipping and some seafaring population is certain,
but the numbers were small.   In peace as in war, the advance of
Rome was directed to the mainland of Italy.   And, though many
citizens in this period left Rome to settle on the conquered lands,
though the blood-tax of the long wars was heavy, still the city itself
was growing.   The population was still fertile, and the capital attracted
men from other towns and country districts.   Citizens of note, such
as Senators, were obliged to keep houses in Rome and to spend
much time there, in order to discharge their public duties: round
them gathered the slaves and freedmen of whom we hear in this
age.   We must think of the city as mainly a collection of low buildings in narrow streets.   The commonest material was sun-baked
bricks [*lateres*], apt to collapse when reached by a Tiber flood, for
fires were not the only peril in Rome.   A platform[2] in the Forum,
from which Magistrates (or others by their leave) addressed the
people, was probably rebuilt in this period, and near it a space[3]
was marked off and fitted up for the proper accommodation of

---

[1] Livy VIII § 20.

[2] The so-called *rostra*, adorned with the beaks of ships taken at Antium. Livy VIII 14 § 12.

[3] The *Graecostasis*, Varro *L. L.* v § 155, compare Justin XLIII 5 § 10.   The name is significant.   It is supposed that the Greeks of Massalia were the first foreigners thus favoured.

envoys from foreign states. To enumerate the various public buildings is beyond our scope. But those meant for secular purposes must
have been very few in number. Of temples there were already a
good many. Several were built in this period in discharge of vows
made during some great crisis : others came down from earlier times.
Small shrines and chapels abounded in the city, some of them very
ancient. But preeminent among religious buildings was the Temple
of Jupiter on the Capitoline hill. The god, whose other temples laid
stress on various special attributes, appeared here as the great divine
president, protector of the Roman state. Juno and Minerva shared
the temple with him. Public works of general utility were not lacking.
The main streets at least were paved, and a system of drains carried
away some of the city refuse or at least enabled flood-waters to run
off. Aqueducts[1] were beginning to pour into the city the boon of
pure water. And all round the city ran the great wall attributed
to king Servius Tullius, while beyond the river on the Janiculan
hill was a fort, occupying a point of vantage and watching against
the coming of an enemy. Walled lines formed a sort of covered way
connecting it with the famous pile-bridge over the Tiber.

231. This very meagre sketch must suffice to convey the impression that Rome in the period of the conquest of Italy was not
a place of any great splendour. There was as yet no sign of a conscious effort to give it that character. Stone had from the first been
used in large squared blocks for the fortification of some of the hills,
and later in the wall of Servius. It was used to construct the
footing-platforms of public buildings, and no doubt their walls also :
but the stone in use was a rough coarse-grained conglomerate of
volcanic ash and sand. Its quality varied : the tufa [*tophus*] of Rome
itself was liable to waste with the weather and needed a covering
of stucco. The 'pepper-stone' [peperino] of Alba or Gabii was better
in every way, but had to be hauled several miles. All stones of
this kind were easy[2] to cut, but did not readily lend themselves to
the finer works of architecture : the use of harder materials seems
to have come in with Greek influences, and perhaps was already
beginning. That the use of concrete, the normal material of construction in the later Rome, was already known, can hardly be
doubted : but its free use on a large scale belongs to a time when
facing materials, such as baked bricks [*testae*] or hard stones, marbles

---

[1] The *aqua Appia* 312, and the *Anio* (*vetus*) begun 272 by M'. Curius, using the spoils of
the Pyrrhic war towards the cost, but not completed for about ten years. See Frontinus *de
aquis* 6. These were led underground till they reached the city, like those of Syracuse and
Samos. See Thuc. VI 100, Herod. III 60.

[2] Hence *saxum quadratum*. Cf. Livy VI 4 § 12, 32 § 1, X 23 § 12.

&c. were at command.   The famous Roman mortar played but a small part in the earlier buildings.   Wood was easy of transport, and extensively used.   Even in the Capitoline temple so much was wood that its chief peril was that of fire.   The columns were far apart, after the Tuscan manner, so that even the architrave was necessarily of wood : no stone beam could have stood the strain of so wide a span.   Artificers from Etruria built the temple and supplied the statues and ornaments of terra cotta both inside and out.   The casting of bronze was another art introduced by Etruscan workers. We hear of statues in public places, and in particular of a group, the she-wolf suckling the twins Romulus and Remus.   The bronze wolf of the Capitoline Museum is thought to be the original figure. Painting as a mode of decoration was not unknown.   The frescoes of the temple of Salus (304—2) were painted by a Fabius, who was thence styled Pictor, and the name became hereditary : from this family came the first Roman historian.   Before we leave the topic of materials I must say a word about the use of the arch.   That the early Romans could and did build arches is true.   This knowledge may also have come from Etruria.   But that the arch became the leading principle of Roman architecture has been shewn to be untrue. By the time when the arched form became common, the use of concrete had been perfected, and what looks like an arch is nearly always a single mass, cast in one piece.

232.   We get now and then a glimpse of the common trouble of primitive communities, helplessness in dealing with matters affecting the public health.   There is reason to think that the practice of sloping roofs inwards [*compluvium*], so that they dripped into a tank [*impluvium*] below, afforded a breeding-place for mosquitos and promoted infection[1] with malarial fever.   We hear of pestilences, sometimes recurring for several years together, and carrying off numbers of all classes.   Sometimes the sickness extended to country districts.   In the absence of professional physicians, religious ceremonies were employed to appease the gods and allay the general alarm.   But the prohibition of burials within the city wall, the introduction of a good water supply, and the general simplicity of diet were perhaps the most effective influences of a sanitary kind.   In 331 the number of deaths was great, and a female slave gave information of a widespread conspiracy of poisoning among Roman matrons.   Many men of position had lately died with a striking likeness of symptoms, and panic fear prompted the reception of the evidence.   Twenty ladies are said to have been caught with poisons in their possession, and to have committed suicide : others (170) were seized and con-

[1] A little book *Malaria* by Mr W. H. S. Jones has lately called attention to this.

demned, no doubt to death. But it may all have been a horrible
mistake: accusations of poisoning were always readily believed till
modern science provided tests. Nor must we forget the oppressive
belief in Prodigies. Any strange occurrence, magnified or conceived
by imagination, was held to portend something, probably some evil,
and to read its meaning and apply the proper treatment [*procuratio*]
was a confessed and urgent need. The fall of a thunderbolt, an
earthquake, showers (real or supposed) of earth stones milk or blood,
moisture appearing on an image so that it seemed to sweat, human
sounds detected in the lowing of an ox, the birth of deformed
monsters,—such events and many others, called for instant expiation.
A regular system of rules for dealing with such manifestations grew up
under the direction of the Pontiffs, who kept their lore to themselves
and found in this superstition a great source of power. Religious
festivals played an important part in Roman public life, and there
were already a good many of them in the year. The keeping of the
calendar was a matter of public importance. When festival days,
unlucky or 'black' days were subtracted, the rest were available
wholly or in part for legal proceedings : only on some of these[1] could
Assemblies be held. The knowledge of the lawful days was another
instrument of pontifical power. The Pontiffs were also the repositaries
of legal tradition, and indeed the first keepers of a sort of public
record in their year-books [*annales*]. They alone were fully acquainted
with the forms of pleading under the statutes [*legis actiones*], in which
a minute accuracy had to be observed if the litigant was not to lose
his case on a technical flaw. It was too much. At the instigation
of the bold Patrician reformer Appius Claudius a blow was dealt at
their monopoly. In 304 Gnaeus Flavius, a dependant of his, published[2] a sort of 'citizen's handbook,' shewing the lawful business-days
throughout the year, and giving the properly-drafted forms of pleading
required in the courts. He is said to have picked up the knowledge
bit by bit, in a course of patient attendance in court and of systematic consultation of the pontiff-lawyers. It would seem to have
been the work of years. Though the Pontiffs still kept a grasp of
the law, the rise of a class of non-priestly lawyers was made possible
by this enterprising step. The hero of the story was the son of
a freedman.

233. We must bear in mind that the public life of Rome was
passed in the open air. The processions of religious festivals, the
games of the Circus, the military processions of the Triumphs that
celebrated victory in war, were naturally outdoor functions. But so

---

[1] *dies comitiales.*

[2] See Livy IX 46, where the other references are given by Weissenborn.

also were the informal meetings [*contiones*] in which the citizens listened to speeches and the formal Assemblies in which they gave their votes. The Magistrates discharged most of their duties under the open sky: halls [*basilicae*] for the holding of law-courts were not yet built. The Forum, and particularly the space known as the Comitium, was the chief centre of public life. Facing the Comitium was the Curia or Senate-house. The Senate alone met indoors. Any building within the city precincts would do for the purpose, if duly sanctified by the taking of auspices. But the doors of the building stood open during the meeting, unless some pressing emergency called for a secret debate. Early hours—it was usual to begin business with sunrise—were suggested by the heat of the climate: but many things could not be despatched in a hurry, and from the utterances of later writers we may infer that the Romans of this simpler age patiently endured much discomfort from the sun and dust. One is inclined to wonder how such work as that of law-courts could be carried on amid the noise of the streets. But wheeled vehicles for passengers seem to have been unknown or forbidden in the city. Ladies and the sick or aged might be borne in litters, but the barefooted slaves moved with silent tread. Drays and carts for transport of goods there were, but the aediles would no doubt see to it that they did not interfere with the transaction of public business. We hear also of special carriages used for processional purposes; but when these were in use there would be no public business going on. And in general the magistrates had ample powers for keeping order: shop-folk and hawkers could at need be silenced. Self-control and respect for constituted authority were characteristic of the Romans in their best days: even in moments of excitement the city, compared with Greek cities, would seem orderly and calm.

234. In such surroundings the young Roman of good family grew up. Reared in the stern unchallenged discipline of home, he willingly attended his father as he went through the duties and occupations of the day. Thus he learnt by actual observation at an impressionable age what things were enjoined or forbidden by ancestral custom. The exact formalities of sacrifices and other religious ceremonies, the dates of festivals and the like, the order of proceedings[1] in Assemblies for elections legislation or judgment: the competence of the various magistrates and minor officials, and the nice distinctions of official etiquette: the usages of the law-courts, the forms of buying and selling, of transfer and contract: episodes of the registration, if a Census was being held, or of the military

---

[1] Whether the sons of senators had in this period already begun to accompany their fathers to the sittings of the House, is not quite clear.

levy, if preparations were on foot for a campaign : these and many other matters would from time to time be present to his eager eyes and ears : he would ask questions and receive explanations, and by the time he was himself of age to begin his career of public functions he would have acquired a considerable store of experience and precedent. As he laid aside the games of childhood, his chief sports were running and riding on horseback in the Campus Martius and swimming in the Tiber. With the completion of his sixteenth year he became a man of military age [*iuvenis*], liable to be called out for service. From that time onwards he remained actually or potentially a servant of the state, at first as a soldier, but more and more in a civil capacity as years went by. His ambition was to be a Roman of Romans, to excel in representing a type of which he and his comrades were not unreasonably proud. And the nobles of this period, judged from this point of view, were as a rule efficient and sturdy patriots, worthy of the support of the sound Roman People, the farmers of the country side.

235. In short, the training of the men who led Rome was good and practical within its own narrow range. It served to build up the Roman power at home : it sufficed for the conquest of Italy. The history of the next 200 years will shew how insufficient it was for producing men of light and leading to deal with greater struggles, with ever-widening interests, and with new and complicated problems of state. The inability of Rome's generals and statesmen to understand new circumstances and meet new difficulties will often be painfully apparent : the strength acquired in the present period alone enabled her to last through conflicts with inferior powers, in spite of atrocious blundering and the needless sacrifice of hundreds of thousands of men : unconquered by foreign foes, the Republic staggered on, to fall under a Monarchy, merely because of political incapacity within. Whether a true intellectual stimulus, a love of inquiry and learning for its own sake, would have saved the Roman Republic, we cannot tell. We can see clearly that the contemptuous indifference to knowledge in and for itself, the confusion of the Seeker with the Dreamer—which was the common Roman attitude—had an evil effect in blinding men's eyes to the true significance of events, and in checking the development of genius. Hence the monotonous series of Roman heroes, good local worthies, all of one type, among whom Appius Claudius the Patrician reformer may pass for a great and original man. We have now to tell how Rome won an empire and shewed herself unfit to rule it.

BOOK IV

ROME AND CARTHAGE

CHAPTER XXI

CARTHAGE

236. UPON the fame of the Phoenicians[1] as the greatest traders of antiquity it is unnecessary to dwell. Nor are we concerned here with their ventures in the eastern Mediterranean, their submission to Persian overlordship, and their competition and collisions with the Greeks in the regions of the Aegean. What bears directly upon Roman history is their systematic occupation of the western Mediterranean, by the spread of their trading-factories and colonies reaching from Malta and Sicily to the strait of Gibraltar and beyond. The district in which they took root most firmly was in the middle of the north coast of Africa, where their settlements throve greatly. Of their collisions with the colonial Greeks of the West we have spoken already. At first both parties suffered from lack of combination. With the Greeks this was an essential feature of their political life: each city claimed to be an independent state. To the more strictly commercial Phoenician it was probably a matter of all-engrossing importance to keep a sure hold on his profitable markets. To attain this end he might well acquiesce in some limitation of local freedom. Accordingly we find that a sort of concentration took place. An union of Phoenician towns was formed, enabling joint resources to be used for common ends. At the head stood the great city of Carthage. As was only natural, the power of the central city tended to grow, and presidency became empire. The concentration and skilful direction of Phoenician resources checked the advance of the Greeks, and enabled the Carthaginians to strengthen their hold on the coasts of northern Africa and Spain. The success of their policy attracted attention everywhere: the stability of their

---

[1] My obligations to O. Meltzer's *Geschichte der Karthager* in this chapter are great, and call for special recognition. There is a good account of the Carthaginian constitution (a very obscure matter) in Mr W. L. Newman's *Politics of Aristotle*, Vol. II, Appendix B.

constitution was a subject of interest to Greek political inquirers in the fourth century B.C. It was held to resemble the much-discussed constitution of Sparta in several respects, particularly in that the real power was normally in few hands, that it was 'mixed,' containing monarchic oligarchic and democratic elements, and that neither anarchic mob-rule nor unconstitutional monarchy (tyranny), the bugbears of Greek political thought, had disturbed the even course of state life. To Plato Aristotle and others it seemed that here was a barbarian community the institutions of which deserved the serious consideration even of Greeks. It is a sad pity that we have no connected account of the Carthaginian republic handed down to us. What we have consists either of criticisms, the true bearing and worth of which we are often through our ignorance of details unable to gather: or of incidental references in writers of very various credit, the expression of which is often loose and the interpretation disputed. What we do really know is very little.

237. The regal element in the constitution was present in the form of two yearly magistrates, the Suffetes, resembling the Roman Consuls rather than the lifelong Kings of Sparta. That the Suffetes had once enjoyed greater powers than we find assigned to them, is highly probable: they may originally have held office for life. We have however no trace of a true regal period, a government of single Kings: to infer such a state of things from the old Phoenician monarchies, such as Tyre and Sidon, is tempting, but perhaps hardly justified. The body in which the chief political power centred was the Council or Senate. We meet with them as a body of 300 members, but the real conduct of state affairs rested with a sub-committee (30 in number[1], apparently including the Suffetes) of the most influential men. This inner Council or Senate proper met often and was in practice the government: the remaining 270 or outer Council seem only to have been summoned on special occasions. Membership was no doubt sought, for it stamped a man as an active member of the ruling class. The Council then stood for the aristocratic or oligarchic element. Over against it was the mass of humbler citizens who formed the Assembly, clearly to be distinguished from the unenfranchised mob of resident or passing aliens, freedmen, and slaves, who were no doubt a large part of the swarming population of Carthage. Few matters came before the Assembly, and these either carefully prepared by the Senate or referred to the popular body because Suffetes and Senators could not agree: for in case of their agreement it was not necessary to consult the Assembly at all. Public trials of state criminals seem to have been unknown. In elec-

---

[1] Perhaps originally a select 10 out of a total of 100.

tions it seems probable that names were submitted to the Assembly by resolution of the Senate, or at least some kind of check placed on the free action of the popular body. But what really paralysed the apparently democratic element of the constitution was the open and recognized bribery, what Aristotle calls the purchase of offices. There is no trace of a group-system such as existed at Rome: probably the Carthaginian citizens voted by heads in one mass, like the normal Ecclesia of a Greek democracy. Yet the Assembly seems never to have made itself supreme in the state. At the time of the wars with Rome its power had grown greatly under the leadership of the famous Barcid family, but this did not lead to democracy. It would seem that the influence of the Barcids shewed itself in causing more questions to be referred to the people than had been the custom hitherto. It seems also that in the Carthaginian Assembly speeches were delivered and new proposals made in the course of debate: it is all the more remarkable that the governing class was never really overthrown. This may have been partly due to an institution compared by Aristotle to the Spartan Ephorate. The court of the Hundred (strictly 104) is said to have been set up in the 5th century B.C. as a check on the great family of Mago, then predominant in the state. They were a select body of Senators, originally appointed to call the magistrates to account for their acts. But they gradually assumed wider functions and in the later days of Carthage seem to have generally controlled the government. But we shall hardly form a fair judgment of the working[1] of the Carthaginian system unless we make allowance for the effect of seafaring commerce. The mass of the common citizens were no doubt often on the move; and, if we reckon those who were at any time afloat, those just embarking on or returned from a voyage, we may guess that a large percentage of the whole took but a secondary interest in politics. Here was a fine field for bribery, and the power of money was the most permanent influence at Carthage. Connected therewith was the admissibility of reelection to office and the lax system by which it was allowable to hold several offices at once. It was probably the reform of these abuses that was eventually undertaken by the great Hannibal.

[1] I omit from the text, as beyond my subject, the Canaanite religion. Baal or Moloch the Sun, with his human sacrifices, Astarte Ashtaroth or Tanith the Moon, with her licentious worship, Melkarth the so-called Tyrian Hercules, Eshmun the healing god, were the chief divinities. Carthage was no doubt a chief centre of dark Phoenician superstitions, and we may well believe that religion was a means of controlling the masses. A learned and brilliant attempt to give a picture of this side of Punic life will be found in Flaubert's *Salammbo*. Many of the Punic names imply the favour of Baal Astarte or Melkarth. Such are Adher*bal*, Hasdru*bal*, Hanni*bal*, Mahar*bal*, Bo*star*, Ge*star*, Bo*milcar*, Ha*milcar*.

238. The Carthaginian empire at its height may be sketched in outline as follows. First, there was the great city itself. We are told that at the outbreak of the third Punic war (149 B.C.) it had a population of 700,000. If this figure includes all classes, it is credible. The citizens have been estimated at from 200,000 to 300,000. In the crisis of 310, when Agathocles invaded Africa, about 50,000 citizens were serving under arms. At all events the city was very populous. Next came the Phoenician towns with Utica at their head, once free allies of Carthage, now subject-allies with considerable powers of local government. These were as a rule strongly fortified, though not to be compared with Carthage itself. Thirdly there were towns and districts where dwelt the half-breed race called Libyphoenicians. These were favoured subjects, and seem to have shared rights of intermarriage and holding of property with their Phoenician rulers. Fourthly there were the subject Libyans in the province directly under Carthaginian rule, carefully watched for fear of their rebellion. Outside of the Home-province lay the bulk of the lands in which Carthage had a greater or less interest. There were allied tribes kept under her influence by trade-connexions and judicious management of their chiefs. This was a common relation in the North-West coast lands of Africa and the South of Spain. Fortified stations, some of them considerable cities, were planted in well-chosen spots on the seaboard: and through these colonial centres, carrying on a brisk trade with the interior, a number of the native peoples were more or less closely connected with Carthage. The utmost jealousy was shewn in the exclusion of foreign traders from access to these ports: and it seems that this exclusion was gradually made more effective by compelling all traffic with the West to pass through Carthage itself, even that from the Phoenician cities. Much the same practice, the control of an unconquered interior by means of a monopoly on the coast, seems to have been followed in Sardinia and Corsica so far as possible, and in the Balearic isles. In Sicily such a policy was out of the question. From her strongholds in the West of the island Carthage ruled and influenced what she could. But she left her subjects more freedom here than elsewhere, and dealt more kindly with her allies: many natives, and some Greeks, preferred[1] her rule to a Greek dominion in its usual form of a military tyranny: nor was the later rule of Rome a change for the better. Indeed there seems to be no reason for thinking that the government of her dependencies by Carthage was bad, judged by the standards of the time. The degrees of subjection and the forms of control no doubt varied greatly according to local circumstances: the subjects were on the whole as loyal as could be

[1] See Diodorus XIV 41, 55, 58.

expected of subordinate peoples exploited in the interest of a great commercial concern. It was rather in the Home province that the danger of Carthage lay. Here the yoke pressed more heavily. To raise a Libyan or Libyphoenician revolt was easy for an invader: the rich estates of the Carthaginian nobles lay open to plunder, and swarms of desperate slaves could be let loose upon the land. Even the walled Phoenician cities might under great pressure desert their mistress.

239. To support her system and perform her imperial tasks Carthage always needed a great revenue and not seldom great armies. The revenue was chiefly got from tributes and customs dues. The armies consisted of (a) citizens (b) contingents of subjects and allies (c) mercenaries. The first had no doubt done good service in earlier days, though the Phoenicians were not a military race. But with the attainment of empire it became more and more the custom to do the work of war by deputy. Citizen troops were only called out in desperate emergencies, or as a general's bodyguard. The governing class supplied officers: the mass of citizens (perhaps partly for political reasons) were left to lose by disuse their aptitude for war. The subjects and allies furnished contingents of various size and character, from the infantry of the Home province to Balearic slingers, and in the later period the famous Numidian horse. But more and more the rank and file came to consist of mercenaries raised among the warlike barbarians of Spain and Gaul, Liguria and Sardinia: till 306 B.C. even Campanian Samnites were freely enlisted in the service of Carthage. Sometimes she employed Greeks, whose splendid capacity she well knew: they were in the market, but rather dear. So a Carthaginian army was in general a motley gathering of hired ruffians without common national feeling, scruple, honour, or shame, hard to bring under discipline, unsteady in defeat, brutal and cruel in the hour of victory. To command such a force was a dreadful task, and it seems that generals in the field had ample powers. They might incur vast losses of men without remonstrance from the Home government, for the blood of mercenaries is not meant to be spared. But it was not the custom to pardon failure: crucifixion or impalement were often the lot of unsuccessful leaders at the hands of the 'Hundred.' If we are to believe hostile tradition, it was wise for even a successful general to dissemble his successes: the jealousy of the ruling class was dangerous to provoke. The last remarks apply equally to admirals of the fleets of war.

240. Of the naval power of Carthage it is most difficult to form a just conception. Tradition attests the skill and enterprise of her seamen, and there is no doubt of their eminence as navigators. But

the handling of a war fleet as a fighting force was a different matter, and the record of naval warfare with Greeks and Romans hardly justifies the high reputation of the Punic navy. The Western Greeks seldom placed on the water a fleet of the first order : when they did, they were generally able to hold their own. The Romans, conscious of their inferiority, followed Punic models in shipbuilding : but, when they had got the ships, they had on the whole the better of the fighting, and ended by gaining the upper hand at sea. If we had fuller information concerning the crews of Carthaginian war ships we should probably find a simple explanation of their failure. It seems certain that the headquarters of the fleet, if not its only important station, were at Carthage. Here was the great arsenal and dockyard. It was a part of imperial policy to centralize naval administration : other cities were relieved of the burden of keeping up local fleets : Carthage found in her responsibility for their protection a guarantee for their obedience and a pretext for exacting tribute. But it does not appear that the Punic fleet, or any great part of it, was ordinarily[1] kept in commission, as was that of Athens in her imperial days. The ships were there, with oars and tackle, no doubt : whence came the crews ? The normal warship of the third century, the quinquereme, needed[2] 300 rowers, and we hear of a Punic fleet of 350 ships. How were a mass of more than 100000 men raised and formed into effective crews ? That all or the greater part were drawn from the Commons of Carthage is surely incredible. If we believe that hirelings and slaves formed a large part of the ships' companies, we have a reason why fleets were not kept ready for service but fitted out and sent to sea in a hurry. To keep such a throng of doubtful characters hanging about the port, perhaps for months, while they were being taught to act together, could hardly be the policy of the jealous rulers of Carthage. We must add 120 men per ship as the fighting crew, whether citizens or not, apparently not a match[3] for Roman soldiers. The navigating officers seem to have been worthy of their great repute as seamen : in other respects we shall do well not to think too highly of the navy of Carthage. The writers from whom we draw, even Polybius, were under strong temptation to enhance the achievement of Rome.

241. Into the vexed question[4] of the treaties between Carthage and Rome it is impossible to enter here. Early in her history Rome

---

[1] See Index under *Naval Powers*.   [2] Polybius I 26.   [3] See Polybius VI 52.

[4] There is Mommsen's discussion, printed in Vol. I of the English translation of the History, that in Mr Strachan-Davidson's *Polybius*, and the relative passages in Meltzer. The present section is not seriously affected by the adoption of any of these views, which do not invalidate the general conclusions.

had been on terms of friendship, perhaps of alliance, with the Greeks of Massalia.   Still earlier, Carthage was leagued with the Etruscans to check Greek encroachment in the West.   It is not in itself incredible that the great trading city should have made a treaty with Rome as early as 509 B.C.   Polybius[1] declares that the text of such a treaty existed in his time.   We hear[2] then of treaties or at least embassies in 348, 343, 306.   So far as the contents of these are given, it appears that regulation of trade and definition of the commercial spheres of the two powers were the chief points dealt with : protection of their respective allies and mutual abstinence from piracy also came in.   The commercial jealousy of Carthage grew with her empire : in the later treaties Roman merchants were more carefully excluded from the ports of the West.   The embassy of 343 may perhaps indicate an attempt to secure a footing in the markets of Campania, then passing under Roman control.   The exclusion of the Romans from Sardinia is perhaps partly due to their having tried to found a settlement there, if that story be true : and the same may hold good of Corsica after the fall of the Etruscan power in 311—308.   The old allies of Carthage in Italy were seen to be a broken reed : naturally we find her shop-keeper-rulers prompt to make the best available bargain with a rising power.   Lastly there comes the treaty of 279.   This seems to have been an actual alliance : it was directed against Pyrrhus, and has been spoken of above.   But by this time the two parties were conscious of their own inevitable rivalry : and the failure of the Epirote king was certainly not brought about by hearty cooperation of these insincere allies.   Pyrrhus is said to have foreseen that they must come to blows over Sicily.   To secure her province there, it was clear that Carthage must complete the conquest of the island : and this Rome's policy and honour alike forbade her to permit.   A solid Punic Sicily would be a menace to her hold on Italy : and she was now in effect the head and leader of the Western Greeks.

---

[1] Polyb. III 22—25.
[2] See Livy VII 27, 38, IX 43, Diodor. XVI 69, Orosius III 7.

CHAPTER XXII

FIRST PUNIC WAR, 264—241 B.C.

242. IN 264 B.C. the smouldering antagonism between Rome and Carthage[1] blazed out into open war. This war dragged out its weary course till the peace of 241, a slow and clumsy struggle stubbornly fought out between rivals well aware of the great vital interests at stake. We are fortunate in having a sketch of it from Polybius, one of the most trustworthy of ancient historians, who wrote about the middle of the second century B.C., when evidence was still plentiful and traditions fairly sound. For convenience sake it may be treated in four periods or sections: (*a*) the early victories of Rome and her appearance as a naval power at the battle of Mylae in 260, (*b*) her advance, and invasion of Africa, ending with the great disasters of 255, (*c*) slack and fitful warfare, till the great Roman victory at Panhormus in 250, (*d*) the exhaustion of the Roman forces in the fruitless siege of Lilybaeum, and the improvement of the Carthaginian position by the exploits of Hamilcar Barcas, till the destruction of the Punic fleet in 242 leads to the conclusion of peace.

243. The immediate occasion for war was found in the Mamertines of Messana. These freebooters were constantly disturbing the quiet of Sicily. The exact details of what happened are not clear, but it seems that Hiero of Syracuse undertook to chastise them, and was in a fair way to capture the city. A party of the Mamertines sought the help of Carthage: this was granted, and the citadel was once more occupied by a Punic garrison. They were now able to withstand Hiero, but meanwhile the situation had been complicated: another party had turned for help to the rulers of their native Italy,

---

[1] In this chapter I have mainly followed the narrative of Polybius, whose chief authorities were Philinus a pro-Carthaginian Greek from Sicily and Fabius Pictor on the Roman side. See Polyb. I 14, 15. Livy's books 16—19 survive only in brief epitomes. The late writers (Florus, Eutropius, Orosius etc.) who drew from Livy had, it is now admitted, before them not the full text but an epitome now lost. Valerius Maximus abstracted many illustrative stories from Livy. Fragments of Diodorus remain. He seems to have been much influenced by Philinus. Attempts have been made to restore the Livian version by ingenious critical examination of the Livian epitomes and copyists. The results are summed up, with references to the extensive literature of the subject, in Max Schermann's *Der erste Punische Krieg* etc., Tübingen 1905. That Livy drew from Fabius Pictor and other annalists, and gave the Roman view or views, is certain.

offering to place Messana under the protection of Rome. Rome was on friendly terms with both Carthage and Syracuse, and she had quite recently purified her own side of the strait by destroying the nest of mutineers at Rhegium. The Mamertines had no sort of claim on her for support. But the danger of allowing all Sicily to pass into the hand of Carthage, as it must if Messana were left to its fate, was great and imminent. Was the work of the last hundred years to be put in jeopardy merely because the turn of events or the clever intrigues of a rival power had made the Roman case seem a bad one? Great powers, we know, are not apt to refrain from their manifest destiny or immediate interest through regard for the quibblings of legality. And the power that had wriggled out of the compact of the Caudine Forks was equal to the occasion now. The Roman Senate, in all decency and order, could not see its way to the resolution that necessity required: they left the decision to the Assembly: and the Assembly, stirred up no doubt by the memory of past sacrifices and the hope of coming gains, voted to succour the Mamertines. Scruples now were laid aside, and consuls and Senate made ready for the war.

244. The presence of the Carthaginian garrison does not seem to have made their cause more popular in Messana. The Roman party gained ground, a Roman agent stole across into the town, and the Punic commander was induced by trickery and threats to withdraw his forces and encamp outside. Carthage and Syracuse came to terms, and besieged the city together. But, before they could take it, the consul Appius Claudius Caudex was at Rhegium. The ways of the wind and tides in the strait had been studied: and, disregarding the threat of Hanno, that 'he would not let the Romans so much as wash their hands in the sea,' Claudius made the passage by night. He soon changed the situation. A proposal, that the assailants should raise the siege on certain terms, being declined by both Hiero and Hanno, the consul first turned upon the Syracusan forces and defeated them. While they fell back upon Syracuse, next day he utterly routed the Punic army. The siege was effectually raised, and this success was followed up by an attempt upon Syracuse. This move, however, was a failure. In 263 both consuls were sent to Sicily with their armies. Numbers of cities came over to the side of Rome: and the sagacious Hiero himself made overtures of friendship, which were readily accepted. He remained Rome's loyal ally till his death in 215, giving much useful help at need: and Rome could command the maritime resources of another great Greek city. Dismayed at this turn of affairs in Sicily, the Carthaginian government raised a great army of mercenaries in Spain Liguria and Gaul, and set themselves to restore their power in the island. The great city of Agrigentum was made their headquarters and occupied in force. In the next year (262) the Romans laid siege to it. They suffered several reverses, and only the timely help of Hiero averted famine : but they held on, and destroyed a force sent to relieve the besieged. So Agrigentum fell. The Punic general cleverly drew out his troops and escaped : the Romans sacked the town, and with a barbarous unwisdom sold as slaves the wretched people, who had had no choice in the matter of resistance to Rome. Thus a chance of winning general goodwill in Sicily was blunderingly lost. The elation of the Senate and people at the successes of the Roman arms inspired a hope that Carthage might now be turned out of Sicily altogether. But it was remarked that the coast towns still adhered to Carthage, in fear of the Punic fleet : and the occasional descent of marauding expeditions on the Italian seaboard reminded the Roman statesmen that to attain their objects the first necessity was a fleet of their own.

245. We are told that they had not a single battleship : hitherto they had made the passage in vessels borrowed from the Greek cities of Italy. Such craft served for running the blockade of the strait, but were not fit to meet the battleships of the period on equal terms. At last a Carthaginian quinquereme ran aground in the ardour of a chase : she was promptly secured as a model, and the problem was solved. The shipwrights addressed themselves to their task with such energy that in sixty days time from the hewing of the timber a Roman fleet of 120 ships (100 of them quinqueremes) was ready for sea. The tale is highly coloured in the course of boastful tradition, but that a great and successful effort was made is clear. While the work went on, the crews were got together and taught to row on dry land. Great wooden stages, with benches built exactly like those on board the ships, were erected, on which the men learnt to swing in time and make the various movements in obedience to the call of the boatswain. Polybius[1] records this without a suggestion of doubt : and indeed the only serious difficulty is the enormous strength that must have been needed in these skeleton ships, if they stood the strain of 300 men swinging together. But the difficulty could be met if clearly seen, and it would be more clearly seen then than imagined now. That ingenious minds were at work in this business is manifest from the invention of the 'ravens.' To counteract the better equipment of the enemy's ships and their superior skill in handling them, it was desir-

---

[1] Polyb. I 21. It is not clear that this plan was a new invention, and it seems certain that it was used afterwards. In Dion Cassius XLVIII 51 § 5 we hear that Agrippa (37 B.C.) having collected his oarsmen, ἐπὶ ἰκρίων ἐρέττειν ἤσκει. For ἴκρια = 'stages' see references in Liddell and Scott.

able to reproduce on the water so far as possible the conditions of a
fight on land. Grappling irons for catching hold of an approaching
vessel were at least as old as the fifth century: the idea was now
carried further. In the bows of a Roman ship was set a stout post or
mast. Revolving freely on this as a pivot was a wooden gangway,
easily raised or lowered by a rope running in a block at the mast head.
It projected some 24 feet from the mast, and at its outer end had on
its under side a large iron spike. This was the raven's beak. The
gangway was hoisted on going into action. When an enemy charged,
it was let go. The spike held fast in his deck long enough for the
Roman soldiers to board, and hand-to-hand fighting[1] took the place of

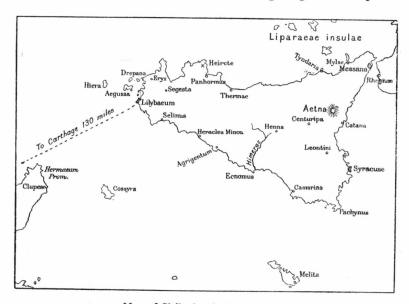

Map of Sicily for the Punic Wars.

nice manœuvres in the decision of a naval battle. The Roman fleet
now put to sea. It began badly. The consul Cn. Cornelius Scipio,
who was in command, started in advance with a small squadron, with
which he was ingloriously captured by a ruse of the enemy. Next
the Punic commander fell in with the main fleet, and in his turn lost
a number of ships through his own carelessness. Duilius the other
consul now took command. Sailing round the N.E. corner of Sicily
he found the enemy near Mylae, with a fleet larger than his own, and

---

[1] We find the same situation reproduced in the great civil war 49 B.C., when the clumsy
ships of the Caesarians defeated the superior fleet of the Massaliots by their stability and the
tactics of grappling and boarding. Caesar *civ* I 57—8.

confident of easy victory. But the 'ravens' served Rome well: Carthaginian tactics were foiled: they took to flight, having lost 50 ships, and their boasted naval supremacy was at an end. Minor operations in the West of Sicily closed the year 260, and Duilius on his return to Rome received, beside the honours of a triumph, exceptional distinctions. In particular a column[1] adorned with the beaks of captured ships was set up in the Forum, to commemorate Rome's first naval victory.

246. Rome was now ready to stretch out her hands across the water. The presence of Carthage in Corsica and Sardinia had no doubt long been silently resented. An expedition[2] now visited these islands and achieved some successes against the Punic fleet. The commander of the latter, Hannibal by name, had managed to escape punishment for his defeat at Mylae: he was now fully qualified for crucifixion, and received it from the enraged survivors of his force. The war in Sicily dragged on (259), but the Romans held their ground with difficulty. And about this time we come upon an obscure[3] story (which can hardly be dismissed as an invention) of a conspiracy among the crowd of captives and slaves (and a body of Samnites with or among them) assembled at Rome for the service of the fleet. It was betrayed and came to nought. But we may perhaps infer what is in itself probable, that slaves, prisoners and pressed Allies supplied many (perhaps most) of the rowers in the ships of Rome. It was a service detested by all, and the higher duties, requiring nautical skill, were probably entrusted to Greeks. In 258 a war of sieges went on in Sicily, and several places were won for Rome. But the consuls could not take Panhormus, and by the fortification of Drepana and a concentration on the western strongholds the position of Carthage was strengthened. This was due to a Hamilcar[4], who had been sent to Sicily after the fall of Agrigentum. Next year (257) a Roman fleet, fitted out for the capture of Lipara, fell in with the enemy off Tyndaris, and an indecisive battle was the result. But the Romans had now lost their dread of Punic skill, and were planning to carry the war into Africa. Great preparations were made on both sides, for the Carthaginians, well aware of the defenceless state of their Home province, were anxious to forestall the Roman design by beating their

---

[1] The inscription on the *columna rostrata* (Wilmanns 609, Wordsworth pp. 170, 412) is now regarded as the genuine copy of the contemporary original. See Schermann p. 51.

[2] In 259 under the consul L. Cornelius Scipio, whose epitaph (Wilm. 538, Wordsw. p. 160) refers to it. Why Polybius (1 24) omits to mention the exploits of a Scipio, is hard to explain. See Schermann pp. 54—5.

[3] Not mentioned by Polybius. Orosius IV 7 § 12 and Zonaras VIII 11 probably got it through Livy and Dion Cassius.

[4] Not the famous Hamilcar Barcas.

fleet at sea and confining the war to Sicily. In 256 the great fleets
met off the headland of Ecnomus on the south Sicilian coast. The
Romans had 330 battleships and about 140,000 men: but were
encumbered by their equipment for landing in Africa. For instance,
they had horse-transports in tow of some of the battleships. The
Punic forces are given by Polybius[1] at 350 battleships with an
estimated strength of over 150,000 men: unencumbered, it would
seem. The tactics of both sides were of little moment, and again
handiness in manœuvring was of no avail against the 'ravens' and the
picked soldiers of Rome. At the end of the day the account stood
thus:—*Carthage*, over 30 ships destroyed, 64 captured: *Rome*,
destroyed 24, captured none. So after refreshment and repairs the
consuls resumed their voyage and landed near the town of Clupea (or
'Aσπίς), which after a short siege they took and occupied as a base of
operations. Plundering next engaged their attention: immense booty
in cattle and slaves was gathered in: but orders came from Rome
recalling one consul and the bulk of the forces. So L. Manlius sailed
home, and M. Atilius Regulus remained at the front with only 40
ships and an army of 15,500 men. He advanced laying waste the
country. The Punic generals handled their army badly and were
beaten by Regulus in a battle. Towns were sacked or drawn over to
the Roman side, among them Tunes near Carthage. Wild Numidians
were raiding parts of the Carthaginian dominions: the city, thronged
with fugitives, was in prospect of siege and famine: when to the
general surprise Regulus offered to negotiate for terms. The Roman
system of yearly change of commanders was the cause of this. The
proconsul was a poor man. His glory was everything to him, and he
preferred[2] to extort the submission of Carthage himself rather than
leave its actual capture (which seemed a mere matter of time) to the
credit of his successor. But he wrecked his own design by the severity
of his demands. Nerved by despair, the Carthaginians prepared for a
further struggle. And at this juncture a body of Greek mercenaries
arrived. Among them was Xanthippus, a Spartan skilled in war, a
man reared in the famous discipline which had kept its high repute
even in the decline of Sparta. This man soon noted the defects of
Carthaginian tactics. He gained public confidence, and was able to
improve the management of the army. The generals followed his
directions, and their superiority in cavalry and elephants was turned
to account by operations on level ground, ending in a crushing defeat
of the Romans and the capture of Regulus. Only a poor remnant

---

[1] Schermann p. 65 thinks the numbers of the forces given incredible.

[2] So Polyb. I 31. The Regulus-Xanthippus episode has left a mass of accounts varying
in almost every detail. See Schermann pp. 70—4.

escaped to Clupea. Xanthippus, it is said, knew better than to stay
in Carthage exposed to Punic jealousy : he took ship and went home.
The Carthaginians now invested Clupea, but made no headway with
the siege, and withdrew. The Romans got ready a fleet to bring off
the relics of Regulus' army, while the Carthaginians prepared one to
prevent them. But the Roman fleet was the stronger (350 to 200
sail), and gained a complete victory off the Hermaean cape, taking a
number of ships. They then embarked their comrades at Clupea, and
started on the homeward voyage, coasting along the southern shore of
Sicily. In this 'naval demonstration' the consuls persisted, though
warned by their pilots (Greeks, no doubt) of the treacherous nature of
the season and the scant mercies of a lee shore. The storm caught
them before they could double cape Pachynus. The seaboard was
strewn with corpses and wrecks : less than a quarter of the great
armada escaped. Polybius moralizes on the headstrong Roman
temperament, too stiff to make allowance for the irresistible forces of
nature. After this tragedy the rest of the year 255 passed without
important movements. Carthage was cheered by the news of the
disaster, and there was no prospect of peace.

247. From Carthage Hasdrubal was sent[1] to Sicily with all the
men that could be spared and 140 elephants. Since the defeat of
Regulus, in which they had borne a great part, the Roman legions
could not be got to face these animals : and from this cause their
operations by land were slack and timid for four years. Both sides
built new fleets : the Roman at least was active. In 254 the Punic
stronghold of Panhormus was attacked by sea and land. Part was
stormed, the rest surrendered : the work seems to have been for once
smartly done, and a garrison was left to hold this important post. In
253 the fleet sailed on a marauding expedition to Africa, and entered
the bight known as the Lesser Syrtis. We must remember that the
practical knowledge of these dangerous waters was in all likelihood
rare, perhaps confined to a few Carthaginian skippers. Falling into
shoal water, the foolhardy Romans found themselves stranded on
banks by the ebb of a local tide. In panic they threw overboard their
heavy things, and with help of the flood got their vessels off. But
they had had enough. They sailed back in haste to Panhormus, and
laid their course for Rome : but on the voyage more than 150 ships, a
good half their fleet, foundered in a storm. And now, weary of
maritime disasters, the Roman government ceased shipbuilding for a
time, and only kept a moderate squadron to maintain communications
with the forces in Sicily. The hopes of Carthage rose. Her army in
Sicily was now in good fighting trim, and her fleet was strong. But

[1] Not until 252, after the Romans had taken Panhormus. Schermann p. 79.

the command of the sea at this time, ascribed to her by Polybius, was
not so decided as to close the waterway to Rome. The few conquests
made by the Romans in 252 and 251 were all on the seaboard: one
was that of the island-town of Lipara. But meanwhile (251) the
growing confidence of Hasdrubal led him to advance upon Panhormus,
where the consul L. Caecilius Metellus was in command. Metellus
by the use of skirmishers lured the elephant-corps close up to the
town, plied them with darts, and drove them back in mad fury upon
their own lines. A well-directed sortie in force[1] turned the disorder
of the Punic army into rout and slaughter: the whole of the dreaded
elephants were among the prizes of this splendid victory. Carried
across the strait on huge pontoon-rafts, they adorned the triumph of
Metellus, and were butchered to divert the populace or to save their
keep. Hasdrubal, it is said, was summoned to Carthage and impaled.
At this time comes in the famous story (ignored by Polybius) of the
embassy[2] from Carthage to Rome, to treat for exchange of prisoners.
It is told how Regulus was sent to forward the business, on oath to
return: how he warned his countrymen to make no terms with the
enemy: how he went back to Carthage to face death under torture.
The tale has been coloured for the use of edifying by the poets and
rhetoricians of later days, but in its main outlines it may be true.

248. We have now reached the year 250—49 and with it the last
stage of the war. The central event is the siege of Lilybaeum. All
the operations are undertaken with reference to the attack or defence
of this fortress. At first the consuls pressed it hard with siege works
and engines of the usual kind. But after a certain point the defenders
under Himilco began to have the advantage. The mere bloodshed
was enormous. Nor could the Romans effectively close the port to
pilots who knew every reef and shoal of that dangerous coast. Reinforcements were thrown into the town, and the Romans had to fight
hard to hold their own lines. Their attempts to keep up a blockade
by sea were set at nought by a bold skipper who sailed in and out as
he chose: only the lucky capture of a peculiarly fast ship enabled
them to stop the blockade-running. A storm wrecked their siege-
works and the besieged set them on fire. After this[3] they settled
down to a simple blockade, and awaited the effect of time. The next
year (249) was disastrous for Rome. The consul P. Claudius Pulcher

---

[1] The battle was probably in 250. Metellus triumphed as proconsul in September. *Fasti
triumph* under year 504 AUC. The elephant is a common symbol on coins struck by Metelli.

[2] To judge from the epitomes it may seem that Livy (18 and 19) placed it before the
battle of Panhormus. But no certain inference can be drawn. Discussed by Schermann
pp. 90—9.

[3] We hear of much sickness and many deaths in the camp. Corn had run short, and
flesh diet brought on a plague. Diodor. XXIV 1 § 4.

set out with the fleet by night, in hopes of surprising and destroying the Punic fleet lying in the harbour of Drepana. The surprise failed, and the coolness and tactical skill of Adherbal gained a decisive victory. The consul escaped with a remnant[1] of his fleet, leaving 93 vessels in the hands of the enemy. Here we have another edifying story, not mentioned by Polybius, how Claudius disregarded the divine warning conveyed in the refusal of food by the sacred fowls, and wilfully sent his fleet to its doom. On his return to Rome he was impeached before the people and sentenced to a heavy fine. The Carthaginian admiral now delivered a counterstroke. He sent Carthalo with a fleet to Lilybaeum, where he found the Roman ships at anchor, and by fire and capture still further reduced their number. Carthalo then sailed along by the southern coast, in hope to intercept the fleet known to be coming with supplies for the Roman army in the West. He chased an advanced squadron and took a few ships, and went on to meet the main convoy under the consul L. Junius Pullus. The luck of Junius was worse than that of his colleague. Carthalo drove him to seek the land not far from cape Pachynus, and himself on the advice of his pilots doubled the cape, where his ships rode in smooth water : while the predicted storm burst upon the Romans, again helplessly exposed to the horrors of a lee shore. The Roman fleet was utterly destroyed, but some at least of the crews seem to have escaped. The men before Lilybaeum had now to be fed by overland convoys, for Rome was again in financial straits, and of late fleets had been built to little purpose. So she gave up ship-building on a large scale. Now was the time for Carthage to sweep the sea and cut off Sicily from Italy. But she did nothing of the kind, and the golden chance went by.

249. At Rome a dictator was appointed, the first for duty outside Italy : but nothing came of this. Junius by a sudden movement seized Eryx[2], the town and temple on the mountain that rises behind Drepana. But the pressure on Lilybaeum and Drepana, though creditable to Roman tenacity, was futile, both places being fed and relieved by sea. So the year 248 dragged on : marauding descents were made by Carthalo at various points of the coast of southern Italy. Such operations were at best useless, and we hear that his mercenaries became mutinous, their pay being in arrear. As the marooning of ringleaders on desert islets or their deportation to

---

[1] The other version, followed by Diodorus, makes his loss 117 ships and 20,000 men. This may serve as a specimen of the variations in the tradition of the war.

[2] According to Polybius I 55, he seized both the temple on the summit and the town a little below, but only left garrisons at the temple and at the foot of the hill. The temple post may perhaps be the one referred to in Zonaras VIII 16 as entrusted to some Gauls, deserters from the Carthaginian army.

Carthage did not quiet the rest, numbers were either butchered or thrown overboard, until order was restored. Meanwhile Rome was engaged in drawing closer the bonds of friendship with Hiero of Syracuse. In 247 the Carthaginian government made Hamilcar Barcas commander-in-chief in Sicily. He had not done great things as yet, but had in some way shewn himself a good officer. His present task was to uphold the cause of Carthage in arms under conditions[1] of the greatest difficulty. It was clear that vigorous naval activity on a large scale was not to be hoped for from the Home Government. Punic mercenaries were no match in pitched battles for Roman legionaries, who had ceased to stampede at the sight of an elephant. So he took the one course open to him and engaged in a guerrilla warfare, prolonged for five years by his genius. After ravaging the Italian coast, he suddenly seized Heircte[2], a natural stronghold of limestone rock, almost inaccessible, standing over the rich plain of Panhormus. Here, though detached from all regular support, he held the Romans at bay for years, raiding the country, harassing their forces with constant skirmishes, cutting up detachments, and causing them trouble and loss. Descents on the Italian coast were made now and then. At last, emboldened by success, he made a dash to the West and seized the town of Eryx. Here he had Roman forces above and below him, and full in view was the beleaguered Drepana. A complicated system of sieges was formed: and as time went by it became more and more clear that the weary wasteful struggle must go on till one side should cut the communications of the other by gaining command of the sea. Both sides were much exhausted. The Roman treasury[3] was empty, but patriotism found a resource. The wealthier Romans, singly or in small companies, provided 200 battleships built on the last improved[4] model. It was a voluntary extension of the old system of the war-tax, repayable if and when victory should enable the state to meet its obligations. The fleet was ready by the season of 242, and Gaius Lutatius Catulus, the consul in command, spared no pains to bring it to the highest state of efficiency. He held the harbour of Drepana, which the slack or over-confident Carthaginians had neglected to secure. Presently he had news of the approach of a Punic fleet under

---

[1] It is said that some of the mercenary Gauls deserted to Rome about this time, disgusted at their treatment, while Roman privateers did damage with impunity on the African coast.

[2] Monte Pellegrino.

[3] Pliny *N.H.* XXXIII 44 tells us that the Roman *as* was reduced in weight to a *sextans* (2 *unciae*), that is to ⅙ of the weight of the original *as*. A previous reduction not mentioned by Pliny, perhaps in 269 when silver was first coined, had brought it down to 4 *unciae*. See Index, *Coinage*.

[4] Polyb. I 59.

Hanno. It had got as far as the 'holy isle' (Hiera). It had on board supplies for the men at Eryx, and was poorly manned. Hanno's plan was to slip through to the landing-place of Eryx, discharge cargo, embark Hamilcar and some of his men, and only then to try, if necessary, the fortune of battle. Lutatius divined his object, and set out[1] to thwart him. Off the island Aegussa, with his ships and crews in perfect trim and a picked force of marines, he lay to and waited. At daybreak the breeze had freshened, foul for the Romans, fair for the enemy, who came on running before it under sail. The consul put out to meet them, resolved not to lose his chance for fear of a contrary wind. Sails and masts were lowered on the Carthaginian vessels, and the fleets closed in unequal combat. Ships, rowers, marines, all, thanks to the blind confidence or neglect of the government of Carthage, were inferior in the Punic fleet. The Romans sank fifty of their ships and took seventy, with nearly 10,000 prisoners. The rest got away, favoured by a change of wind. The war was at an end : one of the two game-cocks (to use the simile of Polybius) had been fought to a standstill at last.

250. Sulkily but promptly the Carthaginian government opened negotiations for peace, and wisely entrusted Hamilcar with full powers to make the best terms he could for his country. Meanwhile they crucified Hanno. Lutatius was very willing to treat for peace, knowing that his victorious fleet was but the last despairing effort of exhausted Rome, that there was no prospect of a speedy capture of Carthage, and that the glory of his achievement must either be reaped at once or left to a successor. On the other hand Hamilcar, the best general of the war, knew that he was helpless, cooped up in Sicily by the Roman fleet. He submitted to fate for the moment, and terms of peace were agreed to as follows :

(1) Carthage to evacuate Sicily,
(2) to make no war upon Syracuse,
(3) to give up all Roman prisoners without ransom,
(4) and pay in 20 years 2200 talents to Rome (over £500,000).

We may perhaps infer a clause dealing with the redemption of their own prisoners, as is indeed stated in one[2] tradition. But all was reserved for the decision of the Roman people. At Rome the draft treaty was doubtfully received, and ten commissioners were sent out to consider and settle matters in consultation with Catulus. Finally they raised the war-indemnity to 3200 talents, reduced the term of

---

[1] The battle *ad Aegates insulas* was fought on the 10th March 241. Lutatius was still consul, for the consular year at this time (see § 75) ran from the 1st May.

[2] Zonaras VIII 17, probably from Livy through Dion Cassius.

payment to ten years, and extended the evacuation-clause to include all islands between Sicily and Italy. So peace was made in 241. The Carthaginian forces were withdrawn to Lilybaeum, and thence shipped off to Carthage in lots, not all together. Hungry and unpaid, they had made a gallant fight for Carthage under the magnetic influence of Hamilcar. They now looked for their reward, and it was thought wise to give the Home government the chance of dealing with their claims in detail.

251. Polybius remarks that the war for Sicily or First Punic War displays the character and resources of the two rival states better than that which followed: and surely he is right. The Punic generals, if successful, were left in command for years together: the Romans were regularly changed year by year, so that a consul was often recalled just as he was getting to know his men and understand the conditions of his task. In the material of the armies we need hardly dwell on the manifest superiority of Rome. But here also the yearly system of reliefs was an obstacle to the attainment of the highest efficiency. We get a glimpse of its working when Regulus is left in Africa with an inadequate force. The Italian farmers disliked serving abroad, and it is doubtful whether the half-measure[1] of relieving only a part of the army each year gave satisfaction to all. It is not unlikely that Roman citizens were more favourably treated than the contingents of Allies. Greek help is probably to be detected on both sides in matters needing cleverness. But here Rome had the advantage, as being to start with more backward in mechanical inventions. It is usual to place Rome's naval victories to the credit of Greeks: and this may be granted so far as shipbuilding and seamanship are concerned. Massalia, Neapolis, Tarentum, Syracuse, allies old or new, not to mention lesser cities, no doubt gave great help. But the fighting crews were Romans, and the rowers must have been got together from any and every available quarter. The mere numbers required make this certain. The cost was surely borne to a great extent by Rome. But when Polybius reckons the naval losses of Carthage in this war at 500 quinqueremes, those of Rome at 700, we must not regard the 700 as all Roman in a strict sense, or the men who perished as all Roman citizens. Nor need we wonder at the goodness of the Roman navy. It is the badness of that of Carthage that is the curious and very significant fact, as has been pointed out above. The war did not develope a Roman prodigy: it did expose a Carthaginian sham. Unless a navy is steadily kept

---

[1] I think this may be taken as certain, though we have little direct evidence of it. The force left with Regulus in Africa and the long siege of Lilybaeum are clear cases of service beyond the ordinary season of campaigning.

up to fighting standard, and used boldly when occasion serves, it is useless.

252. The land of Sicily now fell into two unequal parts. First there was the kingdom of Hiero in the East and South-east. This was left independent, and every care was taken to please the faithful ally to whom Rome owed so much. The bulk of the island had passed under the dominion of Rome, and presented a new problem in government, how best to rule a transmarine district which could not safely be left to its own devices. We do not know the details of the arrangement first adopted, but we do know that the solution was found in the extension of an old Roman principle. Any public duty could be assigned to a state official as his 'sphere' or 'department' (*provincia*). Constitutional precedent required that he should have ample powers within his sphere during his tenure of office, and that the term of office should be a year. So Sicily was made the 'Province' of a Roman official, and a momentous step was thereby taken in the development of the Roman empire. It has been conjectured[1] that these early Governors were either nominees of the Praetor or elected by the Assembly for the special purpose. In any case some kind of charter or scheme was no doubt prepared under the direction of the Senate as a guide for the Governor. All the communities in the Province were not on the same footing. Thus Messana had called in Rome as protector, Panhormus had been taken by assault, while Lilybaeum was only acquired in virtue of the terms of peace. In general it seems that local governments were preserved, but the wealthier burgesses placed in power. A tribute ($\frac{1}{10}$ of yearly produce) was the regular impost: for Rome now began to tax subjects. There were also customs levied at the ports. But these tithes and tolls seem to have been retained from the old regime. The right of dealing and holding property (*commercium*) outside a man's own community seems only to have been granted to a very few favoured communities[2] which had joined Rome early. Whether *conubium* was allowed is uncertain. All arrangements were under the supervision of the Governor. No means were provided by which the Provincials could obtain redress of any oppression on his part. But the Senate of these days had some conscience, and a keen eye for the interest of Rome. No doubt a Tribune would have been found to bring an ex-Governor to the bar of the Assembly if he had injured the Roman state. And Rome was not yet absolute in the Mediterranean. To keep her subjects contented and prosperous was a matter of import-

[1] See Marquardt *Stvw.* I 243.
[2] Such as Centuripa. Mommsen thinks that this town was favoured that it might watch the Syracusan frontier.

ance. The Sicilian province was probably never so well administered under the Republic as in the first years of its existence.

253. However much we may suspect the traditional history of the war, coming as it does through Greek and Roman channels, of placing Carthage in an unfavourable light, we may discern some points in which Rome as a state was at this time superior to her rival. The relation of subject allies to the central power was in her case more wholesome, far removed from commercial exploitation, and in most cases smoothed by kinship. The administration was probably more honest, for Rome had not yet bowed to worship money. Consequently there was in general contentment, and on the whole unanimity, among the citizens. This hardly seems true of Carthage. We find two parties, in violent opposition to each other, spoken of as a matter of course at the time of the outbreak of the Second Punic war. These divisions must have taken time[1] to develope, and it is almost certain that they were at work during the first war. The shameful neglect of Hamilcar Barcas during his gallant struggle (247—2) is only explained on this supposition. A stray notice, which we have no ground for doubting, shews[2] us a great force operating in Africa against up-country natives. It names as commander Hanno, whom we meet later as Hanno the Great, leader of the Senatorial or conservative party. We are told that this war was partly undertaken by him in quest of glory, partly to keep his army employed; and this was at a time when Hamilcar in Sicily had neither money nor food for his men. Again, at the end of the Sicilian war, when it came to paying off the mercenaries who had with difficulty been induced by Hamilcar to wait for their due, the government made delay, and meanly tried to put them off with less than the proper amount. Hanno acted for the government in this matter, and there can be little doubt that base party intrigues were rife at Carthage, for which she paid dearly in the horrors of the Mercenary war. We are in fact getting stray glimpses of the stubborn opposition to the 'popular' party of which we shall hear later, a party which already existed, and whose hero was Hamilcar Barcas.

254. If we turn to the internal condition of Rome in 264—241, the few side-lights available seem to suggest a better state of things. Some things were not well: it was an evil precedent when in 264 Decimus Junius Brutus gave a show of gladiators in honour of his deceased father. But in general what we hear testifies to progress along the old lines and maintenance of sound national spirit. In 252 we find the first Plebeian raised to the office of Chief Pontiff: in the

---

[1] This point is well treated by Meltzer.
[2] Diodorus fragm. XXIV 10, referring to 247 B.C.

same year the censors purged the Senate by a strict revision, thus adding to its dignity.   In 246 we have the story of a gross insult offered to the majesty of the state by Claudia the sister of P. Claudius, author of the disaster at Drepana.   The brother was dead: the sister, vexed at the jostling of the crowd as she was returning from the public games, said 'it's a pity my brother isn't alive and commanding the fleet again.'   The unpatriotic sentiment is said to have been punished by a fine: to hint at such a method of clearing the streets could not, even coming from a lady, be treated lightly.   But it has already been pointed out that stories of the arrogance of members of the Claudian clan are justly suspected of being coloured, if not invented, by party spite in a later age.   In 243 Metellus, the hero of Panhormus, was chosen Chief Pontiff.   In the same year the pressure of legal business, ever increasing with the growth of Rome and the presence of many aliens in the capital of Italy, led to a wise extension of the magistracy.   A second Praetor[1] was to be appointed, to relieve the existing office by taking over all cases in which either litigant or both were aliens.   On this momentous change we cannot at this point dwell.   But its usefulness for the moment was delayed by an instructive combination of circumstances.   In 242 the special priest of Mars (*flamen Martialis*) was elected consul with Lutatius.   He would have gone to the war, but the Chief Pontiff, taking his stand on the religious law, forbade him to leave his priestly duties.   So in order to provide a second commander one of the newly elected praetors[2] was sent out with Lutatius, and this man, Q. Valerius Falto, was actually in command of the fleet at the battle of Aegussa, the consul being disabled by a recent wound.   Valerius is said[3] to have made claim to a triumph, but without success.   In relation to gods and men alike (*auspicium* and *imperium*) Lutatius stood first, and precedent, the embodied instinct of Rome, would not allow the responsible chief to be slighted through the luck of the subordinate.   But meanwhile a new precedent had been created: the increase in the number of praetors had enabled one of them to be employed out of Italy.   We shall see below that this practice was soon carried further.

255.   To illustrate Roman life and its ideals in this age no more striking passage exists than the abstract[4] of the laudatory speech delivered in 222 by the son of the Pontiff Metellus at his father's funeral.   He declared that the old man had aimed at ten things, objects of ambition to wise men, and had attained them all.   He was

---

[1] Livy epit. 19.

[2] According to the *Fasti triumphales* both these commanders triumphed in October, Catulus as proconsul, Falto as propraetor, but on different days.   If correct, this would seem to suggest a compromise.

[3] This is the story told by Valerius Max. II 8 § 2, probably from Livy.

[4] Pliny *N. H.* VII §§ 139—141.

(1) a warrior of the first order, (2) an excellent speaker, (3) a brave general. He had been (4) in responsible charge (*auspicio suo*) during the passage of great events, had (5) held the highest office (dictator 224) of state, was (6) distinguished for wisdom and (7) for his reputation as a Senator. He had (8) amassed a fortune by honourable means, he left (9) a large surviving family, and was (10) the most eminent Roman of his day. Such success, said the orator, was unique in the whole history of Rome. Here we have a picture of the purely Roman type at its very best. It is curious that no reference is made to the vigorous constitution which carried him to a remarkably hale old age, and was undoubtedly one of the main causes of his success. He became one of the familiar figures of Rome in his later years. In the year 241 the temple of Vesta caught fire. In it was kept the Palladium, a very ancient wooden image of the highest sanctity, the destruction of which would bring disaster upon the state. The Chief Pontiff himself rushed into the flames and saved it. But the fire got to his eyes and he never saw again. He was granted special leave to ride in a car through the streets to attend meetings of the Senate. A simple privilege, as was also that granted to Duilius—the escort of a torch-bearer and a flute-player to see him home at night whenever he supped abroad. To keep great merit ever in the public view, to provoke emulation in the young, were praiseworthy objects: and the spectacle of the Roman people, unable to produce men of striking genius, and continuing to be successful by the maintenance of sound moral qualities, is not without a peculiar grandeur of its own.

256. The traces of Roman movements in Italy claim a moment's attention. The colonies of Firmum (264) and Aesernia (263) are mere continuations and completions of the policy of the preceding period. The citizen colony of Aesium (247) and the Latin colony of Spoletium (241), in different parts of Umbria, seem meant to strengthen the hold of Rome in the North, in view of expected conflict with the Gauls. Very different are the citizen colonies Alsium (247), Fregenae (245) and Pyrgi (before 191, year unknown), all on the coast of southern Etruria. These are close to Rome, and seem to have been meant to protect the actual neighbourhood of the city from descents of Punic fleets. For some five or six years (248—3) Rome kept no large naval force of her own. The Latin colony at Brundisium (244) was a most important foundation. It turned the best harbour on the Adriatic into a Roman fortress. True, Rome's direct connexions with Greece and the East were as yet very slight: but thoughtful men might well foresee that the situation was not unlikely to change, and they would remember the visit of Pyrrhus. In short, the great war for Sicily did not prevent Rome from tightening her grip on Italy and preparing to meet future contingencies.

CHAPTER XXIII

ROME, HOME AFFAIRS 241—218 B.C.

257. BEFORE we turn to the story of the second Punic war a few points in the internal history of Rome must briefly engage our attention. In 241 two new Tribes were formed, bringing the total up to 35. This number was never exceeded: after. this, when new districts were added to the land of Rome, the citizens included were put on the roll of one or other of the existing Tribes. Hence, as time went by and citizens from districts not touching each other were enrolled in the same Tribe, the former local significance of the Tribes was lost, and they became mere arbitrary divisions. And it was either now or a few years later that a reform[1] of the system of the Centuries took place, by which the balance of voting power in the Centuriate Assembly was materially altered. Vainly do we look for any account of this great change: we only learn that there was a change, and that it came after the full number of 35 tribes was reached. As to the process by which it was effected, by an act of legislation, or by the mere exercise of the censors' powers on the occasion of a *census*, or by both: whether it was the outcome of agitating struggles or was carried through with general assent: strange to say, we have no tradition on these points. It falls within the period during which Gaius Flaminius was active as a popular leader, and we may fairly guess that he took an interest in the matter. If, as some have thought, he was the moving spirit in the reform, it is even more strange that we find no reference to it among the many passages in which Flaminius is mentioned: and the 20th book of Livy is lost. From expressions used in speaking of the Assembly of Centuries at a somewhat later time a few details as to the nature of the change may be timidly inferred.

258. First, if we set aside the Knights and the odd Centuries of engineers, musicians and supernumeraries, the Centuries of infantry (that is, the great mass of these bodies) were in future to be parts of Tribes, each Tribe containing so many Centuries. The five classes, and the division of Seniors and Juniors, remained as in the Servian

---

[1] The matter is discussed in Mommsen's *Staatsrecht* Vol. III, where the authorities (such as they are) are quoted. I confess that to me many points still remain obscure.

system. We naturally infer that there would be ten Centuries (two of each class) in each of the 35 Tribes. This accounts for 350 Centuries. Add to these the 18 Centuries of Knights and the 5 odd ones, and we have a total of 373. When however we think of them as voting-groups, and remember that by Roman custom an absolute majority was required for an effective result, we are somewhat staggered by the greatness of this number. Even in a legislative or judicial matter, where the issue was simple, not less than 187 Centuries had to vote one way to reach a decision. In case of strong opposition, the other 186 might all have to vote: and to take the votes of 373 groups in one day seems a large undertaking. But let us take a consular election of an ordinary type with four candidates for the two posts: each Century would vote for two consuls, and the number of possible votes must be put at 746. Out of the many possible distributions of the votes four will serve to illustrate the sort of difficulties that might or might not arise on a full poll.

	I	II	III	IV
Votes for A	200	200	200	200
,, ,, B	187	186	186	182
,, ,, C	186	186	185	182
,, ,, D	173	174	175	182
	746	746	746	746

In the first case the election of two consuls is achieved, the second man getting his majority by a single vote: in the other cases only one consul is elected, and the second place will have to be filled up by another voting, when each Century will only vote for one candidate. That such a system as this was deliberately established by practical men is indeed very hard to believe. But we do at least know that it was sometimes found very difficult to bring elections to a definite result; and this may have been partly due to the defects of such a lumbering machine. Beside this correlation of Tribes and Centuries, whatever were its details, it seems that the order of voting was also changed. Hitherto[1] the Centuries had been called to vote in a fixed sequence—Knights, Class I, Class II, and so on, till a majority had been secured. Henceforth, the first vote[2] was to be given by a Century of the first Class chosen by lot: after this, there

---

[1] Livy I 43 § 11, X 22 § 1.

[2] See Weissenborn on Livy XXIV 7 § 12, 9 § 3, XXVI 22, and on the erroneous anticipation in V 18 § 1.

seems to have been a fixed sequence. But we must remember that the tendency to follow a lead was a Roman trait, and that the use of the lot was a method of appeal to the will of Heaven. The example of the first-voting (*praerogativa*) Century had generally a marked influence upon those that followed : it was an object to secure its vote. If, as seems probable, the reformers acted in a democratic spirit so far as they made it no longer possible for the Knights and first Class to override all opposition, the introduction of the lot may have been due to a compromise. For to give a kind of sacred sanction to the vote of a group of wealthy citizens was hardly a democratic move.

259. Of the general working of this strange voting machine it is hard to form any notion. It is clear that the Centuries differed greatly in size : the elder and richer men would be fewer than the young and the poor. The percentage of voters present would no doubt vary a good deal : the citizens were already scattered widely, and those living far from Rome would seldom attend the Assemblies. Small attendance and skilful organization in detail enabled the machine to work somehow, and voting by Centuries went on at Rome so long as Assemblies remained of any importance at all. It is characteristic of Rome that much of the old military framework was retained, though Army and Assembly were now in practice quite distinct. What took place in connexion with the property-assessments of the Classes is by no means clear. But it seems that the fifth Class included those whose property was valued as low as 4000 *asses* (about £17). This was the limit qualifying for legionary service : the poorest citizens and freedmen were, except in great emergencies, only employed in the fleet. Freedmen appear to have been enrolled in all the Tribes (and therefore in the Centuries according to their property) just like the freeborn. But this was a purely censorial question, and it was probably in 220 that the Censors, of whom Flaminius was one, put them all into the four city Tribes. This checked their influence for the time, but their growing numbers gradually rendered all precautions futile, and the freedman-question was one of the standing troubles of the later Republic. We now see a Roman People divided into sections on three different principles, Locality, Wealth and Age. But the local cohesion of the Tribes was, as we have said, now beginning to be destroyed : limits of Age in the Centuries lost their meaning when Army and Assembly were no longer the same : Wealth indeed was a real distinction, but the Classes as such were not voting bodies. The line of cleavage between Rich and Poor became more and more marked as time went by, but it had no relation to the artificial divisions of the Classes.

Distant residence in time of peace, campaigning in time of war, kept great numbers of citizens from the use of their votes. Even if this had been otherwise, if every citizen had voted on every occasion, the system of group-voting, whether by Centuries or by Tribes, told strongly in favour of the minority, that is, the minority counting heads. In short, to repeat what must be repeated, there was no real organ to express the will of the majority of citizens. That the power of the Senate became greater and greater was, so long as that body remained sound, not a matter for either wonder or regret. The growth of the Senate's power was clearly felt, and the reformers of the period seem to have thought it excessive. In 218, or somewhat earlier, a tribune named Claudius, supported by Flaminius alone among the senators, carried through a law[1] forbidding any senator to own more than one ship of burden of ordinary size: this being reckoned enough for the transport of the produce of his estate. This law seems directed to prevent the real governors of the state from becoming a body of merchant princes. We can hardly help wondering whether reports of the corruption and misgovernment of Carthage may not have led the Roman reformers to this curious step: the effects of this exclusion of senators from direct participation in commerce and finance will be considered in a later chapter.

260. I have already mentioned the establishment of the separate Praetorship for purposes of jurisdiction in 367, and of a second Praetorship to deal with cases in which aliens were concerned, in 243 or 242. Of the influence of the Praetors on the development of Roman Law[2] we must speak below. What calls for remark here is their occasional employment for other purposes outside Rome. We have seen them commanding forces in war: and the spread of the Roman dominion, together with the increase of legal business at Rome, made it clear that more officials of high rank were needed for the discharge of public duties. Accordingly, in or about 227, we find the number of Praetors raised to four. Two of these were to act as magistrates in charge of the new departments (*provinciae*) outside Italy. Such was the origin of the series of provincial governors, who play so important a part in later Roman history. To each of them a quaestor was attached, who had charge of financial matters and was useful as a subordinate to whom other duties could at need be delegated. In this increase of the officers of state we see an attempt to secure efficiency, but the smallness of the staff compared with the business to be done still was, and continued to be, characteristic of the Roman state-system.

261. A few stray notices have come down to us which, though

---

[1] Livy XXI 63 §§ 3, 4, Cic. II *in Verr.* V § 45.   [2] See §§ 991, 1373—1377, and Index.

small matters in themselves, give momentary peeps at the life of
Rome in this period. After the close of the first Punic war Hiero
of Syracuse paid a visit to Rome. He was present at some public
games, and is said to have gratified the people by a great largess of
corn. There were precedents for such largesses in Greek cities, where
an idle populace welcomed the ostentatious bounty of contemporary
kings : but the recognition of an urban multitude as a body to be
courted and fed was a step of no good omen for Rome. In 225,
under the alarm of the Gaulish invasion, we hear of a horrid ceremony. A prediction was current that Gauls and Greeks would
possess Rome. To elude the prophecy by fulfilling it in the letter,
a man and a woman of each of these races were buried alive in one
of the public places of Rome. As human sacrifices did not in
historical times form a part of Roman religious usages, this sudden
outbreak of superstition is remarkable. Ihne is perhaps right in
attributing it to Etruscan influence. Another tradition[1] reports that
the first case of a divorce in Roman life occurred in the year 231.
This seems to be not strictly accurate : at least the lower forms of
marriage seem to have been dissoluble from a much earlier time.
But it may shew that divorces were hitherto very rare : and the story
is a striking illustration of Roman views of marriage. The husband
was very fond of his wife, but she was barren. Now at the census, in
reply to the censor's question, Carvilius had made declaration that he
had a wife 'with a view to a family.' Here was a case of conscience.
Roman-like, he called a council of his friends to consider the matter :
and on their advice reluctantly put the lady away. The man in him
revolted, but he had to remember that he was a Roman citizen. Why
he did not adopt somebody we do not hear, and the details given are
perhaps garbled in tradition. About this time one of the Vestal
virgins was condemned for unchastity. But we cannot fairly assert
that at present there was any serious change for the worse in the
morality of Roman life. It is perhaps an index of the development
of the city as a centre of population that in 219 the first free foreigner
settled there[2] as a practitioner of the healing art. He was a native of
Peloponnesus, Archagathus by name, and evidently of high repute.
He was made a Roman citizen, and a surgery found for him at the
public expense. Specializing in operative surgery, he had at first a
large practice : but the too ready use of knife and cautery made him
less sought after in his later years. As a rule the *medici* at Rome
were slaves or freedmen : the former were private property, and the
first duty of each was to keep his owner in repair : if they took
outside practice, it was for their masters' account. The ordinary

---

[1] Valerius Max. II 1 § 4, Gellius IV 3 § 2, XVII 21 § 44.   [2] Pliny *N.H.* XXIX 12—14.

practitioner of the later Republic was a freedman. All, or very nearly all, were Greeks.

262. In this period too we see the first beginnings of a Greek influence destined to have immense consequences. Rude lays and songs had not been lacking among the Italian peoples from early times. Even a kind of rough dialogue had been developed. But no epic like the *Iliad* or *Odyssey* had come to birth in Italy, and the uncouth attempts—to judge from what now followed—of the early singers were probably not of such merit that we need deplore their loss. A new movement began with the attempt of a Greek teacher to supply material for the use of his pupils in the form of a Latin translation of the *Odyssey*. This man, Andronicus[1] by name, seems to have been brought as a slave to Rome from Tarentum at the end of the war with Pyrrhus. On his emancipation by his master (a Livius) he would take the name Livius. He kept a school for many years, and produced a number of tragedies translated from the Greek. He lived to a great age, and was employed to write a sort of processional ode[2] for a solemn ceremony of purification in 207. The few fragments of his works that survive bear out their reputation for uncouthness. But a beginning, however rude, had been made. His younger contemporary, a Campanian named Cnaeus Naevius[3], also made versions from the Greek, but was best known as an original writer. His lampoons on great persons, such as the powerful Metelli, got him into trouble: even, it is said, into prison. At last he had to leave Rome, and seems to have spent his later years in writing his chief work, a poem on the subject of the first Punic war, in which he had fought when young. This was a sort of epic of Roman glory, written, not (like his plays) in metres borrowed from the Greek, but in the old 'Saturnian' verse, a native product of Italy. This poem may be regarded as the beginning and promise of a national literature that never came to fulfilment, being stifled by the inrush of Greek influence. The few fragments of Naevius indicate that the Latin language became in his hands a much more powerful instrument. He is said to have enjoyed the favour of the people, and it is on the whole clear that we are unfortunate in having so slight a record of a very remarkable man. The activity of Naevius was in part a protest against too servile adhesion to Greek models: he and Livius are in this respect a contrast. Both lived till near the end of the second Punic war. But it has seemed best to refer to them here, and not to mix them up with Plautus and Ennius, who belong properly to the next generation.

---

[1] See Teuffel-Schwabe *Rom. Lit.* § 94.   [2] Livy XXVII 37 § 7.

[3] See Teuffel-Schwabe § 95.

CHAPTER XXIV

FOREIGN AFFAIRS, 241—218 B.C.

263. THE short interval between the end of the first Punic war in 241 and the beginning of the second in 218 was not a period of rest. Each of the rival powers was subjected to the severest strain in warfare near home: each emerged victorious, and extended its dominions by conquest: in each the constitution of the state was affected by internal political struggles, of which we have clear indications but no satisfactory record. It will however be observed that the characteristic difference between the two states shews itself unmistakeably in these parallel series of events. The achievements of Carthage are due to the eminent abilities of the Barcid family, backed by the popular party, which gradually wins control of the government. They are the achievements of great men working under difficulties in a corrupt state. The old ruling class are still powerful in the Senate, and are able on occasion to hamper, if not to thwart, the action of the popular leaders. In order to guard against movements of reaction, it was necessary to keep the popular party together, in other words to pay for votes, and, when you had paid for them, to see that you got them. The achievements of Rome are due to the soundness of the state and the good practical working of a clumsy constitution, by which the direction of policy more and more passed into the hands of the Senate, the only body fitted for the work. They do not depend on the production of men of genius, but are carried out by men of fair ability, whose patriotism and sense of duty render them trusty agents to fulfil the designs of the great council. That there was an opposition party is seen from the career of Flaminius: but various indications make it probable that party-spirit was not so embittered as to lead either side to forget the interest of Rome.

264. We remarked above that the Punic mercenaries[1] were shipped from Sicily to Carthage in lots. They were clamorous for the arrears of pay due to them, and for the rewards which their

---

[1] The chief authorities for the war of the Mercenaries are Polybius I 65—88 and the fragments of the 25th book of Diodorus. An elaborate modern picture of this affair is given in Flaubert's romance *Salammbo*.

leaders had on special occasions found it necessary to promise them. To raise money by whatever means, to pay off each detachment and be rid of them before the next arrived, to avoid the folly of irritating armed men by meanness or delay, above all to prevent a concentration of the whole force in the neighbourhood of Carthage, were now necessary points of policy, to fail in which was to court disaster. But the wretched government dallied until the army had all reached Africa, then collected them together at Sicca, and by the mouth of Hanno the 'great' tried to persuade them to abate their claims in view of the financial exhaustion of Carthage. Beside the numerous Libyans, there were men from Spain and Gaul, from the Balearic isles and the Ligurian hills, with mongrel Greeks and other strays. No one language was understood by all: combination was difficult among the various races: they had but one thing in common, their claim against Carthage for service rendered. As it was gradually brought home to them that they were being required to forego a part of what they regarded as their rights, the one bond of sympathy was discovered: they broke out into open mutiny and marched to Tunes, about 15 miles from Carthage. The city walls alone protected the defaulting state from its enraged hirelings. To describe the war that followed would be out of place here. Money was found, and payment made, but too late. Confidence had been destroyed, and agitators found it easy to foster distrust and to make every concession the occasion of some further demand. The ringleaders of the revolt were Spendius, a runaway Roman slave, and a Libyan named Mathos: the Gaul Autaritus also came to the front in the latter part of the war. A Numidian force invaded Carthaginian territory, and most of the Libyans, cruelly taxed to meet the needs of Carthage, rose against their oppressors. Hanno's management was a failure: the enemy held the open country, and laid siege to the Phoenician towns of Utica and Hippo. Yet even so the last hour of Carthage was not yet come. New mercenaries were hired, and the citizens themselves trained to military service: Hamilcar Barcas was put in command, and the tide of disaster slowly turned. A young Numidian chief brought over a number of his countrymen. Though another mutiny led to the loss of Sardinia, and Hippo and Utica soon went over to the rebels, though there was much friction between the joint commanders, Hanno and Hamilcar, still on the whole the Punic cause gained ground. Hamilcar tried to make the resistance of the mutineers less desperate by shewing some clemency after victory, but the artifices of Spendius destroyed the effect of his leniency. In general this 'truceless' war was carried on by both sides with a treachery and barbarity beyond example. Stoning, crucifixion, impalement were every-day scenes: before the spectacle of massacres and tortures the thoughtful Polybius stands aghast and moralizes on the causes and symptoms of the brutalizing of human nature. For more than three years these horrors went on. But Hamilcar had to be placed in sole command of the Punic forces. This must mark a victory of the popular party in Carthage: under the stress of public calamity the old ruling class had to give way at last. The attitude of foreign powers was friendly: Hiero, who for his own sake had no wish to see Rome's rival perish utterly, sent help: Rome herself went so far as to allow her merchants to carry supplies to Carthage but not to the mutineers: for the present she refrained from intervention in Sardinia, though that coveted island lay at her mercy. So Hamilcar got the better of the mercenaries: famine, cannibalism and the courage of despair marked their last struggles with scenes even bloodier than those of the first revolt.

265. Peace was restored in Africa, and it was now time to recover Sardinia. But Roman jealousy had revived, and the preparation of an armament for the purpose was now plainly resented: Rome would treat a Punic expedition to Sardinia as a declaration of war against herself. In short, she now meant to occupy the island rather than see it in the hands of Carthage. She was bent on picking a quarrel: it is said that a declaration of war was actually voted. But Carthage had of course no means for such a conflict. She was granted peace on the terms of abandoning her claims on Sardinia and paying an indemnity of 1200 talents. Corsica was probably thrown in: at least Rome presently occupied both islands as a Province, that is the coast districts: for many years went by, and much blood was shed, before her hold of the interior was peaceful and secure. To take advantage of her rival's misfortunes was a most ungenerous act, but Great Powers did and do act in this manner, tempted by opportunity, and it is vain to revile them. The sympathy with Carthage shewn by Hiero may have had some effect in rousing the jealousy of Rome. As for Carthage, we do not find that her terrible experience taught her not to rely on mercenary armies: that lesson it was probably too late for her to learn. The old governing class seem to have more and more become a peace-party, for the merchant-princes saw a commercial future for themselves if only they could keep clear of collisions with Rome. It was the anti-Roman popular party that now ruled in Carthage, and was ready to support any feasible project of revenge. Soon after the suppression of the mercenaries in 238 Hamilcar carried through a proposal for the despatch of an army to Spain. He made arrangements for the leadership of the party during his absence, and set out to make up for the Punic losses of recent years by a new expansion in the West.

266. For Rome, on the contrary, the years following the first Punic war seem to have been a time of growth. But from 241 to 230 our authorities are very meagre and obscure. The rebellion of Falerii, suppressed in six days, may have been a symptom of some more widespread discontent, but was more probably due to local causes. About 238 we are told[1] that an embassy was sent to Ptolemy III with an offer of help in his war with the king of Syria. Nothing came of it, the war being already over. If this story be true, it shews that the outlook of Roman policy was greatly widened: and Rome would not wish by neglect to leave an opening for Carthaginian intrigue at Alexandria. From 238 to 230 we find the Romans at war with the Ligurian mountaineers. This was no doubt in the main an aggressive movement, connected with the occupation of Sardinia and Corsica. In 230 other enterprises called off the attention of Rome, and the conquest of the hillmen was deferred till after the Hannibalic war. With the Gauls the case was different. They were becoming restless, and we hear of indecisive war with them in 238 and 237. They invited the aid of their kinsmen[2] beyond the Alps, and in 236 a large force appeared before Ariminum, which place with its territory they summoned the Romans to restore. But, as they lay encamped together, they quarrelled among themselves, and the expedition came to nought. In 232 the tribune Gaius Flaminius, a great popular leader, carried a law, in spite of the opposition of the Senate, for distributing in allotments to Roman citizens the strip of land along the coast of Umbria, a district that had been conquered from the Gauls, and to which they had recently laid claim. This act proclaimed that Rome did not mean to draw back: the Celtic tribes saw that she meant to advance further, and prepared to accept the challenge. While these events were passing, a troublesome warfare was going on in Sardinia and Corsica. There was reason to think that the resistance of the natives received encouragement from Carthage, but Roman complaints drew from the Punic government no offer of redress. The two islands were made into a province in 231, but the conquest was by no means complete.

267. The Romans now took an important forward step in foreign policy. By their occupation of Brundisium they had already shewn that they claimed an interest in the Adriatic: and, though we hear very little on the subject, it seems certain that there was in this period a considerable development of Roman transmarine commerce.

---

[1] Eutropius III 1.   [2] Polybius II 21—35.

But the Illyrian coast opposite abounded in islets and safe harbours, from which sea-robbers issued to prey on merchant vessels, and in which they found at need a safe retreat. The chief city and centre of the Illyrian kingdom was Scodra, where Teuta, widow of king Agron, ruled on behalf of her young son. The insolence of the Illyrian corsairs[1] was becoming intolerable to all their neighbours. From the capture of shipping they passed to descents on the coasts of Epirus and Western Greece. No Greek power could withstand them on the water, and in raids on the land they usually slipped off with their booty before a force could be got ready to attack them. In 230 a Roman embassy was sent to Scodra to complain of piratical attacks on Roman merchantmen and seek redress. Teuta tried to shuffle out of responsibility by pleading that privateering was not a state affair but a time-honoured form of individual enterprise. This drew a rough answer from one of the Romans: he was murdered by order of the queen, and Rome at once declared war. The war was of no particular interest. Several states were received into the protection of Rome as her 'friends': such were Corcyra, Apollonia and Epidamnus along the coast, and the Partheini and Atintanes inland. The Romans took several places and beat the Illyrians in various fights. The adventurer Demetrius of Pharos, who had deserted the cause of Teuta and had helped them to win Corcyra, was made ruler of most of Illyria. Thus the year 229 ended, and early in the next year Teuta made her submission. She lost most of the kingdom, and had to give up the ships of war and the freedom of navigation that had been so grievously misused. The result of the expedition was most welcome to the Greek powers. The Aetolian and Achaean Leagues sent their thanks: the Corinthians invited the Romans to take part in the Isthmian games: Athens, it is said, admitted Romans to share the Eleusinian mysteries. Such was the joy of the disunited and helpless Greeks at having found a new and powerful protector. Rome had indeed displayed her power to some purpose beyond the Adriatic. But she had made a new enemy, for the king of Macedon necessarily viewed her movements with suspicion and alarm.

268. We must now shift our scene to northern Italy. The Gauls saw their doom written in the forward policy of Rome, and felt that a great rising, with the object of beating back their enemy, could not safely be delayed. The two chief tribes, the Insubres and Boii, entered into an agreement for the purpose, and by pledges and prospects of booty attracted the support of an immense host of

---

[1] Illyrian War. Polybius II 2—12.

Transalpine Gauls. Leaving a detachment to watch[1] the Veneti and also the Cenomani, whom Roman diplomacy had drawn away from the national cause, they poured over the Apennine into Etruria 70,000 strong. Polybius[2] lays stress on two highly significant symptoms of Italian feeling at this moment. First, the alarm was great and general, in Rome and elsewhere: secondly, the Allies came forward with eager promptitude in a cause which was the cause of them all, not of Rome only. When the Gaulish terror threatened, jealousy of Roman headship was silent: a fact we shall do well to bear in mind in considering the career of Hannibal. In spite of timely preparations, Rome seems to have been in no small danger. The Gauls swept through Etruria unchecked, ravaging the country. They were only three days' march from Rome, when they found themselves followed by a Roman army which had been sent under one of the praetors to operate in Etruria. Upon this force they turned, and defeated it with heavy loss. The survivors were only rescued by the arrival of one of the main armies under the consul L. Aemilius Papus, who had made a forced march from Ariminum. The Gauls now made for the coast, intending to work their way home by that route and to deposit their booty in a place of security. But it so fell out that the other consul, who had been on duty in Sardinia, just then landed with his army at Pisae and set out for Rome. At Telamon he fell in with the Gaulish host. Aemilius was following on their rear, and no escape was possible. The Roman troops had long learnt how to deal with the noise and first rush of the fiery Celt, and the *pilum* and the thrusting sword were far more effective in action than the rude cutting sword of the Gauls. The Roman cavalry too were well handled on this occasion. The slaughter of 40,000 of the invaders, and the capture of 10,000 or more, relieved the general anxiety. The booty was restored to its owners: the golden collars and other spoils of the Gauls were sent to Rome. Aemilius took command of the united armies (his colleague Atilius fell in a cavalry charge at Telamon) and marched to the North. After plundering the lands of the Boii he returned to Rome and celebrated a splendid triumph.

269. In narrating these affairs of 226—5 B.C. we may well pause awhile to reflect with Polybius on the enormous forces now at the disposal of Rome. We cannot quite follow out the details[3] of the

---

[1] For the Veneti see above §§ 17, 132. The Romans seem to have derived no small advantage from their alliance with them. Polybius II 17—24.

[2] Polyb. II 23, 24.

[3] The matter is treated by Beloch, *der Italische Bund* pp. 93—100, *die Bevölkerung der Griechisch-Römischen Welt* pp. 353—67.

numbers, nor is this necessary here. He is speaking on the authority of Fabius Pictor, who fought in this war. He tells us that, beside the great forces actually under arms, a schedule was at this time prepared shewing the entire number of men available for the field-armies. It was no less than 700,000 foot and 70,000 horse: more than half this total were Allies. Rome now moved forward with confidence, wishing to lose no time in coming to a final issue with the Gauls south of the Alps. Not only was it becoming clear to her that the Alps must be the real frontier of Italy: the course of events in Spain made her more and more anxious to have done with the Gaulish complications. So in 224 the weakened Boii were harried into a formal submission. In 223 the great popular leader Flaminius was consul, and the campaign of the year was directed against the Insubres, the strongest of the tribes, who tried bravely to avert their subjection without success. Blunders of generalship seem to have been made on the Roman side: but the Roman soldier nevertheless fought his way to victory. In 222 the stubborn Insubres called in mercenaries from beyond the Alps and made a last vain fight for freedom. Rome wound up the war with a show-campaign: the dashing consul Marcus Claudius Marcellus killed the Gaulish chief in single combat. Victories in the field, in which the cavalry did good work, and the capture of Mediolanum and other strongholds, at last brought the fighting to an end, and even the Insubres acknowledged the supremacy of Rome. In short, it was now effectively claimed that Cisalpine Gaul, the land drained by the Po and its tributaries, belonged to the political system of Italy. That the claim was seriously meant was shewn by a campaign (221) to keep in order some restless neighbours, the native tribes of Istria, by the reconstruction (220) of the northern way to Ariminum as a first-class military road (*via Flaminia*), directed by the censor Flaminius, and by the founding of strong Latin colonies (6000 men each) on the Po at Placentia and Cremona in 218. It was clear that Rome meant to Romanize this rich district; but for the moment her work was interrupted by the Hannibalic war. As a policy this advance was wise, in fact an imperial necessity. But its military effects were not good: commanders learnt to depend on the superior efficiency of the individual Roman soldier as compared with the barbarian Gaul. The art of handling troops so as to produce great results with small means, never a strong point in the early Roman army system, was more and more neglected: and this when the Roman citizen-generals were on the eve of receiving costly lessons in strategy from an unsurpassed professor of the art.

COLONIES OF THE PERIOD 262—201 B.C.

Citizen Colonies	Latin Colonies	Where situated	Remarks
247 Aesium	... ...	Umbria	
247 Alsium (?) Pyrgi 245 Fregenae	... ...	Etrurian coast	To secure coast N. of Rome in first Punic war. See §§ 256, 566.
	244 Brundisium	Calabrian coast	Adriatic port for Greece &c.
	241 Spoletium	Umbria	Attempt to hold line of Po for conquest of Gauls before second Punic war. After Gaulish attacks (200) restored (198—195) and reinforced (190).
	218 Cremona	Transpadane Gaul	
	218 Placentia	Cispadane Gaul	

270. We must turn again to the West and note the progress[1] of the Carthaginian arms in Spain. Hamilcar found things in a bad way, the power of Carthage at a low ebb in consequence of her late disasters. Inspired by a grim hatred of Rome, the Phoenician hero set to work to build up a real empire in Spain as a military base from which the struggle, sure to be renewed, could be carried on with better prospect of success. He knew the fine soldierly qualities of the Spanish tribesmen. He set to work to bring them, tribe by tribe, and the resources of their rich country, under his control, skilfully combining diplomacy with force. He made himself both feared and liked, and had already added a large part of southern Spain to the Punic dominion when he fell in battle. His son-in-law Hasdrubal was chosen (228) to succeed him. This was the act of the army, that is no doubt of the Phoenician element in it, probably not large: and confirmed by the approval of the Home government. Hasdrubal continued the policy of Hamilcar, but was in practice more the statesman than the warrior. As his negotiations extended the Carthaginian sphere, it became plain that the old Phoenician city of Gades was no longer a convenient centre for the Spanish empire of Carthage, however well situated for commerce. Hasdrubal therefore founded on the S.E. coast a new city, the 'New Carthage,' to be the chief seat of the administration, an arsenal and place of arms, and the headquarters of the fleet. This step shewed clearly the ambitions of Carthage, and could not be viewed with indifference by Rome. Accordingly a Roman embassy was soon despatched to Spain, instructed to negotiate with Hasdrubal for the fixing of a boundary beyond

[1] Polybius II 1, 13, 36, Livy XXI 1—3.

which the forces of Carthage were not to operate. Neither side wished for war at the moment, so they came to terms, and drew the line at the river Iber or Iberus. This 'delimitation' implied a sort of recognition of two 'spheres.' But, while the southern sphere was effectively occupied by Carthage, Rome was too busy with matters nearer home to proceed at once with the occupation of the northern. Thus difficulties were likely to arise, for to exclude another power from a sphere for the occupation of which you do not provide is sure to create material of quarrels. Nor indeed does the compact with Hasdrubal seem to have been recognized at Carthage as a valid treaty: it never received (so it was said) the ratification of the Home authorities. The Romans did nothing in Spain for the present beyond forming alliances with some nominally Greek cities on the Spanish coast. The glory of Greek colonial expansion in the West had departed, but mongrel populations might retain some Greek traditions, among which hatred of Carthage, the Phoenician mono-polizer of trade, would probably be one. In particular the alliance with Saguntum was important. The people were Iberians, and the suggestion of an original Greek colony from Zacynthus was not im-probably a mere fiction. The place itself was south of the Iberus, but Rome had not renounced her right to make allies and to protect them when made. The whole negotiation is a suspicious move, and we need not impute sincerity to either party. Each knew that war must come, and they manœuvred for vantage.

271. In 221 Hasdrubal was murdered by the avenger of a private wrong, and the chief command was passed on to Hannibal, eldest son of Hamilcar, a youth of 26 years. He had come to Spain as a boy with his father, and grew up in the camp. He was already a thorough man of war, distinguished in battle and a practised campaigner: he had learnt the military art in the best school, hard service under a great leader: the troops were devoted to him, and the patriot party at Carthage saw in him a worthy successor to the honours and policy of the house of Barcas. His endowments of body and mind were quite exceptional, and as a military hero he remains the equal of the greatest generals of history. Purged from the calumnious inventions of Roman hatred by the impartial scrutiny of Polybius, his moral character stands high in the estimates of modern writers, and it seems almost heresy to detect any weak point in a grand figure whom all critics admire. Yet we shall find that a naturally sound judgment and the most painstaking inquiries did not save him from miscalculating the situation in Italy. Was not this at least partly due to the blinding effect of a lifelong thirst for revenge? To destroy Rome was a passion that grew with him from childhood.

It dominated his whole being, as he confessed in his later years. In his Semitic intensity, under the consuming influence of one negative idea, he may rather remind us of Shylock than of any great statesman guided solely by cool calculation of interest. His glorious and patriotic career was a failure, and he left Carthage weaker than he found her. The chief causes of his failure were no doubt the badness of the Home government, the untrustworthiness of his allies, and the folly of both. But to lay the whole blame on them, in order not to soil the perfection of the hero, is an extreme judgment, unwarranted by the facts. We must now pass on to consider his doings in the West. In 221 and 220 Hannibal was campaigning in north-central Spain, conquering refractory tribes, exacting indemnities, and proving to friend and foe that a great master was there. Money was necessary, not only to pay and feed his men (of whom he took great care), but to keep alive the political fortunes[1] of the patriot party at home. The army now under him was a very different force from the old-fashioned mercenary hosts of Carthage. Those were a sort of journeymen cut-throats, ruffians hired 'for the job.' To be quit of them when the work was done was the first anxiety of their employers: the fewer that lived through the war to claim the final reward, the less was the burden on the treasury. But the army of the Barcids, now brought to its best by the son of Hamilcar, was in effect a standing army. There were a few trusted Phoenicians, mostly, perhaps all, officers: there were Libyans, who under wise treatment made excellent troops. The cavalry were good: no doubt they included some of the finest riders of the day, the famous Numidian horse. The elephants must have been unusually efficient, trained as they were by frequent service in the field. But more and more the strength of the army came to consist of the contingents of the Spanish tribes in alliance with Carthage. They were born warriors: there was no one tribe strong enough to form the nucleus of an independent Iberian nation: the greater the Punic dominion grew, the more it exercised the military magnetism of a strong central power. So long as great leaders represented Carthage in the Peninsula, the supply of recruits was not likely to fail: the devotion of the men to their commander increased with time, and as yet no other great power was competing with Carthage for their allegiance. Hannibal felt strong: he knew that Rome had other work in hand: so he determined to take Saguntum, and make an end of Roman allies within the Carthaginian sphere.

272. The true story of the affair of Saguntum is lost beyond

---

[1] Polybius iii 17.

recall. The traditional narratives are all more or less coloured by the effort to put the conduct of Rome in a favourable light. A few outlines seem fairly trustworthy. There was a Carthaginian party in Saguntum, but the Roman party had the upper hand: Roman arbitration had recently been employed to settle some internal disputes in the city. As suspicion of Hannibal's design grew into certainty in the winter of 220—219, message after message was sent to Rome, imploring protection. The Senate resolved to send ambassadors to warn, first Hannibal, then the Home authorities at Carthage, against attacking the allies of Rome. Before they started, news came that Saguntum was besieged. After fresh debate, new instructions were issued to the envoys: they were to order Hannibal off, and, in case of his refusal, they were to demand from Carthage full satisfaction, including the surrender of the general himself. Hannibal, who had already prepared matters at Carthage, and been authorized to protect their allies against Saguntine aggression (such was his pretext), dismissed the Roman embassy with contempt, and sent off with all speed an agent to give his party their cue before the ambassadors should arrive. He succeeded: vainly did the opposition party advise concession: the Romans were told that the blame for the present trouble belonged to Saguntum, and no redress was offered. All must have known that this meant war. It is said that Roman scruples required the sending of another embassy, formally charged to declare war unless Carthage repudiated the act of Hannibal. There was, however, no repudiation, and war was declared. This was early in 218. Meanwhile, after an eight months' siege, Saguntum was at last carried by storm: butchery or bondage removed[1] its stubborn defenders: and Hannibal turned at once to preparation for his main enterprise.

273. The slow and halting policy of Rome in the affair of Saguntum attracts our attention. Not that slow movement was a new thing at Rome: far from it. But the serious nature of the crisis was well understood: the course of events in Spain had long been watched with uneasiness. The chief cause of the Roman delays was that matters nearer home were at the moment felt to be more pressing. As the wars in northern Italy and the Adriatic had kept them busy, and thus left Carthage free to build up an empire in Spain, so now it was their first care to secure their footing in the valley of the Po. The mere foundation of two fortress-towns such as Placentia and Cremona among the hostile Gauls was itself no small matter. And just at this time the Illyrian war broke out again. The

---

[1] The dramatic account of the desperate resistance and complete extermination of the Saguntines cannot be trusted. See § 296 below.

adventurer Demetrius of Pharos, Rome's ally in the former war, now leaned towards Macedon, and thought that he might safely defy Rome. He attacked Roman allies, and violated the treaty by his piratical enterprises in forbidden waters. In 219 the consuls M. Livius Salinator and L. Aemilius Paullus were both sent to put down this nuisance. This they did with energy, and for the time order was restored in the Adriatic. Demetrius fled to the Macedonian court, where he remained, intriguing against the interests of Rome. The plunder of Pharos had yielded rich booty, of which it was said the consuls had taken a large part for themselves. When later they were brought to trial[1] for embezzlement, Aemilius cleared himself with difficulty: Livius was condemned, and withdrew into a sulky retirement for several years. One may suspect that party struggles had some influence in this trial. These two competent men will appear again, and appear with credit. We must glance briefly at the position of Macedon. Since Rome's former war with the Illyrians, and the establishment of friendly relations with several Greek states, much had happened. The Achaean League, threatened with destruction by the revival of Sparta, had been saved by Macedonian help. King Antigonus had been able to bring the League and other parts of Greece under Macedonian leadership. Not for many years had Macedon been so strong, so influential in the Greek world, as it was now. The young king Philip V, who came to the throne in 220, was active and ambitious, and at present popular. In 220—217 a confused war (often called the Social War) was going on, in which the Aetolian and Achaean Leagues were the chief antagonists. The latter, being worsted at first, called in Philip. The king shewed great vigour, and humbled the Aetolians. But in 217 he made peace with them. His cherished design was to drive back to Italy the intruders whose presence on the east of the Adriatic was a check to the pretensions of Macedon. The early victories of Hannibal in Italy made him hope that his chance was come: but the relations between the king and the Punic leader will be narrated below.

[1] Livy XXII 35 § 3, XXVII 34 § 3, Weissenborn.

CHAPTER XXV

SECOND PUNIC WAR, (a) 218—216 B.C.

274. WE need not enlarge upon the importance[1] of the Second Punic War. All recognize in it a great turning point, not only in the history of Rome, but in that of the whole Mediterranean world. It was a highly dramatic struggle, and has from this point of view been called the 'Hannibalic' war, after the great central figure. And indeed in the central action of the drama, in Italy, the presence of Hannibal was everything: but in the side-actions, in Spain, Greece and Sicily, his absence was not less important, and these side-actions were all parts of the war and went far to determine its result. Nor was the war a private affair of the Barcid family. The Barcid party was dominant in Carthage, and Carthage clearly accepted the issue of battle. The government sent forces to Spain and Sicily, and it seems certain that reinforcements, though inadequate, reached Hannibal in Italy. It was strictly a Punic war. Like the first war, it was a long weary struggle, but it had two points of difference. First, it was decisive. After the first war, the loss of Sicily and Sardinia was a heavy blow, but the foundation of a Carthaginian empire in Spain opened up new markets to take the place of the old, at the same time adding greatly to Carthaginian military strength. The second war deprived Carthage of Spain: henceforth she might heap up money, but no land remained in which she could create another empire. In the second place, it was not a maritime war. No great sea-fight was fought in all those 17 years. A few minor naval operations were carried on from time to time, but the general freedom of movement by sea shews that no effective control of the waterways was established by either side.

275. The military lessons of the war were sharp and plain. That the yearly magistrates of the Roman state should command its armies was absurd. But its absurdity had never yet been exposed as it was now, when Hannibal foiled and beat these brave and

---

[1] I will not apologize for the length of this narrative of the war. So many matters that illustrate the condition of Rome and Italy, not to mention Carthage and other powers, come up in the course of the story, that it can hardly be told briefly. Of the actual battles I have said very little. See additional note on page 340.

respectable soldiers one after another. In hand-to-hand fighting the superiority of trained troops to a raw militia is universally admitted. It was now proved beyond all doubt that the brave but half-trained soldiers of Rome, who had as yet not met their match, were, man for man, by no means equal to the skilled veterans from Africa and Spain. Nor was this all. It was vain to attempt to use an overwhelming superiority of numbers. The larger the army, the greater the skill required to handle it: once thrown into confusion, its very size was a cause of disaster. Again, the Roman armies were weak in light troops, and particularly in cavalry. Hannibal was strong in the mounted arm. His Iberian cavalry were equal to the best Italian, and he filled up the gaps in this force with trained Gauls. But for mobility, whether for rapid flanking-movements or in a pursuit, the pick of his army were the Numidian horse. And the proper use of cavalry, unknown to the Romans, was well understood by the Punic general: perhaps learnt from traditions[1] of its inventor, the great Alexander. How helpless great bodies of foot, not supported by sufficient horse, could be made by good cavalry tactics, was demonstrated on the field of Cannae. Yet the reforms suggested by these plain lessons did not find favour with the Roman government. The defects exposed were in truth part of the Roman constitution: the stress of the great war necessitated some temporary deviations from the regular practice: but when once the danger was past things returned to the old groove. In the course of time we shall find a professional army, and generals in continuous command: the force of circumstances, imperial needs, will have overcome the opposition of the Roman nobles: but, when that stage is reached, the fall of the old constitution is at hand.

276. The story of the war comes down to us in a complete narrative filling ten books of Livy. Written about 200 years after the events, it is based on the works of earlier writers, of whom Fabius Pictor and Cincius Alimentus were contemporary witnesses. Part of the continuous narrative, and a number of fragments, remain of the history[2] of Polybius, written more than 50 years after the end of the war. Polybius[3] not only used the works of his predecessors, but examined public documents, such as treaties, and in particular a long inscription[4] set up by Hannibal himself in southern Italy, recording the chief details of his great enterprise. In the second century B.C.

---

[1] Hannibal is said to have received a partly Greek education. In his later days he wrote a book in Greek. Nepos, *Hannibal* 13.   [2] Used by Livy.

[3] A good sketch of his sources of information is given in Shuckburgh's *Polybius*, Introd. § 2.

[4] Polybius III 33, 56.

tradition was still fresh, and Polybius conversed with survivors of the war. His wide travels brought him into contact with outside views: even Carthage[1] supplied some gossip. To geography and topography he gave great attention, but a want of clearness in exposition, and some false geographical assumptions, lessen the value of his authority in this department. Of later historians, and of the many writers who refer incidentally to the events of the great war, we cannot speak here. But we must say a few words on the general defects of the record, which cause many things in it to be received with distrust. In the first place, Roman misrepresentation has played a great part. This is partly 'patriotic,' the aim being to set things in a light favourable to Rome: partly personal, as when family traditions assign to a member of the house or clan more than his fair share of credit. The former of these is troublesome because, in the absence of a Carthaginian version, it is not possible to detect the full extent of its influence. History as written by Romans was always more concerned to edify the reader than to ascertain truth. Of family traditions we have spoken above: the persistence of this form of corruption may pretty certainly be traced in Polybius' partiality to the Scipios. The illustrious Greek was a genuine seeker after truth: but he lived for years under the protection of the Scipios, had access to their records, and caught some of their prejudices. In short, the second Punic war, though in the main truly historical, is invested with a mythology of its own. We may fairly assume that members of the *gens Fabia* had full justice done them by Fabius Pictor. Partisan colouring has probably given unfair portraits of the popular leaders Flaminius and Varro. But corruption goes further than this: there is at times an uncertainty as to who did this or that. There are also mysteries which cannot be satisfactorily explained: as when Nero, the hero of the Metaurus, after the best piece of generalship shewn on the Roman side during the war, dropped out of military command altogether. Why he was not again employed in war, if he really did perform the brilliant feat ascribed to him, imagination is left to guess. Enough has now been said to justify a hesitation that will be sometimes necessary in a sketch of this momentous war.

277. We left Hannibal in Spain, making all ready for his great design. After the fall of Saguntum in the winter of 219, he sent the booty to Carthage to encourage the popular party, and made a number of military arrangements, no doubt with the approval of the Home government. He had in view three main objects, the defence of Africa, the retention of Spain, and the invasion of Italy. To the western district of north Africa he transferred more than 15,000

[1] Polyb. IX 25.

Spanish troops and a body of Balearic slingers, while he moved on 4000 of the local troops and a few of the Spaniards to Carthage itself. He had thus provided against rebellions in Africa and secured hostages for the fidelity of Spanish allies, avoiding at the same time the concentration of a large military force in Carthage, which would have been rather a danger than a protection to the city and the government. In Spain his brother Hasdrubal was to be governor, under whom were to be left as an army of occupation more than 14,000 African troops, with a few Balearic and Ligurian irregulars, and a handful of northern Spaniards drawn from the Roman sphere. There was also assigned to Hasdrubal a fleet of 50 quinqueremes, 2 quadriremes and 5 triremes: but of these[1] only the 5 triremes and 32 quinqueremes had crews—another illustration of the real weakness of the Carthaginian navy. To these must be added 21 elephants, and the mass of war-material in the arsenal at New Carthage. His own marching army was to be brought to the highest state of efficiency: a wise concession to his Spanish soldiers, whom he meant to lead far from their homes to fight in an alien cause, was the granting of a long furlough. Meanwhile he had sent trusty agents to learn the truth about the Alpine districts, and invite the cooperation of the Gauls settled in Italy, whom he believed to be hostile to Rome. News arrived that the Gauls were eager to join him, and that the passage of the Alps, though hard, was practicable: and he heard that the Roman envoys had met with defiance at Carthage. The time for action was come, and he was ready: he drew together the various corps of his army in the spring of 218, and passed the frontier river at the head of more than 100,000 well-trained men.

278. At this point we may reasonably ask what considerations induced Hannibal to choose the land route, and dare the dangers of the Alps, rather than make the passage to Italy by sea. It has been suggested that the moral effect of a sudden descent upon the Italian plains from the regions of eternal snow was an object consciously present to his mind. This may have been so, for none knew better than Hannibal the power of moral effects in war. But there were simpler considerations of a practical kind. The risks run by a fleet laden with men and stores would be great: the loss of the fleet off the Aegatian islands in 242 had ended the former war in favour of Rome. And the voyage from his headquarters at New Carthage to the Italian coast was five times as long as that from the old Carthage to western Sicily. Besides, to land in Sicily in 242 meant a junction with the Punic force that still held its ground there: in 218 the first

[1] Polyb. III 33, Livy XXI 22 § 4.

object on reaching Italy must be to effect a junction with the Gauls. Now the lands of the Po and its tributaries, where these Gauls dwelt, were shut off from the western seaboard: first by Etruria (held by Rome) and the Apennine range at its back, secondly by the broken mountain district of Liguria, whose wild hillmen were certain to oppose the passage of an army. The coast of Gaul from the Pyrenees to the Alps was chiefly held by the Greeks of Massalia, old allies of Rome. Corsica and Sardinia were no longer held by Carthage: nowhere was there a friendly shore. And, if we allow for no more than the numbers with which he actually crossed the Rhone, it is clear that to transport 46,000 fighting men, 8000 horses, 37 elephants, with all the equipments and stores, would have been a vast undertaking: in the circumstances, a gambler's risk. The way over the Alps was indeed hard—how hard, he could scarcely guess beforehand. But it would at least lead him straight to the Gauls, on whose support his hopes were built. Was not the land march a safer course than to expose his army, the hardly-forged weapon of his country's vengeance, to perish in a single storm?

279. Hannibal's first task after crossing the Ebro was the conquest of the tribes north of the river. Time was more valuable than lives: so he went quickly to work, marching, fighting, storming towns, till he made them submit. An officer named Hanno was left behind with a force of 10,000 foot and 1000 horse, to act as governor and keep open communications with Gaul. He crossed the Pyrenees by a pass near their eastern end. Here he parted with some 10,000 or 11,000 more of his Spaniards, sending them to their homes. His aim in this was, according to Polybius, to ensure the loyalty[1] and confidence of the Spanish tribesmen, that he might be able to rely on reinforcements from that quarter when needed. These various losses so reduced his effective strength that he left the Pyrenees with only 50,000 foot and 9000 horse. But they had no heavy baggage train, and could move freely. The hostility of the tribes of southern Gaul was overcome by peaceful negotiations and gifts to the chiefs, and without serious opposition the army reached its first great obstacle, the Rhone.

280. Meanwhile the Roman government, seeing they were at war with Carthage, took leisurely steps. The consuls of 218 were to take their forces to the expected theatres of war, Publius Cornelius Scipio to Spain, Tiberius Sempronius Longus to Africa. The foundation of colonies to secure the region of the Po was to be carried out at the same time. That this step would enrage the dispossessed Gauls was

---

[1] The story preserved in Livy makes him get rid of over 7000 discontented men, 3000 having already deserted. Polyb. III 35, Livy XXI 23 §§ 4—6.

plain, but they were no longer to be allowed to menace Italy. No extraordinary precautions were taken: it seems that no report of the visit of Hannibal's agents had reached Rome. Before the consuls could set out for their provinces, the great tribes of the Boii and Insubres rose, and drove the colonists of Placentia and Cremona from their unfinished towns. Mutina, held by a Roman garrison, served as a rallying point for the fugitives, but was itself besieged. A praetor commanding a force in the district advanced to its relief, but fell into an ambuscade and only cut his way out with heavy loss: he too was besieged by a multitude of Gauls. The news of this alarmed Rome at last: another praetor, with two legions that had been raised by Scipio, was despatched in all haste to the scene of action: the rising was suppressed, and for the moment order was restored in Cisalpine Gaul. Scipio made up his army by fresh levies, and started for his province by sea, with 60 vessels of war and no doubt a fleet of transports. He coasted along to Massalia, and encamped near the eastern mouth of the Rhone. Here he was surprised to learn that Hannibal was not far off, preparing to cross the river. He could hardly believe this, but he sent a body of cavalry up the eastern bank to reconnoitre and learn the truth, while his seasick recruits were recovering their military tone. In a few days the cavalry returned, having lost some of their number but having beaten and pursued a party of Numidian horse. They reported that the enemy had already crossed the Rhone: and the consul at once marched his army inland, in hopes to find them and bring them to battle. But Hannibal had given him the slip: it was not his plan to fight in Gaul. Scipio saw himself foiled. Duty now called him different ways, for to stop the advance of Hannibal was virtually a part of the Spanish province assigned him. With wise decision he handed over his army to his brother Gnaeus Scipio, and sent them on at once to Spain. He himself took ship with a handful of men and sailed for Italy, meaning to take command of the forces in the North, and with them to encounter the invaders if and when they should issue from the Alps.

281. Hannibal's crossing of the Rhone had not been the work of a day. The strong tribe of the Volcae held the eastern bank in force, but the Punic leader knew how to deal with them. He seized or bought up all the boats and timber in the neighbourhood: his men, helped by paid natives, built pontoons and even constructed huge rafts to carry the elephants. He then sent a detachment to cross the stream at an easier place higher up, and appear in due time on the rear of the enemy. The turning movement was carried out in exact combination with the front attack, the Volcae were put to flight, and the whole army safely landed on the left bank of the river. Its

numbers at this point were 38,000 foot, more than 8000 horse, and probably about 20 or 25 elephants. Time was precious, for the Alps must be crossed before winter blocked the passes, and the season was already waxing late. At this juncture the arrival of a deputation from the Gauls of Italy was a timely help. Hannibal was now able to reassure his men, whose hearts were failing them at the thought of Alpine terrors. Here were friends come over the Alps to lead them by a practicable route into a promised land where brave allies awaited their coming to share with them the spoils of Rome. He broke up his camp and marched up country to the Island, a fertile district between the Rhone and the Isara (Isère). Here he came upon a tribe in sedition and on the point of civil war, two brothers claiming the chieftaincy. In this quarrel he intervened with effect in favour of the elder : and the grateful chief provisioned and equipped the way-worn army. New-shod and new clothed they pushed on to the foot of the Alps, while for fear of the hostile Allobroges their new friend covered their rear. On reaching the foot of the ascent they were left to their own resources, and their troubles began. In the mountains the horses and beasts of burden were an encumbrance, in the narrow gorges a positive danger. First the Allobroges, then the mountain tribes, beset their column of march and inflicted serious loss. Hannibal's skilful stratagems dispersed some of their tormentors : but he had also to deal with gross treachery, only discovered by the help of their Gaulish guides. As they advanced, food became more difficult to procure : how they fed the elephants is a mystery. The march to the top of the pass was an agony of hardships and uncertain fears; in the descent, though no longer molested by enemies, they had to face natural difficulties of the most serious kind. The snow and ice, a sore trial to men from southern lands, were gathering fast, for it seems now to have been our November. And the southern slopes of the Alps have a sharper fall than the northern. We need not doubt the consistent tradition that lays peculiar stress on the perils of this steep and slippery track, in places broken by landslips. That a way had to be found for elephants did not make the labour less. By which pass it was that this terrible journey was made, is a problem that has long had a fascination for scholars and travellers. No certain inferences can be drawn from the loose descriptions of Livy or even Polybius, nor have Alpine topographers been able to agree in a solution. For our purpose it matters not. It is enough that by some pass Hannibal brought down the relics of a splendid army, half-frozen and half-starved, into the lowland of northern Italy, when the winter of 218—7 was just coming on. The number of these survivors is variously given : the lowest and best attested figures are

20.000 foot and 6000 horse. Some elephants also got through. We will now turn from events in the North to the opening of the war in the southern waters.

282. It had been intended that the consul Sempronius should carry the war into Africa, and indeed no other plan of campaign was so likely to bring Carthage to her knees. But this was as well understood at Carthage as at Rome, and it was the Punic government that struck the first blow, in hope to forestall and perhaps prevent invasion. But this wise move was weakly carried out. Sempronius had at disposal a powerful fleet, including 160 quinqueremes. But before he reached Messana and took command, the Carthaginian attack had been delivered. One squadron of 20 ships, sent to ravage the coast of Italy, was scattered by a storm, and three of them fell into the hands of the faithful Hiero, whose fleet was ready waiting for the consul. Learning that another squadron of 35 ships was at sea with the object of surprising Lilybaeum and stirring up rebellion in Sicily, the king sent off a despatch to put the praetor on his guard. Preparations for defence were promptly made; the attempted surprise failed: in the sea fight which followed the Punic fleet was put to flight with the loss of 7 ships and 1700 men. We are told[1] that an insufficiency of fighting men was the cause of their defeat. In other words, the lessons of the former war had not been turned to account: the navy of Carthage was not up to date.

Just at this time Sempronius reached Messana. He was loyally welcomed by Hiero, and informed of the Carthaginian expeditions, and further warned that some of the Sicilian communities were dis-affected to Rome. He sailed at once for Lilybaeum, but was too late to bear a part in the victory. So he made a dash at the island of Melita, still held by Carthage. The natives rose against their oppressors, and handed over to him the Punic governor and a garrison of nearly 2000 men. After a grand sale of prisoners at Lilybaeum, he paid a flying visit to the Liparaean isles, but did not find the enemy. Returning to Sicily, no doubt in hope to hear of a good landing-place on the African coast from his scouts, he was met by unpleasant news. The fleet that had just given him the slip had been ravaging the coast of southern Italy, and the Senate sent word of Hannibal's descent upon Cisalpine Gaul. Africa had seemed within reach: he was now recalled to support his colleague in the North. He left a subordinate to watch the southern coasts with 25 ships, made up the praetor's squadron to 50 ships, and set out to rejoin his army, which he had sent on before him to Ariminum.

283. Things moved fast in the North. Hannibal allowed his

[1] Livy XXI 50.

army a few days for rest and refreshment, but the situation was one in which no dallying was possible : he must keep up the impression of power created by his passage of the Alps. The Taurini were at war with his allies the Insubres : he picked a quarrel with the former, and took their chief town by storm. The near tribes at once joined him : those further to the East, held down[1] by the Roman forces, bided their time. Scipio had by this time taken over the praetors' armies, with which, and a contingent of Gauls, he advanced to meet Hannibal. Both leaders were eager for battle, the one to crush the invader while still weak in numbers, the other to win allies by a great demonstration of his strength. Scipio crossed to the northern bank of the Po, and the first collision took place on the Ticinus, an Alpine tributary of the great river. It was almost wholly a cavalry battle. The Roman horse were badly cut up by the better-handled and probably more numerous enemy. The consul himself was severely wounded, and it was with difficulty that some champion[2] saved his life. He withdrew his little army to Placentia, followed by Hannibal, and many more of the Gauls now openly took part against Rome. Even Scipio's Gaulish contingent deserted to the Punic leader, after murdering a number of their Roman comrades in the early hours of a winter morning. Fearing the enemy's cavalry, and the treachery around him, Scipio shifted his camp to some high ground near the Trebia, an Apennine tributary of the Po. He had a great store of provisions collected at Clastidium, a little further to the West. Hannibal encamped about five miles off, and drew his supplies from the friendly Gauls : but he presently threatened Clastidium, and the commandant (not a Roman but a *socius*[3] from the Latin colony of Brundisium) surrendered the depot for a bribe. Things were getting serious, but at this juncture Scipio was reinforced by Sempronius and his army. The latter was eager to fight at once, before their year of office should expire, and while the disablement of his colleague left him in sole command : we must also remember that he had already been too late in Sicily. His confidence was raised by an apparent advantage gained by his cavalry and light troops in support of some Gauls whom Hannibal was punishing for double-dealing. But the subtle Carthaginian had divined the ambition of Sempronius, and his retreat in this skirmish was a calculated lure. Scipio had to

---

[1] We must remember that the Veneti (see above §§ 132, 268) had long been connected with Rome. It is clear that their help was very useful to Rome in this war. See below, § 284.

[2] His son, afterwards the great Africanus, according to Polybius and the prevalent tradition. But Livy preserves a contemporary version, giving the credit to a Ligurian slave.   [3] Livy XXI 48 § 9.

submit to the decision of his acting colleague, and the battle of the
Trebia was fought. It was a cold December day, cold as a north-
Italian winter can be. The consul was completely outgeneralled.
His men were drawn into battle with empty stomachs and forced to
wade through the icy Trebia: his cavalry were defeated, the legions
outflanked and at last surrounded. That 10,000 of them cut their
way through and reached Placentia shews the wonderful steadiness
and fine condition of the Roman foot. The armies engaged seem to
have been about 40,000 on each side : but Hannibal's men were well
fed before fighting and splendidly handled, and a clever ambuscade
completed his decisive victory. Most of his losses, which were not
small, had fallen on the auxiliary Gauls. The battle had been fought
in a storm of snow and rain, and the weather grew worse : from this
cause he lost a number of men and horses and most of his elephants.

284. The relics of the Roman army—stragglers had followed the
10,000—were quartered in Placentia and Cremona. Supplies reached
them[1] by way of the river: the country round was hostile, and
Hannibal kept his army employed in attacks upon their depots.
Meanwhile alarm reigned at Rome, for the truth about the lost battle
soon became known, in spite of the optimistic tone of official despatches.
At length Sempronius himself appeared. He had eluded the raiding
parties of Hannibal, chancing all risks for the purpose of holding the
yearly elections in due course. The consuls chosen for the next year
were Gnaeus Servilius and the popular leader Gaius Flaminius.
Sempronius then returned to his post, and the consuls-elect[2] set to
work preparing for the next campaign, enrolling armies and establish-
ing depots of supplies on the lines of intended advance. Measures
were taken, no doubt by the Senate, to secure with garrisons exposed
places of strategic importance, such as Sardinia Sicily and Tarentum :
60 new quinqueremes were made ready for sea. The government's
demands on the Allies were clearly great, but seem to have been met
cheerfully. Even Hiero sent 1500 light troops in response to the
call. To destroy this active loyalty of the Roman Allies was one of
the chief means by which Hannibal meant to overthrow his enemies.
Accordingly in this very winter he began the policy of differential
treatment of prisoners, shewing kindness[3] to all that were not Roman
citizens. Next to this bid for Italian support was the military
strength expected to be gained by the alliance with the Gauls. How
far these designs succeeded, how far they were consistent with each

---

[1] Here again we see the profit of the alliance with the Veneti.
[2] They would enter on office in March. See § 75.
[3] He sent a number of them back to their homes, with a message that he was come to
restore Italian freedom.

other, will be considered below. For the present it seems that the Gauls caused him no little embarrassment. They cared nothing for Hannibal and his cause: plunder was their object: might they not be ready to listen to a more promising offer from the Roman side? So thought the Punic leader, and he well knew that the feeding of his army was felt to be a burden. We are told that he used disguises, false hair and changes of clothing, to avoid assassination and enable him by passing unrecognized to learn things not intended for the general's ear. He seems to have kept his troops on the move whenever the weather allowed it. But the references to his movements are most obscure, and we gather little more than that he passed part of the winter in the hill country of Liguria, preparing to invade Etruria in the spring.

285. We must return to Gnaeus Scipio, to whom his brother the consul had entrusted the army destined for Spain. The prestige of Rome among the Spanish tribes had sunk to nothing, thanks to the affair of Saguntum (whatever the true story of it may be) and to the victories of Hannibal north of the Ebro. When Scipio landed at the half-Greek town of Emporiae, just south of the Pyrenees, he had to begin his task from the beginning. Bases on the coast were of the first importance. So he made descents at various points, and took and garrisoned several towns, among them Tarraco, a strong position. This display of Roman activity gained him some allies, and a Spanish contingent joined him when he shortly entered on an inland campaign. He met with great success, gaining over a number of towns, and beating the Carthaginian commander of the district, Hanno, in a pitched battle. Hanno and other important persons were taken prisoners, and the neighbouring tribes promptly threw off their allegiance to Carthage. Punic authority north of the Ebro was at an end. But Hasdrubal, the governor of the old Carthaginian Spain, did not submit tamely to the loss of the new province. With a small mobile force he crossed the Ebro, and fell upon the Roman marine contingent left with the fleet. Taken off their guard, they were driven back upon the ships with heavy loss. Scipio punished the delinquent officers, but Hasdrubal of course was gone. According to Polybius, he withdrew to his own province and was busy organizing his forces there: Livy makes him stir up serious rebellions among the northern tribes, thus necessitating a second campaign on Scipio's part, including the siege of a town where his siege-works were carried on for 30 days in deep snow. Anyhow Scipio won back his lost ground, and wintered at Tarraco. He was, we hear, popular with his army, among whom he divided the rich booty won from Hanno.

286. Early in the spring of 217 Hannibal, anxious to be rid of

the Gaulish chiefs and their plots, made ready to cross the Apennine into Etruria.   In Livy we read of two attempts, the first of which failed owing to a terrible storm.   Polybius mentions one only, and says nothing of an indecisive battle which according to Livy the consul Sempronius fought with the invader when he returned baffled from the hills.   When at last he got through, his task was no easy one.   In order to take the Romans by surprise he had chosen a short but bad route that led through swampy and flooded lands, and for four days the army had not dry ground to sit or sleep on.   The order of march was cleverly arranged: his African and Spanish veterans led the van, the cavalry were the rearguard: between these trusty troops were the Gauls.   By this means Hannibal led and drove those burly ruffians, unfit for toil and hardship, many dropping by the way, on to a land where bloodshed and robbery were to be their reward.   He lost many beasts of burden, and not a few men: he suffered from ophthalmia himself, and lost the sight of one eye: but he bore up bravely and directed the march from the back of his one remaining elephant.   While he rested his men in the rich country of Etruria, he learnt through his efficient scouts the position of the Roman forces and much other useful information as to the state of things in general.

287.   The Romans had meant to invade Africa and humble Carthage, while they tightened their own grip on Cisalpine Gaul. They now saw Hannibal in Italy, and the Gauls backing him: he had beaten the forces opposed to him : a few fortified posts were all that was left of Roman dominion in the valley of the Po.   No wonder that public feeling received a great shock from the disappointment.   No wonder that prodigies were reported on all sides: the most trivial occurrences observed, the wildest absurdities of excited imagination, magnified in talk, served to alarm the ignorant and to give importance to the sacred colleges.   Livy records two separate outbreaks of the prodigy-mania, in the winter and in the following spring.   It would seem that, while the Senate was busy considering these matters with the help of the pontiffs and the guardians of the 'Sibylline' books, and while the Roman nobles in general thought that the proper treatment of these supernatural warnings was the chief thing needed to retrieve past disasters, another view of the situation was gaining strength.   The popular party laid the blame of military failures rather on the mismanagement of the nobles than on the anger of heaven.   Their support had raised Flaminius a second time to the consulship in spite of senatorial opposition.   True to his past, Flaminius was resolved not to be controlled by the Senate.   In acting on his own responsibility as consul he was no doubt only restoring to the magistracy a power of which it had never been formally deprived.

But the quarrel was at the moment most inopportune. Platform eloquence and patriotic motives would hardly stay the advance of Hannibal: the attitude of a refractory consul could only be justified by a great victory in the field. Now Flaminius felt sure that, if he waited on in Rome and entered on his office there in the regular way, every effort would be made to keep him in the city by the obligations of religious duties which, when once consul, he could not well decline. So he gave all such pretexts the slip by going to Ariminum as consul-elect and entering on his office there. Evil omens (such is the tradition of the Roman nobles) attended him, now and to the end. He took over his army, and, as soon as he was able to move, crossed the Apennine into Etruria, where he occupied a strong position at Arretium. The numbers of his army are not definitely given: probably he had between 30,000 and 40,000 men. Servilius the other consul entered on office at Rome and, as soon as he could be spared from his duties there, set out and made his headquarters at Ariminum.

288. Hannibal was in a commanding position. One of the consuls was out of the way: the other, the one committed to an active strategy, was close at hand. The character and political position of Flaminius were no secret to him: such a man could surely be tempted into offering opportunities for his own destruction. So he marched on, laying waste the country as he went, past Arretium towards Cortona: the smoke of burning farms rising to heaven was an insult and challenge to the consul: besides, the invader now stood between Rome and the army on which the city relied. Some officers, probably men who had served in the North and knew the efficiency of Hannibal's cavalry, begged Flaminius not to follow and fight, at least not to bring on a pitched battle without the help of his colleague. But Flaminius could stand it no longer: he broke up his camp and followed his enemy. Not far south of Cortona there lies a broad sheet of water in a pan of the hills. The way from Cortona to Perusia ran along its northern edge, commanded on the left by hills that at some points draw close to the water, at others recede from it. One evening in the early summer Flaminius reached the shore of this mere, called the *lacus Trasumennus*, and encamped. Next morning he entered the defile, eager to catch the enemy and bring him to battle. A thick mist hid the high ground on his left, occupied by the troops of Hannibal, whose scouts watched the Roman army as it worked its way into the death-trap. At the right moment the signal was given and the attack delivered, before the consul could give new orders or throw his column of march into line of battle. Yet the Roman nerve did not easily give way. After three hours

of desperate and disordered fighting, in the course of which a mighty earthquake passed unnoticed, they broke and fled. But those who sought refuge in the water were either drowned or butchered by the cavalry. The 10,000 stragglers who reached Rome must have slipped through gaps in the enemy's lines. One body of 6000 had cut their way out early in the day, and pushed on to the crest of a hill and waited. The mist broke and shewed that all was over. They hurried from the field, only to surrender, exhausted and starving, to the Punic cavalry the next day. The consul, whose lack of military skill had brought about this disaster, died like a brave man: he who had divided Gaulish land among Roman citizens fell by the spear of a Gaul. About 15,000 fell on the Roman side in the main battle. Hannibal's loss is put at 1500 by Polybius, 2500 by Livy, but it seems to have fallen as usual mainly on the Gauls. Many on both sides died later of wounds. Hannibal found himself with some 15,000 prisoners in hand. Such, avoiding vexed questions of topography, was the memorable disaster of Trasimene.

289. The differential treatment of prisoners proceeded as before : Romans were severely kept in confinement, the Allies lectured on the goodwill of the conqueror and his wish to free them from the Roman yoke, and then dismissed to their homes. Meanwhile the news of the lost battle filled Rome with mourning and dismay. As it was gradually perceived that the army of Flaminius had ceased to exist, despair possessed the people: the Senate alone was calm enough to face the crisis, meeting daily from sunrise to sunset to discuss measures of defence. Hardly had they grasped the serious nature of the situation, when they were stunned by the news of another blow. There was at all events, so they reckoned, the whole army of Servilius safe and sound at Ariminum. But it now appeared that the consul, meaning to join his colleague in Etruria, had sent on a body of 4000 horse in advance of his main army, and that Hannibal, getting wind of this move, had waylaid them, killing or capturing the whole detachment. Even the Senate now felt that the time for discussion had gone by. With the growth of the Senate's power the old expedient of a Dictatorship had gone out of favour. But the friction inseparable from collective wisdom must be got rid of in the hour of peril. It was agreed that a Dictator must be appointed. But according to Roman rule—precedent—he must be nominated by a consul. Now one consul was dead, and the other far away, parted from Rome by a district overrun by the enemy. A way was found out of this constitutional difficulty. The people were called upon to elect[1] a Dictator. Quintus Fabius Maximus was chosen,

---

[1] Polybius III 87, Livy XXII 8 §§ 5—7.

and with him Marcus Minucius Rufus as his master of the horse, an officer who in the regular course would have been the dictator's nominee. Fabius, chosen no doubt for the firmness of his character, was a Roman of the old school, full of the scruples of the formal religion of the race. He began by cleansing the state from taint incurred through the irreligious acts of Flaminius, and making good all other negligences and errors that the ingenuity of the religious colleges could discover. When the last ceremony was over, the last temple vowed, the Roman people might breathe again, and claim the favour of their jealous gods. Most of the formalities for which the personal presence of the dictator was not needed were transacted by a praetor: Fabius had enough to do in levying an army and making all ready for the war.

290. Hannibal did not sit still after his victory, but pushed on into Umbria. He soon came upon the Latin colony of Spoletium, a fortress guarding Rome's communications with the North. He seems to have thought that it would surrender under pressure, but here he learnt his first lesson as to the true nature of his undertaking. Of his ravages in their territory the colonists took no notice, and when he assaulted the town they beat him off with loss. He had no siege-train: nor was his army suited to the patient toil of sieges. So he moved on at once into Picenum, and gave his troops that for which they longed, a spell of plundering and ravaging undisturbed by the presence of an enemy. The booty carried off from this rich country was immense: Polybius adds that many of the inhabitants were put to the sword. In this style he reached the Adriatic, and marched along roughly parallel to the coast-line, extending his devastations into the hill country on his right, and filling central Italy with alarm. At some point in this march he seems to have halted for a time and devoted his attention to improving the condition of his men and horses. He also re-armed his African foot with picked suits of armour stripped from Roman prisoners or dead. Probably the lighter shields and corslets meant for the burning climate of their native land were not so well suited as the local armour to the hand-to-hand fighting of Italy. He also resumed touch with the Home government by sending news of his progress to Carthage. His message was received with great joy, and it was resolved[1] to send help to their armies both in Italy and Spain. When at last he reached the Daunian country in northern Apulia, a wide district lay open to his ravages, and he stayed there some time. But neither on the Latin colony of Luceria nor on the other

---

[1] This is only mentioned by Polybius III 87, and may be a misplaced reference to the same resolution as that given in Liv. XXIII 13.

Roman Allies did he make any impression by his destructive raids. None came forward to join the foreign invader, leader of the hated Gauls.

291. Meanwhile the Roman preparations were gradually made. Servilius, no doubt crippled by the loss of his cavalry, could not do much : after a few small affairs with some Gauls, he felt his way southwards, in order not to leave Rome exposed to attack. Hannibal was now working to the East, and the main [Flaminian] road was clear. The dictator, having arranged for the raising of two new legions, went to meet the consul as far as Ocriculum, and there took over his army. Behind him he had left the city preparing for the worst : walls were repaired, most of the bridges in the neighbourhood were broken down, guards were posted at important points. Orders were sent about Italy, warning the country folk to take refuge in fortified strongholds, and to lay waste the country in the line of Hannibal's advance. The superseded consul was at once needed for fresh duty. Fabius sent him to Ostia. A Punic fleet hovering off the Etrurian coast had captured a convoy of transports carrying supplies for the Roman forces in Spain. All available battle-ships were fitted out and manned : to complete the crews a number of qualified freedmen were enrolled for naval service, and Servilius put to sea to protect the coasts of Italy. Fabius drew together his army and started in search of Hannibal by way of Capua and Beneventum. His march was conducted with every precaution known to the military system of Rome : scouting in particular was carried to extreme perfection. All his men were downcast at the recent defeats : some of them were raw recruits : Fabius did not intend to fight a pitched battle with the veterans of Hannibal under such conditions. His plan was to follow the enemy from place to place, allowing him no security or ease, and to weaken him by cutting off stragglers. Thus the prestige of the invader, depending on great successful strokes, would decay, and the exhaustion of the country by his raids would automatically add to his necessities. Meanwhile, a toilsome campaign would make the Roman lads into steady soldiers, and the nerve of the legions be restored by breaking the habit of defeat. To this cautious strategy he steadily adhered, in spite of all the provocations of his adversary and the murmurs of his own army. His second in command, Minucius, made no secret of his contempt[1] for such timidity : he courted a cheap popularity by denouncing the plan of marching from place to place in attendance on the enemy, merely to provide passive spectators of the devastation of Italy. Hannibal knew better the true meaning of the Fabian strategy. Since he had had the slow dictator facing him, he had achieved no great success: if

---

[1] This may be coloured by the Fabian annalist to enhance the glory of Fabius.

he let himself decline into a mere captain of marauders, he would never convince the Italians that he was come to stay. So he broke away over the mountains by way of Beneventum into the dales of Samnium, laying waste the country of the Calor and Vulturnus. His objective was the rich district of northern Campania. Surely a raid upon the garden of Italy would force even Fabius to give him battle. There was also a hope that Capua, the centre of this wealthy region, the second city of Italy, would join him: but for the present the plan failed. And until he held Capua it was premature to try for what he wanted most of all, a good Campanian harbour within easy sail of Carthage.

292. The account of the manœuvres of Hannibal and Fabius in Campania varies a good deal in the different versions. But it seems clear that the former descended into the fertile plains north of the Vulturnus and laid them waste: one raid through the Falernian district reached as far westward as the coast by Sinuessa. The devastation of a country abounding in vines and fruit trees would be more permanent in its effects than that of cornlands. The army of Fabius, looking on at the havoc from the skirts of the Massic hills, came very near to open mutiny. But the dictator stuck to his plan. He saw that Hannibal must move elsewhere for winter quarters: it seemed pretty certain that he would have to return by the way he had come: Fabius meant to entrap his opponent in a gorge of the range known as mount Callicula, and then fall upon him with every advantage of the ground. While engaged in organizing this masterstroke, he sent out an officer with a party of cavalry, under strict orders to confine his men to scouting duty: but they were lured on by Numidian horsemen, and so cut up by the heavy cavalry of Hannibal, that few of them returned. Worse was to follow. The wily Carthaginian guessed the designs of Fabius. He had with him a great number of captured oxen. On their horns[1] he had dry faggots tied and told off a body of men to drive them. At a certain time the faggots were to be set on fire and the oxen driven uphill on to the ridges commanding the gorge. It was well carried out in the dark hours. The fires rushing about the hill sides took the Romans by surprise: Fabius was too wary to risk anything till he understood what it all meant: the men on guard at the outlet of the pass lost their heads and deserted their post. By daybreak Hannibal had got his army and their booty safely through, and the dictator's scheme had failed. The Punic general had now succeeded in discrediting Fabius with the Roman people. It seemed that caution was after all not so very much better than boldness: at least it

[1] This again is a very suspicious tale, but I cannot suggest a good reason for inventing it.

offered little prospect of a speedy ending to a burdensome war. To add to the dictator's unpopularity was Hannibal's object. Well-informed as ever, he found out the position of some lands belonging to Fabius, and left them untouched while all around was turned into a desert. Fabius was at the time negotiating with him for the usual exchange of prisoners. The balance was against Rome, and a cash payment of so much per head was due to redeem the excess of Roman captives. The Senate refused to vote the money, or at least made difficulties: Fabius at once sold the estates that the enemy had spared, and redeemed the prisoners with the money. Such is the story, which may be true. The march of Hannibal seems now to have been to the North, probably along the line of the upper Vulturnus, and to have extended even to the hill country of the Paeligni. Fabius followed on the high ground, keeping between Rome and the enemy, who, bending away to the East, at last found a suitable place for winter quarters at Gereonium or Gerunium near the borders of Apulia. The Roman army took post at or near Larinum.

293. We now come to the affair of Fabius and Minucius, a most important episode in Roman history, the accounts of which present a great variety in detail. No doubt the Fabian side was sympathetically represented by the great Fabian annalist, while the naughtiness and failure of Minucius have been made more heinous through the Roman tendency to point a moral. While the armies were facing each other, it became necessary for Fabius to visit Rome in order to take part in some religious ceremonies. He left the master of the horse in charge, with strict injunctions to follow his own cautious policy and run no risks. Now at this time Hannibal's first care was the collection of ample stores, particularly of grain, to feed his men and horses through the winter. He had not only to provide strong foraging parties, but also to keep under arms a sufficient force to protect them: if it became necessary to advance some distance from Gerunium, he had to guard against a sudden attack on his magazines. To do all these things with speed, while the corn was still to be had, was no easy matter. One day, it seems, Minucius caught him at a disadvantage, and attacked him. The engagement was never a real trial of strength, for Hannibal was at the time more concerned to secure his magazines than to beat the Romans: but the result could be, and was, reported as a victory for Rome. The indignation at Fabius' conduct of the war received a great impulse: the popular party was enabled to override all constitutional rule and precedent. A tribune proposed to give the master of the horse equal powers[1]

---

[1] An inscription is extant in which Minucius plainly describes himself as dictator. See Wilmanns' *exempla*, 24.

with the dictator, thus depriving the dictatorship of all meaning. While this. was under consideration, Fabius was called upon to hold an election of a consul in the stead of Flaminius: and Marcus Atilius Regulus was chosen. Before the equal-powers bill came on for voting, Fabius, unmoved by the attacks made on him, slipped away and rejoined his army. Soon the news came that Gaius Terentius Varro, a rising popular leader of humble origin, had taken up the proposal, and that the Meeting of the Plebs had passed it into law. Fabius took the insult calmly, and kept his temper with the inflated conceit of Minucius. He refused to share powers by alternation of the supreme command: an exact division of the army[1] was made, each taking half, and two separate camps were formed. Hannibal saw his opportunity: in a few days he tempted Minucius into an engagement and led on his men into an ambuscade. Only the arrival of Fabius with his army in the nick of time averted a great disaster. In the fullest version, that of Livy, the story ends with an edifying scene: the contrite Minucius hands back his army to Fabius with an appropriate speech, and resumes his subordinate position, abdicating his equal powers. But the dictatorship[2] never really recovered its prestige as a means of saving the state in emergencies by a brief concentration of supreme executive power in one man. We shall soon see it pass out of use and become an antiquity: the later constitutional lawyers, puzzled by the exceptional circumstances of Fabius' appointment, doubted whether he was ever strictly[3] a dictator. For the moment the important matter was that his six-months term was running out. He and Minucius handed over their forces to the consuls Atilius and Servilius, whom Fabius had sent for: they followed the system of Fabius, watching and annoying Hannibal during the winter.

294. Before we leave this eventful year 217, we must turn to the operations in Spain and the fitful attempts at naval war. Hasdrubal advanced along the coast northwards, his army keeping in touch with his fleet, and Gnaeus Scipio moved south to meet him. The strength of the Punic land forces induced Scipio to confine himself to a naval

---

[1] Polybius represents Fabius as offering either to share powers or divide the army, Minucius as choosing the latter. This seems to me so inconsistent with the character of Fabius, that I follow Livy with confidence. Plutarch in his life of Fabius follows the same version.

[2] It would appear from the note of Festus (under *optima lex*) that the dictator had already been made subject to the right of appeal, at least within the city precincts. The date of this is uncertain. Mommsen *Staatsrecht* would refer it to the *lex Valeria* of 300 B.C. See Livy x 9, and § 149 above.

[3] They suppose him to have been elected to act as dictator, *qui pro dictatore esset*, Liv. XXII 31, cf. VI 6 § 16.

movement: but he took picked fighting men on board his ships, and he had most useful help from some fast cruisers sent by Rome's old ally, Massalia. Off the mouth of the Ebro[1] the fleets engaged. The Carthaginian was larger (40), and had its army drawn up on the shore in its rear: the Roman (35) was evidently far more efficient as a fighting machine. Ill-prepared and perhaps outmanœuvred the Punic line soon gave way. Vessels were run ashore and abandoned by their crews: besides other damage and loss, Hasdrubal saw 25 ships towed off as prizes by the enemy: for the present one hearty stroke had put the Iberian seaboard in the power of Rome. The Romans coasted along, making descents at various points, even near New Carthage itself, doing all the damage they could, and weakening the prestige of Carthage among the natives. They ravaged the island of Ebusus: and their control of the sea was for the time so marked that the favour of Scipio was sought by an embassy from the Balearic isles. So the fleet worked its way back to its headquarters in the North. Numberless tribes from near and far now sent envoys to the Roman general, anxious to make terms with the rising power. That more than 120 communities actually submitted to Rome and gave hostages, is not easy to believe: however small these *populi* may severally have been, the tale is probably due to the family annals of the Scipios.

295. The naval reverse off the Spanish coast roused the Home government of Carthage. To carry out their designs, they felt that they must not give up their hold on the sea. So they sent out a fleet of 70 ships, which sailed to Sardinia and then to the coast of Etruria, a visit to which we have referred above. Unable to find Hannibal, with whom they had hoped to join hands, and hearing of the approach of a strong Roman fleet, they went back home as they had come. Servilius with his 120 ships pursued them: finding that he was too late, he extended his cruise to the African coast. Here he plundered or levied contributions on some islands, but a mismanaged descent on the mainland was repulsed with serious loss. So he withdrew in all haste to Lilybaeum, made arrangements for sending home his fleet, and went off to take command of the land forces in obedience to the summons of Fabius. Meanwhile the sea was clear

---

[1] The accounts of the battle, Polyb. III 95—6 and Livy XXII 19, 20, are very incomplete. If the newly discovered fragment of Sosylus really refers to this affair (see Wilcken in *Hermes* XLI pp. 103—141), it would seem that the clever naval tactics of the Massaliots were a chief cause of the victory. This attribution seems to me very probable. We know from Nepos that Sosylus was a friend and companion of Hannibal. That Polybius (III 20 § 5) sneers at him as ill-informed of affairs in Rome, is not to be wondered at. Even a mere scrap of a Hannibalic version of an obscure event is worth mention. And Polybius also calls attention to the notable services of the Massaliots in the Hannibalic war.

of Punic fleets, and the Romans had without hindrance strengthened their forces in Spain. Publius Scipio, the consul of 218, was continued in his *imperium* as proconsul, and sent to join his brother. He had 20 battleships, 8000 soldiers, and ample stores: the whole convoy of transports was very large. To keep a firm footing in Spain was a main object with the Senate: they saw that the control of the resources of the peninsula bore directly, perhaps decisively, on the issue of the war in Italy. Yet communications with Spain had to be maintained by sea. It was the fatal half-heartedness of Carthage in her naval policy that left this vital waterway open to Rome throughout the war.

296. Publius and his army came at a happy moment. Spanish tribes in alliance with Carthage had lately entered Roman territory and been driven off with loss. Now the Celtiberians, powerful tribes of partly Gaulish blood, were engaged in a much more serious invasion of the Carthaginian sphere. News came of their successes: the Roman leaders seized the chance of backing up their allies: with the fleet cruising in support along the coast, they crossed the Ebro and reached Saguntum without opposition. While encamped about five miles from the town, which seems to have been in a habitable state, a piece of luck befell them. It was known that Hannibal, before he left Spain, had taken hostages for the good behaviour of a number of suspected tribes, and that these hostages, mostly the sons of chiefs, were kept under guard at Saguntum. The device checked rebellion but did not generate loyal feeling; and that the Romans, if they could get the youths into their hands, would turn the prize to good account, could hardly be doubted. It occurred to Abilyx or Abelux, a Spaniard of rank in the Punic service, that here was a grand opening for a bit of businesslike treachery. Forecasting the growth of Roman power in Spain, he wished to join the winning side in good time. To hand over the hostages to the Scipios at this critical juncture would secure him a hearty welcome in the Roman camp: to arrange for their speedy restoration to relatives and friends would add to his already high reputation among his fellow-countrymen. The local commander of the Punic forces, Bostar, was a guileless soldier, and had the fullest confidence in Abilyx. The latter persuaded Bostar to forestall the growing popularity of Rome by restoring the hostages, and offered his services for the transaction. But he had come to an understanding with the proconsul, and betrayed the precious charge to the Romans: he then carried out the scheme of restoration in the name and interest of Rome. Scipio wisely sent some of his own staff to bear a part in this act of grace and collect goodwill. A widespread movement in favour of Rome was now certain, but open action was delayed by the coming of winter.

297. The position of Rome in relation to the war is somewhat illustrated by sundry occurrences during the winter months. A deputation from Neapolis visited the city, to offer what gold cups they could muster as a contribution to the cost of the war, and to declare their intention of devoting all their resources to the cause of Rome. The Senate would not confess exhaustion by taking the bulk of the gold. They accepted but one little cup, and returned the warmest thanks for this cheering exhibition of loyalty. It was however no great wonder that a commercial Greek city should support the Roman cause against Carthage, their ancient enemy. A different excitement next stirred men's minds. Hannibal's spies had served him well. Just now one of them, who had passed undetected for two years, was caught. His hands were cut off, and he was turned out to find his way to the Punic camp. A conspiracy of slaves was discovered, the guilty crucified, the informer rewarded. Diplomacy had its share of attention. The Senate sent out no less than three embassies; one to Philip of Macedon, to demand the surrender of their old enemy Demetrius of Pharos; another to Liguria, to induce the hillmen not to send help to Hannibal, and incidentally to watch the doings of the Gauls; a third to their client the Illyrian king, to recall him to a more punctual discharge of his obligations to Rome. Little or nothing came of these missions, but they served to shew that Rome had not abdicated her position as the great Italian power. Soon a deputation came from Paestum, of the same character as that from Neapolis, and received with the same dignity: also one from the faithful Hiero, bringing supplies of corn, and a contingent of bowmen and slingers. Hearty thanks were voted him: even the gold sent was in this case gladly accepted, being in the form of a statue of Victory, to refuse which would be unlucky. The king's advice, to carry the war into Africa, was so far followed that the fleet on the Sicilian station was increased, in case an opportunity for such a venture should occur.

298. But the all-absorbing interest at Rome in that winter was the election of consuls for the next year. Already the inadequacy of the system of yearly generals had been noted. Senate and Plebs had agreed to suspend all rules[1] restricting reelections of ex-consuls to the consulship. It was another matter to put the new policy into practice by at once electing none but tried men. The Scipios were busy in Spain. Of other possible candidates Fabius had borne the greatest part in the war: but the merits of his strategy were matter of furious controversy. Nor does he seem to have wished to come forward at present: indeed he was wanted in Rome. The masses were discon-

---

[1] Livy XXVII 6 § 7, compare VII 42 § 2, X 15 § 11.

tented at the burdens and sufferings of the war, and Varro, the popular leader of the hour, charged the nobility with allowing it to drag on that they might the longer enjoy the powers and honours of command. The election was delayed by various hindrances, which only inflamed the general irritation. Neither consul would leave his army to preside at the *comitia*. Requested to name a dictator for the purpose, one of them did so : but the augurs found some flaw in the appointment, and the dictator was driven to resign. It was necessary to resort to an *interregnum*, and at last the election took place. There were six candidates : three Patricians, two Plebeians of noble families, and Varro. Of these Varro alone gained the requisite majority, the votes of more than half the Centuries. On the earliest day available for an Assembly he presided at the election of a colleague. The nobles looked round for some man who might hold his own against the hotheaded Varro. Lucius Aemilius Paullus was a soldier distinguished in the Illyrian war : but his former treatment by the people rankled in his mind, and he was living in grim retirement. With great difficulty he was coaxed into standing for what was likely to be an arduous and thankless post, and he was elected. The four praetors chosen were likewise all men previously tried in office. It was no time for experiments.

299. Before the season opened for the campaign of 216, vast preparations were made. A great effort was to be put forth in hope of getting rid of this weary war. The praetor Postumius was to hold down the Gauls in the North with a strong force, which eventually reached a total of 25,000 men. The praetor Marcellus, hero of the Gaulish war of 222, was to command in Sicily. Supplies were collected for the service of the army in Spain. Not only were an extraordinary number of legions raised, but the strength of each legion was increased from a normal 4200 (4000 foot) to 5300 (5000 foot). Beside the regular military oath of obedience, a customary voluntary oath binding the soldiers of each company not to desert one another, a sort of comrades' pledge, was on this great occasion officially required. A new batch of prodigies were scrupulously expiated with the proper ceremonies. Then the newly raised legions were despatched to their destinations, mostly to the seat of war on the Apulian border. For the present the consuls remained in Rome and the command in the field was left to Servilius and Atilius as proconsuls. They carried out their instructions, avoiding a pitched battle, and using every chance that offered to engage in skirmishes and small combats. The blame of previous failures was now being laid rather on the rawness of Roman troops as compared with Hannibal's veterans than on the incapacity of Roman generals : but

Fabius, it is said, knew better.   It was probably summer or the end of spring[1] when the consuls joined the army.   The proconsul Atilius was allowed to go home on the score of age: Servilius was employed in subordinate command.   At first things went on much as before. There appears to have been some hope that failure of supplies would make it impossible for the Punic leader to keep together his motley army: his Spanish troops in particular were said to be on the point of deserting him.   At all events it is true that he was lost if he did not soon fight and win a great battle.   A casual skirmish resulted in favour of the Romans, and gave them a fatal confidence.   Hannibal then tried to lure the Romans into an ambush by a pretended flight, leaving his camp by night, with valuable property lying about in it. The bait took: the men were eager to pursue the flying enemy. Varro would have led them out in spite of his colleague's protests, but Paullus sent word that the sacred fowls had refused their food. Neglect of religion had not been attended with good results, and Varro yielded.   To stop the men was not easy, and they were getting out of hand, when two slaves, prisoners in the Punic army, came in with news that the enemy were waiting for them in ambush beyond the hills hard by.   This stratagem having failed, Hannibal coolly returned to his abandoned camp.   But he felt it necessary to move, so he shortly slipped off into Apulia, where the harvest was earlier.   On the river Aufidus was the small town of Cannae, on rising ground not far from the sea.   It was used by the Romans as a depot for stores.   While the Roman army was following him slowly, Hannibal seized the place and encamped near it, choosing his position with great care.   He saw, as did the reluctant Paullus, that a pitched battle was now inevitable, and he meant to have it fought on the open ground below Cannae.   Here he could use to the full his superiority in cavalry.   He meant also to disconcert his enemy by the blinding dust of that dry plain.   An E.S.E. wind got up daily about the same time: this he must have at his back.   He knew that the Senate had sent the consuls orders to fight, and that Varro was eager to engage, while Paullus preferred to await an opportunity. By feints and provocations he played into the hands of Va.ro: and, as the consuls were commanding by turns on alternate days, the orator-general soon gave the signal for battle.

300.   The tactics and topography of Cannae have had a great fascination for scholars and military critics.   Fortunately the many

---

[1] Polybius makes them take command when Hannibal had already moved to Cannae, only a few days, it would seem, before the battle.   This is surely incredible, and his version includes several errors.   I have chiefly followed Livy, but his account is far from clear. Dates are quite unattainable.

points in dispute do not concern us. The strength of the armies is given in round numbers as follows: Roman, 70,000 or 80,000 foot, 6000 horse; Carthaginian, 40,000 foot, 10,000 horse. The course of the battle was briefly this. The Roman cavalry were cut down or put to flight on both wings. Then the mass of the Roman foot were allowed to force back the much shallower lines of Spaniards and Gauls, whom they blindly followed into a trap. Their exposed flanks were at once assailed by the Africans, while the heavy cavalry, leaving the Numidians to pursue the remains of the Roman horse, fell upon their rear. By degrees this main body, perhaps 50,000 of Rome's finest infantry, lost their order, and were crowded together into a helpless throng, of which only the men on the edges could bear any part in the fight. But they fought on bravely, and fell as the turn came to each: tradition said that they all died on the field: at all events few of this body escaped. What happened to the Roman force left on guard in the larger of their two camps, and to the fugitives who took refuge in the camps, is far from clear: but it seems that 8,000 or 10,000 were taken prisoners, while a few hundreds cut their way out and reached Canusium, picking up stragglers on the way. A few thousands of stray fugitives got as far as Venusia, where they found the consul Varro, who had fled from the battle with a handful of the beaten cavalry. The confusion of the accounts makes it difficult to estimate the total losses: Livy puts the killed at 48,200, and accounts for the escape of 14,550; Polybius allows, killed over 70,000, escaped about 3000. This last can hardly be right, as special legions were afterwards formed out of survivors of Cannae. Prisoners and 'missing' must account for the balance of Rome's great army. Among the killed was the consul Paullus, in after times the hero of Roman writers: Servilius the proconsul, Minucius the late rival of Fabius, and many other men of distinction: of senators, or men qualified but not yet on the roll, eighty had fallen. On the Carthaginian side the loss was small: Livy puts it at 8000, Polybius at 5700, and this is perhaps the more likely figure: 4000 of the 5700 were Gauls.

301. By the time that the last stragglers came in, the number of fugitives at Canusium seems to have been about 10,000, at Venusia nearly 5000. At both towns they were received with warm hospitality. But there was trouble[1] at Canusium. A party of young nobles grew faint-hearted and gave up the commonwealth for lost: their design was to slip away to the coast and take ship for the court of one of the eastern kings. Those monarchs were known to welcome

---

[1] This story is evidently from a source favourable to Scipio. Livy XXII 53 may have copied Polybius, but the passage is lost.

foreign adventurers. This scheme, which at a moment of disaster might have had a fatal influence on the Allies of Rome, came to the ears of young Scipio, one of the two military tribunes whom the refugees had chosen as temporary commanders. With a few armed supporters he surprised the conspirators: under threat of death he made them take an oath of devotion to the cause of Rome, and stayed the plague of despair. When news came that Varro was safe at Venusia, the leaders at Canusium reported their numbers to him and asked for orders: the consul marched to Canusium and resumed his command. The Roman army had been reduced to a pitiful wreck, but the Roman system was unshaken.

302. Polybius, to whom the character of the Roman people was a study of the deepest interest, describes[1] the state of feeling in the city when it was known that the armies were face to face and that orders had been given for a battle. The thought of previous disasters suggested dire misgivings. Oracles and prodigies were the common talk: vows, sacrifices and ceremonies the chief feature of life. 'For,' he remarks, 'in time of danger they have a wonderful way of making their peace with gods and men, and Roman pride and Roman dignity will stoop to any performance of the kind.' Livy tells us that the first news of the battle was that the whole army had perished: the panic and confusion at Rome was more than he can adequately describe. It was indeed a black moment. 'Any other people,' he adds, 'would have been crushed by a disaster like this.' But the leading men soon rallied to meet the crisis. The Senate, those members who survived and were not serving abroad, met to discuss measures of defence. Once more old Fabius came to the front. By his advice scouting parties were sent out to learn the truth, whether some of their army had not escaped, whether the enemy was, as generally assumed, marching on Rome. Guards were posted at the gates to prevent an exodus of the timid, sure to be a contagious movement, and measures were taken to keep mourners within doors and stop the voice of lamentation in the streets. All news was to be brought at once to the praetors, and patience was enjoined on all. These sedative measures were soon followed by the receipt of a despatch from Varro, from which men learnt the number of survivors and their whereabouts, and that Hannibal was still at Cannae. The city breathed again, and measures of defence were actively pushed on. Just then came a call for aid from Sicily. The propraetor reported that the enemy's fleet were making raids on the territory of Hiero, while a well-equipped second fleet was hovering in the West: he could not help Syracuse, because his duty to the Roman province

[1] Polyb. III 112.

kept him at Lilybaeum. But this matter had to wait. Marcellus seems to have been just ready to start for his province[1], and his fleet lay at Ostia. He was now ordered to send 1500 of his marines to help in guarding Rome, and take a full marine legion to Canusium. The consul was to hand over to Marcellus' charge the remains of his army, and himself to return to Rome without delay. He was also instructed to name Marcus Junius Pera dictator. Whether he did this before or after his return to Rome is uncertain, and it matters not: anyhow the appointment was made in due form. The story of the home-coming of Varro is one of the stock scenes on which later writers loved to dwell, as illustrating the steadfast magnanimity of the Roman people. When he drew near the city, he was met[2] by a throng of citizens of all ranks, and thanked by the senators for not having despaired of the commonwealth. It was indeed a moment when patriotism demanded that all should pull together and avoid recriminations: but we must not lay too much blame on the defeated consul. The accounts of his forwardness and temerity have probably been coloured so as to glorify by contrast the virtues or victories of others. Varro was afterwards employed in important military and political duties. He could hardly have continued to be a trusted officer of the Roman state, had the responsibility for Cannae lain wholly at his door.

303. Rome was in a fair way to be herself again, but the nerves of the people had been terribly shaken. The natural result of fear was credulity, which shews itself in a fresh crop of prodigies and horrors: Vestal virgins failing in chastity, punishment of them and their paramours; human sacrifices, such as in the panic of 225. An envoy, Fabius Pictor, afterwards the historian, was sent to Delphi to seek predictions and advice from the great oracle of Greece. This was perhaps better than looking for scapegoats. Meanwhile the new dictator was busy with the levy of troops. Four new legions, with 1000 horse, were raised: but in order to make up this force lads who were only just the military age (17) had to be taken, and some even younger. The Allies, Latins &c, were called upon for their contingents. We must not forget that they furnished at least twice as many cavalry as the Roman citizens. But even so, with the destruction of the cavalry at Cannae before their eyes, knowing (as they surely must have known) that it was by the numbers and efficiency of

---

[1] Sicily.

[2] Legends gathered round Varro. One story is that he was offered the dictatorship, that is to say, invited to name himself dictator, and refused. Another is that he went into mourning and would never again accept office. Livy XXII 61 § 14, Valerius Max. III 4 § 4, IV 5 § 2, Frontinus *Strat.* IV 5 § 6.

his mounted troops that Hannibal maintained his superiority in the field, we do not find the Roman government making serious efforts to strengthen and remodel this important arm. Probably this apparent neglect is a trace of the influence of Fabius, and the abandonment for the present of all idea of fighting pitched battles. How great just now was the strain upon the resources of the state in flesh and blood is shewn by the formation of a volunteer corps[1] of slaves. Of these there were 8000, all bought from their owners by the state: good service in the field was to be rewarded by the gift of freedom. A number of criminals and debtors are also said to have been discharged and embodied for service.

304. At this point comes in the story of the Roman citizens prisoners in the hands of Hannibal. He had as usual picked out the Allies and let them go free. He now changed his former severe treatment of the Romans. He offered to let them be ransomed at prices fixed according to quality, and allowed a deputation to proceed to Rome to negotiate for the redemption. Carthalo, one of his best cavalry officers, was sent with them, instructed to feel his way, and treat for a peace in case he found the Roman leaders disposed to come to terms. The story[2] appears in different versions with much variety of detail. Briefly, Carthalo was not received at all, and the prisoners' delegates met with a negative answer. One or more of them tried by means of a dishonourable quibble to evade the obligation of returning to captivity according to their oath. This conduct aroused general disgust: whether one culprit was arrested and handed over to Hannibal, or whether the ten delegates stayed in Rome for the remnant of their lives, blasted by official and popular indignation, was a matter on which tradition varied. To hand down a striking picture of constancy in the face of disaster, and of a delicacy of honour proof against temptation, is the essential purport of this edifying tale. We are to understand that the Roman government (the Senate, in fact) chose to buy slaves as substitutes for citizens, rather than ransom citizens who had bowed to the Punic yoke to save their lives. We are told that two considerations had great weight in promoting this decision. First, it was reported that Hannibal was in need of money to pay his troops. Secondly, it was suspected that he wanted to establish a notable precedent for the surrender of Roman soldiers. The Senate would not help to fill his military chest: it would not be tempted into a concession that was but too likely to weaken the moral fibre of Roman armies. The picture may be overdrawn: its main features are surely true.

[1] Livy XXII 57 §§ 11, 12, Weissenborn.
[2] Polyb. VI 58, Livy XXII 58—61, Cic. de Officiis III § 114.

305. Hannibal did not destroy his Roman prisoners with every circumstance of barbarity, as malignant fiction asserted. He had use for some of them, as we shall see at Capua. That he sold many into slavery as the market offered, is more than likely. Nor did he march at once upon Rome. He had not the means of carrying on a regular siege: a mere demonstration would be worse than useless, for there was no particular object to be gained by it just then. In invading Italy he had counted on detaching the Italian Allies from Rome. His experiences up to this point had shewn him that no other procedure offered any prospect of success. And now at last he seemed to be near the fulfilment of his hopes. The aristocratic governments generally favoured by Rome were in many towns overcome by the 'popular' parties, men with little to lose, and the towns brought over to Hannibal. He thus won Arpi and other places in Apulia, part of the Sallentine or Calabrian peninsula, the bulk of southern Samnium and Lucania, nearly all the Bruttian country: in short, a large part of southern Italy, to which was presently added Capua and other cities in Campania. But the exceptions to this abandonment of the Roman alliance were weighty and significant. The Latin colonies, such as Venusia, Brundisium, Paestum and Beneventum, stood firm. So for the present[1] did the Greek cities. All the good harbours were still held by Rome.

(b) 215—209 B.C.

306. We have hitherto followed the sensational story of a war in which pitched battles form the main feature. In about two years, from the crossing of the Ebro to Cannae, Hannibal had apparently stricken the power of Rome to the ground. But a war and a battle are different things: it was not necessary to go on gathering the flower of Italian manhood into great armies, and sending them forth under amateur generals to be destroyed by the genius of a master. We now enter upon a time when Rome carries on the war in Italy on different principles. Smaller armies are employed, and more of them, and Hannibal could not be in several places at once. Fortified camps and sieges play an important part in the war, and Hannibal had neither the numbers nor the materials for this kind of warfare. Both sides have now allies to protect and positions to hold, and Hannibal could spare no garrisons to speak of. The policy of Rome no longer wavers with the ups and downs of party strife, as Flaminius or Fabius

---

[1] Both Polybius III 118 and Livy XXII 61 § 12 say that Tarentum went over at this time, but from the later part of their narratives it seems certain that this was not so. Some negotiations may have taken place.

or Varro happen to prevail. The popular party has lost self-confidence, and the Senate quietly takes in hand the government. Fabius, whose previous campaign had earned him the nickname *Cunctator*, the Dawdler or Slow-goer, is the most influential man in the House, and often commands in the field. Beside him the brave Marcellus now comes to the front. Romans called him the sword of Rome, Fabius the shield. He brought into defensive warfare the necessary offensive element. Looked at from a strictly military point of view, the conditions of the war were much less favourable to the invader than they had hitherto been. Nor was the winning-over of Roman Allies so much of a gain as it might at first sight appear. Because the defection of this or that community was a serious blow to Rome, it did not follow that Hannibal won as much as Rome lost. As the southern Greeks had wished to find in Pyrrhus a champion rather than a master, so did the southern Italians now in Hannibal. Of protection they expected at least as much as they had enjoyed under Rome; of freedom, more. Now freedom was apt to mean shirking the burdens necessary for their own defence: and, if coercion was applied, the new yoke was no less galling than the old. Besides, their territories had to be spared, and much land was thus closed to Hannibal's foragers. Of genuine inclination to the cause of Carthage there was no sign. Carthage had no vital imperial system, the blessings of which sanguine allies might fairly hope to share: it is hard to see what could have been the basis of interest common to Carthage and the Italians. A common antipathy to Rome was not enough: it was a negative influence, and merely meant that each of the partners was ready to make use of the other to destroy or weaken Rome. In short, Hannibal had nothing to offer that could rouse enthusiasm in Italy. The tie between him and his new allies was and remained essentially a military one: and the slowness and insufficiency of the support received from Carthage put him at a great disadvantage in dealing with allies who looked to him for protection first of all. Nor was the composition of his army without its drawbacks. We cannot suppose that the Africans and Spaniards were in themselves welcome guests: their presence in Italy would hardly be reassuring. But, if these might be tolerated as means to an end, what about the Gauls? Fear and hatred of these barbarians was widespread in Italy. In no character did Rome command Italian sympathies so certainly as in that of a bulwark against Gaulish invasion. And now here was a strange liberator, with 'freedom' in his mouth and Gauls at his back. Surely men had heard what sort of freedom was enjoyed by the African subjects of Carthage. The horrors of Libyan risings and mercenary wars were not things done in a corner.

307. The truth is that, what with the lukewarmness of his allies, the inadequacy of reinforcements from home, and the wiser direction of Roman policy, Hannibal's prospects in Italy were getting worse and worse. The war moved slowly, and much of its interest centred at Capua and Tarentum. By 209 both these cities had been retaken by the Romans and suffered dire punishment: it was all over with the Punic cause in Italy, unless a new army from abroad should join Hannibal and drive the Roman forces from the field. Already in the winter of 216—5 the great Carthaginian must have begun to feel that his task was not ending but beginning, and that he must seek external help from every possible quarter if he was to have any chance of final victory. Hence his alliance with Philip of Macedon, from which he hoped much: but, though Philip did not make peace with Rome till 205, it was clear by 209 that Macedon was but a broken reed. Hence too his active interest in the affairs of Syracuse, and the effort to drive the Romans out of Sicily: but, thanks largely to Punic mismanagement, Syracuse fell in 212, and Rome was supreme in Sicily by 210. As for Spain, Rome and Carthage were equally alive to the necessity of getting and keeping the upper hand in the peninsula. Both sides kept up their forces, and in 211 it seemed as though Carthage would be the winner: but the cause of Rome was restored and prevailed in the end. The forlorn hope of Hasdrubal, and its destruction at the Metaurus, belong to the next stage of the war.

308. The latter part of the year 216 was an eventful time. Hannibal advanced to Neapolis, and gained a small victory over the city forces: but there was no sign of surrender, and the walls were strong, so he withdrew to a more promising enterprise. The great city of Capua, capital of the rich Campanian plain, able it was said to place in the field an army of 30,000 foot and 4000 horse, had for some time been discontented with its position in the Roman system. The people[1] were Roman citizens without the 'public' rights of voting in Assemblies and holding office at Rome. The 'private' rights of *conubium* and *commercium* would be of little use to any but the wealthy. The policy of Rome had been to support the party of the nobles in all communities. At Capua the wealthy knights (*equites*) had been treated with special favour. By the settlement of 338 they had been endowed with a kind of pensions, a rent-charge on the lands retained by Capua. Thus the nobles were bound to Rome by direct money-interest, by intermarriages, and by common military service. At this very time 300 picked Campanian knights were serving in the Sicilian garrisons, perhaps intended to be also hostages for Campanian

---

[1] The city had been left with its local government. There was a senate, and magistrates, the chief of whom was the Meddix. See § 183.

loyalty. In Capua itself an ambitious noble had by skilful intrigues become all-powerful. He saved the senate from popular violence, but made it subservient to the populace, who, already wishing to shake off the Roman yoke, thought they might safely do so after the disaster of Cannae. After some hesitation, the city was allied with Hannibal, and the senators implicated in the revolt. It is said that there were some in Capua who dreamt of a time coming when the victorious Punic army would be withdrawn from Italy, having done its work, and an imperial Capua succeed to the lost primacy of Rome. If so, the terms made with Hannibal were ill devised to attain that result. To exact from him 300 picked Roman prisoners as a means of redeeming their 300 knights in Sicily, to insist on retaining their own laws and government, were wise and dignified claims. But, when they bargained[1] that no Punic officer should have control over any Campanian, and stipulated for exemption from compulsory military service and contributions, the effect of this ill-timed assertion of freedom was to render their adhesion to Hannibal rather a burden than a support. In the dizzy elation of the moment it is said that the patriot populace seized the Romans who happened to be in Capua and stifled them to death in a bath-house. There was probably a small minority in the city to whom the revolt from Rome appeared a blunder. One highly respected citizen, Decius Magius, had openly denounced the step, and refused to obey the orders of Hannibal. Hannibal dared not leave this man at large, to form a rallying-point for disaffection in case the fickle Campanians should change their minds. He therefore required the senate to agree to the surrender of Magius, and they did not venture to refuse. It was a curious illustration of the freedom[2] of Capua. But circumstances drove Hannibal to act the tyrant. He arrested Magius, sent him to the sea coast, and shipped him off for Carthage. Foul weather drove the ship to Cyrene, then a province of the Egyptian kingdom. Magius took sanctuary, and was forwarded to Alexandria, where he claimed protection from the reigning Ptolemy. The Egyptian court was traditionally jealous of Carthage, and had long been on friendly terms with Rome. Magius was declared free: but in the present state of things, rather than return to Rome or Capua, he preferred to settle down in Egypt and wait for better times.

309. Meanwhile Mago had reached Carthage, and made report to the senate of his brother's successes in Italy, his brilliant victories, the enormous losses of the Romans, the adhesion of a large part of Italy. To impress his countrymen with the greatness of the blow

---

[1] Livy XXIII 7 §§ 1, 2, Weissenborn.
[2] Livy XXIII 10 § 4.

dealt at Cannae it is said that he emptied on the floor of the House one or more large measures or cases. The contents were golden rings. These, he explained, were not worn by ordinary Romans, but only by knights of the first order. Those lying before them were stripped after Cannae from Roman dead. The story may be true, but, like the other scenes reported in the Carthaginian senate, we cannot trace it back to any good authority. The main object of Mago's mission was however to urge the prompt despatch of stores and money to feed and pay their army in Italy, and men to make good the wastage in the ranks and enable Hannibal to use his great opportunity of bringing the war to a triumphant end. To repose on previous victories would be to waste them. It is said that Hanno renewed his former opposition to the war-policy, and maintained that the wisest use of their successes, if genuine, would be to conclude with all speed an advantageous peace. On such situations, imaginary or founded on fact, the moralizing rhetoric of Livy loves to dwell. But the party of the Barcids were in a great majority, and supplies and money were voted, and it was decided to strengthen Hannibal's army by considerable[1] reinforcements. In connexion with these requirements troops were to be raised in Africa and Spain. Voting however was not the same thing as sending, as Hannibal was to learn.

310. At Rome hopes were reviving. Fabius Pictor had come back from Delphi: the religious precautions enjoined by the oracle were observed with minute care, and the favour of the gods secured. The dictator Junius marched for Campania with his miscellaneous army of 25,000 men. The tradition of the war in Campania is so obscured by the want of details of the chronology and topography, and the recurrence of incidents (perhaps repetitions of the same thing) is so suspicious, that only a tentative outline of events can be constructed. How often Hannibal vainly tried to gain Neapolis, whether he was repulsed from Nola more than once, we do not know. It seems certain that in Nola the populace was ready to revolt, and that the promptitude of Marcellus in coming to the help of the aristocratic party was what saved the town for Rome. Whether Marcellus gained a considerable victory under the walls of Nola, is reasonably doubted: anyhow Hannibal withdrew. He succeeded however in taking Nuceria and Acerrae: but this cannot have been a great gain while Nola remained Roman, and the people of these two towns (the Roman partisans, that is) are said to have taken refuge in other places still loyal to Rome. Some versions of the story speak of many being butchered through the cruel treachery of

---

[1] The text of Livy XXIII 13 is defective in the matter of numbers, but it seems that 40 elephants were included.

Hannibal. It is the fashion to reject these imputations on his character, but in face of the barbarities usual in Carthaginian warfare it is safer to offer no opinion. A more striking enterprise was his attack on the town of Casilinum, which commanded the passage of the Volturnus and threatened Capua. No proper provision had been made for the defence of this important post: too much had been staked on the field of Cannae. There were in the town two cohorts: one of Latins from Praeneste 570 strong, the other 460 Allies from Perusia. A few Roman citizens were with them. The brave little garrison beat off his first assault. If it be true that he defeated a

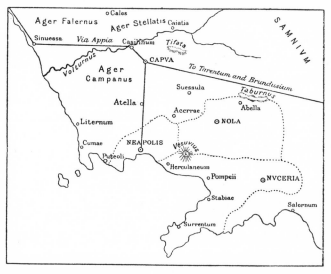

Map of Campania in the second Punic war. Only the chief roads, mountains, etc. are shewn. The territories of three Roman Allies are indicated (after Beloch) by dotted lines: (1) Neapolis, (2) Nola with Abella, (3) the confederation of the four towns headed by Nuceria.

sally of the besieged with the help of elephants, he must already have been reinforced from Carthage. But he had to turn the siege into a blockade. After enduring the extremities of famine during the winter, the remnant surrendered on honourable terms early in 215 and returned home on payment of a fixed ransom. Livy records[1] that the Roman Senate voted a threefold reward to the Praenestines: double pay for the year's campaign, exemption from military service for five years, and Roman citizenship. The last offer they declined. We must grasp the full significance of this. Citizens of an old Latin town, formerly a member of the League (which Rome had broken

---

[1] Livy XXIII 20 §§ 1, 2.

up), were ready to fight for Rome, and yet preferred to keep their old franchise as Latins of Praeneste. Nearly half their number died at Casilinum. If the most-favoured Allies of Rome were so contented with their relation to the dominant power, even the less-favoured had probably little to complain of: and they might hope to better their position by loyal service. In isolation they could not maintain their independence: if they were inclined to forget this, the presence of Hannibal was an effective reminder. As parts of a great system they could be strong: and they knew of no system combining so much efficiency with so little interference as that devised by Rome. They would not lightly despair of the Roman cause, even when Cannae followed Trasimene, and 'freedom' was offered them: the force and blandishments of Hannibal were for the most part vain.

311. Further south, out of reach of the Roman armies, his lieutenant Himilco gained ground in Bruttium. The towns mostly joined him at once, but in a few cases force was necessary. Petelia on a rocky hill stood a long siege with exemplary fortitude, and only surrendered when starved out. Consentia made but slight resistance. Of the Greek towns, Croton, the mere shadow of its former self, fell at once: the still important Locri was brought over, either by treachery within or through the carelessness of the men in command: but they made good terms as free allies of Carthage, and had the good faith to aid the escape of the Roman garrison. An attempt on Rhegium failed, the town being strongly held. Of Thurii we at present hear nothing: but, as in the case of Tarentum, there were hostages held by the Romans for their fidelity: like Tarentum, it was probably garrisoned by Rome. After all these captures[1] and defections, Rome still held all the naval positions of the first importance in southern Italy. Neither Croton nor Locri were harbours of the first order. The dates of these events in Bruttium are not clear, but they seem to bring us to the spring of 215. Meanwhile a large part of Hannibal's army spent the winter at ease in Capua, where they are said to have lost their hardihood in the luxuries and debaucheries of the wicked city. This was an endless theme for the moralizing rhetoric of later times. But the current versions applied the story to the whole army of Hannibal, regardless of the forces engaged in Bruttium or in the lines before Casilinum. The tale does not deserve[2] belief, but it may contain some elements of truth. That his men

---

[1] The capture of these Greek towns is told twice over by Livy, XXIII 30, XXIV 1—3, with differences in detail. The only notable points in the latter version are, the wrath of the Bruttii at not being allowed to sack the towns, and the removal of the remnant of the Greeks of Croton to Locri.

[2] It does not appear in the remains of Polybius; who indeed in XI 19 says that Hannibal kept his forces in the field all through the war.

could not fight well after Capua is simply untrue. What he needed was more men, more food, more money to pay troops.

312. At Rome the government was terribly hampered by the financial pressure of the war. When the propraetors wrote from Sardinia and Sicily begging for supplies of corn and money, that they might be able to keep their fleets and armies efficient, all the Senate could do was to bid them shift for themselves. In Sicily the crisis was met by the generous help of old Hiero: in Sardinia the communities allied with Rome were constrained to make 'voluntary' contributions. At Rome itself the pressing need of ready money in circulation was dealt with by some exceptional[1] measure, perhaps by cash advances on the security of properties for which there was at the moment no market. Also the vacancies in the college of Pontiffs were filled up, and the filling up of those in the Senate was taken into serious consideration. The debate on this matter was the occasion of one of the most remarkable proposals ever made in all the history of Rome. The number of senators was far below the normal 300. The number of citizens who had a claim to be put on the roll as having held offices was far short of the number of vacancies. Free choice would play an unusually large part in the selection: it was not clear that enough men fitted for the dignity and responsibility could just now be found among the citizens. The proposal[2] was that the Roman Senate should select two members of the senate of each of the Latin[3] towns, that the men selected should be made Roman citizens, and at once made members of the Roman Senate. To us it sounds a wise and liberal scheme, likely to please the communities that enjoyed the 'Latin right,' as giving them another mark of superiority to the other Allies. It has in it a suggestion of a representative Senate, which sounds strangely modern. The proposer was an ex-consul, Spurius Carvilius, a man not belonging[4] to one of the great ruling families, who had been in politics an ally of Flaminius, and had risen by the support of the popular party. He was silenced by old Fabius, who had the House with him. The proposal was ill-timed: concessions made at such a moment would seem the result of fear, and only encourage the Allies generally to make demands: surely they were wavering enough already. It was agreed to drop the matter and treat the fact of the proposal as a state-secret. This narrow-minded obstinacy is merely the ugly side of that Roman firmness that brought Rome safely out of so many disasters. To praise or blame it is idle.

---

[1] Livy XXIII 21 § 6.　　　　　　　　　　　　　　　　　[2] Livy XXIII 22.

[3] If we reckon 3 old Latin towns (Praeneste, Tibur, Lauro-Lavinium), 3 Hernican, and 30 Latin colonies then existing, they would furnish 72 members.

[4] Cic. *de Senect.* § 11, Velleius II 128.

313. But the filling-up of the Senate was of the first importance, and it was no time for running the risks of a disagreement between two censors. It was agreed that the eldest living past-censor should be made dictator specially for this purpose. The consul Varro came posting from his army in Apulia, nominated the person designated, Marcus Fabius Buteo, and was off to his camp again. There were now two dictators at once, both having their nomination from Varro. But Junius was a dictator of the old sort with full powers : he was in Campania with his master of the horse : we may add that he was the last of his kind. Fabius Buteo was appointed expressly for the one duty of filling up the Senate, and had no master of the horse. We are now very near the total disuse of this great emergency-office. The new dictator complained bitterly of the evil precedent created by placing the choice of senators in a single hand. But he went on with the business, keeping on the roll all that remained of those enrolled by the previous censors of 220. He then added those who, not being already senators, had held magistracies since the last census. These cannot have been many. The rest were chosen simply on the ground of military distinction. The total of the new members added was 177. Business was promptly taken in hand. It was now winter, and the generals in Campania were summoned to Rome, to consult upon the plans for the next campaign. The annual elections were held by the dictator Junius. The consuls elected were Lucius Postumius, who was away with his army in the North, and Junius' master of horse, Tiberius Sempronius Gracchus. The dictator left Gracchus in Rome to see to the preparations for the next year, and himself returned to Campania. Things were getting .into train again, when suddenly news came[1] that Postumius with his whole army had been ambushed and destroyed by the Gauls. Great was the consternation in the city : of calamities there seemed to be no end. But the Senate, led by Gracchus, soon recovered its nerve. They took stock of the forces available. War with the Gauls might be put off to a more convenient season : but could they raise troops to face Hannibal? Various military arrangements were sketched out, which were afterwards completed and modified. In particular, a second-rate force was to be formed for service in Sicily, made up of the fugitive survivors of Cannae, who were to serve till the end of the war, and of the weaker men picked out of the army of Junius : and Varro was continued as proconsul in the Apulian command.

314. Far more cheerful was the news from the West. The receipt of a small reinforcement from Carthage emboldened Hasdrubal to enter on a forward movement both by land and sea. But his ship-

---

[1] Livy XXIII 24, Weissenborn. Polybius III 118 puts it earlier in the year.

captains[1] were sulky: a number of them deserted, and served the cause of Rome by promoting a native rising against Carthage. His first attempts to put down this rising failed, but success made the barbarians careless, and he presently defeated them with great slaughter. But about this time he received orders from home to start with his army at once and join his brother in Italy. The news of this plan, it is said, leaked out, and the prospect of the withdrawal of the Punic army turned the thoughts of most Spaniards towards Rome. So Hasdrubal wrote to the home government, pointing out that they had utterly miscalculated the Roman power in Spain. He could hardly make head against the Scipios now, and he had no forces to leave as an army of occupation behind him. If he went, a successor even with a strong army would find it no easy task to hold the country for Carthage. But the reply was a repetition of the order, and the despatch of a general with a strong military and naval force. The new-comer found it a difficult and dangerous business even to open communication with Hasdrubal: such was the state of Spain. But the brave son of Barcas did his best to carry out his orders. Before starting however he had to raise money. His brother had bought an unmolested passage through the land of the Gaulish tribes, and had hired Gaulish soldiers: so too must he. But to raise it by levying contributions on the Spaniards of the Punic province did not help to assuage the present discontents. He then marched northwards, and was brought to action by the Scipios. His Spanish troops ran away: the rest were killed or scattered in utter defeat. Wavering tribes hastened to join the side of Rome. Carthage had now to exert herself to keep what still was left to her in the peninsula: the fear of another invasion through the Alps, the Romans' nightmare, was for the present overpast.

315. Before the consular year (215) began in March, sundry religious matters were got over: others were attended to somewhat later. We must never forget the bargaining nature of Roman dealings with the gods. The object was to put pressure on the divine powers by doing exactly the right thing (worship, sacrifices, etc.) in exactly the right way. This successfully achieved, they were bound to lend their aid. In these days of doubt and danger it was of the first importance that the gods should not be let off too easily. This year too had its tale of prodigies: signs in the sky and sea, monstrous births, and other phenomena superstitiously deemed portents of evil: which were punctually 'expiated' as usual. The military picture of the war is projected on a background of religious rites and ceremonies. The military arrangements for the next campaign were

[1] Livy XXIII 26 § 4.

carefully considered. But no changes of quarters or commanders would provide pay for the armies in the field. The Senate decided to double the war-tax [*tributum*] for the current year. It was a pity, but it could hardly be helped. Many sources of revenue were lessened or stopped altogether by the war, the treasury was empty, the need urgent. We shall see that this measure by no means sufficed. An interesting question[1] came up in reference to the 300 Campanian knights, who were now in Rome, having served their time with the army in Sicily. They were loyal to Rome, but who were they? They had been Roman citizens without the 'public' rights. But the revolt of Capua had annulled all this. The matter was dealt with in true Roman fashion, by a fiction. Cumae, which had been on the same footing as Capua, was still loyal. It was proposed that the 300 should be deemed to be citizens belonging to Cumae[2] as from a given date, namely the day before the revolt of Capua, and that (being thus once more half-citizens) they should receive the full Roman franchise. The Tribe-Assembly wisely accepted the proposal. Next a consul had to be elected in the room of Postumius. Marcellus, late praetor and already continued in *imperium* as proconsul, was the choice of the Centuries. But the occurrence of a bad omen led to his resignation, and old Fabius, the 'safe man,' was chosen to fill the place. In order to avoid waste of time, a special arrangement was made for meetings of the Senate to be held hard by the *porta Capena*, the gate by which the chief roads to the South left the city. They were thus more directly in touch with news from the seat of war. The juridical praetors held their courts for the time in the same neighbourhood: in fact the centre of the city life was temporarily shifted.

316. A short review of the position of the Roman forces in 215 will give us some notion of the greatness of the strain on the resources of the state. The actual numbers cannot be ascertained. The consuls, Fabius and Sempronius Gracchus, were in northern Campania, the former with Junius' old army at Teanum, the latter with 25,000 Allies and the 8000 volunteer slaves [*volones*] at Sinuessa. The proconsul Marcellus was on the other side of Capua at Suessula, with the two 'city-legions' [a reserve kept as the nucleus of a garrison in Rome] of the preceding year, and probably some Allies. These forces moved as required, but not far: their function was to watch opportunities in Campania and prevent further revolts. The proconsul Varro was moved into Picenum, with a special commission to raise troops and provide for the defence of those parts. His place in Apulia was taken by M. Valerius[3] Laevinus the *praetor peregrinus,*

[1] Livy XXIII 31 §§ 10, 11.   [2] *Municipes Cumani.*
[3] Livy XXIII 30 § 18, 32 § 16.

who had to let his legal duties slide and turn to the work of war: with him were two legions recalled from Sicily. He took over also the army left by Varro, but this he posted at Tarentum under a subordinate: he had also a squadron of 25 ships to guard the coast from Tarentum to Brundisium. It was known that danger threatened from the East, and this command might at any moment become of first-rate importance. Q. Fulvius Flaccus the *praetor urbanus* could not be spared from the city, but he too had military responsibilities. He had 25 ships to guard the Latin and Etrurian coasts, and probably two newly-raised city-legions in Rome. He had also to deal with a sudden emergency in Sardinia. Roman supremacy in the island was menaced, and Mucius the new praetor was sick. Fulvius had to raise an extra legion for the service, and to appoint a deputy of his own [Manlius] to take the command. It seems certain that some naval force was despatched thither, and the forces in the island rose this year to over 23,000 men. To Sicily, which was beginning to cause anxiety, were sent the praetor Appius Claudius, with an army of inferior quality, and a deputy-commander to command the fleet at Lilybaeum: this was T. Otacilius, who had been previously employed on the same station. Of a force in Cisalpine Gaul we have no direct mention, but it seems that the idea of abandoning northern Italy for a time was not carried out. There was a certain Pomponius in the so-called *ager Gallicus* with a force of some kind, probably at Ariminum: we hear of his being continued in command for the year 214. And, beside all these forces maintained in fighting trim in Italy and the adjacent islands, there were the strong army and fleet under the Scipios, doing the work of Rome in Spain. When we reflect on the task of feeding all these bodies of men and of providing for the transmission of supplies and intelligence by land and sea, the magnitude of the whole undertaking is most impressive. No wonder the fabric of the state was severely tried by the strain.

317. It was a wise policy for the Romans to be active at many points, watching for something to give way somewhere. They had no tactician capable of handling great armies and bringing the war to an end by one or two great battles. But the interest of Carthage was just the opposite. She was far behind Rome in military resources, but she had a great general. It was her business to back him up, whatever else might have to be put off. Every man ship horse or elephant placed at the disposal of Hannibal was, for the service of Carthage, more than twice as useful as the same employed elsewhere. Once strike down Rome in Italy, and her power outside Italy would be at an end. Spain Sicily Sardinia Corsica could be gathered at leisure as the fruit ripened. And indeed the Punic

government had made ready a force to support Hannibal: 12,000 foot, 1500 horse, 20 elephants, 1000 talents of silver: the transports were to be convoyed by 60 ships of war.   All was ready, Mago, Hannibal's brother, in command, when news came of the disaster in Spain.   This caused alarm and hesitation: and it was soon followed by an appeal from Sardinia, where the leading chiefs, weary of Roman rule, were ready to rise in revolt.   The rulers of Carthage lost their balance under the stress of fear and hope.   To save Spain, they despatched Mago and his forces, not to Italy, but to Spain.   To gain Sardinia, they fell to preparing another armament of about the same strength. Hannibal had to wait.   It is hardly too much to say that the blind folly of this decision marks the turning-point of the war.   We are told that during this year's campaign some of Hannibal's Spaniards, even a few Numidians, deserted him and took service with Rome. Whether this be true or not, the story is in keeping with his situation. The moral effect of his great victories was dying down.   The prestige of conquest easily becomes stale while the conquest is incomplete.

318.   The appearance of a new party to the struggle raised the hopes of Hannibal.   Philip of Macedon had never relished the intervention of Rome in Illyria.   But he was busy with war in Greece. The news of Trasimene converted him to a new policy.   Under the advice of Demetrius[1] the refugee from Pharos he made peace with his Greek enemies, and prepared to turn to account the misfortunes of Rome.   After Cannae he ventured to send an embassy to form an alliance with Hannibal.   Landing near Croton, they proceeded safely towards Capua, but in Apulia they fell into the hands of the praetor Valerius.   With cool effrontery—they were Greeks, of course—they declared that they were come on a mission to the Roman government ; and the honest praetor sent them on with an escort into Campania, meaning them to negotiate with the consuls.   But they gave their escort the slip, and reached the camp of Hannibal, with whom they soon came to terms.   We have two versions[2] of the treaty agreed to.   Polybius gives what purports to be the actual text, or very near it : but it consists mainly of commonplace clauses guaranteeing mutual support.   The intention to deprive the Romans of their possessions east of the Adriatic is however clearly expressed.   Livy gives a version of its general drift to this effect.   Philip was to co-operate in the Punic conquest of Italy, by land, and more particularly by sea.   This achieved, Hannibal was to do the same for the king in Greece.   All territory and spoils of war acquired in the Greek peninsula were to belong to Macedon : in Italy, to Carthage.   That

---

[1] In 217 Rome had demanded the extradition of this troublesome person, but in vain.
[2] Polyb. VII 9, Livy XXIII 33, 34, 38, 39.

this at all events preserves the secret understanding as to common policy, is highly probable. The envoys made their way back safely to their ship, taking some Carthaginians with them, to receive from Philip his confirmatory oath. But, when they were at sea somewhere off the heel of Italy, they fell into the hands of the Roman squadron patrolling the coast. The chief Greek was ready with a lie of much the same kind as before, but the presence of the Punic envoys aroused suspicion. A search disclosed the treaty and a letter from Hannibal: so the local commander at once forwarded them, documents and all, to be examined by the consuls or at least by the Senate. They were sent all the way round by sea, no doubt for safety. Off the Campanian coast the ships were challenged by the fleet of the consul Gracchus, who was at Cumae. He read the documents and sent them on to the Senate by land, the prisoners by sea. Thus was the first embassy from Philip intercepted. Later in the year a second one was sent, which made the double journey safely: but the delay caused by the capture of the first party was of no small advantage to Rome.

319. The Roman Senate saw the state menaced by a new danger at a moment when its resources were already strained to the utmost. But they set themselves to deal with the danger coolly and wisely. They now reaped the reward of their care of the fleet and the coasts. There was a squadron on the south-eastern coast, and an army at Tarentum. More ships were sent out, and a fleet made up of over 50 sail: the officer, a deputy of the praetor Valerius, was ordered to embark troops from Tarentum and cruise in the Adriatic. He was to find out all he could as to the prospects of war with Macedon, and report to his superior. If hostilities appeared imminent, the praetor was himself to take command of the armament, invade the territory of Philip, and so keep him employed at home as to prevent him from invading Italy. Thus, with a minimum of disturbance and little new preparations, a great deal was done to guard against contingencies: it was a sort of extension of the Brundisium-Tarentum district command. The necessary funds were got by deferring the repayment of a loan to Hiero: and just now the loyal old king sent a welcome contribution of corn. Fortune also favoured the Romans in Sardinia. The armada from Carthage, intended to support the local rebellion, was caught in a gale from the East, and reached the Balearic isles in so shattered a state that its repairs caused long delay. Meanwhile Manlius had beaten the rebels in a great battle, and the Punic forces arrived too late. The natives were already cowed, but joined the Carthaginians. A second great victory over the joint forces destroyed the whole strength of the rebellion. Manlius levied contributions of corn and money, which he handed over to the proper officials. He brought back the reinforcements that he had taken out with him, leaving the regular garrison behind: he handed over his Punic prisoners to his principal, the city-praetor. So peace and discontentment were smartly re-established with the sword in the island of the Sards.

320. In Italy during the summer the war dragged on in a succession of minor operations. Gracchus surprised a Campanian force and slaughtered a number of them in a night attack, by which act he is said to have forestalled their treacherous designs on Cumae. Hannibal, watching all movements from his camp on mount Tifata, came to aid and avenge his allies, but too late. At their entreaties he laid siege to Cumae, but he could neither storm the walls nor tempt the consul into any rash step: he withdrew foiled. We hear of a small Roman success in Lucania, the details of which are very obscure: also of a short campaign made in the Hirpinian country by the praetor Valerius, operating from Apulia. He is said to have punished severely the rebels of that district. Nor was the Campanian plain itself left in security: the consuls never went far from Capua, and watched for opportunities: weakly-guarded posts now and then fell into their hands, garrisons and all. Nola, it seems, was still causing uneasiness, but the intrigues of the popular party were forestalled by the return of Marcellus with his army. We hear also of the fleet from Lilybaeum making a descent on the African coast and even fighting a successful action with the Punic fleet homeward bound from Sardinia. Nor was Appius Claudius idle in Sicily. The convoy of reinforcements for Hannibal was expected. In hope of intercepting it Appius made a dash over to Locri, but was too late. It was not a happy time for the great general in his camp on Tifata, tied by the duty of protecting his new allies, and with his army weakened by the inevitable wastage of war. His hopes from diplomacy outside Italy were as yet hopes only: meanwhile the Roman forces were everywhere alive. He was soon approached by a deputation from the Hirpini and Caudine Samnites, claiming protection. This time it was Marcellus, raiding from Nola, who had laid their country waste. They had made no effective defence: yet it is hardly likely that, as Livy makes out, all their fighting men were serving in Hannibal's army. Hannibal marched upon Nola. He soon found that all was ready for his reception, and that there was no hope of gaining the town by treachery within. But he was now joined by the reinforcement from Carthage, and he ventured to deliver a general assault. This was repulsed. The tradition followed by Livy goes on to say that two days later a pitched battle was fought in front of Nola, in which Marcellus gained a splendid victory. This may be a fiction of some Roman annalist: or Livy may have confused matters and made two battles of Nola out of one, for his chronology is very hard to follow: or again it may be true, for the new troops from Africa were probably very raw. The desertion of some of Hannibal's cavalry to the Romans is placed by Livy after this battle.

321. The season was now waxing late, and Hannibal retired to winter quarters, sending his new troops into Bruttium, and taking his old army to Arpi in Apulia. Fabius had bided his time. He now moved upon Capua, and laid waste the Campanian plain. No serious fighting took place, and he went into winter quarters in the camp by Suessula, a commanding position. Part of the army at Nola was sent home for the winter to save expense. Gracchus marched his army from Cumae into Apulia, to winter at Luceria and keep an eye on Hannibal. Valerius was moved on to Brundisium, to guard the south-eastern seaboard and make preparations in view of the impending Macedonian war. The progress of the Scipios in Spain was still satisfactory, and we hear of two great victories gained in the latter part of the year's campaign. Whether this story deserves belief is very doubtful: the details at least suggest the exaggerating touch of Scipionic family tradition. But Rome did well in Spain, and she was ready to make every effort to keep the upper hand there. In the summer an urgent call for supplies had reached Rome: money and other things, most of all food and clothing, were needed to enable the Spanish army to keep the field. All agreed that this call must be met, but the treasury was empty. Many sources of revenue were dried up: the direct war-tax could not be raised further: yet it was becoming less productive, as the number of the citizens was reduced by the war. The Senate appealed[1] to the patriotism of the capitalists. It was an old custom at Rome to let out state works [*publica*] to contractors. It may well be that the system had been greatly developed in the course of the preceding half-century. Anyhow we meet now for the first time with the joint-stock companies or syndicates [*societates*] which play so important a part in the later history of the Roman Republic. In tendering for the supply of the army in Spain contractors were invited to accept a promise of cash payment to be made as soon as the treasury could meet its liabilities, and not to insist on payment by a fixed date. That the companies agreed to these terms is represented by the rhetorical moralists of later times as an act of the purest patriotism. But the men of money had a keen eye for a bargain. They stipulated for their own exemption from military service during the continuance of the contract, and also that

[1] Livy XXIII 48, 49.

any losses at sea through storms or act of the enemy should be made good to them by the state. We shall see later to what abuses and frauds this insurance-clause led. Meanwhile, public spirit was in fashion, and credit enabled the Senate to feed and clothe the distant armies.

322. The war was already spread over a sufficiently wide area: but hitherto Sicily, save for a few stray descents of the Punic fleets, had been at peace. The death[1] of king Hiero in 215 threw all into confusion, and the island became a theatre of horrors. In his long life (he was over 90 when he died) he had been the greatest of benefactors to Syracuse and the district that made up his kingdom. His policy of keeping friends and not making enemies was the only reasonable course for a minor power, anxious to preserve independence in the neighbourhood of the giant forces of Rome and Carthage. Once an ally of Rome, his loyal support was never withheld: and the republic owed him an immense debt for men money corn ships and information, promptly supplied in many a moment of distress. Yet he bore no ill-will to Carthage, and lent her a helping hand in the death-struggle of the mercenary war. When a disastrous earthquake wrought havoc in Rhodes, Hiero was one of the most generous of those kings and cities who contributed to the relief of the calamity. In short, his consistent aim was to be on good terms with all the world, and to promote the honour and well-being of Syracuse. He ruled unostentatiously and wisely: agriculture and trade flourished: his patronage of artists was recorded in the splendour of the city, adorned with temples and other public buildings, with pictures and statues. Under him Theocritus for some time lived and sang: one of his topics was the praise of Hiero. But nothing proves the sound judgment of the king more surely than his engaging the services of Archimedes. The great mathematician was no doubt an useful man to have on the spot for many purposes. Given a free hand, his mechanical skill doubled or trebled the strength of the already famous defences of Syracuse: the man of Science turned aside for a moment to shew himself the first of artillerists and engineers. The city, governed with benevolence and enlightenment, enjoyed under Hiero its greatest prosperity. No form of government other than monarchic had been found to work at Syracuse. The population, originally Greek, had long been contaminated with foreign elements. Native Sikels, freedmen and slaves of various origin, mercenary soldiers of various races, the nondescripts that gather in a seaport; these and descendants of these thronged the city still ostensibly Greek: and to

---

[1] The chronology is disordered, but this seems the most probable date. It is accepted by Holm, *Geschichte Siciliens* III 45.

these were now added deserters from armies and navies, particularly slaves and other 'naval allies' who had escaped from the onerous service of the Roman fleet. Whatever power of self-government the early Greek citizens may have had, nothing of the kind was to be found in this mongrel crowd.

323. Hiero had hoped to hand on his kingdom to his son Gelo, whom he had trained to be fit for the responsibilities of monarchy. But Gelo died before his father, leaving a son Hieronymus, who was 15 years old at the time of his grandfather's decease. All the old man's advice and precautions were vain. The boy fell under the influence of a knot of intriguing men connected with the royal house, who inflamed his ambition and turned the genial royalty of Hiero into a suspicious and cruel despotism. They thought that the power of Rome was broken, and aimed at aggrandizing Syracuse and themselves by an alliance with Carthage. Hannibal welcomed the advances made in the name of Hieronymus, and sent two brothers, Hippocrates and Epicydes, of mixed Syracusan and Carthaginian descent, as his agents. With the entry of these men into the city all chance of peace disappeared. Vainly did the praetor Appius Claudius protest and warn the boy-king: a treaty was made with Carthage, the final form of which conceded to Hieronymus the possession of all Sicily, a concession which in the event of victory was certain to be annulled. But a few months of the new tyranny had disgusted many men, and conspiracies began to be formed. In 214 Hieronymus was assassinated. A violent revolution took place in Syracuse. But the recovery of freedom was signalized by the murder of all connected with the royal house, a blunder which was turned to account by the malignant cleverness of the Punic agents. Hippocrates and Epicydes came into power on the top of a wave of reaction in popular feeling. An attack on Roman frontier posts began actual war: and when Marcellus, who was now in Sicily, replied by storming Leontini and executing a number of deserters found there, the military element became bitterly hostile to Rome. It is said that a body of Cretan mercenaries, survivors of a contingent sent to Rome by Hiero and dismissed free by Hannibal after Trasimene, took the lead in the movement: the civic government of Syracuse was overthrown, slaves and criminals were set free, and in a pandemonium of robberies and murders the two Punic agents conducted the city to its doom.

324. We must turn to Rome, and the preparations for the campaign of 214. The elections seem to have been held somewhat later than usual, and we hear[1] of a strange scene, which illustrates the extensive powers of the presiding magistrate, on this occasion

[1] Livy XXIV 7—9.

the veteran Fabius.   When the Century to which the lot had assigned
the first vote [*praerogativa*] was called, it was clear that the majority
in it were voting lightheartedly for two consuls of ordinary type, just
as if Rome were not engaged in a struggle for existence.   Before
these two were actually returned and the vote made irrevocable,
Fabius stopped proceedings.   He read the voters a lecture on the
needs of the situation and their duty to the state.   Then he called
on the 'prerogative' Century to vote over again : this time they voted
for Fabius himself, and Marcellus the hero of Nola.   The other
Centuries followed suit, and the thing was done.   Of the four praetors
one, Q. Fulvius, was kept on from the previous year, and specially
marked out for the city praetorship.   Rome thus sent her two best
generals to the front and kept an officer of tried efficiency as head
of administration and acting chairman at the centre of affairs.   The
officers commanding armies were continued in their commands,
among them M. Pomponius, who it seems had after all been watching
the Gauls in the North.   Two praetors were appointed to Sicily,
but events there soon required the presence of the fighting consul.
The usual crop of prodigies appeared early in 214 and much ceremonial was necessary to set the minds of the people at ease : discomfort and damage also resulted from an excessive rainfall, by
which the Tiber was twice swollen so as to flood the low-lying ground
in and near the city : but the business of national defence went on.
The task was more gigantic than ever.   Livy accounts for 18 legions
without including the three in Spain.   Taking 21 legions at 5000 men
each, we get 105,000 men : the Allies were probably about the same
number.   Then there were the rowers of the war-ships, mostly slaves,
perhaps from 40,000 to 50,000 men.   Nor must we forget the men
in the colonies, whether citizens or Latins, who were at any given
moment not serving in the field but standing to arms in defence
of their own towns whether on the coast or inland.   Though we hear
little of this service, we may be sure that by commanding roads, by
securing depots, and by affording local bases of operations, it was
all-important in determining the final issue of the war.   On the
whole, an estimate of 250,000 men employed on the Roman side is
probably far below the truth.

325.   In view of the danger threatening in the Adriatic (for
Philip's schemes were taken seriously) a fleet of 150 vessels of war
was to be kept in commission.   But there was a lack of men to row
them, and it was found necessary[1] to resort to an exceptional measure.
Taking the census-tables of 220 as a basis, the more well-to-do classes
of citizens were declared liable to provide rowers and pay in proportion

[1] Livy XXIV 11.

to the amount of their property : a senator had to find eight rowers and pay for a whole year, and so down to the single rower and six months' pay found by the lowest class affected. We hear that this was imposed by a notice of the consuls acting on an order of the Senate. Several points in this arrangement are interesting. We see senators treated as a class whose wealth is assumed to come up to a certain standard: later we know that a certain fortune was required in a member of the Senate, but no such fixed rule seems to have existed at this time. It is probably due to the seriousness of the crisis that so great an extra burden was imposed without a regular act of popular legislation. We must not confuse this case with the subscription fleet raised in the first Punic war, which was a voluntary offering. No doubt the wealthier classes, led by the Senate, did make sacrifices for the state in this hour of need. In the year just past (215) a sumptuary law had been carried by the tribune Oppius, restricting the ostentation of wealth in the dress and equipage of Roman ladies. It seems to have been approved by the Senate: at least we hear of no opposition. It was perhaps a demonstration, somewhat cheap, of the patriotism of the classes who had opposed the popular policy of Flaminius, and the *lex Oppia* was only in force for about 20 years.

326. The great efforts of Rome soon became known, and all notion of her giving way was utterly belied. There was reasonable alarm in Capua. To the appeal of the Campanians for protection Hannibal responded by marching from Arpi and occupying his old camp on mount Tifata. But what to do in Campania when he had got there was no longer a question easily answered. The Romans would not give themselves away in pitched battles. He was driven to try attacks on places. There was no chance for him at Neapolis or Cumae. But a good deal of shipping had taken of late to using the harbour of Puteoli : if he could gain this town, he would at last have the long-desired port on the Bay. But in the last winter the place had been fortified and garrisoned by old Fabius, and Hannibal could make no impression on it. Nor did he gain much by laying waste parts of the country ; and a movement upon Nola was again forestalled by the watchful Marcellus. Great hopes however were aroused in him by the visit of a party from Tarentum. They were some of the men whom he had let go free after his great victories, and they now made him an offer. If he would bring his army into the neighbourhood of Tarentum, they would stir up the populace and deliver the city into his hand. The offer was of course gladly accepted. Tarentum had the finest harbour in Italy, and was so situated as to promote the expected cooperation of the king of Macedon. But things in Campania were not going well for Hannibal.

The Roman generals were on the alert. It may be patriotic exag-
geration that represents him as decisively beaten in front of Nola,
and declares that only the blundering of a lieutenant of Marcellus,
one, Gaius Claudius[1] Nero, prevented the defeat from being a set-off
against Cannae. Anyhow he did not get Nola. Casilinum too was
threatened by Fabius. Marcellus was soon able to bring a force to
his aid, and the two consuls recovered this important post for Rome.
Marcellus, always a rough man of blood, seems to have acted with
brutal treachery to some Campanians who formed part of the garrison.
And meanwhile an unexpected collision had taken place at Beneventum. When Hannibal moved into Campania, Fabius had called up
Gracchus from Luceria. The design seems to have been to close in
on the enemy and, while avoiding pitched battles, to deprive him of
freedom of movement. But Hanno, who had wintered in Bruttium
with the new troops from Africa and a large force of Lucanian and
Bruttian levies, was marching up the country, and came upon Gracchus
at Beneventum with his army chiefly made up of slave-soldiers. A
hard-fought battle went in favour of Rome, and Gracchus felt bound
to give his men the freedom they had earned. But some Lucanian
troops of his (there were it seems Lucanians on both sides) were soon
after badly cut up by Hanno. Fabius laid waste parts of Samnium and
Lucania. His son, the praetor Fabius, was active in northern Apulia:
Marcellus for a time lay sick at Nola. Hannibal had left Campania,
where he could make no head-way, and marched to Tarentum. But
here too he met disappointment: the Romans had strengthened the
garrison, and the Tarentine democrats dared not stir. He withdrew
into Apulia, where he occupied the town of Salapia on the coast. At
this centre he collected all the food and forage that he could get, and
formed winter quarters. Here he could communicate with Carthage
and look out for news from Philip, while his men were training
captured horses as remounts for the cavalry.

327. In this year there were censors appointed, and in the lull of
disaster (it was now two years since Cannae) they did their work. It
is said[2] that they inflicted degradation on two sets of men by whom
the name of Rome had been disgraced: first, those who after Cannae
had proposed to abandon Italy, and secondly, those who had by an
unworthy quibble broken their promise to return to Hannibal if not
ransomed. There are difficulties about this story which we cannot
consider here. Evasions of military service were detected and punished.
The general aim of the censors' action is clear enough. On the
financial side of their department their activity was cramped by the

---

[1] Livy XXIV 17.   [2] Livy XXIV 18.

want of funds. The capitalists offered to tender for contracts as usual, and to let payment stand over till the end of the war: but we do not hear that the censors launched out into great expense on the strength of this offer. Owners of slaves set free by Gracchus refused to draw on the treasury for the price of the men till the end of the war. Guardians of infants and heiresses advanced on loan to the state the moneys of their wards. Even in the armies the more highly paid soldiers (knights and centurions) declined to draw their pay at this time of need. Such is the tradition.

328. To return to Syracuse. Marcellus can hardly have reached Sicily till the year 214 was far spent. But he was not sent there for

Syracuse in 214 B.C.

nothing: it meant that the Senate were not going to make the mistake of trifling with a serious danger. After various attempts at negotiation had failed, as they were bound to do with the city in the hands of desperate men, a regular siege began, carried on by sea and land. Syracuse was famous for the extent and strength of its walls, which ran for much the greater part of their course along the edges of the limestone plateau upon which the bulk of the city was built. The space enclosed was not all inhabited: the great triangle of Epipolae would be in part open ground. But Dionysius had acted wisely in enclosing it: if left open, the city was certainly vulnerable on that side. This enclosed, there was but a very small part of the enceinte against which battering-rams could, from the nature of the ground, be employed to any purpose. At the Euryalus or western end of Epipolae was a grand fort, able to defy all means of force then available, and guarding the natural point of approach for supplies and succours from inland. On the sea side splendid harbours made easy the relief of the city by naval enterprise. To carry the city by storm was hardly possible, and was never achieved. And, when an assailant was driven to undertake a blockade, he had no easy task to shut out succours both by land and sea. In the choice of his own camps he must exercise great care. The position nearest to the weakest point in the walls was close to the swamp in whose deadly exhalations the armies of former besiegers had wasted away. Besides, if an enemy's fleet gained even temporary control of the Great Harbour, the besieger inside it was at once himself the besieged. On the foreland of Plemyrium there was no water, and it was a bad landing-place. To maintain a blockading force in safety before Syracuse it was necessary[1] that it should operate mainly from the North. This Marcellus seems to have recognized from the first.

329. But it had not yet come to blockading. At the end of 214, or early in 213, he delivered a series of attacks on the northern walls and on the sea front of Achradina, hoping to break in somewhere. Every machine and device known to his engineers was used freely in the effort to make a lodgment, but in vain. The engines of Archimedes, directed by the man of science himself, baffled every attempt. After great loss in killed and wounded, and the failure of the land attack also, the Roman forces drew off, and the siege had to be turned into a blockade. The war now spread into other parts of Sicily. While Appius remained in charge before Syracuse, Marcellus took a number of towns that had belonged to Hiero's kingdom. But a Carthaginian force was landed in the West: Agrigentum fell, and sympathizers with Carthage began to draw other towns into revolt. Even from Syracuse a strong force slipped out to support the movement : but Marcellus came upon them unawares by a lucky accident, and cut most of them to pieces. The Carthaginians moved on to Syracuse, but could do nothing : the admiral Bomilcar found his fleet too weak[2] and sailed home to Carthage : Himilco drew off the army

---

[1] We hear of *Leon* and *portus Trogiliorum* (see Thucyd. VI 97, 99) as places connected with these operations. But they cannot be identified with any certainty. I have long been convinced that the little peninsula of Thapsus was all-important as a shelter for ships. Of the many sieges of ancient Syracuse, the Roman was the only one conducted mainly from the North.

[2] Livy XXIV 36.

to support other towns in revolt.   At this juncture came horrible news from the centre of the island.   The hill-stronghold of Henna, a town honoured throughout Sicily as the seat of the worship of Ceres and Proserpine, was held by a Roman garrison.   The commandant knew that the citizens wished to go over to Carthage.   If they once admitted the enemy into the town, his position in the citadel would be greatly imperilled.   Lieutenants of Marcellus knew that they must hold their posts at any cost: as to means, the consul was not so nice. This officer then invited the people of Henna to an assembly on the pretext of ascertaining the true wishes of the majority, and had them butchered by his soldiers.   The news thrilled through Sicily like a lightning shock.   Henna was saved for Rome, and Marcellus passed no censure on the deed.   But its inhumanity drove a number of wavering towns over to the Punic side.   Marcellus, perhaps for this reason, after getting in stores from the country, returned to his camp before Syracuse.

330.   The story of the famous siege had best be completed at once.   There was a Roman camp to the SW of the city on the small hill where stood the Olympieum, or temple and precinct of Olympian Zeus.   This was the only eligible post commanding the approaches from the South.   The main force was on the North, in direct touch with the fleet.   As the year 213 went by the hope of starving out the besieged grew less and less.   It was in fact impossible to keep up an effective blockade by sea, and Punic convoys revictualled the town. However, before giving up the task and operating elsewhere, Marcellus tried to negotiate for the betrayal of the city through some Syracusan citizens.   They were themselves betrayed to those in power, and put to death.   But soon after this an agent sent to king Philip was captured by the Roman guard-ships.   In his eagerness to recover the man, Epicydes was led to hold conferences with the Romans near the northern wall.   One of them took this chance of estimating carefully the height of the wall at a favourable spot.   Learning from a deserter that a religious festival was shortly to be celebrated in Syracuse, Marcellus had ladders made, picked out special men for a forlorn hope, and sent them to scale the wall by night.   The feast had told upon the sentinels, and the plan succeeded.   Marcellus was master of Epipolae before the city was well awake.   Roman fancy depicted the proconsul as he looked out that morning over the other quarters of Syracuse, populous and splendid, and thought of all its ancient glories, and the long loyalty of Hiero ; and declared that he wept.   It was indeed a pity that so fair a city should be given to the flames.   So he tried to open negotiations for the surrender of Achradina on terms.   But the Roman deserters on guard there, themselves

beyond pardon, refused to treat. Marcellus now encamped between Tycha and Neapolis. Here he had the impregnable fort of Euryalus in his rear, and to win it was his first object: in a short time the commandant, despairing of relief, surrendered the post. Tycha and Neapolis had already submitted. The people were not butchered, and the houses not burnt: but looting was carried out systematically, with strong guards posted to prevent a surprise.

331. It throws light upon the hopelessness of a naval blockade, when we hear that at this very moment there were 90 Carthaginian ships[1] in the harbour. On a night of foul weather Bomilcar ran out with 35 of them and bore news to Carthage of the imminent fall of Syracuse. Great efforts were made to relieve it in time. Hippocrates brought his army from the West, and both divisions of the Roman forces were attacked, but without success. The autumn season was unhealthy, but the pestilence was as usual most deadly to the Carthaginian army encamped on the ground near the swamp. They are said to have perished to the last man: their native allies from the Sicel towns went off to their own homes. The Romans on the high ground also suffered, but in a much less degree. Soon after this Bomilcar returned from Carthage, bringing[2] (if the numbers are to be trusted) 700 vessels of burden laden with supplies, convoyed by 130 ships of war. Marcellus, though outnumbered, set out to fight this new armada, but Bomilcar declined the battle. He ran out to sea and made for Tarentum, and ordered the supply-ships back to Africa. The fall of Achradina and Ortygia (the 'Island') was now merely a question of time. Delegates appeared to treat for surrender, but the deserters as before prevented its being carried out. In the confusion which followed, as the divergence of interest between these men and the mercenary troops became clear, a plan for the betrayal of Ortygia was arranged with one of the mercenary captains, a Spaniard named Moericus. In carrying out this the Roman troops also effected an entry into Achradina. The surrender now finally took place. The richest part of the city was thoroughly sacked, not without some violence and bloodshed: to the great annoyance of Marcellus, one of the victims was Archimedes. The long agony of Syracuse seemed likely to be followed by a famine, for supplies were running short. This was averted by the action of the Roman admiral[3] at Lilybaeum. In striking contrast to the naval timidity of Bomilcar, he made a dash over to the African coast, surprised a number of ships of burden in the harbour of Utica, raided the country round, and

---

[1] Livy xxv 25 § 12.   [2] Livy xxv 27.
[3] Otacilius. Livy xxv 31.

brought back 130 vessels laden with corn and other booty. This corn relieved the need of Syracuse.

332. The year 214 saw also the beginning of war with Philip of Macedon. If we may believe Polybius, the king had brought a large fleet into the Adriatic before he came to terms with Hannibal. But he knew it to be inefficient, and a false alarm of the approach of a Roman squadron sent him flying. He now began to attack the Roman allies on the Illyrian coast, where he took Oricum and besieged Apollonia. But M. Valerius Laevinus, the praetor commanding at Brundisium, came at once to protect the allies. In a short time Oricum was retaken, the king's camp before Apollonia surprised and his siege-engines taken, a large part of his army killed or captive, his retreat by sea cut off, and Philip himself with the wreck of his forces in full retreat by land, leaving his ships on fire behind him. Later, apparently in 213, he took Lissus and made considerable progress in Illyria: but his movements do not seem to have effected anything in the way of help to Hannibal. War was also going on in Spain. The confused account given by Livy deserves little credit. It speaks of several Roman victories, but betrays that these successes, if ever gained, were of no lasting effect. The Punic armies in Spain had been reinforced, and it seems that native recruits still joined them in numbers. In the next year (213) a quarrel between king Syphax of western Numidia and the government of Carthage opened up hopes of finding an ally for Rome in Africa itself. Embassies were exchanged between the Scipios and the king: a Roman centurion stayed with Syphax in order to train a force of Numidian infantry on the Roman model. Carthage turned to Gala, ruler of eastern Numidia, whose troops, joined with a Punic army and led by his young son Masinissa, routed with great slaughter the forces of Syphax and drove him in flight to the West. Things were not going well for the Romans in these parts. Nor was it a great source of strength to them that they now took to hiring mercenaries in Spain. We do not know exactly how things were mismanaged, but probably long success and ignorance of the present strength of the Punic forces induced the Scipios to believe that they could by one great effort decide the Spanish war in favour of Rome. They divided their forces in the summer of 212, meaning to attack simultaneously and destroy the two main armies of the enemy. But one division found itself threatened by a force of Spaniards as well as by the regular Punic army: in the endeavour to cut their way out of a position of great danger nearly all perished: the Numidian horse led by Masinissa were the chief agents in the destruction of this body. Publius Scipio was among the slain. The whole Punic force now turned upon

Gnaeus and his division, whom their faithless Celtiberian mercenaries had left to their fate. Gnaeus also fell, and most of his men. The work of years seemed to be wasted, and the power of Rome in Spain at an end. But a brave officer, Lucius Marcius, a knight, gathered the fugitives from the armies and held his ground north of the Ebro till succours could arrive. It is even said that he checked the victorious enemy after the last battle, and slew a great number of them in a night-attack on their camp. There were many different versions of the story: the truth is out of our reach. That Marcius kept together the remnants of the army of the two Scipios, may be believed.

333. Little has come down to us concerning the war in Southern Italy during the year 213. Probably the want of sufficient numbers kept Hannibal from attempting large operations: and he was no doubt preoccupied with his designs upon Tarentum. For Gaulish recruits to reach him was no longer easy: three Roman forces, at Ariminum, in Picenum, and near Luceria, lay north of the Apennine, between his camp and the region of the Po. The temper of his Italian allies was doubtful, for the unexpected revival of Rome caused misgivings to those who had abandoned her. The case of Arpi in Apulia is significant. Hannibal had been master of the town for about two years: he had wintered there: he had now a garrison of 5000 men there, not counting 3000 armed citizens of Arpi. But an offer from a leading citizen to betray the place was followed by the approach of a Roman army. A bold escalade under cover of a storm of wind and rain placed the town at the mercy of the Romans. In the street-fighting that ensued the local troops went over to the Roman side, and the Spaniards in the Punic garrison, only stipulating for the safe withdrawal of their comrades, followed the example. This affair cost Hannibal a strong town and the services of about 4000 men at arms. Soon after, a small body of Campanian aristocrats slipped out of Capua and made their submission to Rome. There was also news of a victory gained by the praetor quartered at Ariminum, which would tend to remove the unforgotten danger from the Gauls. In the South one or two Bruttian communities returned to the Roman alliance: small successes were gained in Lucania. But in Bruttium the Punic general Hanno routed a Roman force with great slaughter. This force (a sign of the disorder of the times) was a large band of brigands, slaves and others, raised on his own account[1] by a Roman capitalist of bad character, said to have defrauded both the state and his fellow-shareholders in companies of contractors.

---

[1] Livy XXV i §§ 3, 4, 3 § 9.

We shall presently meet with another of these rogues, whose appearance should be noted as ominous for the future of Rome.

334. In Rome itself there was a good deal of unrest. At the end of 214 a tribune undertook to call the censors to account for their severity lately shewn, but proceedings were blocked by his nine colleagues. Festivals were not neglected. Four days given to stage plays remind us that a drama had begun to appear as a regular form of public entertainment. In 213 were some prodigies as usual, and much damage caused by a fire in the city. But real trouble was caused by an outbreak[1] of superstition, that is, of addiction to fancy rites and ceremonies not of Roman origin. The old gods of Rome had not granted her the success that she looked to receive at their hands,—had not carried out their part of the bargain. The city swarmed with soothsayers and quacks, who drew after them the ignorant and credulous majority. The aediles were powerless: but early in the year the city praetor, backed up by the Senate, took measures that checked these irregularities for a time. Some vacancies in the sacred colleges were filled, and early in the next year a new selection of a Chief Pontiff took place. Whether the preference of a young and vigorous man to elder members of the college with strong claims had any connexion with the recent vagaries or not, we do not know. In the elections of magistrates for 212 we find in the list of praetors the name of C. Claudius Nero, of whom we shall hear again. And one of the curule aediles was young P. Cornelius Scipio, afterwards famous as the great Africanus. The latter was only just 22 years old, and objection was taken to his candidature on this ground, but vainly. We hear that the aediles celebrated on an unusually lavish scale the public games of which they had the charge, and also gave as largess a dole of olive oil: a custom greatly developed later, of which we may here note the small beginnings. In assigning the departments of the magistrates the only notable points were the combination[2] of the two juridical praetorships in the same person, and the substitution of Etruria for Picenum as the sphere of one of the minor armies. The former step was probably due to the decrease of litigation in time of war and the need of extra praetors for military duties : the latter perhaps indicates that disaffection was suspected in some Etruscan towns. The disposition of forces was much as before, but new troops had to be levied to supply drafts for keeping the legions up to their strength. Livy gives the total of legions under arms as 23, not speaking of the Allies. So great was now the difficulty of raising recruits in sufficient numbers, that special

---

[1] Livy XXV 1 §§ 6—12.   [2] Livy XXV 3 § 2.

commissioners were sent round the rural districts occupied by Roman citizens, charged with the conscription of able-bodied youths, even though under military age.

335. But nothing stirred the public mind so much at the beginning of this official year, as the trial of a state contractor [*publicanus*] for fraud.   Since the state had agreed to take upon itself the storm-risks incurred in transporting supplies to the forces abroad, it had been possible to defraud the treasury by deliberately scuttling old hulks laden with rubbish, and claiming compensation as for vessels and cargoes of great value.   This was what Marcus Postumius Pyrgensis had done.   His partner T. Pomponius Veientanus was a prisoner in the hands of the enemy.   Their frauds had been found out in the preceding year, but the Senate, thinking the time unsuited for a collision with the capitalist class, took no steps.   But the scandal became known, and popular indignation encouraged two tribunes to take up the case.   They laid on Postumius a heavy fine : he appealed[1] to the Tribes.   When at last they met for final voting, the excitement was so intense, that a friendly tribune did not dare to block the proceedings as had been expected.   The *publicani* then drew together and burst into the space before the bench of the tribunes : a riot ensued, and the meeting had to be broken up.   The Senate was summoned : strong protests were uttered against this intolerable use of violence against the rights and dignity of the Roman people. Hereupon the two accusers dropped the procedure by fine, and brought an indictment against the offender on a capital charge of high treason [*perduellio*].   Having either to find sureties for his appearance in due course, or to submit to arrest, he took the former alternative, and presently bolted, leaving his sureties to forfeit the bail.   The criminal trial thus fell through, but a further step remained to be taken.   The two tribunes carried a resolution in the Assembly of the Tribes, fixing a date by which Postumius must appear to stand his trial.   In case of default, he was to be treated as self-condemned, and recognized as being in exile, that is, as having given up his Roman citizenship : his property was to be confiscated, and himself outlawed. Postumius once dealt with, they went on to punish in the same way others concerned in the recent breach of the peace, who mostly went into banishment like the chief offender.   The whole affair is interesting as illustrative of the clumsy but vigorous ways by which the public conscience made itself felt at Rome, and of the system of voluntary exile, by which the death penalty was practically abolished though not formally repealed.

[1] Livy XXV 3, 4, seems to regard the meeting as a *plebis concilium*; but he speaks of it also as *comitia*, and it may have been a regular Assembly of the Tribes.

336. At this time the Senate is said to have received, through a despatch of Marcellus, a pathetic appeal from the survivors of Cannae. They had been formed into two special legions, and sent off to serve in disgrace as the garrison of Roman Sicily till such time as the war should come to an end. The war with Syracuse broke out, but they were not employed in it: they were kept in the background for mere defensive work. They had petitioned to be granted an opportunity of shewing their valour in the field. The Senate would not even now treat them as the equals of other soldiers. They left the decision to the discretion of the proconsul, but added that, in case he saw fit to make use of these men, no services on their part were to be rewarded with the privileges and distinctions usually bestowed upon the brave. The episode has been so dressed up for edification of later ages that we cannot rely upon the details. And the question, why the rank and file should have been so harshly treated, while the officers—Varro for instance—were still in positions of high trust, is one that calls for a satisfactory answer. The Senate may very well have known something the tradition of which is now utterly lost. But, as in Roman politics the nominal equality of citizens was in practice overridden by the influence of great families, so in the army the higher officers were in practice all drawn from the wealthier classes, and able to command influence denied to the rank and file.

337. The usual prodigies, met as usual by special ceremonies, appeared in this year. Special commissions for repair of the city walls and other public works were appointed. But a more alarming event soon occurred. The hostages detained as security for the loyalty of some southern Greek cities, in particular Tarentum and Thurii, were induced to attempt to escape. They were caught and put to a shameful death. This ill-timed severity at once strengthened the party in Tarentum that had for some time been seeking to betray the city to Hannibal. A plot was soon formed: Marcus[1] Livius, commanding the Roman garrison, was put off his guard: and one night the Punic army made its way into Tarentum. A great number of Roman soldiers were butchered in detached parties: Livius, fuddled with excessive dining, had enough sense left to let his slaves take him round to the citadel in a boat. Hannibal had now got the town, but not the citadel. This stronghold, which, like the island Ortygia at Syracuse, represented the original city of the first colonists, stood on what was virtually an island, and commanded the narrow channel connecting the inner harbour with the roadstead outside. At first Hannibal tried to take it. His

---

[1] M. Livius Macatus (Livy XXVII 25 §§ 3—5, 34 § 7, for Cic. *de Senect.* § 11 is wrong). See Polybius VIII 26—36, who calls him *Gaius*. Livy XXV 7—11.

operations for the purpose are of no interest. In short, he failed, and a wearisome blockade began. Hannibal had the Tarentine fleet dragged over land from the inner harbour to the outer sea. But the Romans were not cut off from help for long. Heraclea and Metapontum soon followed the lead of Tarentum. A garrison had to be withdrawn from Metapontum: it was sent to reinforce the Tarentine citadel. When Thurii did the same, the remainder of the defeated garrison was shipped off to Brundisium. But, of these towns, only Tarentum was of first-rate importance. To get full control of the Tarentine harbour was with Hannibal a prime object, which he could not gain. How far his occupation of the city was a real advantage to him in the war, is not clear. He had to leave a garrison there, and

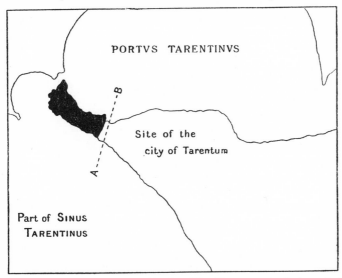

The outer roadstead is sheltered by two islands. The old entrance to the inner harbour was spanned by a bridge, probably in part a drawbridge, in ancient times. The citadel is marked in black. *AB* is the line of the artificial cut, dating from the 15th century of our era, enlarged in the 18th, and recently adapted to admit the largest vessels of war. See Nissen, *Italische Landeskunde*, II pp. 865–70.

the Tarentines had stipulated for freedom: they were not even to pay a tribute. Meanwhile Roman officers ran cargoes of corn into the harbour and revictualled the citadel.

338. The chief religious excitement of the year 212 was the publication[1] of the 'prophecies of Marcius,' an ancient Roman (at least Latin) soothsayer of whom tradition has left nothing but the name. They had been seized in the inquiry of the previous year.

[1] Livy XXV 12, Weissenborn.

Their great antiquity is very doubtful: Greek influences can be detected in them, and they are said to have led to the institution of the 'games of Apollo' [*ludi Apollinares*] which became an important item in the festivals of the Roman year.

339.   The punishment of Capua, long delayed, was now seriously taken in hand.   There was to be no miscarriage in this business.   It was to be an object-lesson to rebels and waverers in Italy, and full preparations had been made to ensure a successful result.   Puteoli had been fortified, and Casilinum retaken : a fortified depot was now established at the mouth of the Volturnus: corn came by sea from Sardinia and Etruria, and the besieging armies would have secure bases of supply.   The Campanians grew uneasy.   Their own tillage had been interrupted by Roman raids.   But, when Hannibal at their entreaty granted them a quantity of corn, he found that he must send a force to protect the convoy.   Hanno was moved from Bruttium to near Beneventum on this service.   But the consuls heard of it : Fulvius came up with his army, to whose bravery is attributed the victory which followed.   The account is clearly exaggerated, but at least the corn seems not to have reached Capua.   The danger of the city must now have been plain to all.   But the actual formation of complete blockading lines was delayed by a series of disasters which befel the Romans at this time, partly it would seem in consequence of their own folly.   Gracchus was drawn into a trap and killed with a number of his men, through the treachery of a false Lucanian : his army of emancipated slaves, whose attachment to him was perhaps largely personal, is said to have melted away.   Great efforts were made to find them and bring them back to the ranks.   The story seems to have come down in many various forms.   But the prevalent tradition asserts that Hannibal honoured the fallen proconsul with a magnificent funeral.   When the Roman forces began to draw near to Capua, timidly, and not unchecked by the Campanian cavalry—one of the regular stories of a duel between champions comes in here— Hannibal himself appeared upon the scene.   It is clear that he broke up the siege for the time: the Roman armies dispersed in different directions.   But when he drew off they returned and began again. While in pursuit of one of these armies he met with a piece of luck. A certain Centenius, a time-expired centurion, volunteered[1] to continue in the service as leader of a detached corps, with which he boasted that he would out-hannibal Hannibal and clear up the mystery of Roman defeats and Punic victories.   The Senate in a weak moment gave him 8000 men, and he gathered in numerous volunteers.   Before he had even got his force into order, he had the

[1] Livy xxv 19 §§ 9—17.

misfortune to encounter Hannibal seeking an enemy to destroy, and was destroyed. A worse disaster[1] followed. A Roman army was as usual operating in Apulia. The praetor in command, seeing the enemy busy elsewhere, grew careless and let his men get out of hand. Suddenly Hannibal appeared, brought him to battle near Herdonea, and cut his army to pieces. Thus in a short space of time two of the secondary Roman armies had ceased to exist. The hand of the great master had not lost its cunning.

340. But at this moment the main issues of the war were being decided at the three great cities. Syracuse fell, and was completely at the disposal of Rome. In Tarentum Rome held the citadel and harbour, Hannibal the city. Capua was wholly Hannibal's. But the main armies of the two consuls and the praetor Nero now closed in on the doomed city. Three camps were built at different points, and regular blockading lines with inner and outer ditch mound and palisade were steadily pushed forward to unite the camps. Sorties from the town were repulsed : a last offer was made to all who might wish to quit Capua by a day named, an offer treated with contempt. Messengers were sent from the besieged to Hannibal, calling for prompt relief. For the time he was preoccupied with vain attempts on the citadel of Tarentum and on Brundisium. But he promised to appear in due time and scatter the Roman armies as before : the message reached Capua none too soon, for the circuit of the siege-works was nearly complete.

341. The elections for the year 211 and the arrangements of the various spheres of duty were made as usual. Livy reckons the forces for the year at 23 legions, but takes no count of the two city legions or of those in Spain. At least 150 ships of war[2] were in commission, counting only the Sicilian and Adriatic fleets. Spain was a matter of great anxiety. It was agreed to elect a new commander for the charge of that war, but the matter seems to have stood over for a time. The consuls of 212 were kept on duty as proconsuls at Capua, till the place should fall. The new consuls were kept in Rome and did not command armies till late in their year of office. The survivors of the shameful rout of Herdonea were sent to serve in disgrace in Sicily with the men of Cannae till the end of the war. But their inefficient general did not escape. This man, Gnaeus Fulvius, was said to have let down the discipline of his army, and in action to have been the first to run away. A tribune[3] brought him to trial, at first by way of the ordinary fine-process : but, as the facts came out more and more at the successive hearings, and popular

---

[1] Livy xxv 21.   [2] Livy xxvi 1 § 12.

[3] Livy xxvi 2, 3.

indignation was fully roused, the accusation was changed to one of high treason, and the capital penalty demanded. Before the Assembly of the Centuries could vote on his case, Fulvius took the usual course of going into voluntary exile. He was a brother of the proconsul Quintus Fulvius, commanding before Capua, who was ready to come to Rome and beg him off: but the Senate wisely refused their consent to this step.

342. The Roman commanders had now for several months kept a tight grip on Capua. Provisions were nearly run out: all attempts at breaking through the Roman lines had failed: with great difficulty a messenger slipped through and bore an urgent appeal to Hannibal. It was a sore trial for the Punic chief, to have to give up the siege of the all-important citadel of Tarentum: but he had in fact no choice. The eyes of all Italy were on him, and to desert his allies was to throw up the game. He marched with all speed into Campania, but he found things sadly changed since his last visit. To break through the completed lines was no easy task. Backed up by a sortie from the town, he made an attempt to carry part of the Roman works by storm. One account says that he did at one point pierce the outer rampart with the help of his elephants: but the beasts were driven out again with torches and the lost ground regained. It is certain that the assault was a failure, and probable that the losses of the assailants were heavy. The sortie from the town was also beaten back. After this it was impossible for Hannibal to sit helpless and see the city taken before his face. There was however just one more chance. If he marched on Rome, would not the Romans lose their heads and call off their armies from Capua? For this enterprise there were preparations to be made, and information of his plan to be conveyed to the besieged. Meanwhile some inkling of it had reached Fulvius (Appius was severely wounded) by means of deserters, and news was sent to Rome. The alarm was great, but the Senate, led by old Fabius and others, kept cool: day by day, in permanent session, the great council sat for the despatch of business, ready to order and advise. The consuls and the city praetor were at hand. It was agreed not to abandon the siege of Capua, but to leave it to the discretion of the proconsuls to bring succour to Rome, so far as this could be done without relaxing the blockade. The city itself was by no means defenceless. Not to mention the help of volunteers, always available in such an emergency, there were the two city legions. And according to Polybius[1] there were by a lucky chance two (if not four) legions newly enrolled by the consuls, the men of

[1] Polyb. ix 6.

which reported themselves at Rome in obedience to their oath on the very day when Hannibal appeared. Livy[1] mentions 1200 Numidians, deserters from the Punic army. Appian[2] says that, on hearing of Rome's danger, a body of 2000 men from the Latin colony of Alba by lake Fucinus marched off at once and took their place in the defence of the city. From Capua came the proconsul Fulvius with a force of 16,000 picked men. The walls of Rome had lately been repaired. Nor is it probable that Hannibal ever thought of assaulting the city. On his march from Capua he seems to have been more concerned to lay waste the lands of the colonies and allied towns than to reach Rome at the earliest possible time. This may well mean that he hoped by these ravages to provoke the Romans to a pitched battle and repeat the experience of earlier years. But, though he came within three miles of the city, no general engagement took place. This episode, Hannibal's march on Rome, the panic, the steadfastness of the Senate, has come down to us encumbered with a vast amount of fictitious detail. The early annalists (senators to a man) did not let the story lose in the telling: the later rhetoricians developed it so as to make more and more out of a favourite theme: to the poets[3] it became a part of their regular stock. We know little more than that Rome's great enemy came and went away again. After a very short stay he departed, taking a different route but ravaging the country as before. No doubt what he heard about Capua was not calculated to tempt him to further efforts for its relief. It was a confession of failure when he marched on and left the beleaguered city to its fate. Still victorious on the battlefield, for he had given his Roman pursuers a good beating on his march from Rome, he nevertheless found himself playing a losing game. The new warfare was slow and laborious, unsuited to his army and beyond his resources. He now tried a bold stroke. By forced marches he pushed rapidly to the South, in hope to surprise Rhegium. He was just too late to capture the town and port: booty and prisoners caught outside were not a permanent gain.

343. The fall of Capua was not long delayed. The populace compelled the Senate to assemble: all men shunned responsibility in that dreadful hour. It was agreed to send a deputation to surrender the city. A minority of senators, convinced that no mercy was to be expected, dined and drank together for the last time and then took poison. When the town was handed over, the remaining senators were sent away in chains, some to Teanum, the rest to Cales. The proconsuls differed[4] as to the course to be followed in dealing with

---

[1] Livy XXVI 10 § 5.   [2] Appian *Hannib.* 39.
[3] As late as Claudian *bell. Gild.* 83 *attonitae iam proximus Hannibal urbi.*
[4] Livy XXVI 15.

these men. Appius Claudius was for awaiting the decision of the Roman Senate: Fulvius feared that this might lead to mercy, and resolved to forestall it. With a cavalry escort he rode off in the night to Teanum, ordered the local magistrate to bring out the prisoners, and had them all scourged and beheaded in the early morning. He then turned back to Cales. While preparations were being made for a repetition of the executions there, it is said that a packet forwarded by express from Rome was put into his hands. He guessed the purport of its contents, and deferred opening it till the work of blood was complete. There were other versions of the story, but varying only in details. The surrender of Atella and Calatia, minor towns in dependence on Capua, was followed by similar executions of local senators. A number of Campanian nobles were thrown into prison, some handed over to the charge of the authorities of various Latin towns: sickness and neglect made their days few and evil. The mass of the citizens were sold as slaves. Who bought them, we are not told: Sicily was now quieting down, and there may have been a market there. Such was the fate of the great city of Capua, so far as concerned the people of the city and territory. We must not apply modern sentiments of humanity in judging the vengeance of Rome. The Romans do not seem to have been shocked by the bloodthirsty act of Fulvius. Rome was no worse than her neighbours, and an example had to be made: she was fighting for existence. The city of Capua itself was not destroyed. In so rich a district many dwellings and other buildings would always be needed: farmers must have some place of meeting. The object was to make it a centre of population utterly devoid[1] of communal life. There were to be no local Magistrates Senate or popular Assemblies: the administration of justice was to be conducted solely by Roman officers sent for the purpose. Thus, with every trace of common organization destroyed, it would not be easy for the inhabitants to combine for common action. The whole territory of Capua and the dependent towns [ager Campanus] was to become Roman state-property. Farmed out to lessees, the rents from this grand estate were one of the safest sources of revenue for the later Republic. In the next year (210) a number of survivors, professing to be guiltless of the rebellion or making out that they had been away at the time, appealed[2] to be left their freedom and some of their property. Some of them were allowed to keep part of their moveable goods and escaped slavery. But they were sent away from Campania to live elsewhere. It seems that of the old inhabitants none but freedmen and aliens—non-Campanians in short—were left in the place. All this retribution

---

[1] Cic. *de lege agr.* II § 89, Livy XXVI 16.   [2] Livy XXVI 33, 34.

Hannibal had not been able to prevent, a fact which set many men thinking in the length and breadth of Italy.

344. It is time to return to affairs in Spain. The Romans still held their footing in the country north of the Ebro, but their gains in the further districts had been lost with the Scipios. Carthaginian influence predominated, and would perhaps have been even more powerful if the leaders had acted in harmony. In 211 after the fall of Capua, the Senate, anxious about Spain, and wishing to put an end to the provisional arrangements by appointing a regular commander, sent out the propraetor Gaius Claudius Nero with a picked force. Nero seems to have gained no great[1] success: we hear that he did on one occasion outmanoeuvre Hasdrubal so that he had him at his mercy: but then, duped by pretended negotiations for the evacuation of Spain, let the enemy slip through his fingers. So the war in the West stagnated, and there was uneasiness at Rome. At this point comes in the story[2] of the appointment of young Scipio to the command. It is full of fictions, the motive of which it is not always easy to determine with certainty. That the choice of a general was left by the puzzled Senate to the chance nominations of a popular Assembly, and that the young hero of 24 was unanimously elected to the post of danger and honour to which Rome's veteran officers had not the nerve to aspire, is a situation dramatic but incredible. It is morally certain that it was the influence[3] of the great Cornelian House that led to young Scipio's being entrusted with the charge of this almost hereditary war. It was no mere chance that raised a military tribune, who had held no office higher than that of aedile, to the position of a proconsul commanding an army in a sphere so far removed from direct senatorial control. But legend has obscured the process by which Senate and People were led to take this leap in the dark.

345. The new commander was no ordinary man. He had little of the formal stiffness generally found with Roman solidity. A sympathetic nature enabled him to understand the feelings of other men: ambition moved him to please or at least impress them. Quick to seize opportunities, and gifted with dramatic tact, his influence with the people was immense: jealousy alone could withstand his charm. Over soldiers he exercised the magnetic power of a born leader. Yet he was not a man of the first order of genius, even in strategy: in civil life he failed as he grew older, lacking the stolid conformity on

---

[1] Livy XXVI 17, Appian *Iber.* 17.　　　　[2] See Weissenborn on Livy XXVI 18, 19.

[3] The power of the *gens Cornelia* began long before this and was at its height now or a little later. Ihne IV 8 has some good remarks on the Scipios, in particular referring to the conscious pride shewn in their famous epitaphs.

which Roman life rested and which Roman institutions required. From his youth up he is said to have been fond of mystery and to have gained reputation by reserve. Frequent visits to the temple of Capitoline Jove suggested that he enjoyed special divine favour and guidance, which he would neither assert nor deny. When it was whispered that he was, like the heroes of ancient myth, of divine origin on the father's side, he was at no pains to discountenance the rumour. Reared among the high traditions of a great Patrician family, he was a loyal citizen of the Roman Commonwealth. But his education was wider and more stimulating than that of most Roman youths of his day. That he became impatient of Roman narrowness was no doubt due partly to Greek influences. In him we first meet the type of 'new Roman,' for whom it was not enough to win victories in war and serve state offices with credit. Greek literature was the highest interest in the cultivated circle[1] that he gathered round him. He was a patron of the poet Ennius. He declared that he was never so busy as in the intervals of business, never less lonely than in solitude. Like all ambitious men of those days, he seems to have been affected by the example of the great Alexander: but there was no room for an Alexander in Rome.

346. The young proconsul set out, accompanied by M. Junius Silanus as propraetor to help and advise, and fill the position now occupied by Nero. He took reinforcements for the army and 30 ships of war. Escorted by the friendly Massaliots, he reached his province safely, and set to work at once getting all things in order for the campaign of the coming spring. He inspired confidence in the friendly tribes, cheered up the troops who had stood to bay so doggedly after the disasters of the previous year, and praised with generous candour the services of Marcius. In short he was all things to all men, which was just what was needed at the time. So passed the winter months in Spain, the Punic forces wintering in three different places. Towards the end of this year we get a peep into the situation[2] at Tarentum. A Carthaginian fleet was brought over from Sicily to blockade the citadel. This it did, but the citadel had by this time been revictualled, and suffered little inconvenience. The city on the other hand was worse off than before: the presence of the fleet added greatly to the number of consumers, while it was found impossible to increase the imported supply in the same proportion. Surely Carthage could have met this need if she had chosen. But things dragged on, and at last the Tarentines were relieved to see the fleet put to sea and give up the blockade.

---

[1] This is of course not the more famous 'Scipionic circle,' that which gathered round the second Africanus.   [2] Livy XXVI 20 §§ 7—11.

347. To continue the story of Sicily. The severity of Marcellus after the fall of Syracuse in 212 was not well-timed. Kindness might have led to the voluntary submission of many towns, but now none yielded to anything but immediate fear. Nothing outraged local feeling more than the brutal appropriation of treasures of art. Each statue and picture in the public places of Syracuse had, besides its beauty, a special meaning. There was still left in the great city enough Greek feeling, even Greek blood, to set great store by these things. Figures of their fathers' gods, memorials of the great princes heroes and athletes of the past, scenes of Greek mythology or records of their ancestors' valour,—all were endeared to the people by old associations and significant where they stood. They were shipped off, first to adorn the triumph of Marcellus, and then to be used for the decoration of Rome. It was a barbarous act: unfortunately it set an example often followed afterwards by Roman generals. The war in Sicily was not ended by the capture of Syracuse. True, the other towns in the Syracusan kingdom made haste to submit and get what terms they could from the conqueror. One or two had done so before the fall of the city: these Marcellus treated as friends, the others as conquered enemies. But in the West the rebellion promoted by Carthage still went on. The Punic headquarters were at Agrigentum, and Hanno, a Phoenician noble, in command: but the life of the war centred in a Libyphoenician half-breed named Muttines or Myttonus, who commanded a roving band of Numidian horse. His raids spread the fear of Carthage so that the Romans had little hold on the country districts. But, like many another dashing cavalry officer, he was touchy and vain. Hanno treated him with less respect than he thought his due, while profiting by his exploits: and jealousy, as in Spain so in Sicily, was the ruin of the Carthaginian cause. When Hanno advanced to the river Himeras, facing Marcellus, Muttines went off to coax back some discontented Numidians: the rest, already tired of the Carthaginian service, let Marcellus know that they would bear no part in the impending battle. Marcellus defeated Hanno with heavy loss, and returned to Syracuse, where he had no doubt plenty to do. Towards the end of the summer of 211 he went to Rome, having already forwarded for his triumphal show cargoes of rich spoils, works of art, elephants, and the now famous engines of Archimedes. But there was still war in Sicily, and his sulky troops, left behind in the island, were perhaps grimly content to hear that their general had been refused a full formal triumph on this ground. He had the minor triumph [*ovatio*]. No doubt the punctilious Senate was willing to take a chance of asserting itself. The effect of the great war, in

giving to successful generals a power not easily controlled, had not escaped the notice of the Fathers. At the same time those who, like Moericus[1] the Spaniard, had helped Rome by perilous acts of treachery, were richly rewarded. Meanwhile a Punic fleet landed a fresh force in Sicily, and M. Cornelius Cethegus the praetor had no easy task to protect allies and subdue rebels. But in 210 Marcellus' old army was withdrawn, and the consul Laevinus came over with a new one. His task was made easy by the discord of his opponents. Muttines, deprived of his command by the jealousy of Hanno, opened a gate of Agrigentum to the Romans. Bloodshed and plunder, the scourging and beheading of the chief rebels, the sale of the rest of the citizens as slaves, completed the restoration of the supremacy of Rome in a city that in its palmy days had been one of the most opulent and splendid centres of Greek life. We hear that some 66 towns remained to be won in Sicily; but of these 40 made their submission at once, 20 were betrayed from within: only six had to be taken by storm. Rome was now unchallenged mistress of all Sicily: what she did with it will be considered below. Muttines had his reward[2] in a sum of money and the citizenship of Rome. Hannibal's hopes of advantage from Sicilian risings were at an end.

348. There were however other quarters from which he expected help. But Philip of Macedon, who had not hitherto effected anything, was at this time more useless than ever. Laevinus with a Roman fleet commanded the Adriatic, and made Roman influence felt on land. In 211 he induced the warlike Aetolians, always jealous of Macedon, to form an alliance with Rome. Into this alliance several of the minor Greek states were drawn, also Attalus the king of Pergamum, who feared the ambition of Philip, and the leading chieftains of Thrace and Illyria. All chance of Philip's coming to the help of Hannibal now disappeared: the king had his hands more than full at home. If he moved southwards, his own realm was overrun by neighbours always on the watch for a chance of plunder and revenge: when he turned back to restore order in the North, the Aetolians made conquests among his allies in the South. In short, with a moderate fleet and skilful diplomacy Rome achieved her object—the neutralizing of Philip. No great exertion was needed: that her allies should win a complete triumph, and perhaps become too strong, was hardly part of the Roman programme.

349. In the winter of the years 211 and 210 various interesting events occurred in Rome. At the elections for 210 the helplessness of the Assembly[3] was again illustrated. The leading Century gave its votes for two consuls one of whom was nearly blind. He appealed

---

[1] Livy XXVI 21 §§ 12, 13.   [2] Livy XXVII 5 §§ 6, 7.   [3] Livy XXVI 22.

to the presiding officer for leave to speak before the announcement of the result made the vote irrevocable. A few words convinced them of their folly. The Century (juniors) conferred with the corresponding Century of seniors, and voted again: their new nominees were Marcellus and M. Valerius Laevinus the hero of the Adriatic war, who were elected by an unanimous vote. The games in honour of Apollo were kept up, but do not seem to have been made a regular yearly festival till 208. Prodigies as usual were reported and expiated with due ceremonies. Vacancies in the religious colleges were filled up as usual. But it was not long before a scene[1] occurred, quite new in the experience of Rome, and important as foreshadowing the trials of provincial governors in a later age. A deputation of Sicilians came to Rome to complain of the severities of Marcellus: another was being prepared at Capua to beg some alleviation of the severities of Fulvius. No court existed in which they could prosecute a Roman official: they sought redress from the Senate as the effective directors of Roman foreign policy, and only arraigned the conduct of the proconsuls in order to justify their claims. When Laevinus reached Rome, the consuls cast lots for the two 'provinces' reserved for them. Laevinus drew the command against Hannibal: Sicily, at this time chiefly a naval command, fell to Marcellus. Hereupon the Sicilian envoys broke out in despairing appeals to the Roman nobles, and are said to have found some sympathy, at least from those jealous of the consul's fame. Marcellus, who is represented as a model of conciliatory gentleness, offered to exchange commands with his colleague: and so Laevinus commanded in Sicily in 210, as we have seen above. When the petition of the Sicilians was heard in the Senate, the Fathers agreed to commend the Sicilians (that is, Syracuse) to the favourable attention of Laevinus, but in general approved the acts of Marcellus. Nor did the Campanians gain much by their appeal, as we have already remarked. The Roman Senate was not the body, nor was this the moment, lightly to throw over successful officers, or weigh too nicely the conduct which had accompanied the suppression of rebellions. To the Campanian petition the time was particularly unfavourable, for a fire[2] which had caused much damage in Rome was attributed to Campanian incendiaries. In the case of the Sicilians we see the beginnings of an institution common in the later Republic, the clientship of Provinces. Having failed in upsetting the decisions of Marcellus, the deputation devoted their efforts to soothing his resentment. The gentle Marcellus was all forgiveness, and undertook at their request to be their patron and protector. Henceforth the provincials of Sicily had a recognized claim to the

---

[1] Livy XXVI 29—32, Weissenborn.   [2] Livy XXVI 27.

good offices of the Claudii Marcelli whenever any matter affecting their local interests came up for settlement at Rome.

350. Among the most important questions of the moment was the manning[1] of the fleets. While Carthage seemed blind to the necessity of naval activity for the successful conduct of a widespread war, the Roman Senate had thoroughly grasped the main fact of the present situation. The various hostile forces must be kept apart at all costs, while their own freedom of movement was secured. To keep Philip employed in Greece and Hasdrubal in Spain, to isolate and weaken Hannibal, to guard their own coasts and keep open the waterways, while alarming the African seaboard by occasional descents,—these were Rome's immediate strategic objects, which she could not hope to attain without a strong and efficient navy. But how, with an empty treasury, was the cost of adequate naval armaments to be borne? If eight years of deadly warfare had taught useful lessons, they had also drained resources: and an attempt on the part of the consuls to make the well-to-do citizens provide rowers in proportion to their property, as had been done in 214, led to a general outcry of irresistible protest. But the Senate, it is said, rose to the occasion: on the motion of Laevinus they voluntarily placed all their money and valuables at the service of the state, each man retaining only a small pittance for family needs. The contagion of their example infected the knights and lower orders, and out of the abundance of patriotic offerings it was found possible not only to buy rowers but to provide their pay. But the financial strain was intense, and was probably the main reason for the reduction of the forces in this year (210). Livy only reckons 21 Roman legions, and the number of Allies under arms was also less. How supremely important it was to keep up the fleets was presently shewn by a disaster[2] on a small scale. The supplies of corn for the citadel of Tarentum were brought from Etruria, until the revival of agriculture in Sicily under Laevinus opened up a nearer source of supply. In either case it was brought by sea, and the vessels of burden were convoyed by a squadron of ships of war. Rhegium was the headquarters of this squadron, but it seems that its brave commander had not a force sufficient for the work to be done. While guarding a convoy as usual, a Tarentine squadron met him and brought him to action: after a sharp struggle his war-ships were all taken, sunk, or driven ashore: the corn-ships escaped by hoisting sail and running for the open sea. Apparently steps were taken to prevent the recurrence of such a mishap, for we soon hear of supplies and reinforcements being thrown into the beleaguered citadel. It is worthy of note that the one naval

[1] Livy XXVI 35, 36.   [2] Livy XXVI 39.

defeat of the Romans in this great war was suffered at the hands not of Carthaginians but of Greeks. Later in the year the fleet at Lilybaeum made a sudden descent on the African coast and returned bringing prisoners and much booty, above all the important news that the present aim of Carthage was to reinforce Hasdrubal in Spain and hurry on the second invasion of Italy from the North. Another expedition against Sicily was also in preparation. Nothing came of this, but a Punic fleet made a descent on Sardinia: the booty taken can hardly have repaid the cost of the expedition, and it had no effect whatever on the general result of the war.

351. We must now follow the fortunes of the struggle in the West, a task which errors of chronology and the fictions and distortions of the Scipionic legend render extremely difficult. Certain main facts alone can be trusted. It seems that Scipio spent the winter of 210 in preparations and gathering information. The three Punic leaders wintered in separate camps to the South and West: none of them was less than ten days' march from New Carthage, their chief arsenal and military base. There were kept the army-chest, and the hostages taken to secure the allegiance of many Spanish tribes: the garrison was weak. Scipio set out in the spring of 209 and marched[1] with all speed upon this town, the fleet under Laelius moving in support along the coast. A vigorous assault on the walls masked an attack on the weaker works of the harbour-front. Scipio had been at pains to learn the ways of the local tide in the lagoon: a party waded through the shallow and falling water to an undefended spot, and the Romans were in possession of New Carthage before Hasdrubal and his colleagues could know of its danger. It was indeed a prize. There were 18 ships of war, which were added to the Roman fleet. Better still, there were a number of able-bodied residents, who were drafted into these ships as rowers or added to the short-handed crews of the other ships. A fine staff of skilled slave-artisans became the property of Rome. Both these classes were promised their freedom on condition of doing good work for Rome up to the end of the war. In the port were taken 63 vessels of burden, some with their cargoes still on board. The quantity of corn, arms, timber, metals, and naval stores, was immense. Military engines (the artillery of the day) were there in great plenty and of all sizes. A large sum in gold and silver more than doubled the resources of Scipio's army-chest. The actual citizens of the town, probably a mixed body of Africans and Spaniards, were left free on the understanding that they would be loyal subjects of Rome. But in no respect were the fruits of victory more skilfully turned to account than in the treatment of the Spanish hostages.

[1] Polyb. x 8—20, Livy xxvi 41—51.

Protected from violence and insult, they were freely restored to their relatives, and a number of strong tribes were by this means added to the Roman alliance. It is in connexion with this transaction that we read how Scipio refused to accept a beautiful maid of Spain, reserved by the soldiers as a special prize for their young commander. He restored her to her parents and (with a dowry) to her betrothed. The story[1] furnished material to the moralizing writers of later times: the 'continence of Scipio' was a hackneyed topic of literature, a scene added to the classical gallery of Roman worthies. But the strict business of the war was not neglected: the walls of the town were strengthened, weapons and armour were turned out in great quantities from the workshops, the army and fleet trained to higher efficiency. Having provided for the security of his new conquest, Scipio withdrew to Tarraco, where he passed the winter in receptions of native chiefs and negotiation of alliances. Here we must break off and return to the war in Italy, the fortunes of which were at this time largely dependent on the operations in Spain.

352. As time passed by, and the weary war fell more into a yearly routine, the position of Hannibal became weaker. In 210 he was still holding the Bruttian country save Rhegium and one or two other towns: parts of Apulia and Lucania were still in his power, but a tendency to fall away and make peace with Rome was shewing itself among his allies. Salapia was betrayed to Marcellus, and a garrison of 500 men, the flower of his Numidian horse, were put to the sword. Much the same happened elsewhere. Even Bruttium, where his strength lay, was harried by bands of freebooters operating from Rhegium: a choice collection of mercenary ruffians, whose lives the Romans had spared in Sicily on condition of their doing this risky but congenial work: if Hannibal should cut them to pieces, nobody would be the loser. So his only hope in Italy was to regain his old prestige by sheer fighting, and trust to something turning up from Spain or Macedon: even Carthage might yet awake and send him strong reinforcements. Accordingly we find him active in Apulia and Lucania. But his army was no doubt a far inferior force to that which five years before the Romans had been unable to face. Many of his best veterans must have perished ere this: and the Gauls and Italians who may have filled their places would not be their equals in spirit or military skill. The reinforcements hitherto received from Carthage had clearly been insufficient, and they were not inspired by memories of Trasimene and Cannae. Naturally enough the fighting

---

[1] Livy XXVI 49 calls attention to the wonderful discrepancy in detail of the various versions of the capture of New Carthage, but this highly coloured story is given without reserve. Polybius no doubt had it from the Scipios.

that followed was no unbroken course of Punic victories. However much we may distrust the story in detail, the general outline is credible enough. Hannibal marched into Apulia and cut up the army of a second Fulvius in a second battle of Herdonea. Next he is engaged with Marcellus at Numistro in Lucania. Roman tradition claimed a drawn battle, followed by the retreat of Hannibal, with Marcellus in pursuit. This may mean no more than that Hannibal was not able to press an advantage gained: for the great war-artist was working with inferior tools.

353. At Rome confidence was steadily growing. We hear of negotiations for friendship with king Syphax of Numidia, who had made advances: and also of a renewal of the old friendship with the reigning Ptolemy of Alexandria. But the financial distress was great, and Polybius[1] tells us that the motive of the embassy to Egypt was to procure supplies of corn. There was a dreadful scarcity in Rome: corn was at famine prices, and the new supply from Sicily had not yet begun to pour into the Roman market. Prodigies were reported and dealt with as usual. A dispute arose[2] about naming a dictator to hold the elections for 209. Laevinus, summoned from Sicily, was to have made the nomination, but he stood out for an independence of choice which the Senate would not concede. The difference was ended by the tribunes backing up the Senate, the withdrawal of Laevinus, the transference of the function to his colleague Marcellus, who nominated the Senate's man, Q. Fulvius, the executioner of Capua. But, when Fulvius accepted his own nomination for consul, two tribunes made objection. They did not however venture to block proceedings: the question between them and the dictator was referred to the Senate, who decided in the dictator's favour. This episode well illustrates the effective supremacy of the Senate in the Roman state at this time. There was plenty to be done: we hear of matters connected with religion, the filling-up of vacant priestly offices, celebration of games, expiation of more prodigies. The Senate welcomed the good reports from Sicily and Spain, but was uneasy at confirmation of the news of the intended coming of Hasdrubal: Laelius, who had brought the chief prisoners taken at New Carthage, was ordered back to the province at once. Scipio and Silanus were continued in command during the pleasure of the House, and a last reserve of public money, the accumulated fees[3] on emancipation of slaves, was drawn upon to provide clothing for the army in the West. It also helped to supply necessary means for the proconsuls, Marcellus in southern Italy and P. Sulpicius Galba in the

---

[1] Polyb. IX 44, Livy XXVII 4 § 10.   [2] Livy XXVII 5 §§ 14—19, 6 §§ 2—12.
[3] Livy XXVII 10 §§ 11—13. See index, *aerarium*.

Adriatic, for L. Veturius Philo in Cisalpine Gaul, for old Fabius
(a fifth time consul) in a movement on Tarentum. The consul Fulvius
was to operate in Bruttium. While Marcellus and he kept Hannibal
busy, the old 'Slow-goer' was to gather the fruit now judged ripe.
Etruria and Sicily were not neglected: from Sicily 30 ships of war
were sent to support Fabius, the rest sent off on a predatory cruise.
The campaign of 209 was to be a supreme effort. Its real object was
to forestall a possible junction of Hasdrubal and Hannibal. First,
it was hoped that the former would be kept in Spain: secondly, that
the loss of the city of Tarentum would convince Hannibal of failure
and induce him to evacuate Italy: Hasdrubal then would either not
come at all or come too late. These hopes were foiled by the loyalty
and grit of the sons of Barcas: nevertheless this year's work did much
to give the final victory to Rome.

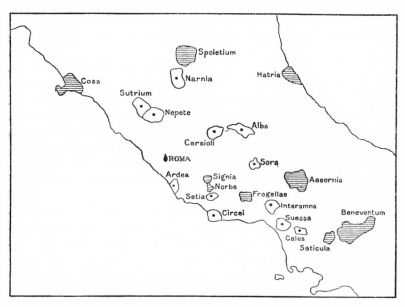

This map shews the Latin Colonies near Rome. It includes some of those which stood by
Rome in the crisis of 209 B.C., marked in line shading, and the whole (12) of those
which withdrew their support, marked in outline with a dot. [Partly adapted from
Beloch, *Der Italische Bund*.]

354. But just at this juncture, when all was in preparation, Rome
received a blow, to all appearance a worse blow than had fallen on
her as yet. The relics of the second army cut up at Herdonea were
sent to Sicily to share with their predecessors the ignominious garrison-
service of the 'legions of Cannae.' It happened that they were mostly

Allies, in great part drawn from the Latin colonies. It is said that their hard treatment brought to a head[1] the discontent long gathering in these communities. Anyhow the normal demand for the yearly contingent of conscripts was in this year met by 12 colonies with a refusal. They declared that they had come to the end of their resources : they had no more men to serve or money to pay them. And they declined to reconsider their decision. It was no movement for joining Hannibal, but a determination no longer to bear their share in the defence of Italy. The consternation of the Senate was naturally great. How well these colonies had served the Roman cause in the war has been pointed out above. Through their sturdy loyalty Rome had kept her hold on Italy in the darkest season of defeat : if these Allies of the first and favoured class grew weary of the common burden, what could be hoped from the ordinary Allies leagued with Rome on less favourable terms? But there were then in all 30 Latin colonies, and the discovery that the other 18 meant to do their duty as hitherto had a calming effect. To them the Senate and People voted the warmest thanks. As to the defaulting 12, we are told that for the present they were simply ignored. Rome would not scold them : if all went well, their time would come. It is a tempting question, what was the cause of the different conduct of the two sets of colonies. It is possible that long distance from Rome, and a feeling of inability to stand alone in an exposed position, may have quickened the loyalty of the colonies in southern Italy or in the region of the Po. And the distant colonies were in fact loyal. The disloyal 12 were all within a moderate distance of Rome, but so were a number of the 18. It is probable that in different places different causes were at work : if we knew from what places the soldiers came who were disgraced or abandoned by Rome on various occasions during the war, we might possibly find some clue to the mystery. But we are not likely to know this. Nor do we know how, if at all, the deficiency in the year's recruiting was made up. Probably more Roman citizens were called out. We are told that in the census[2] held this year strict measures were taken to punish those who ought by rights to have been serving in the cavalry but had evaded that duty. It would seem that already the possession of a certain amount of property bound a citizen to serve on horseback, that there was in fact something corresponding to the 'Knight's rating' [*census equester*] of the later Republic : also that the wealthier citizens already shewed reluctance to serve as troopers.

355. The campaign of 209 in Italy went on much as it was meant to do. Hannibal was kept employed in the field, while old Fabius

---

[1] Livy XXVII 9, 10.   [2] Livy XXVII 11.

dealt with Tarentum. We hear of two battles fought by Marcellus in Apulia, the first a Roman defeat, the second a victory, the truth and the details of which are of no importance: also of attacks on Hannibal's posts in Bruttium. It appears that Marcellus' army was greatly crippled by the severe fighting, but that when Hannibal moved to the South a movement set in among his remaining allies in Lucania and southern Samnium. Town after town submitted to Rome, and any Punic garrisons left in them were handed over to the consul Fulvius. Meanwhile Fabius was busy organizing a general attack on the city of Tarentum by land and sea. The sea was open: of the Tarentine fleet we hear nothing, and a Punic fleet that had previously been stationed there had now been withdrawn to support Philip in his Aetolian war. Nor was the defence of the city satisfactorily provided for: the armed Greek populace were not by themselves sufficient for the purpose, and Carthalo the Punic commander, to whom Hannibal had only left a small guard, thought it necessary to supplement his forces by employing a body[1] of Bruttians. Why Hannibal left so weak a garrison in his most important post, we do not know: he left garrisons in posts of little value, though ill able to spare the men. Perhaps he may have feared to rouse the jealousy of the Greek demagogues. Be this as it may, the task of Fabius was made easy beyond expectation. The captain of the Bruttians was got at through his mistress, a Tarentine lady of a family loyal to Rome, and agreed to betray to the Romans his section of the wall. The treachery was carried out under cover of an assault at other points, and the city was taken. The Greek leaders fell fighting, and the usual indiscriminate butchery took place. Even the Bruttians were many of them cut down in the first fury: the malignant suggestion[2] that this was in part a deliberate act, that success won by treachery might seem to be the fruit of valour, seems to come from Roman sources. Then came the plundering. We hear of 30,000 persons sold into slavery, of immense booty in gold and silver, statues, pictures, and works of art generally. As to the statues, tradition varied. Some at least seem to have been left where they stood: whether because they were too heavy to be easily removed, or through the moderation of Fabius. It depends on the bias of the authority followed.

356. Hannibal, drawn off to the South in aid of his allies, had no doubt reckoned on the city's holding out long enough to enable him to come to its relief. The betrayal of the wall upset his calculations,

---

[1] Livy says that the Bruttians were left there by Hannibal. The version given in Appian seems more probable.

[2] Livy XXVII 16 § 6, Plutarch *Fabius* 22. Was it a suggestion of some Scipionic writer jealous of Fabius' glory?

and forced marches only brought him back too late. With astounding readiness he at once arranged a sham offer of betraying to Fabius the Greek city of Metapontum. The Greek agents are said to have got from Fabius a promise to appear at Metapontum at a fixed time, and Hannibal to have laid an ambush for his destruction. But, whether it was the warning from the birds, or the defective entrails of a victim, or the misgivings of the suspicious consul himself, that made the scheme miscarry, Fabius did not walk into the trap, and lose the fruits of his victory. The consequences of this victory we shall see below.

(c)   208—201 B.C.

357.   The effect of the recapture of Tarentum in strengthening the position of Rome was immense. First, there was the moral effect in Italy. Roman vengeance was not lightly to be risked, and it seemed now to be a certain consequence of rebellion. If Hannibal could not hold a city accessible to him by sea as well as by land, how could his protection be trusted? Thus the lessons of Capua and Syracuse were driven home, and all hope of raising the Italian Allies against Rome was at an end. Secondly, the material difficulties in the way of an invasion of Italy by sea became as great as they had ever been, or greater. To land a large force (small forces were to little purpose), and to keep pouring in for its use the foodstuffs that the wasted country could not supply, was in any case a heavy task: a harbour of the first order and a safe depot were almost indispensable for such an undertaking, subject to vicissitudes of wind and weather. Whatever prospect there had been—we are concerned with hopes rather than with facts—of effective support from Philip or from Carthage itself, was now necessarily less. It is therefore no wonder that we find Hannibal looking for help to the North, to the coming of his brother with an army from Spain and Gaul. When Hasdrubal's desperate venture ended in disaster, the cause of Carthage was virtually lost.

358.   Whether the capture of New Carthage is rightly placed in 210 is perhaps doubtful. Livy[1] was not certain on the point. At some stage of his Spanish campaigns Scipio seems to have been occupied with long negotiations and arrangements for strengthening his position in the country. On the whole it is perhaps more likely that these operations belong to the year 209. The progress made in winning over the Spanish tribes emboldened him to advance early in 208 into the heart of southern Spain. No Punic fleets were

[1] Livy XXVII 7 §§ 5. 6, Weissenborn, and § 351 above.

molesting the eastern coast, so Scipio took the step of arming the crews of his ships[1] and adding them to his marching army. Of the campaign we can only gather that at least one battle was fought, in which the Romans claimed the victory. That the victory was not a decisive one seems clear from what followed. Hasdrubal's main object was to get away safely into Gaul and join his brother in Italy. This by the Roman admissions he seems certainly to have done. His arrangements were no doubt already made: he drew off his army of Africans and Iberians, not forgetting his elephants and a large sum of money, marched to the Pyrenees, crossed them by one of the western passes while the Romans were waiting for him in the eastern district, and made his quarters for the winter among the friendly tribes of Gaul. The chief purpose of Roman efforts in Spain was thus defeated: the second son of Barcas had got away safely and was on his way to Italy. The failure of Scipio has been much blamed by modern critics, and we must admit that he does appear to have been outgeneralled by Hasdrubal. The latter effected his main object. To his later fortunes we shall presently return. As for Scipio, he no doubt already had his eye fixed on Africa as the destined scene of the final acts of the war. A young Numidian prince fell into his hands, and was promptly turned to account: he was set free and allowed to return to his uncle Masinissa, thus opening up a friendly connexion destined to bear good fruit for Rome. The young general in looking to the future also guarded against the jealousy with which, as he knew, many of his influential fellow citizens regarded him. When his Spanish admirers saluted him[2] as King, he publicly repudiated the invidious title, meaning doubtless that his action should be reported at Rome: the story was an integral part of the Scipionic legend, a subject for rhetoricians.

359. The general restlessness engendered by the strain of the war was illustrated in the winter of 209 by the endeavour to make[3] a scapegoat of Marcellus. He had been obliged to rest and recruit his army, crippled by his bloody battles with Hannibal. But, when a tribune accused him of prolonging the war by his slackness and proposed to take away his *imperium*, the Roman people would none of it, and the next day elected him once more consul. The unrest in Etruria still caused uneasiness. The chief centre of disaffection was at Arretium. Threats of military occupation were only of temporary effect. Soon it was found necessary to take hostages from the Arretines, to garrison the town, and to employ a flying column to forestall attempts at local risings. Thus, under the direction of Varro,

---

[1] Livy XXVII 17 § 6, Polyb. X 35.   [2] Polyb. X 40, Livy XXVII 19 §§ 3—6.
[3] Livy XXVII 20, 21, Weissenborn.

an Etruscan rebellion was averted.   The other arrangements for the year (208) consisted mainly of extensions of command.   The consuls were both to operate against Hannibal.   But it was rumoured that Carthage was at last making ready to send to sea a strong fleet: hence we read of exceptional naval activity[1] on the part of Rome. For the Macedonian war, in which Rome was beginning to have the help of maritime allies, the present squadron sufficed.   The Punic attack was expected in the waters nearer home.   So the Sicilian fleet was raised to 100 sail, and Laevinus was given leave to cruise as far as Africa if he saw fit.   From the fleet idle in Spain, where naval war had ceased, 50 ships were drawn to form a squadron for Sardinia. Another force of 50 ships was fitted out to guard the Italian coast near Rome.   This activity was wise: to command the sea was in itself most important, and it went a long way towards the desired isolation of Hannibal.   The question of the future treatment of Tarentum was discussed in the Senate and the decision deferred till quieter times. All we know is that in some form the city lost its freedom.   To unmake it like Capua was out of the question: such a port-town was far too valuable for that.   Matters of religion as usual claimed their share of attention: technical scruples about a temple vowed by Marcellus in the Gaulish war of 222, the plans for which had to be modified, and which he did not live to dedicate: the exceptional difficulty found in expiating the prodigies of the year, a failure of sacrifices telling of disaster to come.   There was also much sickness about: hence it was agreed to turn the games of Apollo the healing god from an irregular festival vowed and held in and for the current year into a regular yearly festival on a fixed date.

360.   The consul T. Quinctius Crispinus opened the campaign by moving upon Locri, but the approach of Hannibal soon sent him to join Marcellus in Apulia.   The consuls were eager to fight.   Hannibal faced them, biding his time : meanwhile he cut off by an ambush a Roman detachment marching to renew the siege of Locri.   The growing impatience of the consuls at length gave him his chance. Tempted by the prospect of seizing a strategic point apparently unoccupied, the two Roman leaders fell into a trap.   In the ensuing struggle Marcellus was killed outright, Crispinus carried off by his escort, badly wounded.   It is particularly noted[2] that of the 220 horse taken with them by the consuls on this occasion 40 were Latins from Fregellae, who mostly fell in defence of their generals ; the rest were Etruscans, who ran away.   Considering the recent evidences of disloyalty in Etruria (Marcellus himself had been sent on a mission there in 209), this trust in the Etruscan Allies is remarkable.   As

---

[1] Livy XXVII 22.   [2] Livy XXVII 26, 27, Polyb. X 32.

horsemen they would belong to the wealthier classes, and may have been Roman partisans in their several cities. If so, they would have been of more use at home. We may remark that this escort included no Roman citizen cavalry. Probably the Romans qualified by property for this service were mostly serving as officers, and the number required for the great forces now under arms (citizens and Allies, horse and foot) would leave few over for service as troopers. The accounts of the disaster of the consuls seem to have varied greatly in detail. A story of the sequel is interesting. One of the first cares of Crispinus, after drawing off the Roman armies into safety, was to send notice round the neighbouring towns, warning those in charge to pay no attention to orders[1] purporting to come from Marcellus, whose signet ring had fallen into the enemy's hand. And indeed Hannibal had paid great funeral honours to the fallen consul, but had reserved his ring for the purpose of a military trick. A forged despatch sealed with Marcellus' seal reached Salapia: the consul would be there that night, all must be ready for his reception into the town. The Salapians, well aware that the Punic leader owed them an ill turn, promised to obey, but laid a clever trap for him. Having a double gate the outer entrance of which was closed with a portcullis, they admitted the 600 leaders of the column of march, dropped the portcullis, and massacred them at leisure. Upon those following they shot missiles from the wall. The affair was a serious disaster to a general who had no spare strength to waste. He lost most of his Roman deserters here, having put them in the very front that their Latin speech might aid the deception. And these would be some of his most desperate fighting men. He marched away southwards and again relieved Locri, but he could not do more for the present. Meanwhile the Senate made arrangements for the temporary command of the consular armies. There was great mourning for Marcellus. In a short time news came that Crispinus also was dead, and the Republic without a consul. Before his decease he had named a dictator for the formal duties of holding games and the elections for the next year.

361. Before we turn to that election and the crisis of 207 we must glance at the detached operations outside Italy. The Sicilian fleet[2] made a descent on the African coast, fought a successful action with a Carthaginian fleet, and brought home an immense booty. In Greece there was a confused scene of wasteful war. Clear-sighted men were beginning to see that this weakening of the Greek states could only turn to the profit of a foreign power. Mediation was attempted by the maritime states of Rhodes and Chios, whose interests were bound

---

[1] Livy XXVII 28.   [2] Livy XXVII 29 §§ 7, 8.

up with peace and commerce.   With them were acting Athens, and Egypt, distrustful of all disturbances of the *status quo*.   But the time for peace was not yet come.   Both combatants had gained help from outside; Philip that of Prusias king of Bithynia, with whose aid and a Punic squadron he hoped to dispute the naval supremacy of his opponents; the Aetolians now had the fleet of Attalus of Pergamum on their side as well as the Roman squadron.   On the whole the latter had the best of it not only in the Adriatic but in the Aegean. But on land the King of Macedon did better.   His energy was surprising: he beat the Aetolians, checked Attalus' enterprise against Euboea, cut up a party of raiders landed from the Roman ships on the Peloponnesian coast, and seems to have appealed with some success to a feeling of 'Greece for the Greeks.'   But, though no one was eager to provoke the active intervention of the Romans and Attalus, the peace proposals laid before the conference at a federal diet of the Achaean League came to nothing.   After a defeat by a force of Aetolians and Romans in Elis, Philip left a small body of troops to aid his allies and returned to Macedonia, where his presence was needed to deal with invaders.   The Roman squadron sailed round to join that of Attalus in the Aegean, and the combined fleet wintered at Aegina.

362.   The election of consuls was a very urgent matter.   We hear that C. Claudius Nero stood out among possible candidates, but was thought to need a discreet colleague to moderate his venturesome temper.   So Marcus Livius (known later as Salinator), a relative of his namesake spoken of above, was drawn reluctantly from retirement and elected with Nero.   The story[1] is dressed up by later writers for edification, and the details cannot be trusted.   Livius is the indignant Roman noble, sulking for years at his condemnation to a fine on the score of embezzlement in the Illyrian war (219), a sentence which he regarded as unjust.   Sour and surly, a marked type of Roman, he will hardly consent to be consul on any terms.   He seems to illustrate a kind of general proposition, that a very disagreeable man may nevertheless be useful.   A further difficulty arose as between the two colleagues: Nero had given evidence against Livius on the occasion of his trial, evidence which Livius declared to be false.   With much ado the Senate induced the pair of personal enemies to lay aside their hatred, at least for the moment, and pull together for the good of the state.   The whole situation was an extraordinary one, and we have no means of telling how far the accuracy of the tradition has been corrupted by the misrepresentations of partisan annalists.   As for Nero, his military career had not so far been a notable success.

[1] Livy XXVII 34.   Above § 273.

Why he should have been regarded as the man of the hour is not clear. Unluckily we have no authority for this episode earlier than the Augustan age, when the Claudii (especially the Nerones) were connected with the emperor and made much of[1] by obsequious writers. We may fairly guess that his Claudian origin helped Nero to the consulship quite as much as his past exploits, and that his share in the great victory of 207 has at least not been minimized by later tradition.

363. The serious nature of the present crisis was fully recognized in Rome, and the winter of 208 was spent in careful preparations. From loyal Massalia came the news that Hasdrubal was wintering and raising troops in Gaul, and would appear in Italy so soon as the melting of the snow opened the passes of the Alps. We hear of a census being held, in which a great falling-off[2] in the number of citizens came to light. How all the long and intricate arrangements for which censors were responsible were carried out in the extraordinary pressure of public business is not explained. Religious matters took up much time. Games, dedications, sacrifices, were held: also solemn processions, in one of which was chanted a lay or litany composed by Livius[3] Andronicus. For in this hour of trial the ever-recurring prodigies gave the nerves of the superstitious people no rest. Special care was taken in assigning the various commands of the year, the one great object kept in view being to prevent a junction of Hannibal and Hasdrubal. To Nero fell the chief command in the South, to Livius that in the North: other forces watched important points, such as Tarentum, and Etruria was overawed by Varro. With 23 legions, with the Latin and other Allies, with large and efficient fleets, Rome must have had 250,000 men under arms, perhaps many more. More than half of these were probably in Italy. But the dread of Hannibal was still a mighty force, and Hasdrubal was the great unknown. Nothing was allowed to hinder[4] the bringing of the armies up to full strength. Even the time-honoured exemption from field service enjoyed by the Romans of the citizen colonies (more or less out of date, it is true) was suspended, and all save Ostia and Antium were drawn upon for filling up the legions. One tradition declared that Scipio sent 11,000 men, mostly Spanish Gaulish or Numidian mercenaries, from Spain—a doubtful story. That light troops were borrowed from the Sicilian army is more likely. So great was the pressure that the enlistment of slaves was

---

[1] See especially Horace, Odes IV 4.
[2] Livy XXVII 36 § 7. See Beloch, *die Bevölkerung der Griechisch-Römischen Welt*, p. 346.
[3] See § 262.   [4] Livy XXVII 38.

resorted to once more. To insure the highest possible efficiency in the two principal armies, the consuls were allowed very wide powers for the transference of picked men from one corps to another.

364. News came from the praetor in Cisalpine Gaul that Hasdrubal was on the move for Italy. He had with him some veteran troops, Spanish and probably also African: these formed the trusty core of his army. But a large part of his forces consisted of recently-enlisted Gauls, very untrustworthy, or of Ligurian hillmen, notoriously fickle though brave. He crossed the Alps with comparative ease, the mountain tribes offering no resistance now that they knew themselves not to be threatened. So he reached the plains of northern Italy sooner than expected by friend or foe. According to Appian[1], he had with him 56,000 men. In an evil hour he gave way to the temptation of besieging Placentia. The colony had been held firmly by the Romans, and was now a well-established fortress town. Hasdrubal had no siege-train, and by blockading a town that he could not storm he wasted time to no purpose. To stop his advance two armies were waiting, Livius with his base at Ariminum, and L. Porcius the praetor, acting under the consul's orders. The anxiety in Rome was of course extreme, and meanwhile it would seem that Nero was only just able to keep Hannibal occupied in the South. Livy has stories of fighting and heavy losses on the Carthaginian side: how it came that, beaten again and again, Hannibal moved about freely in southern Italy from Bruttium to Apulia, is not explained. Probably there was fighting and loss on both sides, and Hannibal, having no reserves to draw on, was somewhat crippled. If we wonder at his not moving northwards to meet his brother, we must remember that he had to cover Bruttium. He could not start to join Hasdrubal until he knew when and where to seek him. At this point[2] it was that fate dealt him the deadly blow. Hasdrubal broke up the investment of Placentia and set out on his way to the South, first despatching mounted messengers (Gauls and Numidians) with full written particulars to Hannibal. Near Tarentum they fell into the hands of the Romans and were brought to Nero. The consul saw his chance and seized it. Leaving the bulk of his army with a lieutenant to watch Hannibal, he set out that night with 8000 of his best men, the pick of a picked army. An express message to the Senate instructed them what strategic steps to take in order to cover the city and give the means of retrieving a possible reverse. Couriers hurried along the intended line of march, to bid the loyal inhabitants to have food and drink ready by the wayside and bring beasts and carts to give a lift to the footsore. All was carried out as planned. Hannibal was deceived, and the march

---

[1] Appian *Hannib.* 52.   [2] Polyb. XI 1—3, Livy XXVII 43—51.

of the 8000 through Italy roused the country side to wild enthusiasm.
How many they were whom Nero led into Livius' camp at Sena, we
do not know, for volunteers old and young had joined them as they
passed.   Livius' men packed them into their tents, not enlarging the
camp, lest the enemy should discover what had happened in the
night.   Hasdrubal was close by.   He had been skilfully watched and
checked by the praetor, who had fallen back before him, and was now
encamped beside Livius.   The total Roman force present is not stated
in our authorities, and it is perhaps rash to estimate the numbers.
So far as an estimate is possible, it would seem that it was about
50,000 men.   But these were men fighting for their country, they were
mostly picked men, they were bred up in a common discipline.   If
Hasdrubal really had 56,000 men (which is possible) they were on the
average of far inferior quality.   In the morning various signs led him
to suspect that something was wrong: presently the sound of the
double bugle-call in Livius' camp convinced him that the other consul
was also there.   To fight at once, before he knew what it all meant,
would be an act of blind despair.   He decided to retreat for the
present, and not to fight until he knew what he was doing.   But this
movement to the rear, however well-judged, had doubtless a demoral-
izing effect on his Gaulish contingent.   During the night march the
guides slipped away and left the column to flounder about in the
dark.   Dawn found the weary and disheartened army waiting to
discover a ford for crossing the river Metaurus.   While they moved
searching vainly, the Romans appeared in pursuit, and brought them
to battle.   Hasdrubal posted his Gauls in an inaccessible position on
his left.   Nero, facing them, found that he could not get at them, and
they had no mind to close with him.   So he left his place in the line of
battle and hurried to the help of his colleague, hard pressed by
Hasdrubal's Spaniards.   He burst on the flank and rear of the
enemy's right wing, and all was soon over.   Few of the Spaniards
escaped : the Ligurians in the centre fared little better, between the
Roman sword and the wild return-rush of wounded elephants : in due
course came the slaughter of the unresisting Gauls as they lay
sleeping the sleep of drunkenness or sheer exhaustion.   Not until the
last hope was gone did Hasdrubal yield to despair : he died fighting
bravely, as befitted a son of Hamilcar Barcas.

365.   If I have for once turned aside to describe a battle at some
length, it is because the affair of Metaurus is one of the electric
moments in the history of the world.   That Rome would have gone
under, if Hasdrubal had won the day, I do not believe.   It suited the
later rhetoric so to conceive the situation, and modern criticism has
often been only too ready to accept this view.   But that Rome after

her long efforts, after her gradual recovery in Italy, her success in Spain, her vigorous display of naval power, would have succumbed to a defeat and the junction of the Punic brothers, is to me incredible. That the agony in Rome, when it was known that Nero had started for the North and the result was yet doubtful, was intense, that the first reports of victory were discredited, that confirmation of the news led to outpourings of joy and thanksgiving to the gods, is probably as true as it is dramatic. It is also true that it was by the victory of the Metaurus that the miscarriage of Carthaginian designs was made clear to the contemporary world. The loss of a single mercenary army had paralysed Carthage. She could no longer pour armies into Italy by sea, and the Alps, even if left undefended in future, were not sufficient as an open door. The expedition of Hasdrubal was a forlorn hope, the tragic end of which made it a famous literary theme, a crown of Roman glory. But it was the issue of the great sieges—Syracuse, Capua, New Carthage, Tarentum—that vitally determined the result of the deadly duel. When matters had come to this, that the one combatant could both win and keep, while the other could not, not all the genius of the house of Barcas could have arrested for more than a brief moment the pitiless course of events. The buoyancy of Rome is characteristically shewn in the effect of the news from the North on the money market. Dealings in money were no small part of the life of the Romans, who were born investors and usurers. For some days no one would buy or lend on any terms: cash, portable value, was the one thing in demand. With the return of confidence, business revived at once. Meanwhile Nero marched back in haste, bearing the news of his own triumph, and stirring up patriotic joy along the length of Italy. He broke the news to Hannibal in brutal fashion, by flinging the head of Hasdrubal in front of his camp. To Hannibal the nearness of the end was now plain: he drew in his scattered posts, and, taking with him some of his remaining adherents, effected a concentration to the rear. He had still forces enough to hold the Bruttian country, and there he for the present decided to wait.

366. After the departure of Hasdrubal for Italy, the war in Spain loses most of its interest, being now less directly connected with the general struggle. But it went on, for neither side could afford to resign to its rival a country so rich in the elements of fighting strength. The remaining Punic generals, Hasdrubal son of Gisgo and Mago son of Barcas, were joined in 207 by a fresh army from Carthage under one Hanno, and began to gain ground again in Celtiberia. We hear that an expeditionary force under Silanus surprised the Punic army, killed or scattered the Celtiberian auxiliaries, and drove the remains of the African troops in flight from the district. These fell back

to join Hasdrubal in the South-west.   On the advance of Scipio, Hasdrubal retired upon Gades, now the base of Carthaginian operations. He quartered his army in separate detachments in fortified towns, and left the Roman to exhaust himself in sieges.   Scipio sent his brother Lucius to take one of these places.   This he is said to have done with small loss : but the Carthaginian's calculations seem to have been justified, for Scipio shortly withdrew his army into winter quarters within the Roman sphere.   It is clear that not much progress had as yet been made towards an effective conquest of Spain.   But the despatch of Hanno and other important prisoners to Rome served to keep up the interest and confidence of the citizens in the young general to whom was entrusted the cause of the republic in the West. In the next year the war went on as before.   We hear of the enlistment of natives on both sides : neither side could really trust the Spaniards when fighting in their own land for a cause not their own. We read of minor operations followed by a great battle, in which the wise tactics of Scipio gave him the victory over a far more numerous enemy.   The usual adhesion of local chiefs and towns to the winning side took place : Hasdrubal fell back, and was badly cut up in the pursuit : Scipio left Silanus to finish the capture or destruction of the Punic army, whose leaders had escaped to Gades and left it to its fate. The general himself returned to Tarraco, dealing out rewards and punishments to chiefs and towns on the way.   The details of this campaign are far from certain : the chronology is confused beyond hope of restoration.   But we may accept as fact the important result that the Carthaginians were never again able to place large armies in the field to contest with Rome the dominion of Spain.   And it would seem that Scipio now assumed the character of a sort of Governor-general, representing a dominant power : Carthage having no longer the leading position in southern Spain, any limitation of the Roman sphere was out of date.   Thus it is with the resistance of native Iberians that Rome has henceforth to deal : the bloody conquest was only completed in a period of about 200 years.

367.   But it was not on Spain that the thoughts of Scipio were fixed.   His aim was to carry the war into Africa and there bring it to a decisive end.   He had as yet no power to undertake that enterprise, but he meant to have it soon : meanwhile he strove to form useful connexions and alliances for the furtherance of his object in due time. He knew that the efficiency of the Punic forces in Spain depended largely on the Numidian horse, who were devoted to their leader the young prince Masinissa.   Masinissa cared nothing for Carthage, and he saw that in Spain the Punic cause was lost.   He therefore made secret proposals to Scipio, who received them warmly.   It was

arranged that the Numidian should return to Africa, establish himself on the throne of his father, and act as an ally of Rome. But Scipio was not less anxious to make sure of the friendship of Syphax, king of western Numidia, an established potentate who had large forces at his disposal. Laelius was sent over to sound him, and was so well received that Scipio himself, it is said, made at great risk a flying excursion to the Masaesylian[1] court. The presence of Hasdrubal (son of Gisgo) on a similar errand in the interest of Carthage made the occasion interesting. The king secretly pledged himself to Scipio, but was in truth waiting on events. On his return to Spain, Scipio found some signs of unrest, and decided that it was necessary to make a few examples among the disloyal towns. Illiturgi, guilty of former treachery, was stormed and all within put to the sword: Castulo was driven to surrender, and spared: the whole population of Astapa perished either in a desperate sally or in self-inflicted slaughter and flames. Not long after this the general fell ill, and was reported to be dying or even dead. The news moved to rebellion the chiefs of north-eastern Spain, old allies of Rome, but disgusted at the prospect of now becoming her subjects: coupled with inaction in the camp, it produced a serious mutiny[2] among some of the Roman troops. The long service away from Italy, with pay in arrear, was the main grievance. It seems to have been chiefly troops of the Allies that were involved in the mutiny: at least their chosen leaders were a Latin (from the colony of Cales) and an Umbrian. But Scipio rallied and with the support of the loyal troops and the use of craft, put down the rising and executed the ringleaders: it seems that at the same time he thought it wise to provide for more punctual payment of the men. Even now Carthage still kept a footing in the peninsula, for Mago clung to Gades. An offer to betray this stronghold and its garrison induced Scipio to send a mixed force there. But the plot was discovered: nothing could be done by land against the island-city: a naval action[3] fought in the strait was claimed as a Roman victory, but decided nothing. So the enterprise was abandoned. The rising of the north-eastern tribes was a serious matter, but a short and vigorous campaign reduced them to throw themselves on Scipio's mercy and pay a heavy war indemnity.

368. At this time we hear of a sudden change in the war-policy of Carthage. Now that it was too late, and Spain virtually lost, the Home government recognized the supreme importance of the war in Italy. Mago, who was still ready to keep up the contest in Spain, was ordered to withdraw from Gades. Money was sent him, with

---

[1] See § 380.   [2] Polyb. XI 25—30, Livy XXVIII 24—29.
[3] Livy XXVIII 30.

instructions to proceed by sea to northern Italy, to raise a large army of Ligurians and Gauls, cut his way through to Hannibal and revive the Italian war.   He set out, but was tempted in passing to attack New Carthage, and was repulsed with heavy loss.   Gades would no longer receive him, and presently surrendered to the Romans.   He then cruised along the islands, picking up recruits where he could : but in the chief of the Balearic isles he met with a hostile reception. The fortunes of his expedition will concern us later on.   Meanwhile the autumn of 206 was at an end, and the Carthaginian power was at last swept out of Spain.   Scipio handed over his charge to the two proconsuls appointed to succeed him, and took ship for Rome. Formal reasons[1] prevented his receiving the honour of a triumph. He had not yet held a Magistracy in the strict sense.   The *imperium* of a proconsul was only effective in his province, and he had not yet been consul or praetor with *imperium* not locally limited.   The *imperium* was necessary for a solemn triumph : if the Senate had wished it, probably the full *imperium* might have been conferred temporarily.   But some authorities suggest that the jealousy of the Roman nobles would not go out of its way to glorify the rising general, who appears to have lost no opportunity of bringing his own merits to the notice of the Roman people.   The elections were just coming on.   Scipio was chosen consul by an unanimous vote of the Centuries : the province assigned him was Sicily.

369.   Before we relate the decisive steps by which the great war was brought to an end, we must take a cursory glance at affairs in Greece.   In 208 we find Philip beset on all sides.   From Euboea, Boeotia, Acarnania, even from the Achaean League, came urgent calls for help : while his own kingdom was threatened by Illyrian, Thracian, and other restless neighbours in the North.   But he again rose to the occasion, and kept up a not unequal struggle in central Greece, operating from bases in southern Thessaly, and organizing a telegraph service of fire-signals[2] in order to be able to move quickly upon threatened points.   Oreus in Euboea was surrendered to the allied Roman-Pergamene fleet.   But upon Chalcis they could make no impression, thanks to the loyalty of the garrison and the violent squalls and currents of the strait.   The Aetolians tried to stop Philip at Thermopylae, but he put them to rout and restored his authority to the south of the pass : Attalus fled at his approach, and soon after returned to Pergamum to resist the invasion of his kingdom by Philip's ally Prusias of Bithynia.   The Roman fleet withdrew again to Aegina.   Philip advanced into the Peloponnesus.   His Achaean allies were now better able to take care of themselves than in the

---

[1] Livy XXVIII 38.   [2] Polyb. X 43—47.

days of their former leader, Aratus, who had allowed the army to become inefficient : great reforms had been effected by their new general Philopoemen. But the Aetolians had a footing in Elis, and Machanidas the tyrant of Sparta was in league with them. The news of Philip's coming caused Machanidas to abandon a threatened expedition, and the king attended a general diet of the Achaean League. He cheered up his allies, and then set out on a naval raid in the Corinthian gulf, where he looked for the cooperation[1] of a Punic fleet. This hope seems to have failed him, for the Carthaginians, fearing to be caught if they ventured into the gulf, remained outside. Philip however raided the coast-land of Aetolia, and then, sending his army home by land, himself took the risk of capture by the Roman fleet and returned by way of the Saronic gulf, Sunium, and Chalcis. He had now become convinced of the necessity of an efficient fleet, and began shipbuilding in earnest : meanwhile he marched inland to provide for the defence of his northern frontier. It seems to have been in the next year (207) that the Achaeans gained a great victory in Peloponnesus, when Philopoemen slew Machanidas and laid Laconia waste. So far Philip's side was strengthened, but a new and worse tyrant, Nabis, seized power at Sparta, and there was still trouble in southern Greece. But of the Macedonian war after this we have hardly any record, and the chronology is most obscure. It seems that after the withdrawal of Attalus the Romans made no exertion to keep up the naval operations, thinking Philip sufficiently occupied in the land warfare, and caring little that their neglect was leaving their Greek allies in the lurch. And the Greeks in general were beginning to be weary of warfare in which they gained (and could gain) nothing : they could only regard with misgiving the intervention of Rome in Greek affairs, now that the cause of Carthage was on the decline. The attempts at mediation on the part of Rhodes and the other peace-powers had only failed because Rome wished the war to go on : now Rome seemed indifferent, and a second invasion of Aetolia by Philip brought even the war-loving Aetolians to their senses. In 205 they sued for peace. They did not ask the concurrence[2] of Rome, as they were by treaty bound to do : perhaps they had good reason to expect a refusal. They accepted Philip's terms, and gave dire offence at Rome. The king's hands were now free, and he moved into Illyria. There he found a strong Roman force just landed. But neither side seriously wished for a conflict. The Romans would not at present fight singlehanded, and they could not rouse the Aetolians : Philip was genuinely anxious for peace. After some negotiation terms of

---

[1] Livy xxvii 30 § 16, xxviii 7 §§ 17, 18, 8 § 8.   [2] See § 428.

peace[1] were agreed upon and sent to Rome, where the prospect of being able to give undivided attention to Carthage ensured their ready acceptance. Some small territorial rearrangements were made: Rome even ceded the mountain district of Atintania to the king. But it was in truth a hollow compact for momentary convenience: an inevitable struggle was only deferred, clearly to the advantage of Rome. The allies of each party were included in the treaty. Philip claimed Prusias of Bithynia, the Achaean League, and the looser unions of Thessaly, Boeotia, Acarnania, and Epirus: Rome's list included the people of Ilium, Attalus of Pergamum, Pleuratus of Illyria, Athens, Nabis of Sparta, and also the Eleans and Messenians. The last two had become allied with Rome through being allies of the Aetolians, and of the Aetolians there was no mention. We can hardly doubt that Rome meant this as a hint of her intention to support these peoples while leaving the Aetolians to shift for themselves. And we may note that the other names indicate a widening of Roman ideas. Rome could now with propriety intervene to aid allies in a much wider area than before the war. This may have been an intentional piece of far-sighted policy, or it may not.

370. In Rome itself the close of the year 207 was marked by the triumph[2] of the consuls. The battle of the Metaurus had been fought in Livius' province. Livius' army was recalled to march in the procession: that of Nero could not be spared for the purpose. Livius rode in the triumphal car, attended by his troops: Nero rode on horseback alone. The arrangement was probably in accordance with Roman etiquette: Livius would have the right of the auspices on the day of battle, and this would give him precedence in the triumph, a function of religious character. But tradition, perhaps derived from a Claudian annalist, lays stress on the sweet concord of the colleagues: they concerted a plan for meeting by appointment at Praeneste and approaching the city together, and Nero was content to play a second part in the show. Nay more, it being found desirable to have a dictator to hold the coming elections, and the nomination resting with Nero, he named Livius. The story is dressed up by the pictorial instinct of Livy, and the general recognition of Nero as the true saviour of Rome is insisted on. But all this must be received with suspicion. Within three years we find the feud between this strange pair as bitter as ever. The elections for 206 were got over, games were held, and the business of the new year began. The commands and governorships were allotted: both consuls were sent to face Hannibal in the South: the Sicilian fleet[3] was reduced, all but

---

[1] Livy XXIX 12 Weissenborn.　　　　　　　　　[2] Livy XXVIII 9.

[3] Livy XXVIII 10 § 16.

30 ships being laid up at home. Etruria still needed special care: Livius went there as commissioner to discover the persons guilty of correspondence with Hasdrubal, and stayed on as proconsul. Prodigies as usual were not lacking, nor the ceremonies of expiation. Sacrifices were offered to appease the wrath of Vesta, the sacred fire in her temple having been let out by a careless Vestal virgin : that the offender was flogged was not enough. At this point we hear[1] of an attempt to get the Plebs back upon the land. Most of Italy was now reasonably safe, and it was desirable that the farmer-refugees should get them back to their farms and till the soil. It was not however a simple matter. Many had fallen in the war, some doubtless leaving no successors: the small farmer had no stock to start afresh with, and his farmstead was in ashes : the large proprietor could not find the necessary hands, for his old slaves had gone to earn their freedom in the battle-field, and the slave-market was empty. Still we hear that under pressure from the consuls a good many were induced to return to rural life. The account is very unsatisfactory. It is made to refer specially to the parts of Italy near Rome, which had been undisturbed for years, at the least since the recovery of Capua, and had never been subject in this war to continuous and searching devastation like the unhappy districts of the South. A reluctance on the part of refugees to leave the city is intelligible enough. Corn was brought there by sea from Egypt and Sicily, perhaps already from Sardinia. In 207 a large quantity was brought from Africa, the fruit of a raid on Punic territory and a victory of the Roman fleet. There were periods of comparative scarcity, but on the whole the supply of food was regular, for the government could not afford to neglect the matter. There was thus a temptation for those unwilling to resume rural labour to remain in Rome, and a city rabble was beginning to form, an idle and steadily deteriorating populace. It may well have been an object with the Senate to thin out this multitude, now that the country was practically safe. During the years of extreme danger the whole guidance of the state had been left to the Senate, but with returning security the Assemblies shewed an inclination to resume their powers. They had grown weary of the slow-going Fabian policy, and we shall presently find Scipio relying on their support to give effect to his designs. Another matter taken in hand was the maintenance of the great colonies of Placentia and Cremona. They had been of the greatest use to Rome in the war, but their lands were often laid waste by the Gauls, to overawe whom it had not always been possible to provide a sufficient force. The troubled life had caused many colonists to desert their post, and the

---

[1] Livy XXVIII 11 §§ 8—11.

hold of Rome on the plain of the Po was thus weakened.　Orders were issued commanding the wanderers to return, and the praetor in the district was bidden to provide for the effective protection of the colonial territories.　After this the consuls began a campaign in the South of which we have no trustworthy detail : it would seem that their successes were mainly achieved by keeping out of Hannibal's way and forcing isolated Italians to return to the Roman alliance.

371.　We said above that Scipio was elected consul for the year 205.　He had returned from Spain resolved to carry the war into Africa.　It is said that he made no secret[1] of his intention, declaring that if the Senate refused to authorize this step he would bring the matter before the Assembly.　Strong opposition there was, led by old Fabius; but in the end the Senate, too discreet to provoke a certain rebuff, had to give way.　Concession was disguised in compromise. Africa was not officially named as a consul's 'province.'　Scipio was appointed to a command in Sicily, but expressly authorized to cross over to Africa if he judged it advantageous so to do.　He was not governor of the province Sicily : that post was as usual filled by a praetor.　When he set about making his preparations, the Senate, bent on discouraging what they could not prevent, refused[2] him leave to hold a military levy.　The fleet and army at present in Sicily were at his disposal : for the rest, he might raise volunteers if any would offer to enlist.　Scipionic tradition may have aggravated this spiteful obstinacy of the Senate : we have however no means of checking the tradition.　It seems clear that there was no real sympathy between the rising general and the majority of the state council : they were over-cautious, and their jealousy blinded them to the change of circumstances calling for a change of strategy : he was ambitious and impatient, and ready to use his popularity to put pressure on them. We hear of an embassy from Saguntum about this time, conveying thanks for the services of Rome during the war, for the reestablishment[3] of their city and the restoration of the surviving Saguntines. If the account be true, we may suspect that the step was not taken without the knowledge of the general to whose merits it formed a testimonial.　Soon after, before starting for his province, he celebrated splendid games in discharge of a vow made at the time of the mutiny in Spain.　This added to his popularity and made his preeminence still more oppressive to republican nobles, whose ideal was the domination of a class, not the supremacy of a man.　There was indeed some excuse for the governing class if they viewed the rise of Scipio with uneasiness.　Flaminius was dead, and Varro was tamed:

---

[1] See Livy XXVIII 40—45.　　　　[2] Livy XXVIII 45.

[3] See the inscription given in § 688 (a) below.　Livy XXVIII 39.

but they had shewn that a popular leader could on occasion shake the power of the Senate. What might not happen, if the drowsy and fitful Assembly were roused and guided by a member of the great Cornelian house? The actual working of the Roman constitution at this time is illustrated by the way in which the compromise was arranged between Scipio and the Senate. It was done through the tribunes: they appear as entirely obedient to the Senate, and, as they could prevent even the consul from laying a proposal before the Tribes, Scipio had to yield to their pressure, unless indeed he were willing to attempt a direct breach of the constitution. So a very dangerous collision was avoided.

372. Scipio had to start with only 30 ships of war and the two legions composed of the fugitives of Cannae and Herdonea. He set to work to make an army and navy without imposing heavy burdens of taxation on the impoverished citizens. The Umbrians and Sabines furnished volunteers for his army, the Marsi and other peoples of central Italy helped to man his ships, one Umbrian community sent him a fully equipped cohort of 600 men. But far more notable were the contributions of the Etruscan cities. Arms and armour, axes and tools for field work and fortification, mills to grind corn, knee-timber planking and iron for shipbuilding, canvas for sails, corn in great quantity, perhaps money to pay ships' crews—from one city or another such things poured in. The account, preserved in Livy, is very imperfect, and the disaffection of the Etruscans in recent years makes it highly improbable that all this was the outcome of pure good will. Either we have a garbled version of a requisition meant to punish the disloyal Etruscans, or the gifts were 'voluntary' in the sense that they were given to appease Roman anger and in hope to avert punishment. The difference between these alternatives is slight. Shipbuilding was pushed on with such vigour, under Scipio's eye, that 30 ships of war were launched in 45 days from the laying of their keels. Here was a man whom even senatorial obstruction could not turn from his designs. He took on board 7000 volunteers[1] and sailed to Sicily.

373. Scipio's colleague was P. Licinius Crassus, who was chief pontiff. As head of the state religion he was bound not to leave[2] Italy, and accordingly had put forward no claim to the charge of the transmarine war. He held a command in Bruttium, where he bore a part in watching Hannibal. A religious precaution taken at this time was the despatch of a gift (from the spoils of Metaurus) to the Delphic

---

[1] This is not given as the total of his volunteers. Weissenborn on Livy XXVIII 46 § 1 takes these to be the Roman citizens, not including the Allies. We have no clear account.

[2] Livy XXVIII 38 § 12.

Apollo : it was thought well to conciliate a god of so great repute.
But money for the expenses of war was scarce, and to raise it the
state sold some of the forfeited Campanian land near the coast. And
the war, even in Italy, had not yet ceased to bring fresh anxieties, for
news came of another invasion from the North. Mago had sailed
from the Balearic isles, landed with 14,000 men on the Ligurian
coast, and taken Genua. This move caused considerable alarm at
Rome, and the forces in northern Italy were duly strengthened. But
Mago soon became mixed up with the local feuds of the hillmen :
precious time was wasted, and his enterprise, from which Carthage
hoped much, never became a serious menace to the power of Rome.
Indeed, if the Alpine passes were hardly an open door into Italy, the
broken Ligurian hills, with their ravines and rock-forts held by high-
land robber tribes, were even less so. It was a far cry to Croton in
Bruttium, where Hannibal was standing at bay, with wondrous skill
keeping together his motley army. Many of the men were sick, and
it was only with difficulty that he could find food for them. Fighting
had almost ceased. The Roman generals trusted to wearing him
out, and they also had many sick. It was now that Hannibal set up
near the temple of Hera on the Lacinian foreland the inscription,
Phoenician and Greek, of which Polybius made use. It was about
this time, according to Livy[1], that a fleet of merchant vessels sent
with stores to relieve his distress was driven by foul winds into
Sardinian waters. The praetor of Sardinia fell upon them with his
ships of war, and out of 100 only 20 escaped. So says Appian, who
adds that there were not only supplies of food on board but reinforcements. It seems that an effort had at last been made to give serious
support to their one great general, but that naval bungling had as
usual made havoc of the Carthaginian design.

374. When Scipio reached Sicily, he had everything to do and
little to do it with. But he wisely resolved to win the hearts of the
provincials by kindness and justice, and he was soon as popular in
Sicily as he had been in Spain. And if his graciousness was un-
Roman, no Roman had a keener eye to business. He picked out 300
young men of the first families in the island to serve as a cavalry
corps : they were to report themselves, each with his charger and full
trooper's equipment, on a certain date. He had counted[2] on finding
them unwilling to serve abroad in an alien quarrel, and so it was.
When drafting his volunteers into tactical units, he had kept 300
young men apart, not assigned to any century or maniple, or provided
with arms. The Sicilians gladly compounded for exemption from

---

[1] Livy xxviii 46 § 14. See Appian *Hannib.* 54.
[2] Livy xxix 1 Weissenborn.

service by each handing over horse and outfit to one of the young Romans, and agreeing to take his substitute home with him and train him in military horsemanship.   Scipio thus was enabled to put in the field a select mounted corps of undoubted spirit and loyalty at no expense whatever.   He also raised supplies of corn from the Sicilian communities: on this he fed his men, and saved up the supplies from home for the actual campaign.   How he managed to increase the numbers of his expeditionary force (as he must have done) we are not clearly informed, owing to the inconsistencies in Livy's account[1]. It was a long business, and he was not able to start till the next year.   But meanwhile he felt his way by sending a force under his friend Laelius to make a descent on the African coast.   This was not one of the isolated raids of which we have often heard, but a part of Scipio's bold forward policy, and meant to be followed up.   We do not know whether he had yet heard of the successful suppression of a native rising in north-eastern Spain: but Laelius' voyage seems to have been late in the season of 205, and it is possible.

375.   Laelius landed in Africa[2] by night, and fell to raiding at dawn.   We have a rhetorical picture of the travelling of the news and the panic at Carthage.   While engaged in measures of despair— getting the fleet ready for sea was one of these—they heard that the invaders were only a small force, and that Scipio was not in command. In calmer mood they (probably the senate is meant) resolved on a number of characteristic steps.   Embassies were sent to draw closer the ties of alliance with African princes, especially with Syphax, who seems to have already dropped his connexion with Rome.   A large sum of money was offered to Philip, to induce him to land a force in Italy or Sicily, a proposal that came too late for any practical effect. Urgent orders were sent to Hannibal and Mago, that every means of pressure must be used to keep Scipio at home.   To Mago indeed strong reinforcements were sent war-ships men elephants and money: he was to hire troops, advance on Rome, join Hannibal: in short to do in a hurry and at an unfavourable moment what could only be done under very favourable conditions, if at all: for the chance of taking the Romans off their guard was gone by.   How much of this picture is due to imagination is uncertain: the details are at least in the true Carthaginian style.   The strength of the Punic government is abroad and in its material resources: mercenary armies and subsidized allies outside: ships, arms, engines, elephants, and money, at home. There is no sign of a coherent population in their country, loyally

[1] Weissenborn on Livy XXIX 1 § 12, 13 §§ 3, 6.
[2] At Hippo Regius, says Livy XXIX 3 § 7, but Weissenborn shews this to be improbable, owing to the distance from Carthage, and suggests Hippo Diarrhytus.

ready to respond to their rulers' call. Numbers and wealth were there, but not the community of sentiment which is the soul of nations. Just at this time Syphax was busy with troubles on his own borders: Masinissa, though for the moment a wanderer, had still much influence in Numidia. He came to see Laelius, and urged him not to dally on the African coast with his small squadron, but to return and hasten the coming of Scipio. For his part, he would give useful support when the time came. Laelius followed this advice, and took back quantities of plunder to Sicily.

376. Neither Scipio nor his men wished to delay their expedition to Africa; but there was much yet to be done, and a smaller affair engaged his attention elsewhere. An opportunity offered[1] of recovering by betrayal the city of Locri. It had now been in Hannibal's power for nearly ten years, and exiled Locrian aristocrats urged Scipio to seize the present chance. The attempt succeeded, one of the two citadels was occupied. Hannibal came to relieve the place and drive out the Romans, but Scipio got there in time to repulse his attack, and he was compelled to withdraw and leave Locri to its fate. It was a bad one. Pleminius, left in charge by Scipio, was a ruffian of the worst type, and his men were as their leader. The scene that followed illustrates the deep demoralization created by the long war. Any wrong that the Punic garrison had done was soon forgotten in the robberies cruelties and abominations of the Romans. The treasures of the temple of Proserpine were at last plundered: but it was remarked that, as evil came upon Pyrrhus after his sacrilege, so these later robbers came to no good. The rascals fell out among themselves. Two subordinate commanders, military tribunes, headed the opposition, and acts of frantic violence ensued. Pleminius had the tribunes flogged, but in the riot kindled by this he had his nose and ears cut off by the mutineers. Scipio came to inquire into the matter, and decided to leave Pleminius still in charge, while he imprisoned the tribunes, meaning to send them to Rome. As soon as his principal's back was turned, the mutilated lieutenant took his revenge. He tortured to death the tribunes and those Locrians who had borne the complaints of his conduct to Scipio, and set to work to outdo if possible his previous course of horrors in the suffering town. But early in the next year (204) a deputation of Locrians[2] reached Rome and laid before the Senate the tale of their woes. The genuine indignation aroused by the story was reinforced by the jealousy of the party hostile to Scipio. It was agreed to bring Pleminius in chains to Rome to stand his trial on a capital charge, to redress as far as

---

[1] Livy xxix 6—9 Weissenborn.
[2] Livy xxix 16—22, Diodor. fragm. xxvii 4.

possible the wrongs of the Locrians, to make double restitution of the temple treasures with sacrificial expiation of the sacrilege, to ship off the garrison to the army in Sicily and put some Latin Allies in their place. In regard to Scipio the extreme proposals at first made were not carried, but a commission, headed by Pomponius the new praetor of Sicily, and including two tribunes of the commons, an aedile and ten selected senators, was appointed. They were given large powers extending even to the arrest of Scipio himself: if he had already sailed for Africa, they were to follow and fetch him: of course, only in case of *prima facie* evidence of guilt. The commissioners went first to Locri, where they saw to the redress of wrongs, and comforted the Locrians with the assurance that Rome gave them back 'their freedom and their own laws,' that is, a measure of local self-government while obedient to Rome. They offered the Locrians every facility for bringing charges against their oppressors, even Scipio. But the Locrians thought it wiser to let Scipio alone, and merely undertook to support by evidence their case against Pleminius and his accomplices; who were put in chains and sent to Rome. The usual clumsy machinery of a popular trial was set in motion by the tribunes, with its several hearings and adjournments, but it seems not to have been carried through to a final decision. The wrath of the people was losing its keenness through delays, when the death of the criminal in prison brought proceedings to a close. Such was the tradition that prevailed : but there were other stories of Pleminius and his latter end. From Locri the commissioners went on to Syracuse[1] to inquire into the truth of the general charges against Scipio. It was said that, leaning as he did to Greek ways (an abomination in the eyes of Fabius and men of the old school), he had laid aside Roman dress and Roman seriousness; that the example at headquarters had corrupted the rank and file, and discipline and efficiency were ruined. Scipio grasped the situation, and he knew his countrymen. He concentrated his army and got his ships into full trim. He said not a word in self-defence, but gave his visitors such a treat of sham fight, naval manœuvres, inspection of arsenals and magazines, and the like, that they were overwhelmed with the display. They wished him good luck in his enterprise, and returned to Rome blessing the man they had been sent to curse. The Senate, elated by their report, was now all for the bolder strategy of Scipio, and seems to have taken some step towards strengthening his

---

[1] It was during Scipio's stay in Sicily that the quarrel between him and his quaestor M. Porcius Cato broke out. Cato was of the old school, and regarded Scipio's conduct as extravagant and lax. At last the consul let him go home. The two men could not possibly work together. See Nepos *Cato* 1 § 3, Plutarch *Cato maior* 3.

forces: what this step was[1] cannot be made out, for Livy (as often) is inconsistent with himself.

377. At both ends of Italy the war languished. Mago seems to have done his best to carry out his orders from home, but he could not bring about a general rising of the Gaulish tribes. Taught by experience, the chiefs would not lightly undertake such a move, watched as they were by two Roman armies. It was on them that the retribution would fall if the venture failed. All Mago could do was to hire mercenaries among them and take advantage of their good will to procure supplies of food. The Ligurians were willing enough to bear a hand in the invasion of the lowlands: but to set them in motion took time, and Mago may have doubted their fitness for operations involving pitched battles with the disciplined armies of Rome. And those armies were ready. Livius marched from Etruria and joined Lucretius the praetor in Gaul, where they awaited the movements of the Punic general: the 'city legions' were sent into Etruria. Meanwhile in Bruttium there was even greater stagnation. Sickness continued to disable the opposing forces, and it was thought wise to disband one of the two Roman armies. At Rome the ever-active desire for supernatural aid in the struggle took the turn of bringing in a foreign[2] worship from the East. Led by a prediction said to have been found in the Sibylline books, and the report of a favourable utterance of the Delphic Apollo, the Senate sent a deputation to Asia charged to bring the 'Mother of the Gods' or 'Great Mother' from Pessinus. The worship was Phrygian: Pessinus was in the part of Phrygia now held by the Asiatic Gauls. With the help of their new friend Attalus of Pergamum the envoys made their way into Galatia. They found that the goddess was worshipped there under the form of a stone. Attalus procured for them what was said to be the genuine stone, with which they set out for Rome. By order of the Delphic oracle the goddess was to be received by the best man of Rome : it is notable that the choice fell on young P. Scipio Nasica, son of the Gnaeus Scipio who fell in Spain in 212, and so first cousin of the general now in Sicily. We have here another testimony to the acknowledged merits of the great Cornelian house. The goddess, lodged for the time in the temple of Victory, was also known as the Idaean Mother, Rhea, Cybele, and by other names. Her worship was of an orgiastic character, and in it the religion of excitement, a product of the East, first gained a footing in Rome. In it games naturally played a part : and the *Megalensia*, as they were called, became a regular festival in the Roman calendar.

---

[1] See Weissenborn on Livy XXVIII 10 § 13, XXIX 1 §§ 12—14, 13 § 3, 22 § 12, 25 §§ 10 —14.   [2] Livy XXIX 10—11 Weissenborn.

378. The elections for 204 were held by a dictator named for the purpose. Games, dedication of a temple, and the expiation of prodigies, occurred as usual. In the appointments for the year we find the now usual continuation of commanders, particularly in distant Spain. Care was again taken to provide for defence and order in Gaul and Etruria. It was perhaps in connexion with this department that a naval squadron was provided to cruise off the coast. And now came the time for dealing with the 12 Latin colonies[1] that had refused their contingents in the year 209, and had furnished no troops since. Their punishment took three forms. First, they were at once to furnish contingents twice as strong as the strongest hitherto furnished in any year since Hannibal entered Italy: the men were to be raised from the better classes, and were to be employed in the unpopular service over seas. Secondly, a direct tax of $\frac{1}{10}$°/$_0$ was imposed on them as a yearly burden. Hitherto the Allies had paid nothing corresponding to the *tributum* of Roman citizens, and this impost was perhaps only meant to be paid while the war lasted. Thirdly, they were to lose the right of conducting their *census* in their own way. The Roman censors were to issue periodically to the local censors a model schedule copied from that in use at Rome: according to this form the local *census* was to be conducted, and the roll, duly attested by the oath of the local censors, was to be delivered by them in person to the censors at Rome. This also was an interference hitherto unknown, and was a move in the direction of uniformity. There was of course a chorus of protests from the magistrates and chief senators of the several colonies who had been summoned to Rome to hear their sentence: to raise double contingents was pronounced impossible. But under steady pressure, and the fear of worse consequences ensuing from delay, even this requisition was fulfilled. Another important act of this time was the provision for repayment[2] of the voluntary war-loan of the year 210. Though we still find the state in difficulties for money, credit had improved greatly, and it was found possible to pay off one third of the sum at once and the rest in two instalments in two and four years' time.

379. While all this was passing at Rome, things were moving in Africa and Sicily. Carthage was now thoroughly alarmed: but some encouragement was found in finally securing the alliance of the wavering Syphax. This was brought about through the influence of Hasdrubal son of Gisgo, who gave his daughter in marriage to the king. The lady is said to have been previously betrothed to Masinissa: be this as it may, the adhesion of Syphax to Carthage served to bind Masinissa the more firmly to Rome. Syphax was now

---

[1] Livy XXIX 15.   [2] Livy XXIX 16 §§ 1—3.

induced to send a message over to Scipio, withdrawing his former promises, and explaining that in the present changed circumstances he would feel compelled to help Carthage in resisting invasion. If Hasdrubal thought that this threat would stop the dreaded landing in Africa, he was mistaken. Scipio felt that to lose Syphax was a blow to his hopes, but his mind was made up: he gave out that the envoys had been sent to chide him for delay, and at once began to requisition merchant vessels for transport, and effect a general concentration of his forces at Lilybaeum. What was the total number of soldiers (not reckoning ships' crews) is quite uncertain, and was so already in Livy's time. But the total does not seem to have been large. It comprised two legions, but these were of exceptional strength (each 6200 foot, 300 horse) and had many veterans in the ranks. The mobilization[1] was carried through without a hitch, thanks to the efficiency of the departmental officers, commissariat included. The voyage also, though delayed by fogs at sea, was marred by no disaster. So complete were the instructions, so thorough the discipline and skill. Yet it was no light undertaking to take over safely 400 ships of burden, convoyed by 40 war-ships, even though the voyage was short. That it should have been done without molestation is astounding. In all probability there were plenty of ships in the dockyards of Carthage ready for sea. Why were they not afloat[2] and active, when the danger of the hour was well known?

380. Scipio landed on the Hermaean promontory, a cape jutting out somewhat east of Carthage. The traditions of the passage and landing differed from each other greatly, nor are the details of the following operations clear and trustworthy. It seems that the Romans found the country undefended. After a successful cavalry skirmish a vast amount of booty was secured and shipped off to Sicily. But the main fleet was sent on towards Utica, a city on which Scipio had designs. The first important event was the appearance of Masinissa in the Roman camp. He brought with him only a small force of cavalry, for his fortunes were just now at a low ebb; but Scipio had discerned the value of this Numidian prince, one of the most remarkable men of his time. Of the tribes occupying the region loosely called Numidia by the Romans the chief were the Masaesyli to the West and the Maesuli or Massyli, lying between them and the Carthaginian Home Province. The former were under the rule of Syphax, but among the Massylians, since the death of Gala the father of Masinissa, no one had become permanently established on

---

[1] Livy XXIX 25—27.

[2] Appian *Pun.* 9 has a notice of the purchase of 5000 slaves about this time to serve as oarsmen.

the throne.   Masinissa himself had won it and held it for a moment:
Carthage had reason to mistrust his designs, and her jealousy set
Syphax in motion.   With inferior resources Masinissa made a stubborn
fight for his kingdom, but in vain.   At the time of his visits to Laelius
and Scipio he was for the third time an exile from his country : but
he had many adherents among the population, who were fascinated
by his warlike daring and the romance of his career.   He soon
began to do good service for Rome.   The Punic government sent to
summon Syphax and Hasdrubal to their aid, and meanwhile formed
a new force of cavalry in which a number of the chief citizens seem
to have been enrolled.   This force threatened the position of Scipio,
then close to Utica.   The skilful Masinissa drew them into an ambush, where they were cut up badly, and Scipio now besieged Utica
by sea and land.   The ancient and famous city, older than Carthage,
could not be left to fall without an attempt to relieve it.   But Hasdrubal
did not dare to shew himself, though he had got together 33,000 men
of some sort, till Syphax appeared with 60,000 men.   Scipio, who had
hoped to find a good base of operations at Utica, was for the time
forced to raise the siege and withdraw his forces to winter quarters
on a promontory hard by.   They were well provided for: corn poured
in from Italy and Sicily : and the zealous praetor of Sardinia sent not
only corn but supplies of clothing as well.

381.   No striking events were at this time occurring in Italy.   A
close watch was kept on affairs in the North.   We hear again of disaffection in Etruria, where the expedition of Mago roused vain hopes
of shaking off the Roman yoke.   In this part of Italy it seems that
the wealthy nobles were not, as elsewhere, loyal supporters of the
Roman interest.   Discontented, but degenerate and unable to effect
anything by their own efforts, they were ready to welcome a deliverer
from abroad, and the long continuance of the war may have blinded
them to the real superiority of Rome.   They were now taken in
hand.   A consul held Etruria as his province: his army made resistance impossible.   He went round the cities, holding judicial
inquiries and punishing the guilty, and with the removal of the leaders
active disaffection was quelled.   In the South we hear of two collisions
with Hannibal, the first confessedly a Roman defeat, the second
claimed as a victory.   But the Roman generals seem to have been no
nearer to turning their great enemy out of Italy.   With Croton as his
base he firmly held the little district under his control.   The Romans
picked away at the edges, and won back two or three towns: but, if
properly reinforced, he would probably have resumed the offensive
and prolonged the war.

382..   In this year a census was held at Rome.   The censors were the consuls of 207, M. Livius and C. Claudius Nero. After the preparation of the roll of the Senate, and the ordinary business of the state contracts, they turned to devising a new source of revenue. This they found in salt. In leasing the salt-works (*salinae*), which were state property, they issued a schedule of prices at which the lessees were bound to provide salt on demand. Hitherto the price had been the same for Roman citizens all through Italy. In the new tariff different prices, but all higher than the old rate, were fixed for different places. In Rome itself the old price was kept. By this change the lessees were enabled to pay a higher rent. Livius, who was known to be the prime mover in this matter, was nicknamed *Salinator*. The preparation of the roll of citizens took some time, owing to the inclusion of those on service[1] in the various armies. A new function of the censors on this occasion was the reception of the census of the 12 colonies from the local officials, and the preservation of this record of their military and financial sufficiency as a state document. The roll of knights and the complete citizen-roll remained to be issued. And here the two lately-reconciled colleagues, partners in the glory of Metaurus, thought fit to give an exhibition of the lengths to which the hard unaccommodating Roman nature would go, not shrinking from bringing even public official acts into contempt. Nero struck the name of Livius off the equestrian roll, on the ground of his having been tried and found guilty by the popular court: as if his consulship and services had not cancelled or condoned his long-past offence. To this pedantry or spite Livius replied by doing the same to Nero, alleging that he had borne false witness on that very trial, and that their reconciliation had been on his colleague's part no more than a hollow pretence. So also in the classified list of citizens, an appendix of which was the black-list of those liable to public burdens but not entitled to public rights. Nero included his colleague by name among these *aerarii*: Livius included the whole Roman people, Nero with the rest, excepting only one of the 35 Tribes. The Maecian Tribe, he grimly remarked, had neither voted for his condemnation though guiltless, nor for making him consul and censor when under a public stigma. Probably the acts in which the two censors did not concur[2] were not recognized as valid, and so nobody would be directly harmed by the doings of cross-grained censors: but the work can hardly have been well done under such conditions. There was grumbling, and a tribune thought to turn the situation to account by bringing the ex-censors to trial for their misconduct. But

---

[1] Livy XXIX 37 makes this seem to be an innovation, which is very doubtful. See Beloch, *Bevölkerung*, p. 349.

[2] Mommsen, *Staatsrecht*, II 346.

the Senate saw that this would never do, and by judicious pressure contrived to have the charge dropped. If the censorship was to be of any use in the working of the constitution, practical irresponsibility was a necessary attribute of the office. The annual elections, appointments to vacancies in the sacred colleges, offerings, and games, brought the year 204 to a close.

383. In the assignment of the various commands for the coming season much the same precautions were taken as in the preceding year. But the extension of Scipio's command was now made, not for a year, but till the conclusion of the war in Africa. There the final issue must be decided, as all now began to see: even the old opposition party in the Senate bowed to accomplished facts, and their veteran leader Fabius seems to have been failing fast. The adoption of wider views of strategy is shewn in the attention paid to the securing of the sea-routes[1] of the central Mediterranean. Scipio had 40 ships of war with him: by repairing old and building new vessels the naval forces were increased, and three fleets of 40 ships each cruised off the coasts of Sardinia, Italy and Sicily. All had good fighting crews as well as oarsmen, the first condition of naval efficiency in the clumsy fighting of those days. It was thought that Carthage, now pressed by land, would recall her traditions of a nautical past and desperately endeavour to save herself by gaining the mastery of the seas. This Rome wisely determined to prevent at all costs. Busy though magistrates and priests were with solemn games and the expiation of prodigies, the main interest and hope of Romans at home or abroad now centred on the African war. Arms clothing and corn came to Scipio from Sicily and Spain: like the governor of Sardinia, all were eager to bear a hand in the great enterprise. Never was the power of cooperation, Rome's great lesson to Italy, shewn to more advantage than now.

384. Meanwhile from his winter camp Scipio had been watching Utica and preparing for his next campaign. News came that Carthage had a fleet ready to attack his communications by sea. Negotiations with Syphax led to nothing. The king was too deeply committed to change sides again at present, and his attempt at mediation, on the terms that each power should evacuate the other's territory, was out of date and absurd. Scipio however played with these proposals, employing the frequent exchange of notes to enable a number of his most trusty centurions to become acquainted with the enemy's camps. These lay close together, and consisted of sheds hastily built of wood, reeds, matting, and the like. When preparations were complete, and the enemy thrown off their guard, a pretext was

[1] Livy xxx 2.

soon found for breaking off negotiations. A feigned resumption of the siege of Utica served to conceal his real design. Suddenly he marched off by night and set fire to the enemy's camps, causing indescribable panic and confusion in the darkness. Butchered as they ran out, or crushed in their own crowd, mixed up with frightened horses and elephants, a vast number perished: others were taken prisoners, and only a small remnant escaped with Syphax and Hasdrubal. Polybius, in whose narrative the sharp practice[1] of Scipio bears an even more deceitful colour than it does in Livy, regards this successful ruse as his hero's most brilliant achievement. After this several African towns submitted to the Romans, and Scipio appears to have hoped that he would now be free to deal with Utica. But he had not yet disposed of Syphax, who, urged by his young wife and encouraged by finding Carthage still ready to shew fight, raised new hordes of Numidians. At Carthage some wanted to sue for peace, others to recall Hannibal: but it was decided to raise a fresh army and fight on. According to Livy[2], this was because the war-party, led by Hasdrubal and the 'Barcid interest,' was still in power. Just at this time a body of mercenaries hired by Punic agents landed from Spain, picked men, and well aware that they would get no mercy from the Romans. So Scipio found that he had, probably with much smaller forces, at once to face an army of 30,000 men. He did not hesitate, but in a short time brought them to action at a spot called the Great Plains. It is to be noted that the victory of his cavalry on both wings determined the fortune of the day, and that the honours did not all rest with Masinissa and his Numidians. The Roman horse had evidently been greatly improved by the care of Scipio. The Celtiberian mercenaries were surrounded and cut to pieces, and survivors of Cannae enjoyed a dramatic revenge.

385. The eyes of the Carthaginians were now opened to their own imminent danger, and in all haste they turned to preparations for standing a siege. Two definite steps were resolved upon, to recall Hannibal to the defence of his country, and to use their idle fleet in an attack on the Roman squadron engaged in the siege of Utica. Scipio, who had been busy gathering the fruits of his victory, and setting free from slavery the Romans captured by Hannibal years before, advanced and seized Tunes close to Carthage. But the movement of the Punic fleet[3] drew him back in hot haste to Utica. He

---

[1] In dealing with the events of this time I have followed in outline the accounts of Polybius and Livy. A very different tradition is found in the later writers, particularly as to the relations between the Carthaginians, Masinissa and Syphax. Polyb. XIV 3—5, Livy XXX 3—5, Appian *Pun.* 21—23.

[2] Livy XXX 7.   [3] Polyb. XIV 9, 10, Livy XXX 9—10.

was just in time to save his ships of war. They were dismantled as fighting-machines and serving as the floating platforms of siege-engines: by a sudden attack from the sea they might all have been destroyed with ease. But the Carthaginian fleet, fresh from harbour and timidly led, dallied on the way, and missed their chance. They found facing them a line of transports three or four deep, bound together by spars lashed firmly and forming gangways from ship to ship. Behind this barrier lay the vessels of war in safety. An assault upon the barrier failed: at the most only a few of the transports were torn away with grappling-irons and towed off to Carthage. In the main the clumsy merchantmen served their purpose well, and from the higher level of their decks the Roman missiles told with effect upon an enemy compelled to shoot from below. The expedition made prize of six hulks, and did not relieve Utica. Meanwhile Laelius and Masinissa had followed up Syphax as he fled westward. In another battle they broke up the new army hastily raised by the king, and took Syphax himself prisoner: Cirta, his capital, surrendered to the victors. At this point comes in the tragic story of Sophoniba, daughter of Hasdrubal and wife of Syphax, told with many minor variations, but in the main as follows. She fell into Masinissa's hands and begged his protection from Roman violence. The passionate Numidian married her that very day, thinking that his wife would be sacred to his allies, and that there the matter would end. Soon after he returned with Laelius to Scipio's camp, bringing the lady. News of his high-handed action had preceded him: and Syphax, wishing to requite the kind treatment extended to him as prisoner, and from other motives, warned Scipio (speaking from experience) that the influence of Hasdrubal's daughter on her new husband would not be exerted in the interest of Rome. The Roman dealt with the awkward question[1] in a truly Roman way. He pointed out that the war was the war of the Roman people, whose property all prize of war strictly speaking became. To decide on the assignment of special booty was for the Senate. Sophoniba must therefore be forwarded to Rome, where Masinissa would no doubt put in a weighty claim. Finding that Scipio would not give way, the Numidian sent to Sophoniba news of what awaited her, and poison therewith: this she took, and the daughter of Carthage escaped from the grasp of Rome.

386. Various details, among them a story of internal dissensions[2] at Carthage and the deposition of Hasdrubal from his command, appear in some versions of the war-tradition. Livy either did not find them in his authorities, or omitted them as interrupting the course

---

[1] Livy XXX 14 §§ 8—11, Appian *Pun.* 28.　　　　[2] Appian *Pun.* 24.

of his dramatic narrative : Polybius is just here in fragments again. Scipio it seems made a second move to Tunes, and so alarmed the Carthaginians that they sent a solemn embassy to sue for peace. Scipio dictated provisional terms and offered an armistice, referring them to the Roman Senate for final negotiation. The offer was accepted, and an embassy sent to Rome : but, if we are to accept the view of our authorities (Roman, of course), the real object of the Punic government was to gain time[1] for the return of Hannibal. At Rome the receipt of so much good news filled Senate and people with joy and the temples with the voice of thanksgiving. The enlarged imperial position of the Senate was shewn in the petition presented by envoys on behalf of Masinissa. The Numidian had been soothed by presents and public praise, and provisionally recognized as king of the Massylians, perhaps of all Numidia. For confirmation of Scipio's acts he now appealed to the Roman Senate : and the Senate, by voting its approval, and sending the king complimentary presents, took a great step towards the position in which we shall meet it henceforth, that of world-umpire and adjudicator of thrones.

387. We now come to the evacuation of Italy. In the summer of 203 Mago was operating in the region of the Po, when he was met and brought to battle by the combined armies of the praetor and proconsul then watching the North. A desperate fight ended in a Roman victory. Mago, himself wounded, drew off the remains of his army to the Ligurian coast, where he found awaiting him the order of recall. He gladly obeyed the summons, and at once embarked with his mercenaries for Carthage. But he died of his wound in midpassage, and a few of his ships, parted from their company, fell into the hands of the Roman cruisers. Hannibal had long seen that he would be called home to avert if possible the consequences of the blind and wavering policy of the government. But he clung on to the patch of ground by Croton. Roman force could not dislodge him : but the call from Carthage came at last. He too obeyed, and we may be sure that the lamentations and regrets attributed to him are the idle fictions of a later age. Far more serious is the question whether we ought to believe the persistent Roman tradition[2] that he butchered, before leaving Italy, those Italians who refused to go with him. We have not here the help of Polybius. Modern delicacy shrinks from imputing such barbarity to the high-minded general who paid funeral honours to Marcellus. But the head of his brother Hasdrubal had been flung to him since then, he was maddened and desperate, and the right of making away with those who might hurt you or help your

---

[1] Livy XXX 16 § 14, Appian *Pun.* 31.
[2] Livy XXX 20, Diodorus XXVII 9, Appian *Hannib.* 59.

enemies was liberally interpreted in ancient warfare. Hannibal was not an ordinary ruffian, but a superb Carthaginian: and his fellow-countrymen impaled their own unsuccessful generals as the natural thing to do. It is therefore safer, as in an earlier case of a similar charge, to offer no judgment[1], than to acquit the accused on *a priori* grounds.

388. Livy[2] tells us, perhaps truly, that the news of the departure of Mago and Hannibal was followed by misgivings at Rome, fears that the combined forces in Africa might prove too strong for Scipio. Of the numbers and quality of those forces it was no doubt difficult to form a notion. Just at this time some Punic recruiting agents were caught with money in hand hiring men in Spain. But it was felt that the real danger of the war was over, and the Senate decreed official thanksgiving and sacrifices. At this point occurred the arrival and audience of the peace-envoys from Carthage. Livy reports (no doubt from some early authority) the debate in the Senate, giving the gist of the various motions laid before the House: according to this tradition the ambassadors were ordered to quit Italy, and a message sent to Scipio, bidding him press on the war. Dion Cassius[3] says that the embassy came while Hannibal and Mago were still in Italy, and was refused audience on that ground: but after the evacuation the truce was accepted, and Scipio's terms approved, though not without much dispute. Appian has a quite different story: that the Senate, unable to agree, sent commissioners to Scipio: he was to consult with them, but was himself empowered to decide upon the final step. According to this version, which sounds probable, it was Scipio who concluded the treaty, the breach of which embittered the last months of the war. But according to Polybius it was the armistice that was violated by Carthage: the treaty was enthusiastically accepted at Rome by Senate and people, but news of this did not arrive until the armistice was already broken: the treaty therefore never took effect. This last account is the most probable and has the best authority: the variations illustrate the easy-going methods of ancient historians and the slippery footing on which modern inquirers stand.

389. The rupture referred to was on this wise. Under protection of the truce great quantities of supplies were shipped to Scipio from Sardinia and Sicily. A large convoy had almost made their destination, when a sudden change of wind drove them from their course. The guard-ships with much ado were rowed into safety: the merchant

---

[1] The act imputed to him in Appian *Pun.* 33 is of the same character. Livy does not mention it. See above, §§ 305, 310.

[2] Livy xxx 21.

[3] Frag. 57 §§ 74—5. Strictly construed, his account differs very little from that of Polybius. See Polyb. xv 1, Livy xxx 17, Appian *Pun.* 32.

vessels were driven to land within sight of Carthage. The temptation was too much for the populace of Carthage. Vainly the senate refused to consent to a breach of the truce: the mob, already somewhat pinched for food, defied all restraint, and forced the admiral to put to sea and take possession of the helpless transports. Scipio sent envoys to complain of this and to demand redress: they spoke plainly, and hardly escaped violence at the hands of the furious multitude. They were got away safely for the moment, but a treacherous attempt, very nearly successful, was made to kill or capture them on their return voyage. Thus not only had the temporary truce been broken, but the rules of international right long and generally recognized had been set at nought. Just at this juncture the Punic ambassadors returning from Rome fell into Scipio's hands. He refused to avenge on them the crime of their countrymen. But he at once resumed hostilities and prepared to fight it out to the bitter end. And now Hannibal landed in Africa, at some distance to the south of Carthage. We may fairly conjecture that he kept away from the city for good reasons. He had to recruit and reorganize his army for a new kind of campaign, to collect horses and supplies, and effect a general concentration of forces. It would have been far harder to carry out his plans with effect, had he brought his army into immediate contact with Carthage, where in the hour of danger the senate was becoming weaker and weaker under the pressure of the mob. To seize the civil government with his own firm hand would have taken him away from the still more necessary army.

390. Even at Rome there were still moments of uneasiness. Old Fabius had died somewhere about the autumn of 203, after a long career of cautious mediocrity in strong contrast to that of Pericles, with whom it pleased Plutarch to compare him. The forebodings of disaster in Africa, utterances of his dotage, had not come true. But it was disquieting to hear that Philip of Macedon, not content with wronging Rome's allies in Greece, had sent a corps[1] of 4000 men and a sum of money to the aid of Carthage. An embassy, headed by the still trusted[2] Varro, was sent to denounce the king's conduct as a breach of treaty. The general tone of the Roman populace was doubtless cheerful; for, though fire and flood had troubled the city, corn was very cheap, owing to resumption of tillage in Italy and large importation from Spain. It was sold to the people by the aediles at a very low rate. But the peace for which men longed was not as yet actually won, and no one could feel sure of final victory with Hannibal still at the head of an army in the field. Much more serious

---

[1] See Livy XXX 33 § 5, 42 §§ 4—6, Frontinus *Strat.* II 3 § 16.
[2] Livy XXX 26 §§ 2—4.

in truth, as we can now see looking back upon the past, was the growth of selfish ambition among the Roman nobles. It may have seemed an isolated case of the greedy quest of glory when the consul[1] Gnaeus Servilius, finding that Hannibal was gone, crossed over from Bruttium to Sicily, meaning to follow the great enemy to Africa, and take part in the transmarine war. The Senate could find no better way of checking the headstrong magistrate than by getting a dictator named for the purpose. Recalled by a superior officer, the consul had perforce to obey. So the matter ended for the time. But, when it came to the assignment of the 'provinces' for the season of 202, it was seen that the desire of a field for display was no personal peculiarity of the late consul. Both consuls wished Africa to be treated as a province of the year: each hoped to get the command himself. The proposal seems to have been rejected, the majority of the Senate not being prepared to vote for superseding Scipio directly. The question of the African command was laid before the Assembly, and the Tribes with one consent confirmed the appointment of Scipio. But Livy[2] tells us that in spite of this decision the Senate did make Africa a consular province, and that it fell by lot to Tiberius Claudius Nero. He was to have a fleet of 50 battle-ships, and was to cross over to Africa and share Scipio's command. We have no ground for doubting the story: probably the party jealous of Scipio had for a moment got the upper hand. The sequel was disappointing. The consuls were detained in Rome by public games, and when Claudius at last[3] put to sea he met foul weather. From shelter to shelter he crept along the Etruscan coast to Elba Corsica and Sardinia, plagued with storms: off the last island his fleet was quite disabled. In refitting the season went by, and the fleet had to be taken home without result. Truly the stars in their courses fought for Scipio. The forces employed in 202 included only 16 legions, a significant reduction.

391. The events that immediately preceded the final battle are variously told and not of much importance. Some traditions imply that sheer mob-rule prevailed at this crisis in distracted Carthage. At all events for other reasons Hannibal, having got together all the army he was likely to get, was anxious to fight. He moved inland to Zama, and Scipio, reinforced by Masinissa, moved to meet him. When his spies were caught in the Roman camp, it is said that Scipio had them shewn round and sent back safe. This is a characteristic scene of the Scipionic legend, but may be a fact: Scipio, like all great

---

[1] Livy XXX 24 §§ 1—3.   [2] Livy XXX 27.

[3] Livy XXX 38 says that he was sulky at a resolution of the Senate reserving the negotiation of peace to Scipio, and hence dilatory.

generals, understood the value of moral effects. Hannibal had probably the larger army, but inferior in quality. It was knowledge of its defects no doubt that led him to seek an interview with his opponent and try even at this late hour to procure peace without bloodshed on moderate conditions. They met, but met in vain. The one offered somewhat less than the terms agreed to before: the other demanded somewhat more as penalty for the breach of truce and the right of nations. So they made ready[1] for battle. It was apparently fought near a place Naraggara, but the name of Zama can hardly be displaced now: the time probably somewhere in the autumn. The means available for the defence of Carthage are well shewn in Hannibal's order of battle. *First*, eighty elephants to throw the enemy into disorder: *second*, the mixed mercenaries, Ligurians Gauls Mauretanians and Balearic slingers, to wear out and perhaps defeat the mass of the Roman foot: *third*, the Carthaginian and other African troops, in whose steadiness he had little trust, but who could not wholly shirk their duty, because *fourth* his veteran army brought from Italy were drawn up in their rear. The battle was long and hard-fought, but decisive. The elephants were mostly rendered ineffective by the ingenious tactics of Scipio. The mercenaries, not vigorously supported by the native troops behind them, at last broke, and in their flight even came to blows with the Carthaginians. The hardest struggle was that with the troops from Italy: joined to any surviving relics of his original army, or later reinforcements, Hannibal had a number of Italians and some Roman deserters, and these men fought desperately. But here comes in the circumstance that shews how conditions had changed since the days of Cannae. Scipio had made his mounted Romans and Allies superior to any heavy cavalry on the other side: by winning the support of Masinissa he had the advantage even in Numidian horse. Victorious on the wings, Laelius and Masinissa checked their pursuit in time, fell on the rear of Hannibal's veterans, and all was over. It was admitted on all hands that Hannibal had handled his army with extraordinary skill. But it had ceased to exist, and Carthage was at the mercy of Rome.

392. Hannibal with difficulty escaped to Hadrumetum, and so to Carthage, where he had never been since he left for Spain with his father about the year 238. Scipio sent Laelius home with the news, and his army towards Carthage. He returned himself to Utica, took over 50 war-ships that had just escorted a convoy of supplies, and sailed off to view the sea-front of the great city. He presently fixed his headquarters at Tunes. The first news was that Vermina, son of Syphax, was advancing with a Numidian army to the aid of Carthage.

[1] Polyb. xv 9—14, Livy xxx 32—35.

This force was speedily cut off, and the coast was clear. An abject embassy from the Punic government received a stern answer. But this was in part a dramatic attitude assumed in order to humble and make submissive a stubborn enemy. Scipio well knew that to take the city would be a long and difficult business. He knew that many were jealous of him at home, and he had no wish to share with a successor the glory of bringing the weary war to a triumphant end. So he sent for the envoys again, and dictated conditions[1] of peace. These may be set forth thus:

(i) *Status of Carthage* (internal). The cities and territory in Africa owned by Carthage before the outbreak of this last war were still to remain in her possession. No garrison was to be placed in the city, and there was to be no interference with the government.

(ii) *Status of Carthage* (external). Carthage was not to go to war with any extra-African power on any pretext, nor with any African power without leave from Rome. Accordingly she was to restore to Masinissa whatever belonged to him or had belonged to his ancestors within certain boundaries to be hereafter defined. She was to surrender to Rome all her ships of war save 10 triremes, and all her elephants.

(iii) *War indemnity.* Carthage was to pay 10,000 talents to Rome, that is £2,350,000 or £2,400,000 of our money, in yearly instalments of 200 talents.

(iv) *Temporary provisions.* All Roman prisoners, deserters, and runaway slaves, were to be given up. The merchant vessels captured in violation of the truce, and all goods taken therewith, were to be restored at once as a necessary condition[2] of a fresh truce. Food and pay were to be provided for the Roman forces for a space of three months, to allow time for receiving the final acceptance or rejection of the terms from Rome. Lastly, 100 hostages between the ages of 14 and 30, selected by the Roman commander, were to be handed over as security for the good faith of Carthage in these negotiations.

The effect of these provisions was to reduce Carthage to a purely African power and to place her foreign policy in the control of Rome. The financial burden laid on her seems to us light, as indeed it turned out to be. The really dangerous clause was that relative to Masinissa, for it left a great latitude to unfriendly interpretation in the future. That this was intentionally so framed we cannot certainly say, but we cannot ignore the fact that the leaving of 'open questions' plays into

---

[1] Polyb. xv 18, 19, Livy xxx 37. [2] So Livy, credibly.

the hands of the stronger of two negotiating powers.   On the face of it the terms were merciful.   Scipio was in a hurry, that the peace might be his own work.

393.   The true greatness of Hannibal never came out more clearly than it did now.   He undertook the unpopular task of convincing his fellow-countrymen that they must submit, and be glad that things were no worse.   He made them accept the terms, and at once set about collecting the merchant ships and making the required restitution, with compensation in place of anything that could not be found. A truce was then granted, and a Punic embassy accompanied by Roman delegates was sent to Rome.   There the strain of waiting for news had led to the adoption of various measures of precaution, and with public feeling nervously excited there was naturally a fresh outbreak of prodigies.   Signs from heaven broke up Assemblies, and the year of the present magistrates ran out before the dictator appointed to hold the elections could perform his office.   Some subordinates of the aediles were convicted of robbing[1] the state chest.   But the arrival of the news of the great victory threw the city into a paroxysm of joy. And now besides the embassy from Carthage there was also one from Philip of Macedon.   Business was however blocked for a time by the ambition[2] of one of the new consuls, who tried to secure by this obstruction the African command.   It seems that he was resisted by two tribunes, acting no doubt in the interest of Scipio.   In the account of Livy the Senate plays a doubtful part, as not daring to set aside the popular favourite, yet wishing if possible to give the consul an excuse for interference.   The various commands for the year (201) were arranged with a view to the quieting of disturbed districts in Italy and abroad.   The number of legions was reduced to 14, that of war ships in commission to 100, in hope of a speedy return to a state of peace.

394.   But the matter of Philip's embassy[3] was ominous of further war.   The Roman ambassadors sent to the king had done their errand and returned.   They had however left one of their number behind in Greece to organize the defence of their allies' frontiers from Macedonian raiders.   Philip now repudiated the charges made against him and retorted by complaints of the acts of Roman allies and the conduct of the Roman emissary.   The bickering became serious when the question of the help sent by the king to Carthage was raised.   Philip wanted to recover his men, prisoners with Scipio: the very mention of this Macedonian corps only deepened the anger of the Senate. The Macedonians were sent away without any concession, and with

---

[1] Livy XXX 39 § 7.   [2] Livy XXX 40 §§ 7—16.
[3] Livy XXX 42 §§ 1—10.

threats of war. Such is the story in Livy, perhaps true, but possibly a later invention of writers concerned to find a decent pretext for the high-handed policy of Rome towards Macedon. We cannot be sure that there was a Macedonian corps serving in Africa at all: the accounts of the actual battle make no mention of it. Livy no doubt had some foundation for his story: but it may have been a mere report. The embassy from Carthage[1] was chiefly composed of members of the old peace-party, and is said to have been kindly received. But the consul Lentulus tried to block the peace, and was only thwarted by two tribunes carrying the whole question before the Assembly. The Tribes voted to conclude peace, to leave Scipio full powers as to terms and the details of evacuation of Africa. The Senate granted the free release of 200 prisoners, friends of the envoys, partly perhaps with an eye to fostering the pro-Roman element in Carthage, which we afterwards find powerful. On the return of the embassy peace was solemnly concluded and the terms carried out. It is said that the ships of war handed over amounted, great and small, to 500. They were taken out to sea and set on fire, probably because the Romans did not want them, but partly perhaps to bring home to the mob of Carthage the fact that their pretensions to naval power must henceforth cease. Then came the punishment of the surrendered deserters. These were divided into two classes: the Latin Allies (and probably other Italian Allies as well), and the Romans, of whom doubtless many, if not most, were only half-citizens, Campanians and others. But the treason of one who was a Roman citizen in any degree was a more serious crime than the bad faith of an Ally. So the 'Latin' deserters were beheaded, the 'Roman' crucified.

395. Scipio withdrew his army and returned to Rome for his triumph. A notable figure in the procession was a senator, Q. Terentius Culleo, wearing the cap of freedom, the mark of a newly-emancipated slave. He had been set free by Scipio from Punic bondage, and was doing honour to his liberator as a freedman to his patron. The laxity of the old annalists is well shewn even here. Polybius[2] declares that Syphax was led in triumph, and died soon after: Livy denies this, and says that he died shortly before the triumph, and that attention was directed to his death by his being granted a state funeral. Great indeed was the glory of Scipio: nothing like it had appeared in the history of Rome. Camillus was a great and glorious memory, but it was a far smaller Rome that he had saved from barbarous Gauls. Scipio had relieved the mistress of Italy from the fear of conquest by the wealthiest state of antiquity, served by the greatest soldier of the age. And the fact of his success having been won in spite of opposition

[1] Livy XXX 43 Weissenborn.   [2] Polyb. XVI 23, Livy XXX 45.

at home made it impossible to pretend that the credit was not all his own. The personal devotion of Laelius, the loyal aid of Masinissa, were parts of the good service done to the commonwealth by an inspiring and dexterous leader. But the exceptional position of Scipio was in no respect more clearly marked out than in the relations between the general and his troops. The larger and better part of the victorious army was made up of the disgraced fugitives of Cannae and Herdonea or of volunteers. To the latter Scipio was the commander of their own express choice: the former owed to him the chance of wiping out an undeserved stain: he had taken them out in degradation and brought them home in honour. Besides, he had set free a number of Roman prisoners, whose relatives and friends were bound to him by strong ties of gratitude. Nor must we forget that his father and uncle had died in battle for Rome, and that to be one of the Cornelii was in itself no mean heritage. And yet the position of the hero of the hour was more glorious than comfortable. The constitution of Rome did not provide for the recognition of such preeminence as his. Even the continuance of skilled generals in command had only been brought about for a time through the force of circumstances: the nobles, competing for opportunities of distinction, insisted on returning at once to the old system of yearly change. As if to invite rivalry, Scipio was by popular consent styled *Africanus*. Henceforth every land where troubles arose was viewed by Roman nobles as the potential source of a nickname of honour. In civil life too the prospect of being ruled by a succession of mediocrities was no doubt a trial to the patience of any active and distinguished citizen: and Scipio was not remarkable for patience. Liberality was a popular trait in his character, but it appealed chiefly to his intimates and to the mass of ordinary citizens. If the Romans of the old school shook their heads at his excessive popularity, it was not without some reason: that one man should so stand out above his fellows was in truth a strain upon republican institutions. But, whatever nervous patriots and jealous rivals might forebode, open friction was for the time avoided, and all Italy rejoiced that the long war was at an end.

For a detailed study of the problems of the Second Punic War see the valuable articles of Prof. J. S. Reid in the *Journal of Roman Studies*, 1913, 1915.

CHAPTER XXVI

THE SITUATION CREATED BY THE WAR

396. IT is perhaps well to pause on reaching the end of the great struggle of 218—201 B.C., and review briefly some of the phenomena that appear in its course, considered as illustrating the condition of the Roman state and preparing us for the changes that meet us in the succeeding period. It is customary to defer doing this till after the Macedonian and Syrian wars, or even the destruction of Carthage and Corinth. But the eastern conflicts were wholly different in character from the second Punic war. Rome was then never in any real danger. Delays and even defeats there were, due to stupid mismanagement: but, when the drowsy giant woke up in earnest, one buffet laid the rash opponent in the dust. And this virtual security abroad reacted upon policy at home: the practical working of the Roman constitution, and the relations of Romans to other Italians, changed rapidly when the check of a great present danger was removed. I venture therefore to treat briefly by themselves certain matters that fall within the 17 years of the great war, the true meaning and tendency of which we should often miss if we had not the clue supplied by the sequel.

397. In speaking of the working of the constitution we are primarily concerned with the relations of Magistracy Senate and Assembly to each other. We have had frequent occasion to notice the general direction of affairs by the Senate: in moments of extreme danger all looked to the Senate for guidance, and so it more and more assumed the conduct of the war. This was natural enough; the power of the great council had long been growing: but we must observe that this was not for lack of an opposition. The popular movement under Flaminius was still strong when the war broke out, and was not ended by the death of its leader. It raised Varro to the consulship, and then died down under the depression caused by Cannae. But with the return of hope it so far revived that by popular support Scipio was able to push his way to the front in spite of the jealousy of the nobles. Not that Scipio was a demagogue, or that the power of the Senate was permanently shaken by his popularity. That the fabric of the state had not fallen to pieces under the stress of disaster and despair, was the Senate's doing: and its supremacy in the next period, not seriously challenged for more than 60 years, was the reward. But its intrepid coolness amid the risks of war was not more remarkable than the wise patriotism with which it conciliated the remains of the popular party. Thus the state was held together, and recrimination hushed in a common devotion to duty. The most striking instance is the reception of Varro after Cannae. The defeated consul was only too glad to be welcomed home in his hour of disgrace by his political opponents: thenceforth we find him, in thorough harmony with the Senate, serving the state in many important posts, and the popular party, cowed by public disaster, had for the present also lost their leader. In short the Senate avoided an ill-timed conflict and gained authority by a well-timed act of grace. Readiness to recognize the power of the sovran people had been shewn in the preceding year, when no consul was within reach to name a dictator: it was surely on the proposal of the Senate that the place was filled by popular election. That the prestige of the office was destroyed by the affair of Minucius was probably not regretted by the Senate: its immense powers were not to the taste of the aristocratic council. Again, the way in which the Senate was filled up after the havoc of Cannae, when a number of new members, not of noble families, were on the ground of public service added to the roll, was calculated to please the multitude or at least their leading men. The same tendency may perhaps be traced in 207, shortly before Metaurus, when the number of military tribunes elected[1] by the people was raised from 16 to 24. So also it has been remarked that senatorial opposition to popular laws, such as the *lex Claudia* of 218, seems to have been dropped later, as the course of events made it clear that all must pull together to save the state. Thus the *lex Minucia* of 216, appointing three financial commissioners (that they were intended to find means of relieving the financial crisis[2] is a fair inference): the *lex Oppia* of 215, a sumptuary enactment: the *lex Cincia* of 204, forbidding patrons to receive fees and presents from their clients for services, chiefly in connexion with the law courts: these and probably other laws of like tendency passed without the opposition, or even with the support, of the better part of the nobility. There occur also not a few cases[3] in which the Senate

---

[1] Livy XXVII 36 § 14.

[2] Lange, *Römische Alterthümer* § 104, from which I have borrowed several suggestions in this chapter. Perhaps the lowering of the standard of the currency by making the *as* $\frac{1}{18}$ of the *denarius*, recorded by Pliny *H. N.* XXXIII 45, was their work. Livy XXIII 21 § 6.

[3] Lange § 104, II² pp. 166—7.

apparently went out of its way to refer important matters to a popular vote with punctilious and conciliatory legality.

398. Enough has been said to shew the fine discretion with which the effective direction of public policy was kept in the hands of the Senate. The Patricians of earlier times had always known when the hour was come to give way, and the mixed Patricio-Plebeian nobility had the same delicate instinct. But we must never forget that the government of the Senate was the outcome of gradual encroachments, and rested on no basis of constitutional right. In the last resort the People was sovran: but even in time of peace it exercised its rights with difficulty. The difficulty was greatly increased by war. Many citizens were away serving in the field armies: others were locked up in the citizen colonies and other garrisons: the scattered owners of the country farms would be loth to leave home in troubled times, unless compelled by the approach of the enemy. The Assemblies must have been made up almost wholly of (*a*) residents in Rome, (*b*) voters from the immediate neighbourhood, (*c*) some men of the two 'city legions,' (*d*) refugees from districts held or threatened by the enemy. Refugees in country towns would not attend: how many there may have been at any time in Rome itself we cannot even venture to guess. The chances are that some of the 35 Tribes were represented by a very small percentage of their members. An Assembly of the Centuries, if there were indeed now more than 350 of those bodies, must surely have been an utter absurdity. Yet the Assemblies were held as usual. If the absence of many of the best citizens, and great inequality of the voting bodies, would seem to a modern observer to deprive the Assembly of the moral right to express the people's will, to a Roman such considerations would have seemed irrelevant: provided that all formalities were duly observed, and that no tiresome bird had perversely given unfavourable auspices, a solitary voice might lawfully speak on behalf of a Century or even a Tribe and carry as much weight (one vote) as the 100 or 1000 voices that determined the vote of another Century or Tribe. Contrasts less extreme than this probably occurred often in this period of war. Whether occasional strange scenes at elections, such as that in 211 at the election of consuls for 210, were perhaps partly brought about by these contrasts, it is impossible to say: but it is quite credible that Centuries of few voters may have been especially ready to follow a lead, and so have increased the influence of the 'prerogative' vote. On the other hand, we are entitled to look for the chief cause of devotion to formality, and indifference to a gross inequality of voting power, in the religious[1] character of the whole

---

[1] Mommsen, *Staatsrecht* I[2] pp. 94—5, Lange § 121, II[2] pp. 443—5.

proceeding. The previous auspices, the solemn prayer uttered by the presiding officer, and (in case of the Centuriate Assembly) the divine will expressed in the casting of lots for the first vote, all appealed to men there present, men reared in the religious notions underlying these formal acts. The force of religious scruples is shewn in such cases as the resignation of Marcellus in 215. Elected consul amid general enthusiasm, he had just entered on office when a clap of thunder was heard. The augurs pronounced it ominous, and like a good Roman he laid down his office at once. In short, the absence of any religious flaw (*vitium*) was more important than number of votes in giving validity to the people's choice: the acquiescence or approval of the gods was greater than the voices of men. This was especially true of the Centuries, now almost wholly confined to elections. But the Tribe Assembly had its religious side also, and it consisted of the same persons as the Centuries. By it was now transacted the legislative and general business of a Roman Assembly. And, in estimating the influence of the Senate on the popular body, it is not irrelevant to remember the atmosphere of restraint in which that popular body was accustomed to work. Men who had seen even unanimous decisions invalidated by a thunderclap, and were unacquainted with modern doctrines of the rule of the majority, may very well have yielded to pressure in a way that would seem astounding to us.

399. In respect of the Magistracy, we find the old tendency, for magistrates to fall under the control of the Senate, still at work, but greatly checked and modified for the time by the necessities of the war. The dictatorship, the occasional organ of brief but absolute power, had been useful in the old days of short wars ended by single battles. It had been dropping out of favour for some time as an active office, and the experience of the Hannibalic war brought it to an end. Continuous commands held by competent men were found to be the need of the time. The use of the office for special limited purposes occurred very often, the most notable instance being in 216 when a dictator was appointed to do emergency-work of a censorial character. The last active dictator also held office in 216, the last special dictator in 202. The consulship was adapted to circumstances by allowing frequent reelections to the office itself, and by generally continuing successful generals in command as pro-consuls, sometimes for several years. Gradually it ceased to be rule that the actual consuls held the two chief commands of the year: it had not worked well in the early years of the war. Reluctantly the nobles, whose ideal was to share all important posts equally among their own select circle, had to submit to these changes. The cry for efficiency was

irresistible, and in the vigorous campaigns of Scipio in Spain and Africa we see a foreshadowing of the one-strong-man system which begins in earnest some 100 years later. The four praetors were elected year by year as usual, but the effect of the war was felt in this office also. Legal business no doubt fell off, and officers were wanted to hold the minor commands in the field. So it became the practice to combine two sets of duties in one person. The 'alien' department[1] of the *praetor peregrinus* was joined with a military command, or taken over by the city praetor. The continuation of useful men as propraetors was common. Of the censorship there is naturally not much to be said in the time of a great war. The office was one on which the noble families set much store, for it was a means of exercising some control over the composition of the Senate. Hence the scandal of the quarrel of Livius and Nero in 204 was carefully hushed up. The tribunate was another office without *imperium* and so more noticeable in time of peace. On the whole the tribunes continued to be rather the agents of the Senate than the special mouthpieces of the popular will. It seems to have been usual for ex-tribunes to be placed on the roll of senators at the next revision, but this does not[2] appear as an actual right at present in the case of any but 'curule' offices. The aedileship was now beginning to acquire a new importance from its connexion with the public games and shows. It was possible to win popularity by lavish outlay, and the number of such festivals was growing. The evil effects of this system were soon to appear. As for Plebeian offices in general, we hear of a restriction to the effect that any man whose father or grandfather was living and had held a curule office was ineligible as tribune or Plebeian aedile. The case of C. Servilius[3] is interesting. His father, when on a mission in connexion with the colonies on the Po in 218, fell into the hands of the Gauls and was given over for dead. After some nine years it came to the son's ears that his father was still alive in captivity. Meanwhile he had been both tribune and Plebeian aedile, and disagreeable persons questioned the legality of his position. But he does not seem to have been publicly attacked: probably because people had other things to do, with Hannibal still in Italy.

---

[1] Livy XXIII 30 § 18, 32 §§ 2, 4, XXIV 44 § 2, XXV 3 § 2. I suppose that in the former case this praetor would issue his own Edict, while in the latter the City praetor would issue both Edicts. But I know of no direct authority. In the next period this plan of combination was often resorted to under direction of the Senate. This seems to shew that the lawsuits involving aliens were not specially numerous. See Mommsen, *Staatsrecht* II 201 —2, and § 260 above.

[2] Mommsen, *Staatsrecht* III p. 862. Otherwise Lange II² p. 161.

[3] See Livy XXVII 21, XXX 19, with Weissenborn's notes. Reference to XXI 25 will shew how doubtful some details are.

In 203 Servilius was consul, operating with an army in the North. One of his chief exploits was the release of his own father. To guard against all chance of future molestation for the illegality (of which the old man's restoration supplied certain evidence) it was thought well to procure an express bill of indemnity: and this was passed by the Assembly. The restriction thus seriously treated was clearly no ancient survival: it did not touch Patricians, but aimed at preventing the wealthy Plebeian nobles from appropriating bit by bit all the powers of the Roman Plebs to the members of a few families, as was happening in the case of curule offices. It has been reasonably held that it was part of the reform movement of Flaminius, and so of quite recent origin.

400. In speaking of the army, we speak of the flower of the population, Citizens or Allies. Few able-bodied males can have escaped bearing some part in the war. The equipment of the foot was so good that Hannibal armed his men with spoils of Roman prisoners and dead. It was the brain of the army that was weak, but both generalship and organization shew some improvement in the course of the struggle. Thus we see the cavalry better trained and better handled. Polybius[1] notes the readiness of the Romans to learn. But there was no standing army and no permanent war-department in the Roman Republic: hence lessons were easily forgotten, as in this case. The legionary officers were often men of great merit, but there was no way by which a man could rise to high command through the display of simple military virtues. He might stand for the consulship, but all the forces of the nobility would be against him. And defeat would not leave him where he had been: commanders would look askance on one who had made pretension to command. It is hard indeed for us to enter into the spirit of a system under which civil and military office were combined. No doubt the consuls and praetors were men who had seen service: but of education for the strategic work of warfare we find no trace. As for the Allies who served Rome so well, we already see the tendency to lay on them rather more than their fair share of duty. It began no doubt in pressure of necessity, which is seen also in the employment of slaves as soldiers, some of whom lived to win the Roman franchise. The area from which the contingents of Allies could be drawn was greatly reduced by the defection of most of southern Italy. But the Campanian revolt was a defection of half-citizens (not Allies), and even the recovery of Capua did not restore to Rome the use of what had been a valuable recruiting-ground for the citizen part of the armies. The distinction between Citizen and Ally was strictly preserved, and we sometimes

[1] Polyb. VI 25.

find the front line of battle made up of equal parts of the two classes. The distant campaigns in Spain and the ceaseless pressure of war nearer home made it necessary to keep the troops more continuously under arms, and financial distress caused the pay at times to fall into arrear: hence arose discontents, and on one occasion even a serious mutiny. It was impossible to put a check on plundering and the barbarities that often accompanied it, and under such conditions it was not wonderful that the Roman discipline lost somewhat of its fine temper. Fabius and the old school blamed Scipio for this, but stress of circumstances was surely the prime cause. A few years of such service brutalized the men, and many grew to enjoy the vicissitudes of a life of bloodshed and rapine. Sooner than begin country life from the beginning on some derelict and weed-grown farm, these men went back to war in hope of loot and largesses: they were the volunteers of whom we hear in the latter days of the war. Good soldiers, to be sure; but not the stuff of which to make good patient citizens to build up in peace the exhausted vigour of the state.

401. Of the navy we may say that on the whole it does credit to the Roman government. But it was assuredly the scandalous inefficiency of the Carthaginian navy that gave preeminence to that of Rome. I will repeat that in those days of clumsy war-ships, propelled by the rowing of slaves and pressed men, the presence of first-rate fighting-crews was necessary for the successful mobilization of a fleet. Accordingly Rome could always mobilize, Carthage could not. This will also partly explain why peace (as we shall see) regularly in later times brought decay of the navy: there was no standing army to furnish the necessary troops. As to navigation, the technical skill needed was found among the Greek Allies.

402. The relations of the Allies to Rome in respect of military service have been spoken of. Certain events during the war give us an indication of the inferior position that they were presently to occupy when it was over. The determination of Rome to be mistress is seen in the fate of Carvilius' proposal[1] in 216: what she would not concede through fear, she was not likely to bestow as an act of grace. And this scheme had in view only the favoured Latins, not the ordinary Italian Allies. In 209 the different behaviour of the two groups of Latin colonies might have furnished a pretext for placing the 18 loyal ones on a superior footing to the other 12. But it does not appear that any permanent change of the kind was made. The revolted Allies in Samnium, Apulia and Lucania returned to their allegiance bit by bit as the war was more and more confined to the extreme South. Those that made the earlier submission got the

---

[1] See above, § 312.

better terms, but we have scarcely any details on the subject. The Bruttians were the last to be subdued, and they met with exemplary punishment. Great districts of Bruttium became domain land of the Roman state, and the natives were made into a sort of public slaves destined to serve the magistrates in all tasks of a degrading kind, a people of 'common hangmen.' Confiscations of land no doubt took place in various parts of Italy where disloyal tendencies had appeared, for instance in Etruria. But the dominion of Rome was no longer confined to Italy: there were other lands, ruled as 'provinces.' Sicily and Sardinia already had praetors for governors, and a more or less complete system of administration: it was soon found necessary to follow the same course in Spain. The distinction between Italian and Provincial Allies was clearly marked, for the former had no Roman governor set over them: but it was nothing to that between Romans on the one hand and Allies of any kind on the other. From Rome (not from Italy) came orders: the great war finally settled that these orders must be obeyed by Allies of all classes. All the governors of provinces were Romans: and, the more provinces there were looking to Rome as their head, the more imperial became Rome's position as compared with that of her Allies in Italy. All foreign policy was in the hands of the Roman Senate, and the war only confirmed its power. The outlook of Roman policy had become wider in the course of the war. Not only had the old friendship with the Ptolemies been strengthened by events, but the Aetolian league and the king of Pergamum were ready to act, and had acted, with Rome against their enemy the king of Macedon. Masinissa on the Numidian throne watched Carthage. But of all Rome's friends and allies none perhaps were more permanently useful, or better treated, than the two maritime Greek cities of Massalia and Neapolis. We hear very little of them; but long patient service, not of a theatrical kind, was not a theme to attract the rhetorical writers of later times, and we find them still Greek, still prosperous, still favoured allies, in the time of Augustus.

403. We have noticed the financial strain of the war on the resources of Rome. How much longer she could have kept up the struggle, we cannot tell. Her exhaustion is represented as extreme. There was of course the *tributum* to be repaid, but that was an ordinary incident of war: now however there was an extra war-loan outstanding, and payments due to contractors, deferred by consent till the end of the war, the total amount of which was certainly large. The war-indemnity was no doubt a help, but it was payable in instalments, and to find enough ready money to meet the state's obligations was likely to be no easy matter. And here we must

briefly refer to the lowering of the standard[1] of the current coin. The old Roman unit was the copper or bronze *as*, which is said to have had originally the full weight of a Roman pound (*libra*), divided into 12 ounces (*unciae*). The *as* was in course of time reduced in weight: in the first Punic war[2] it had sunk to 2 ounces (*sextans*). In 217 we hear that the busy reformer Flaminius proposed a law for relief of debtors (*lex Flaminia minus solvendi*): it seems not to have been passed till after his death at Trasimene. It was an attempt to put an end to the uncertainties of the currency, and so accepted the necessities of the situation, frankly reducing the *as* to a single *uncia*, $\frac{1}{12}$ of its old traditional weight. We must remember that since 269 there had also been a silver coinage, the unit of which was the *denarius* of 10 *asses* value, a Roman equivalent of the Greek *drachma*, a coin widely current in the Mediterranean. For about 50 years Rome had thus a double standard, the new silver beside the old copper. This was a transitional state of things, and we see that the old duodecimal system was giving way to a decimal one. But in 217 the *denarius*, which had been falling in weight, was probably fixed by law at a reduced weight and made the equivalent of 16 of the new uncial *asses*. A small table will shew the position more clearly.

Coin	Symbol	269. Value in *asses* of 4 *unciae* each	217. Value in *asses* of one *uncia* each	Weight in silver. Fractions of Roman *libra* 269	217
1 *denarius*	X or ⚹	10	16	$\frac{1}{72}$	$\frac{1}{84}$
½ *denarius* or *quinarius*	V or ⚹	5	8	$\frac{1}{144}$	$\frac{1}{168}$
¼ *denarius* or *sestertius*	IIS or IIS	2½	4	$\frac{1}{288}$	$\frac{1}{336}$

Thus the sesterce of 217 took the place of the *as* of 269 (4 ounces). For various religious and legal purposes it long remained customary to reckon by the old *as* of 4 ounces, though that coin was no longer in circulation: but in ordinary business the sesterce gradually became the unit of reckoning. In fact the Roman currency was after 217 on a single silver standard, and the copper coins were tokens. This important change, said to have been brought about in the interest of debtors, remained in force for about 280 years. Another measure, of a desperate character, is said to have been resorted to about the same time. This was the issue of *denarii* made of copper and plated with a thin coat of silver, a mere fraud on the part of the state itself.

[1] See references in Marquardt *Stvw*, II pp. 16—18.   [2] See above, § 249.

404. With regard to agriculture, how far its decay in the following period was directly due to the great war, it is very hard to form an opinion. We know that large tracts of land were laid waste, but we have no statistics: nor do we know how long various districts lay waste, how soon tillage was resumed as Hannibal fell back. It is not improbable that the actual devastation due to the war has been exaggerated. It was a far more serious thing that the pressure of need led to large importations of foreign corn. Some of it came in as a present from allies such as Hiero or Ptolemy, some was captured in raids or on the high seas, some was bought, and in the latter part of the war it began to pour in as provincial tribute from Sicily and Sardinia. Partly it served to feed the armies: but there were many hungry mouths in Rome, and the government could not give undivided attention to the war if it were embarrassed by the clamours of a starving mob. So it yielded to the temptation of pacifying the city population by selling corn cheap. Thus an Italian farmer who grew corn to sell found his market spoilt: he had to bear war-burdens but did not get war-prices. This would not tend to encourage the growth of corn in Italy; the olive and vine were profitable, but their culture took time, and only the man of capital could afford to wait for slow returns. The prospects of farming on a small scale were therefore not good. Moreover corn could be regularly produced in other countries more cheaply than in Italy, partly owing to favourable natural conditions, partly to the large scale of operations carried on by slave labour. Foreign competition was thus not likely to cease with the ending of the war. Again, the large-scale tillage could be introduced into Italy itself, wherever natural conditions favoured it: and after 17 years of war slaves were no rarity. Here was another danger threatening the small farmer. Nor was it unimportant that with the return of peace the repayment of loans and the discharge of contract obligations began. The rich began to have free money to invest, and revived confidence suggested the purchase of Italian land, of which there was no doubt plenty for sale. In the case of senators, the legal obstacles to the pursuit of commerce even tended to restrict them to this form of investment. Thus to the small farmers' losses by devastation and the pressure of unfair competition was added the further danger of absorption. The effects of these economic forces will be considered below. Here we need only point out that they were intensified by the demoralization resulting from the long war. Not only were many thousands of adults unfitted for patient toil by the excitements of a military life: many of the younger generation had doubtless grown up imperfectly habituated to the monotonous arts of peace.

405. The necessities of the long war had compelled the Roman government to depend largely upon the private enterprise of contractors for equipping and provisioning of armies, and probably for other purposes also. By allowing payment to be deferred these capitalists had established great claims on the state. It was not merely that large sums of money were owing to them: they enjoyed the moral advantage which is the portion of the successful patriot. If they should choose hereafter to employ their capital in ways not strictly consistent with the true interest of the state, it would not be easy to check them. In this direction there lay a serious danger. To grant leases of state lands at low rents had from very early times been a means of gratifying those who were at any time influential. The practice had by great political efforts been a good deal checked in recent periods, but it might at any time revive. And we must not forget that the careful management of property and judicious investment of money was not only a part of the Roman character: it was honoured and consciously practised as a virtue. The money-making spirit might easily run to excess and become a social disease: the recent development of joint-stock companies supplied a machinery for large enterprises, and greed had been stimulated by reports of the large-scale agriculture of Punic Africa and the rich mines of Spain. It is enough at this stage to point out the obvious risks of the situation created by the war.

406. That Greek influences found their way into Rome and pervaded Roman life, we shall see later. Little of this can be traced during the troubled period of the war. In the department of religion, the uneasy craving for foreign worships, of which we hear in 213, was partly satisfied in 204. But the worship of the Great Mother was not really Greek, though introduced through the agency of the Greek king of Pergamum. The old relations with the Delphic oracle were kept up. The statues brought to Rome from Syracuse (and perhaps from Tarentum) helped no doubt to convey some notion of Greek ideas of beauty, perhaps also to promote anthropomorphic ideas of divinity and the identification of Italian with Greek divinities. In literature the period of the war is most important, for it was at this time that the following of Greek models became an established practice, and independent literary development in Latin came to an end. The Campanian Naevius indeed seems to have lived through the war, but his latter years were passed in exile. The chief figures[1] were T. Maccius Plautus

---

[1] The exact dates of the three do not concern us. The received dates, Naevius 269—199, Plautus 254—184, Ennius 239—169, give to each just 70 years, which is strange. See Teuffel-Schwabe-Warr, §§ 95—104.

from northern Umbria, and Q. Ennius from the Calabrian heel of
Italy, a man perhaps partly Greek by descent, at least Greek-
speaking.   Plautus earned a hard living at Rome partly by manual
labour, partly by translations or adaptations of Greek comedies.   For
this purpose he chose works of the later 'comedy of manners,' the
personal attacks and scurrilous tone of the earlier political comedy
not being suited to the decorum of Roman public life.   His plots,
such as they are, are Greek: and the way in which he at times brings
in Greek words, clearly with intent and to lay stress on some point,
presupposes at least a fragmentary acquaintance with Greek among
a Roman audience.   But if he makes Latin words march to Greek
metres, iambic, trochaic, anapaestic and other, he is very far from
hellenizing the Latin language.   His style and spirit are Latin of
the Romans, and no writer used the Latin tongue more freely or
developed it more happily.   His great popularity is attested by the
practice of attributing to him the work of others.   Out of a mass of
plays bearing his name only 21 were pronounced genuine beyond
doubt by Varro, the great scholar of the Ciceronian age: but it
seems certain that he did in fact produce many more.   In his free
treatment of his Greek models the fine edge of Greek wit was of
course lost, but Plautus had a broad—at times very broad—wit and
humour of his own, well suited to the coarser fibre of his Roman
hearers.   Nor does the laying of his scenes in Greek surroundings
prevent him from making references to Roman or Italian matters:
allusions to the legal phraseology and procedure of Rome are very
numerous, and that though the Greek origin of his plays is marked
by speaking of Italians as *barbari* (βάρβαροι, non-Greek).   In one
passage[1] he refers to the war, wishing the audience victory over
Carthage.   The comedies of Plautus long kept possession of the
stage.

407.   Ennius was a man of a different bent.   His dramatic
activity was most successfully employed in versions of Greek
tragedies.   In comedy he was far behind Plautus.   He wrote also
some national dramas after the example of Naevius, but we know
nothing of them.   He wrote also a number of miscellaneous works
in verse, all apparently either versions from the Greek or composed
under Greek influences.   He had earned his living as a teacher of
Greek at Rome: and as a means of introducing Greek thought, and
so leavening Roman culture, the importance of his work is second to
none.   His fame is chiefly derived from the long poem called *Annales*,
the 'story of the years,' a work containing the traditional Roman

---

[1] *Cistellaria* 197—202, doubtless one of his earlier plays.   Most of his dramatic work
was after the great war.

history from the legendary coming of Aeneas, told in 18 books of hexameter verse. It was a rude attempt to compose a Roman epic, and Roman partiality regarded it as a great poem, though its repute rose and fell with the changes of taste in later times. The many surviving fragments shew that it was rough and strong: and in the absence of a more artistic national epic it remained long the honoured voice of Roman patriotism. The use of the Greek hexameter metre was a literary revolution. It became the favourite measure of Latin poets, and had far-reaching effects on the Latin language. The *Annales* seems to have been a work of his old age. Books VIII and IX contained the Hannibalic war. The career of Ennius illustrates the way in which an Italian could profit by the patronage of influential Romans. In 204 he was serving in Sardinia, and somehow attracted the attention of M. Porcius Cato, then quaestor there. When Cato returned to Rome he took Ennius with him, and the latter earned his living as a teacher of Greek. After this he enjoyed the favour of Scipio Africanus, and seems to have become a client of his house and one of the literary circle that gathered round the great conqueror. In 189 the consul Fulvius took him abroad in his suite, to witness and sing his victories in the Aetolian war. In 184 Fulvius' son was a commissioner for founding a citizen colony in northern Italy, and rewarded his father's laureate by assigning to him an allotment of land and making him a Roman citizen: a boon to which Ennius proudly referred in the line

nos sumus Romani qui ·fuimus ante Rudini,

Rudiae being the name of his birthplace. His life and influence mainly belong to the period after the second Punic war: but he was a child of the war, and the greatest fact in his history is that he both witnessed and sang the triumphant agony of Rome. His most famous line is the appreciation of Fabius Cunctator

unus homo nobis cunctando restituit rem,

and it can hardly be a violation of historical perspective to consider him in connexion with the struggle in which he bore a part.

408. Of the state of things in the city of Rome we can form but a very imperfect notion. Occasional fires and floods have been noted in the course of our narrative of the war: as also the ever-recurring prodigies and the public games, processions, sacrifices, and other ceremonies employed to avert evil and calm superstitious fears. The observances of religion must have formed a great part of the life of the city during the war. After the disasters of 218—216 the strain of long waiting for news, now that the old proud confidence

was gone, must have been extreme. A strange story, the full meaning[1] of which we are hardly in a position to gauge, appears under the year 209. A certain C. Valerius Flaccus, who had led a wanton and reckless youth, was made priest of Jupiter [*flamen Dialis*] and solemnly admitted to the office under strong pressure from the Chief Pontiff. It is said that the course of ceremonies and formalities to which his appointment devoted him wrought an entire change in this man's life and character. He became so virtuous as to win the approval of the most respectable citizens, and the office, of late somewhat fallen in repute, gained prestige from the holy decorum of its new holder. At the same time the election of a Plebeian to a religious office[2] hitherto reserved for Patricians seems to indicate that religion was becoming more and more a political matter, and detached from the venerable traditions of primitive Rome.

409. On the whole, though some things were just beginning to change for the worse, the Roman state was still in a thoroughly sound condition. A patriotic people were led by a steady and experienced Senate, virtually if not formally the government of the state,—far the most efficient governing body of the age. And, if no great military genius appeared on the Roman side, the war brought out a number of generals fully competent to command against an ordinary enemy. Fabius, Marcellus, Laevinus, Livius Salinator, Nero, Scipio, had all done good service in different ways. Nor was there a dearth of young men to provide leaders for the next generation. Cato and Flamininus both served in the war, and the Paullus who fell at Cannae left a son destined to win great honour and renown. But yet all was not well. To us, looking back upon the situation with a knowledge of the sequel, it is clear that Rome was now in a fair way to become a great imperial power as or when she might choose, or even against her will. But to the men who saw the end of the Hannibalic war the future was of course hidden. They could not know how far the empire of Rome was destined to extend: that they would bit by bit become responsible for the peace and prosperity of the whole Mediterranean world. They could not know that to govern subject peoples with consistency and justice, as the common interests of all required, was a most difficult art: that it could not be put in practice without a civil service of trained men under the effective control of a strong central power. They could not know that the growth of the provincial system would weaken the central power and make its control a mockery: that the evils

---

[1] Livy XXVII 8. See an interesting paper by Mr W. W. Fowler in *Classical Review*, VII 193—5, and his remarks in his *Roman Festivals*, concluding chapter.

[2] That of *curio maximus*. Livy XXVII 8.

developed under the rule of a degenerate nobility would become wholly unendurable: and that after a hundred years of reforms and reactions, blind and bloody struggles, the republican government, past mending, would be ended with the sword.

410. Great ruling peoples do not deliberately go into training to fit themselves for prospective duties. Blundering on into a position for which they were not fit, the Roman people simply did as others. Nor, even supposing they had wished to train themselves, was there any school of past achievement in which it was possible to learn. To extend the organization used in Italy to alien subjects beyond the seas was out of the question. The peoples of the North and West, loosely grouped in tribal units, offered no imperial lesson. From Carthage came economic suggestions, and those evil: her imperial enterprises had failed. The Greek or partly-Greek East had more to shew. There were the famous city-states of the past, and the federations of the present: there were the great monarchies, derived from the vast transitory empire of Alexander. But it was only these last that afforded examples of a central government ruling large territories as dependencies or subject provinces. Now Rome by the structure of its government was a city-state, and a city-state in which a body of nobles, a small ruling class, were virtually supreme. No system could be more opposed to monarchy than this, the firmly-rooted republican growth of three centuries. We shall do well to bear in mind that the issue of the second Punic war brought Rome face to face with what proved to be an insoluble problem: how, with the constitution of a city-state, to exercise functions of empire that had hitherto been found to some extent possible only when supreme power was concentrated in a single hand.

31504